AMERICAN ETHNICS AND MINORITIES

Readings in Ethnic History

Second Edition

Editor
Alfred J. Wrobel

El Camino College

KENDALL/HUNT PUBLISHING COMPANY
4050 Westmark Drive Dubuque, Iowa 52002

Library of Congress Catalog Card Number: 94-78136

ISBN 0-8403-9983-9

Printed in the United States of America
10 9 8 7 6 5 4 3 2

To
the incomparable Olga

CONTENTS

PREFACE

As a history major at Swarthmore College in the 1950s, I was aware that any discussion of the illusive concept of ethnicity would show up under the heading of immigration. Furthermore, any recognition of my working class Slavic heritage would have to wait for the post 1960s Civil Rights movement. It was at that time that ethnics became associated with Eastern Europeans.

Today there is a much broader view of ethnicity—especially since it constitutes the heart of the American experience. This revised edition of the *American Ethnics and Minorities* is an attempt to show how various ethnic groups (apart from the Native Americans) dealt with their shock of entering American society. Their adjustments—despite prejudices and dilemmas of organization and loyalties—is for the most part an inspiring and enduring record.

But this record also points to the redefinition of the national identity. It may be that, as Ronald Takaki has shown, we need to see ourselves in a "different mirror."[1] The tenacity and persistence of ethnicity—symbolic or otherwise—within the Native Americans, African Americans, Asian Americans, Hispanics and European Americans underscores the need for a greater understanding of multiculturalism and its off-spring, diversity.

In this confusing post-communist world, the United States could take the lead as a multicultural world power. Indeed one of the greatest achievements of this country in the twenty-first century would be to demonstrate the validity—if not the vitality—of the United States as a multi-ethnic and multiracial society with an emerging common culture.

I would like to thank my contributing colleagues, as well the many students who have provided insights and support for another edition. To provide some perspective on immigration policies, I have added an article on the Immigration Laws of 1986 and 1990. And to further the debate on ethnicity, Michael Novak's views on the "new" ethnicity have been included as well.

I hope you find these readings in ethnic and minority history a rewarding exercise into the meaning of race relations in the United States.

NOTES

1. Ronald Takaki, *A Different Mirror, A History of Multicultural America* (Boston, 1993).

SELECTED BIBLIOGRAPHY

Alba, Richard D. *Ethnic Identity*. New Haven, Connecticut, 1990.

DeConde, Alexander. *Ethnicity, Race, and American Foreign Policy*. Boston, 1992

Gladsky, Thomas S. *Princes, Peasant, and Other Polish Selves. Ethnicity in American Literature*. Amherst, 1992.

Gleason, Philip. *Speaking of Diversity*. Baltimore 1992.

Schlesinger, Jr., Arthur M. *The Disuniting of America*. New York, 1991.

Ueda, Reed. *Postwar Immigrant America*. Boston 1994.

Waters, Mary C. *Ethnic Options. Choosing Identities in America*. Berkeley, 1990.

THE NEW ETHNICITY

MICHAEL NOVAK

The word "ethnic" does not have a pleasing sound. The use of the word makes many people anxious. What sorts of repression account for this anxiety? What pretenses about the world are threatened when one points to the realities denoted and connoted by that ancient word? An internal history lies behind resistance to ethnicity; such resistance is almost always passional, convictional, not at all trivial. Many persons have tried to escape being "ethnic," in the name of a higher moral claim.

There are many meanings to the word itself. I have tried to map some of them below. There are many reasons for resistance to the word "ethnic" (and what it is taken to represent). Rather than beginning with these directly, I prefer to begin by defining the new ethnicity.

The definition I wish to give is personal; it grows out of personal experience; it is necessitated by an effort to attain an accurate self-knowledge. The hundreds of letters, reviews, comments, invitations, and conversations that followed upon *The Rise of the Unmeltable Ethnics* (1972) indicate that my own gropings to locate my own identity are not isolated. They struck a responsive chord in many others of Southern and Eastern European (or other) background. My aim was—and is—to open up the field to study. Let later inquiry discern just how broadly and how exactly my first attempts at definition apply. It is good to try to give voice to what has so far been untongued—and then to devise testable hypotheses at a later stage.

The new ethnicity, then, is a movement of self-knowledge on the part of members of the third and fourth generation of Southern and Eastern European immigrants in the United States. In a broader sense, the new ethnicity includes a renewed self-consciousness on the part of other generations and other ethnic groups: the Irish, the Norwegians and Swedes, the Germans, the Chinese and Japanese, and others. Much that can be said of one of these groups can be said, not univocally but analogously, of others. In this area, one must learn to speak with multiple meanings and with a sharp eye for differences in detail. (By "analogous" I mean "having resemblances but also essential differences"; by "univocal" I mean a generalization that applies equally to all cases.) My sentences are to be read, then, analogously, not univocally; they are meant to awaken fresh perception, not to close discussion. They are intended to speak directly of a limited (and yet quite large) range of ethnic groups, while conceding indirectly that much that is said of Southern and Eastern Europeans may also be said, *mutatis mutandis*, of others

I stress that, in the main, the "new" ethnicity involves those of the third and fourth generation after immigration. Perhaps two anecdotes will suggest the kind of experience involved. When *Time* magazine referred to me in 1972 as a "Slovak-American," I felt an inner shock, I had never referred to myself or been publicly referred to in that way. I wasn't certain how I felt about it. Then, in 1974, after I had given a lecture on ethnicity to the only class in Slavic American studies in the United States,[1] at the City College of New York, the dean of the college said on the way to lunch, "Considering how sensitive you are on ethnic matters, the surprising thing to me was how American you are." I wanted to ask him, "What else?" In this area one grows used to symbolic uncertainties.

The new ethnicity does not entail: (a) speaking a foreign language; (b) living in a subculture; (c) living in a "tight-knit" ethnic neighborhood; (d) belonging to fraternal organizations; (e) responding to "ethnic" appeals; (f) exalting one's own nationality or culture, narrowly construed. Neither does it entail a university education or the reading of writers on the new ethnicity. Rather, the new ethnicity entails: first, a growing sense of discomfort with the sense of identity one is *supposed* to have—universalist, "melted," "like everyone else"; then a growing appreciation for the potential wisdom of one's own gut reactions (especially on moral matters) and their historical roots; a growing self-confidence and social power; a sense of being discriminated against, condescended to, or carelessly misapprehended; a growing disaffection regarding those to whom one had always been taught to defer; and a sense of injustice regarding the response of liberal spokesmen to conflicts between various ethnic groups, especially between "legitimate" minorities and "illegitimate" ones. There is, in a word, an inner conflict between one's felt personal power and one's ascribed public power: a sense of outraged truth, justice, and equity.

The new ethnicity does, therefore, have political consequences. Many Southern and Eastern European-Americans have been taught, as I was, not to be "ethnic," or even "hyphenated," but only "American." Yet at critical points it became dear to some of us, then to more of us, that when push comes to shove we are always, in the eyes of others, "ethnics," unless we play completely by their rules, emotional as well as procedural. And in the end, even then, they retain the power and the status. Still, the stakes involved in admitting this reality to oneself are very high. Being "universal" is regarded as being good; being ethnically self-conscious raises anxieties. Since one's whole identity has been based upon being "universal," one is often loathe to change public face too suddenly. Many guard the little power and status they have acquired, although they cock one eye on how the ethnic "movement" is progressing. They are wise. But their talents are also needed

The new ethnicity, then, is a fledgling movement, not to be confused with the appearance of ethnic themes on television commercials in television police shows, and in magazines. All these manifestations in the public media would not have occurred unless the ethnic reality of America had begun to be noticed. In states from Massachusetts to Iowa, great concentrations of Catholics and Jews, especially in urban centers, have been some of the main bastions of Democratic Party politics for fifty years. The "new politics," centered in the universities, irritated and angered this constituency (even when, as it sometimes did, it won its votes). Thus there is a relation between the fledgling new ethnicity and this larger ethnic constituency. But what that relationship will finally be has not yet been demonstrated by events.

Those who do not come from Southern or Eastern European backgrounds in the United States may not be aware of how it feels to come from such a tradition; they may not know the internal history. They may note "mass passivity" and "alienation" without sharing the cynicism learned through particular experiences. They may regard the externals of ethnic economic and social success, modest but real, while never noticing the internal ambiguity—and its compound of peace and self-hatred, confidence and insecurity.

To be sure, at first many "white ethnics" of the third generation are not conscious of having any special feelings. The range of feelings about themselves they do have is very broad; more than one stream of feeling is involved. They are right-wingers and left-wingers, chauvinists and universalists, all-Americans and isolationists. Many want nothing more desperately than to be considered "American." Indeed, by now many have so deeply acquired that habit that to ask them point-blank how they are different from others would arouse strong emotional resistance

For at least three reasons, many white ethnics *are* becoming self-conscious. As usual, great social forces outside the self draw forth from the self new responses. First, a critical mass of scholars, artists, and writers is beginning to emerge—the Italians, for example, are extraordinarily eminent in the cinema. Second, the prevailing image of the model American—the "best and the brightest" of the Ivy League, wealthy, suave, and powerful—has been discredited by the mismanagement of war abroad, by racial injustice at home, and by attitudes, values, and emotional patterns unworthy of emulation internally. The older image of the truly cultured American is no longer compelling. Many, therefore, are thrown back upon their own resources.

Finally, the attitudes of liberal, enlightened commentators on the "crisis of the cities" seem to fall into traditional patterns: guilt vis-a-vis blacks, and disdain for the Archie Bunkers of the land (Bunker is, of course, a classy British American name, but Carroll O'Connor is in appearance undisguisably Irish). The national media present to the public a model for what it is to be a "good American" which makes many people feel unacceptable to their betters, unwashed, and ignored. Richard Hofstadter wrote of "the anti-intellectualism of the people," but another feature of American life is the indifference—even hostility—of many intellectuals to Main Street. In return, then, many people respond with deep contempt for experts, educators, "limousine liberals," "radical chic," "bureaucrats"—a contempt whose sources are partly those of class ("the hidden injuries of class") and partly those of ethnicity ("legitimate" minorities and unacceptable minorities). The national social class that prides itself on being universalist has lost the confidence of many. Votes on school bond issues are an example of popular resistance to professionals.

In my own case, the reporting of voting patterns among white ethnic voters during the Wallace campaigns of 1964 and 1968 first aroused in me ethnic self-consciousness. Descriptions of "white backlash" often put the blame—inaccurately I came to see—upon Slavs and other Catholic groups. The Slavs of "South Milwaukee" were singled out for comment in the Wallace vote in Wisconsin in 1964. First, South Milwaukee was not distinguished from the south side of Milwaukee. Then, it was not noted that the Slavic vote for Wallace fell *below* his statewide average. Then, the very heavy vote for Wallace in outlying German and British American areas was not pointed out. Finally, the strong vote for Wallace in the wealthy northeastern suburbs of Milwaukee was similarly ignored. It seemed to me that those whom the grandfathers called "hunkies" and "dagos" were now being called "racists," "fascists," and "pigs," with no noticeable gain in affection. Even in 1972, a staff advisory in the Shriver "trip book" for a congressional district in Pittsburgh called the district "Wallace country," though the Wallace vote in that district in 1968 had been twelve percent, and the Humphrey vote had been fifty-eight percent. I obliged the staff member to revise his account and to call the district "Humphrey country." It is one of the most consistently liberal districts in Pennsylvania. Why send this constituency the message that it is the enemy?

Jimmy Breslin was once asked by an interviewer in *Penthouse* how, coming out of Queens, he could have grown up so liberal. Actually, next to Brooklyn, there is no more liberal county in the nation. A similar question was put to a liberal journalist from the Dorchester area, in Boston. The class and ethnic bias hidden in the way the word "liberal" is used in such interviews cries out for attention.

One of the large social generalizations systematically obscured by the traditional anti-Catholicism of American elites is the overwhelmingly progressive voting record in America's urban centers. The centers of large Catholic population in every northeastern and north central state have been the key to Democratic victories in those states since at least 1916. The hypothesis that Catholics have been, second only to Jews, the central constituency of successful progressive politics in this century is closer to the facts than historians have observed. (Massachusetts, that most Catholic of our states, stayed with McGovern in 1972.) The language of politics in America is, however, mainly Protestant, and Protestant biases color public perception. Protestant leadership is given the halo of morality and legitimacy, Catholic life is described in terms of negatively laden words: Catholic "power," "machine politics," etc.

There are other examples of odd perception on the part of American elites with respect to Catholic and other ethnic populations. The major institutions of American Life—government, education, the media—give almost no assistance to those of "white ethnic" background who wish to obey the Socratic maxim: "Know thyself." One of the greatest and most dramatic migrations of human history brought more than thirty million immigrants to this land between 1874 and 1924. Despite the immense dramatic materials involved in this migration, only one major American film records it: Elia Kazan's *America! America!* That film ends with the hero's arrival in America. The tragic and costly experience of Americanization has scarcely yet been touched. How many died; how many were morally and psychologically destroyed; how many still carry the marks of changing their names, of "killing" their mother tongue and renouncing their former identity, in order to become "new men and new women"—these are motifs of violence, self-mutilation, joy, and irony. The inner history of this migration must come to be understood, if we are ever to understand the aspirations and fears of some seventy million Americans.

When this part of the population exhibits self-consciousness and begins to exert group claims—whether these are claims made by aggregated individuals or claims that are corporate—they are regularly confronted with the accusation that they are being "divisive." ("Divisive" is a code word for Catholic ethnics and Jews, is it not? It is seldom used of others: white Southerners, Appalachians, Chicanos, blacks, native Americans, prep-school British Americans, or others who maintain their own identity and institutions.) Earl Raab writes eloquently of this phenomenon in *Commentary* (May, 1974): "Modern Europe . . . never really accepted the legitimacy of the corporate Jew—although it was at its best willing to grant full civil rights to the individual Jew. That, for the Jews, was an impossible paradox, a secular vision of Christian demands to convert . . . [And] it is precisely this willingness to allow the Jews their separate identity as a group which is now coming into question in America." Individual diversity, yes; group identity, not for all.

The Christian white ethnic, like the Jew, actually has few group demands to make: positively, for educational resources to keep values and perceptions alive, articulate, and critical; negatively, for an equal access to power, status, and the definition of the general American purpose and symbolic world. Part of the strategic function of the cry "divisive!" is to limit access to these things. Only those individuals will be advanced who define themselves as individuals and who operate according to the symbols of the established. The emotional meaning is: *"Become like us."* This is an understandable strategy, but in a nation as pluralistic as the United States, it is shortsighted. The nation's hopes, purposes, and symbols need to be defined inclusively rather than exclusively; *all* must become "new men" and "new women." All the burden ought not to fall upon the newcomers.

There is much that is attractive about the British American, upper-class, northeastern culture that has established for the entire nation a model of behavior and perception. This model is composed of economic power; status; cultural tone; important institutional rituals and procedures; and the acceptable patterns of style, sensibility, and rationality. The terse phrase "Ivy League" suggests all these factors. The nation would be infinitely poorer than it is without the Ivy League. All of us who came to this land—including the many lower-class British Americans, Scotch-Irish, Scandinavians, and Germans—are much in the debt of the Ivy League, deeply, substantially so.

Still, the Ivy League is not the nation. The culture of the Ivy League is not the culture of America (not even of Protestant America).

Who are we, then, we who do not particularly reverberate to the literature of New England, whose interior history is not Puritan, whose social class is not Brahmin (either in reality or in pretense), whose ethnicity is not British American, or even Nordic? Where in American institutions, American Literature, American education is our identity mirrored, objectified, rendered accessible to intelligent criticism, and confirmed? We are still, I think, persons without a public symbolic world, persons without a publicly verified culture to sustain us and our children.

It is not that we lack culture; it is not that we lack strength of ego and a certain internal peace. As Jean-Paul Sartre remarks in one of his later works, there is a distinction between one's identity in one's own eyes and one's identity in the eyes of others. In the United States, many who have internal dignity cannot avoid noticing that others regard them as less than equals, with a sense that they are different, with uncertainty, and with a lack of commonality. It is entirely possible that the "melting pot" would indeed have melted everyone, if those who were the models into which the molten metal was to be poured had not found the process excessively demanding. A sense of separate identity is, in part, induced from outside-in. I am made aware of being Catholic and Slovak by the actions of others. I would be sufficiently content were my identity to be so taken for granted, so utterly normal and real, that it would never have to be self-conscious.

The fact of American cultural power is that a more or less upper-class, Northeastern Protestant sensibility sets the tone, and that a fairly aggressive British American ethnocentricity, and even Anglophilia, govern the instruments of education and public life. Moreover, it is somehow emotionally important not to challenge this dominant ethnocentricity. It is quite proper to talk of other sorts of social difference—income, class, sex, even religion. To speak affirmatively of ethnicity, however, makes many uneasy. Some important truth must lie hidden underneath this uneasiness. A Niebuhrian analysis of social power suggests that a critical instrument of social control in the United States is, indeed, the one that dares not be spoken of.

In New York State, for example, in 1974 the four Democratic candidates for the office of lieutenant governor (not, however, for governor) were named Olivieri, Cuomo, La Falce, and Krupsak. It was the year, the pundits say, for "ethnic balance" on the ticket. But all four candidates insisted that their ethnicity was not significant. Two boasted of being from *upstate,* one of being a *woman*, one of being for "the *little* guy." It is publicly legitimate to be different on any other account except ethnicity, even where the importance of ethnic diversity is tacitly agreed upon.

If I say, as I sometimes have, that I would love to organize an "ethnic caucus" within both the Democratic Party and the Republican Party, the common reaction is one of anxiety, distaste, and strained silence. But if I say, as I am learning to, that I would love to organize a "caucus of workingmen and women" in both parties, heads quickly nod in approval. Social class is, apparently, rational. Cultural background is, apparently, counterrational.

Yet the odd political reality is that most Americans do not identify themselves in class terms. They respond to cultural symbols intimate to their ethnic history in America. Ethnicity is a "gut issue," even though it cannot be mentioned. A wise political candidate does not, of course speak to a longshoreman's local by calling its members Italian American and appealing to some supposed cultural solidarity. That would be a mistake. But if he speaks about those themes in the cultural tradition that confirm their own identity—themes like family, children, home neighborhood, specific social aspirations, and grievances—they know he is with them: he does represent them. In order to be able to represent many constituencies, a representative has to be able to "pass over" into many cultural histories. He may never once make ethnicity explicit as a public theme; but, implicitly, he will be recognizing the daily realities of ethnicity and ethnic experience in the complex fabric of American social power.

According to one social myth, America is a "melting pot," and this myth is intended by many to be not merely descriptive but normative: the faster Americans—especially white ethnic Americans—"melt" into the British American pattern, the better. There is even a certain ranking according to the supposed degree of assimilation: Scotch-Irish,

Norwegians, Swedes, Germans, Swiss, Dutch, liberal or universalist Jews, the Irish, and on down the line to the less assimilated: Greeks, Yugoslavs, Hungarians, Central and East Europeans, Italians, Orthodox Jews, French Canadians, Portuguese, Latins and Spanish speaking. . . . (The pattern almost exactly reflects the history and literature of England.).

Now it was one thing to be afraid of ethnicity in 1924, in confronting a first and second generation of immigrants. It is another thing to be afraid, in 1974, in confronting a third and fourth generation. Indeed, fears about a revival of ethnicity seem to be incompatible with conviction about how successful the "melting pot" has been. Fears about a "revival" of ethnicity confirm the fact that ethnicity is still a powerful reality in American life.

What, then, are the advantages and disadvantages in making this dangerous subject, this subterranean subject, explicit?

The disadvantages seem to be three. The first one on everyone's mind is that emphasis on ethnicity may work to the disadvantage of blacks. It may, it is said, become a legitimization of racism. It may "polarize" whites and blacks. Nothing could be further from the truth. Those who are concerned about the new ethnicity—Geno Baroni (Washington), Irving Levine (New York), Barbara Mikulski (Baltimore), Ralph Perrotta (New York), Steve Adubado (Newark), Otto Feinstein (Detroit), Stan Franczyk (Buffalo), Kenneth Kovach (Cleveland), Edward Marciniak (Chicago), and others—have given ample proof of their concern for the rights and opportunities of black Americans. Many got their start in the new ethnicity through their work among blacks. The overriding political perception among those concerned with the new ethnicity is that the harshness of life in the cities must be reduced by whites and blacks together, especially in working-class neighborhoods. Present social policies punish neighborhoods that integrate. Such neighborhoods should be rewarded and strengthened and guaranteed a long-range stability.

But fears about ethnicity require a further two-part response. Racism does not need ethnicity in order to be legitimated in America. It was quite well legitimated by Anglo-American culture, well before white ethnics arrived here in significant numbers, well before many white ethnics had ever met blacks. Indeed, there is some reason to believe that, while racism is an international phenomenon and found in all cultures, the British American and other Nordic peoples have a special emotional response to colored races. Not all European peoples respond to intermarriage, for example, with quite the emotional quality of the Anglo-

Saxons. The French, the Spanish, the Italians, and the Slavs are not without their own forms of racism. But the felt quality of racism is different in different cultures. (It seems different among the North End Italians and the South Boston Irish of Boston, for example.)

In America, racism did not wait until the immigrants of 1880 and after began to arrive. Indeed, it is in precisely those parts of the country solely populated by British Americans that the conditions of blacks have been legally and institutionally least humane. In those parts of the country most heavily populated by white ethnics, the cultural symbols and the political muscle that have led to civil-rights and other legislation have received wide support. Liberal senators and congressmen elected by white ethnics—including the Kennedys—led the way. Even in 1972, both Hamtramck and Buffalo went for George McGovern. McGovern's share of the Slavic vote was fifty-two percent. Nixon won the white Protestant vote by sixty-eight percent.

It will be objected that white ethnic leaders like Frank Rizzo of Philadelphia, Ralph Perk of Cleveland, and others are signs of a new racism on the part of white ethnics in the Northern cities, of a retreat from support for blacks, and of a rising tide of anti-"crime" and antibusing sentiment. The proponents of the new ethnicity perceive such developments as a product of liberal neglect and liberal divisiveness. The proponents of the new politics talk well of civil rights, equal opportunity, economic justice, and other beautiful themes. But the new politics, in distinguishing "legitimate" minorities (blacks, Chicanos, native Americans) from "less favored" minorities (Italians, Slavs, Orthodox Jews, Irish, etc.), has set up punitive and self-defeating mechanisms. The new politics has needlessly divided working-class blacks from working-class whites, in part by a romance (on television) with militance and flamboyance, in part by racial discrimination in favor of some against others, not because of need but because of color.

The second part of this response is that the politics of "the constituency of conscience" (as Michael Harrington, Eugene McCarthy, and others have called it)—the politics of the liberal, the educated, the enlightened—is less advantageous to blacks than is the politics of the new ethnicity. The new politics is less advantageous to blacks because it is obsessed with racial differences, and approaches these through the ineffectual lenses of guilt and moralism. Second, it is blind to cultural differences among blacks, as well as to cultural differences among whites; and sometimes these are significant. Third, it unconsciously but effectively keeps blacks in the position of a small racial minority outnumbered in the population ten to one.

By contrast, the new ethnicity notes many other significant differences besides those based upon race, and defines political and social problems in ways that unite diverse groups around common objectives. In Chicago, for example, neither Poles nor Italians are represented on the boards or in the executive suites of Chicago's top 105 corporations in a higher proportion than blacks or Latinos—all are of one percent or less.[2] In Boston, neither white ethnics nor blacks desire busing, but this highly ideological instrument of social change is supported most by just those affluent liberals—in such suburbs as Brookline and Newton—whose children will not be involved.

The new ethnic politics would propose a strategy of social rewards—better garbage pickup, more heavily financed and orderly schools, long-range guarantees on home mortgages, easier access to federally insured home improvement loans, and other services—for neighborhoods that integrate. As a neighborhood moves from, say, a ten percent population of blacks to twenty percent or more, integration should be regulated so that long-range community stability is guaranteed. It is better long-range policy to have a large number of neighborhoods integrated up to twenty or thirty percent than to encourage—even by inadvertence—a series of sudden flights and virtually total migrations. Institutional racism is a reality; the massive migration of blacks into a neighborhood does not bring with it social rewards but, almost exclusively, punishments.

There are other supposed disadvantages to emphasis upon ethnicity. Ethnicity, it is said, is a fundamentally counter-rational, primordial, uncontrollable social force; it leads to hatred and violence; it is the very enemy of enlightenment, rationality, and liberal politics. But this is to confuse nationalism or tribalism with cultural heritage. Because a man's name is Russell, or Ayer, or Flew, we would not wish to accuse him of tribalism on the ground that he found the Britons a uniquely civilized and clearheaded people, thought the Germans ponderous and mystic, the French philosophically romantic, etc. A little insular, we might conclude, but harmlessly ethnocentric. And if it is not necessarily tribalistic or unenlightened to read English literature in American schools, just possibly it would be even more enlightened and even less tribalistic to make other literatures, germane to the heritage of other Americans, more accessible than they are.

The United States is, potentially, a multiculturally attuned society. The greatest number of immigrants in recent years arrives from Spanish-speaking and Asian nations. But the nation's cultural life, and its institutions of culture, are far from being sensitive to the varieties of the American people. Why should a cultural heritage not their own be imposed unilaterally upon newcomers? Would not genuine multicultural adaptation on the part of all be more cosmopolitan and humanistic? It would be quite significant in international affairs. The Americans would truly be a kind of prototype of planetary diversity.

Some claim that cultural institutions will be fragmented if every ethnic group in America clamors for attention. But the experience of the Illinois curriculum in ethnic studies suggests that no one school represents more than four or five ethnic groups (sometimes fewer) in significant density. With even modest adjustments in courses in history, literature, and the social sciences, material can be introduced that illuminates inherited patterns of family life, values, and preferences. The purpose for introducing multicultural materials is neither chauvinistic nor propagandistic but realistic. Education ought to illuminate what is happening in the self of each child.

What about the child of the mixed marriage, the child of *no* ethnic heritage—the child of the melting pot? So much in the present curriculum already supports such a child that the only possible shock to arise from multicultural materials would appear to be a beneficial one: not all others in America are like him (her), and that diversity, as well as homogenization, has a place in America

The practical agenda that faces proponents of the new ethnicity is vast, indeed. At the heights of American economic and social power, there is not yet much of a melting pot. Significant ethnic diversity is manifested in the proportion of each group studying in universities, on faculties, in the professions, on boards of directors among the creators of public social symbols, and the like. In patterns of home ownership, family income, work patterns, care for the aged, political activism, authoritarianism, individualism, and matters of ultimate concern group differences are remarkable. About all these things, more information is surely needed. Appropriate social policies need to be hypothesized, tried, and evaluated.

Ethnic diversity in the United States persists in the consciousness of individuals, in their perceptions, preferences, behavior, even while mass production and mass communications homogenize our outward appearances. Some regard such persistence as a personal failure; they would prefer to "transcend" their origins, or perhaps they believe that they have.

Here two questions arise. What cultural connection do they have with their brothers and sisters still back in Montgomery, or Wheeling, or Skokie, or Pawtucket? Second, has their personal assimilation introduced into the great American superculture fresh streams of image, myth, symbol, and style of intellectual life? Has anything distinctively their own— formed in them by a history longer than a thousand years—been added to the common wisdom?

The new ethnicity does not stand for the Balkanization of America. It stands for a true, real, multicultural cosmopolitanism. It points toward a common culture truly altered by each new infusion of diversity. Until now, the common culture has been relatively resistant to internal transformation; it has not so much arisen from the hearts of all as been imposed; the melting pot has had only a single recipe. That is why at present the common culture seems to have become discredited, shattered, unenforceable. Its cocoon has broken. Struggling to be born is a creature of multicultural beauty, dazzling, free, a higher and richer form of life. It was fashioned in the painful darkness of the melting pot and now, at the appointed time, it awakens. ✦

NOTES

1. This Slavic American course—in a happy symbol of the new ethnicity—is housed in the Program of Puerto Rican Studies, through the generosity of the latter.
2. Cf. "The Representation of Poles, Italians, Latins, and Blacks in the Executive Suites of Chicago's Largest Corporations." The Institute of Urban Life, 820 North Michigan Avenue, Chicago, Illinois 60611.

IMMIGRATION REFORM

RECENT TRENDS AND LEGISLATIVE

1986 Immigration Act in Historical Perspective

Although other nations may receive larger numbers of immigrants in relation to their population, no other nation willingly accepts as many new settlers as does the United States. Significant changes in U.S. immigration law in 1986 and 1990 have reaffirmed this country's openness to immigrants. The legislative acts address significant changes in the numbers, origins, and legal status of the nation's immigrant population that have occurred in the past three decades. Recent work by Urban Institute researchers Michael Fix and Jeffrey S. Passel puts both laws into historical context and assesses the likely effects of the 1990 legislation.

Legal immigration to the United States has increased steadily over the past five decades, from about 1 million immigrants in the 1940s to some 6 million in the 1980s. More immigrants live in the United States now than at any time in history—more than 17 million. But the rate of immigration in the 1980s was not the highest our nation has experienced. The number of arriving immigrants peaked at 8.8 million in the first decade of the twentieth century, when our population was about one-third of what it is today.

Moreover, while recently the proportion of foreign-born persons in the United States has been increasing steadily, from about 4.9 percent in 1970 to about 7 percent in 1990, this does not even approach the levels of the nineteenth century. Then, about 1 person in 7, or almost 15 percent of the population, was foreign-born. This ratio of foreign-born to native-born began a steady decline in 1932. The immigration cutbacks

---

From *Policy and Research Report*, Winter/Spring 1991, pp. 11-20, published by the Urban Institute.

can be traced to a number of factors, including the restrictive immigration laws of 1921 and 1924, the inhibiting effect of the Great Depression and World War II, and the aging of earlier groups of immigrants.

The impact of immigrants on the labor force also is less today. In 1907 alone, for example, the number of immigrants who found jobs when they arrived added about 3 percent to the U.S. Labor force. An equivalent amount of immigration today would mean an annual flow of 9 million persons into the United States—more than ten times current numbers.

In the nineteenth century, virtually all immigration to the United States was from Europe and Canada; this trend continued into the 1950s. By the 1980s, however, only 14 percent originated from Europe and Canada.

The most dramatic change is an increase in the proportion of Asian immigrants, which rose from 13 percent in the 1960s to 44 percent in the 1980s. In this same period, immigration of Mexicans and other Latin Americans remained steady, at 14 percent and 26-27 percent, respectively.

The explosive increase in the immigration of Asians to the United States—2.6 million arrived in the 1980s—can be traced to the legal changes incorporated into the Immigration Act of 1965. That law put immigrants from all countries on essentially equal footing and eased restrictions in force since 1885 against immigration from Asia.

As total immigration increased during the 1980, so did the number of illegal immigrants. The estimated number of illegal aliens in this country rose from 2.5 to 3.5 million in 1980 to 3 to 5 million by 1986.

Enactment of the Immigration Reform and Control Act (IRCA) in 1986 authorized legalization of immigrants who had resided illegally in the United States since before January 1, 1982. Since the law's passage, some 2.5 million formerly illegal aliens have attained legal status; the estimated number of illegal aliens remaining is 1.8 to 3 million.

These estimates of the undocumented population are lower than might be expected, considering recent media publicity given to apprehensions of illegal aliens along the U.S.-Mexico border. Such publicity, however, obscures two important factors: First, much of the inflow from Mexico consists of temporary labor migrants; and second, there is a large, unreported reverse flow from this country back into Mexico.

The impact of immigration, both legal and illegal, is uneven across the country. Three-quarters of all immigrants who arrived in the United States in the 1980s came to only six states—California, New York,

Texas, Florida, Illinois, and New Jersey. During this period two states—California and New York—received more than half, about 3.3 million of the total 6 million. Of these, 2.3 million arrived in California and 1 million in New York.

This uneven impact played a key role in the redistribution of U.S. population during the 1980s, a decade of considerable population growth. For example, California's huge population increase, confirmed in the 1990 census, was fueled mainly by immigrants. Texas received significant numbers of both immigrants and internal migrants. But the arrival of large numbers of immigrants in New York and Illinois nevertheless failed to offset the exodus of residents out of these states in the 1980s.

These shifts in the numbers, origins, and geographical distribution of immigrants provided the impetus for the Immigration Act of 1990, which addresses primarily the issue of legal immigration. The act defines the family unit, labor, and other criteria for admitting immigrants to the United States.

1990 Immigration Act and Its Likely Effects

The Immigration Act of 1990 was enacted at a time of extreme economic uncertainty, when the nation was poised on the brink of a recession and the outbreak of war in the Persian Gulf. In an era when other industrialized countries are making their immigration laws more restrictive, the 1990 act authorizes an *increase* in legal immigration to the United States. In so doing, it complements the 1986 attempt of the Immigration Reform and Control Act (IRCA) to close the "back door" of illegal immigration with a legislative strategy for keeping open the "front door" of legal immigration.

This liberalization allows entry of many more family members of immigrants and creates a temporary "safe haven" for as many as 500,000 undocumented Salvadorans already in the United States. Thus, it stands in sharp contrast to IRCA, which focused primarily on limiting illegal immigration.

Passage of the 1990 act was driven by three imperatives:

- Economic—to forge a closer link between immigration and human resources policy, in order to avoid the anticipated mismatch between the numbers and skill requirements of future U.S. jobs and the numbers and skill levels of future immigrants.
- Cultural—to encourage more diversity in the immigrant stream.
- Social—to promote family unity.

The provisions of the 1990 law, according to Fix and Passel, signal two important conceptual shifts in U.S. immigration policy: a stronger focus on labor market concerns and an interest in diversifying the immigrant stream, principally by increasing the number of immigrants from Europe.

Cap on Immigration. The new law places a yearly cap on total immigration for the first time since the 1920s. For 1992-95 the limit is 700,000 persons; for the years thereafter, 675,000.

The cap, however, may be more symbolic than real because the law allows an unlimited number of visas for immediate relatives of U.S. citizens (now about 220,000 per year), while at the same time setting a floor of 226,000 visas for other family-based immigration.

Employment-Related Immigration. The number of visas reserved for workers under the new law will increase significantly—from the current level of 58,000 per year to 140,000. However, only about 40 percent of the total is expected to be workers; the others are likely to be members of workers' families. The new law emphasizes admission of skilled workers by capping the number of visas for unskilled workers at 10,000, about half the number allowed under previous law.

Diversity. Perhaps the most interesting innovation in the Immigration Act of 1990 is the class of diversity visas it creates to "seed" immigration from countries that have sent comparatively few migrants to the United States in recent years. However, the diversity criteria are not demanding enough to ensure such an outcome. In fact, during the three years following the law's enactment, national origin and not human capital considerations will largely determine who obtains a visa.

Family-Based Immigration. An important sign of the new law's pro-immigrant character is its approach to family-based immigration. These provisions are driven by congressional interest in promoting the nuclear family, by an interest in eventually diversifying the immigrant stream, and by a less publicized interest in reducing the size of the nation's illegal population.

The provisions increase the number of persons who may enter based on the family categories. Admissions of immediate family members of United States citizens remain unlimited under the act; the preexisting preference system has been updated; and 55,000 visas per year for three years will go to immediate family members of immigrants who have attained legal status under IRCA's so-called amnesty programs.

Thus, despite public attention given to the increase in employment-based immigration, the bill did not increase workers at the expense of family-based admissions.

Reducing the Size of the Undocumented Population. Several lesser-known provisions of the new law best demonstrate its generous, inclusionary nature. The legislation, for instance, prohibits the deportation of, and grants work authorization to, all spouses and children of the 2.5 to 2.8 million persons who will eventually attain legal status under IRCA, if the spouses and children were in the United States before May 5, 1988.

Another provision creates a temporary "safe haven" for a minimum of 18 months for an estimated 350,000 to 500,000 Salvadorans who, although living in the United States, were generally ineligible for legalization and remain undocumented.

Agencies in Charge of the Implementation. The liberal values that characterize the bill are striking, especially in areas related to public health. Whereas in IRCA the principal agency of enforcement was the Immigration and Naturalization Service, under the 1990 bill responsibility for implementation is assigned to Health and Human Services, which is given the authority to determine whether a person "has a communicable disease of public health significance" or "has a physical or mental disorder that could or has in the past posed a threat to others." The former made possible a recently announced, sweeping revision of the nation's policy on immigration and AIDS. The latter substantially eliminates most grounds for excluding those with a physical or mental disability.

Passage of the 1990 act should quiet the concerns of many who feared that enactment of IRCA in 1986 signaled a new, restrictive era of immigration policy. The various programs have the power to change the legal status and work eligibility of more than 1 million persons. In terms of sheer numbers, immigrants in the United States under the legalization and safe-haven provisions clearly outnumber the 34,000 new skilled workers admitted annually under the bill. ✦

THE AMERICAN INDIAN IN U.S. HISTORY

DONALD J. HALEY

INTRODUCTION

When one speaks of the United States as a nation of immigrants, one usually ignores the fact that the ancestors of Native Americans were the first immigrants to the Western Hemisphere. Anthropologists and archeologists widely believe that the Paleo-Indians, who were the ancestors of the modern American Indian, crossed into the Americas from Asia via the landbridge of Beringia, now covered by the Bering Sea, sometime between 38,000 and 11,000 B.C. Different waves of migrants followed until the Western Hemisphere was populated from the Arctic Circle to Tierra del Fuego by at least 9,000 B.C.

Adapting to varied conditions and environments in such a vast area as the Western Hemisphere, these migrants and their descendants developed innumerable cultures. Such development would, of course, also apply to the Indian peoples within the borders of the United States of America.

However, before focusing on the major categories of Indians in the United States, one can identify certain common, broad characteristics within the diversity of Western Hemispheric Indian cultures. For example, Indian political organizations of tribes revolved around kinship. These socio-political units usually held real property in common. With a few exceptions, the Indian lacked the European concept of individual ownership of land. This difference became a great source of conflict

---

The author wishes to thank Dr. Wayne G. Bramstedt, Professor of Anthropology, El Camino Community College, for his helpful suggestions, recommendations, and encouragement.

between the two and, since the European had the technological superiority to enforce his concept, the white man resolved the differences in his favor. The Indian was also very religious. Every known pre-Columbian culture possessed religious institutions and most had specific individuals (priests or "medicine men") to tend to its spiritual needs.

The pre-Columbian Indians made immense contributions to contemporary mankind. Not only did they develop maize, beans, and squash, but approximately one-half of the crops raised in the world today were first cultivated by anonymous Indian horticulturalists. Among these crops were tobacco, peanuts, pineapples, avocados, tomatoes, and both the sweet and white potato. The so-called Irish potato was first developed in the Andes of South America. Modern medicine is indebted to the Indian for quinine and coca, from which cocaine and novocaine are derived. The Indian also deserves credit for cultivating rubber and inventing such items as the hammock and snow shoes. This brief catalog should dispel the myth of the red-skinned, ignorant savage.

There were, of course, certain items that the Indian did not possess—and which the European did. Most notably, the wheel as a transportation device was not used anywhere in the Western Hemisphere. Other than for use on children's toys by the Aztecs of Mexico, the Indian had no practical use for the wheel. Unlike the Eastern Hemisphere, the Western Hemisphere lacked large domesticated animals such as the horse, donkey, and ox. Aside from the llama of South America, man was the main animal of burden in the New World.

ADVANCED NATIVE CULTURES WITHIN THE UNITED STATES

Scattered throughout this hemisphere, advanced Indian cultures and civilizations appeared at different times and places. Although the Aztec, Maya, and Incas are the most famous, there were within the borders of the present continental United States some advanced native cultures that are worthy of note.

An example of these were the desert cultures of the Southwest which included the Hohokam of Arizona; the Mogollon of Arizona and New Mexico; and the Anasazi of Arizona, New Mexico, Colorado, and Utah. Living in agricultural communities—one of which stood on a 300 acre site—and watered by a vast, technically sophisticated network of irrigation canals in southern Arizona, the Hohokam achieved some outstanding feats. In the period between 900 and 1100 *A.D.,* the

Hohokam used their engineering skills to construct small pyramids and ball courts. They were also the only New World inhabitants to discover the process of etching—centuries before the Europeans had mastered this artistic skill. By using saguaro cactus juice as an acid, they made engravings on sea shells. The Mogollon culture, which existed from 250-1150 A.D., was noted for its pottery and the development of multi-roomed masonry pueblos. The Anasazi, no doubt influenced by the Mogollon, continued the masonry tradition and lived in sizeable mountainous communities, one of which had about 800 rooms. The Anasazi had irrigation canals, although not as large as the Hohokam, to water their crops. As a distinctive culture, the Anasazi disappeared around 1300 A.D. However, their influences were perhaps transmitted to the Pueblo cultures along the Rio Grande.

In the Ohio Valley, several mound-building cultures existed. The Adena culture (500 B.C.-200 A.D.) was followed by the Hopewellian (100 B.C.-400 A.D.). Both of these cultures evidently possessed a large population. While part of the populace was engaged in food production, another sizeable part inexplicably constructed large earthen mounds, some of which reached as high as 70 feet and stretched for miles. The size and effort needed to construct these suggest a comparison to the pyramids of ancient Egypt. Archeologists have discovered within these mounds many artifacts and materials that were not available in the Ohio Valley. Consequently the Hopewellians, in particular, must have had a vast trading network which included most of the continental United States.

An example of Mississippian mound-building culture is Cahokia, situated near present-day East St. Louis, Illinois. This site was inhabited from 700-1500 A.D. and supported a population of about 30,000. It possessed a large circle of posts for solar observation similar to those of Stonehenge in England. Located there is the spectacular "Monk's Mound" that is 1,000 feet long, 800 feet wide, and 100 feet high, which means that an estimated 50 million cubic feet of earth had to be moved to accomplish its construction.

Continuing the mound-building culture was that of the Natchez, who lived in nine villages near modern Natchez, Mississippi. This culture continued to exist as late as the early 18th century when it was destroyed by the French.

GEOGRAPHICAL CLASSIFICATION OF U.S. INDIANS

When the European explored all the different regions within the continental United States, he was confronted with a bewildering array of different Native American tribes. Because it would be partially impossible to discuss each Indian tribe, we shall briefly examine the Indian cultures found in the various geographical regions of the United States.

The Northeast Woodlands region corresponds to the area located from the Atlantic to the Mississippi and from the Great Lakes to the Ohio River. Here various tribes engaged in hunting and agriculture and lived in small palisaded communities. One of the first powerfully organized Indian societies that the European encountered here was the Iroquois. "Iroquois" is the collective term given to a confederation of five—later six—tribes. These people had developed a sophisticated governmental structure in which each tribe retained its local autonomy but cooperated with the others on larger matters such as war and diplomacy. It has been suggested that the Iroquois Confederation may have served as an inspiration for principles later incorporated into American government.

Directly to the south were the Southeastern "Five Civilized Tribes": the Choctaws, Chickasaw, Creeks, Cherokees, and Seminoles. These people too engaged in hunting and agriculture and resided in small villages presided over by two chiefs.

Crossing the Mississippi, one discovers the Indians of the Great Plains, stretching from the Canadian border to Texas. Here lived various cultures heavily dependent upon the buffalo. This animal provided most of life's necessities—not only food, but clothing, shelter (tipis), and warmth (buffalo chips). Great Plains' societies hunted the buffalo on foot until the horse was introduced by the white man. As a result, these societies were more mobile than the eastern tribes.

The Indians of the Great Basin, located between the Rocky and Sierra Nevada mountains, had to endure a hostile, semi-arid environment. Indian cultures there were dependent upon primarily rabbit-hunting and gathering almost anything edible for subsistence. Since usually a given environment could not support a permanent settlement, these tribes, also, had to be constantly on the move. The adaptability of these people is seen in their ability to survive under such adverse conditions. Another example of their flexibility are the Comanches, who were originally a people of the Great Basin. But by readily adopting the horse, the

Comanches successfully evolved into a tribe of the Great Plains, where they were noted for their ferocity, courage, and horsemanship skills.

The Southwest was, and is, the home of the Pueblo Indians, often acknowledged as the "most advanced" native culture residing in the United States. Although these people belong to different linguistic groups, they shared common traits in agriculture, political, and religious institutions. At the time of the Spanish arrival in the middle of the 16th century, there were approximately 70 pueblos (Spanish for "village") stretching from Texas into Arizona. In this area also lived the Apaches and Navajos, linguistic relatives to each other (but not to the Pueblos) who migrated from the north into the Southwest perhaps as early as 1000 A.D. Today, the Navajo is the single largest tribe in the United States with a reservation larger than New England and a population near 200,000.

The Pacific Northwest Indian culture was concentrated on the coast from the Alaskan Panhandle to Northern California. The ocean provided these people with their main supply of food. In large wooden boats, these people put to sea in order to fish and hunt seals and walruses. A unique feature of this culture was the *potlatch* ceremony, during which an individual either conspicuously destroyed or gave away accumulated wealth. One individual's *potlatch* ceremony, in turn, stimulated others to amass wealth so that they too could host a *potlatch.* Although wealth was put to a different use, it has been stated that the Pacific Northwest Indians were the only pre-Columbian peoples whose economic value system approximated that of the European, even to the extent that the Pacific Northwest peoples understood the concept of ownership of real property.

The borders of the modern state of California form the final geographical area of pre-Columbia cultures. California possessed one of the largest and most varied native populations in North America. Reflecting this diversity, linguists have pointed out that a number of different language families and languages were spoken in California. In addition, there were various levels of cultural, social, and economic patterns of existence among the California tribes. In the northern part of the state, for instance, lived branches of the Pacific Northwest tribes such as the Hupa and the Yurok, who resided in coastal fishing villages. In southern California there were tribes like the Gabrielinos of Los Angeles, who lived in small hamlets and relied upon small game, fish, shellfish, and ground acorns for food. California desert tribes such as the Agua Caliente of Palm Springs led a nomadic existence gathering whatever they could find in the waste lands. In other words, California, with an aboriginal population estimated to be between 100,000 and 250,000, formed a cultural microcosm, much as modern California does for the world's peoples of today.

WHITE-RED COLONIAL CONTACTS

As is usually true between cultural strangers, many unfortunate misunderstandings occurred during the early period of contact between the European and the Indian. In 1524 one of the earliest explorers of the Atlantic coastline, the French-hired Giovanni da Verrazano, used force and intimidation to solicit information on the location of a mythical water-route through North America. In 1540-42, Spaniards seeking legendary lands of gold also engaged in barbaric acts towards the Pueblo Indians during their forays into the Southwest.

Although English seamen occasionally killed or kidnapped Indians along the Atlantic, the initial contacts between the English and the Indian were free of official overt hostilities. Both even experienced benefits from the other. The Indian might have been dazzled by the novelty and beauty of mirrors and beads, but he immediately recognized the utility of European weapons, iron implements, and textiles. On the other hand, the outright survival of early English settlements depended upon the goodwill and compassion of their Indian neighbors. The Powhattan Confederation Indians, for example, brought food to early Virginia settlers. Further, had it not been for the timely aid of Squanto and Samoset of the Wampanoags, the famous Pilgrims of Plymouth might have perished through starvation.

Relations between the Indian and the English settlers, however, soon soured. As more and more settlers arrived, the Atlantic Coast Indian began to realize that the white had come to stay. Ignorant of or indifferent to earlier Indian aid, later English immigrants felt no particular respect or obligation toward the Indian. The Indian discovered that his food and land, sometimes even his women and children, were coveted by the whites. If the Indian resisted white encroachments, the technological superiority of English culture triumphed and forced the Indian either to migrate or submit. Migration meant the Indian would have to break forever his strong spiritual and emotional ties with his ancestral lands. If these Indians attempted large-scale migration into the interior, they aroused the enmity of Indian tribes there. So they chose to remain on ever-shrinking tribal lands, where they faced a life of humiliation from the settlers and authorities or the risk of death from European diseases. The fate of the Atlantic Coast tribes was sealed: they disappeared from the stage of history.

The fate of interior tribes was complicated by international considerations. As the English moved across the Appalachians into the Ohio Valley, they encountered the French. The two European groups saw the opportunities of the Ohio Valley differently. The French desired to maintain the wooded wilderness for its fur trade potential and to use the area as a defensive barrier against English expansion. Although the English saw the economic opportunities of the fur trade, they also sought to build permanent settlements, homes, and farms which would ultimately tame the wilderness and displace the native inhabitants.

While many Indian tribes recognized that the French represented a lesser threat to their cultural survival, Indians could not always agree—let alone cooperate—with each other on what would benefit all Indian peoples. English and French agents alike tried to cajole or bribe different tribes in order to gain allies in the struggle for supremacy in the interior. Some tribes, such as the Hurons, allied with the French, while others, such as the Iroquois, became allies of the English. However, if the Europeans hoped to use the Indian for their purposes, the Indians, in turn, hoped to use the European to wage war more effectively upon their own tribal enemies. Hence, we discover that both the French and English had Indian auxiliaries during the various colonial wars of the 18th century.

At the conclusion of the French-Indian War (1754-63), Britain was in undisputed control of the interior woodlands. No longer could tribes maintain a degree of freedom by playing off Europeans against one another. Now the Indian faced British law and policy directly. Parliament, aware of some of the tribes' difficulties, passed the Proclamation of 1763 in order to restrict white settlement in the Ohio Valley and protect the tribes from the more aggressive white settlers. This policy, however, angered many settlers and formed an important background grievance that partially contributed to the American Revolution.

The American Revolution again forced the various tribes to choose between the white combatants. Those who sided with England often felt the fury of the colonists' wrath. The Iroquois, for example, suffered a devastating invasion from a Continental force which fired their settlements and crops in 1779. So bitter was this experience that a group of Iroquois, along with many of their Anglo counterparts, found it necessary to migrate to Canada after the Revolution. However, other

Indian tribes, no matter how they had sided during the Revolution, had to await the Indian policies of the newly independent United States of America.

U.S. INDIAN POLICY

Official United States policy toward the numerous tribes was to recognize them as independent, sovereign nations. The authority to deal with the Indian was exclusively vested in the national government under both the Articles of Confederation and the Constitution. In practice, this usually meant that Indians were handled by the War Department or, later, the Department of Interior with Congress providing advice and consent. Generally, the government attempted to negotiate treaties with the Indian tribes.

The purpose of treaty negotiations was to avert Indian-White hostilities by getting the Indian to accept the loss of part or all of his tribal lands in order to open them up to white settlement. In exchange for this loss, the Indian would receive monetary or gift considerations accompanied by a U.S. guarantee and confirmation of ownership of remaining tribal lands. Following these guidelines, it has been estimated that the U.S. government negotiated over 370 Indian treaties from 1778 to 1871.[1]

Treaties presented the Indian with endless difficulties. Often problems of interpretation and misunderstandings resulted in later disagreements between the Indian and U.S. negotiators as to a treaty's contents. Indian negotiators all too commonly felt that they had been purposely misled. U.S. promises of gifts or monetary compensation would either arrive too late or fail to materialize at all. Another difficulty was that the terms agreed to by Indian "leaders" recognized by the American government would not be accepted by other tribal members. To compound the difficulties, it seemed to the Indian that no sooner had a treaty been negotiated when new government agents would appear demanding new Indian concessions. There soon developed among the Indians the belief that neither the U.S. government nor its agents felt honor-bound to obey or enforce their own treaties. As Chief Sitting Bull once remarked, "There is no use talking to these Americans. They are all liars, you cannot believe anything they say."[2]

PHYSICAL REMOVAL AND RELOCATION

On some occasions in American history, the American government has demanded the outright physical removal and relocation of Indian tribes to lands far from their ancestral homes. At times, the government insisted on this in order to remove and protect the Indian from physical harassment and abuse from lawless white elements. However, to the Indian, considering his deep spiritual links to his tribal lands, this demand seemed to be a particularly unreasonable and cruel one.

In 1830, Congress passed the Indian Removal Bill that empowered the president to initiate exchanges of eastern tribal lands for those in the west. The purpose of this law was to place pressure on Indian tribes to cede desirable eastern lands and then force their migration to lands in the distant west which would be designated as Indian Territory (present-day Oklahoma). This measure was supposedly designed to "protect" the Indian, but its true purpose was to remove Indians from lands coveted by whites.

Because most Indians had no desire to migrate to unknown western lands, whites had to find a means to force Indian removal. An example of this ploy was seen in the Southeast. In the states of Georgia, Alabama, and Mississippi, the Five Civilized Tribes possessed millions of acres of potentially valuable cotton lands. When it became apparent that the tribes would not voluntarily exchange their lands, the three states enacted laws placing Indians under state—rather than federal—jurisdiction and further legislated that an Indian could not testify against a white. The intent of these state laws was, in effect, to encourage white harassment of Indians to force their westward migration. Some Indians saw the handwriting on the wall and left, as in the case of 4,000 Chickasaws who moved west in 1831.

Others, however, recognized that state laws violated the U.S. Constitution which had placed Indian policy under federal control. Unfortunately, appeals made to President Andrew Jackson fell on deaf ears. Another legal recourse was to turn to the judiciary, which was exactly what the Cherokee nation did.

The Cherokees owned vast amounts of land in northern Georgia which had been guaranteed to them in a formal treaty by George Washington. The Cherokees had adopted the American system of government for their tribal political structure. They had also created a public school system which taught both Cherokee and English. In many ways, except for red skins, the Cherokees were indistinguishable in their life styles from their white neighbors.

Yet, this similarity did not mean that whites accepted the Cherokees as equals. Many white Georgians resented the prosperity of the Cherokees and the discovery of a small gold strike on tribal lands further whetted white appetites for Cherokee lands. In violation of federal law, Georgia declared Cherokee land open to white settlement. The Supreme Court, in the case of *Worcester v. Georgia*, ruled that Georgia's actions were indeed unconstitutional. However, President Jackson made a famous response: "[Chief Justice] Marshall has rendered his decision. Now let him enforce it." In other words, the chief law enforcement officer in the United States would not defend the Cherokees.

Ejected from their homes, the Cherokees attempted to live in the wilds, as their distant ancestors had done. But this was not to be their fate. A federal army was sent to round up the Cherokees, and, after a group of renegade Cherokees signed a treaty ceding tribal lands, approximately 16,000 Cherokees were then force-marched to Oklahoma along what has been termed the Trail of Tears. En route an estimated 4,000 Cherokees died from exposure, hunger, and disease.

CONQUEST/GENOCIDE: THE CALIFORNIA AND PLAINS INDIANS

Another example of the Indian experience in the U.S. is seen in the fate of the California tribes which, as has been previously noted, were quite varied and numerous. The California coastal tribes, in particular, had experienced great cultural shock and dislocation under the Spanish and the Mexicans, who had enticed the Indians into missions where they labored long hours for the missionary fathers. However, at the very least, Hispanic civilization saw the Indian as a simple creature who needed discipline in order to save his soul.

After California had been acquired by the United States, a different attitude prevailed which resulted in large-scale destruction for the Indians. As one of John C. Fremont's men remarked, "We killed plenty of game and an occasional Indian. We made it a rule to spare none of the bucks."[3] In other words, the Indian was seen as a wild animal that was nothing other than an impediment to the development of the area's resources. Reflecting this viewpoint, miners cut down oak groves to use the wood for shaft supports and blocked rivers and streams rich with fish to pan for gold. These acts resulted in destroying a major source of food [acorns] for the Indian. The large numbers of miners who arrived in California also served as carriers of Occidental and Oriental diseases against which the Indian had no immunity. The upshot of the American impact upon California's Indian population was genocidal; for in 1850, there were approximately 100,000 Indians, which became 30,000 in 1870 and 16,000 in 1916.

The arena for the final military conflict between Indian and white cultures in the United States was in the Great Plains region. This was the last untamed frontier region and here the Indians had to make their final stand against the white American onslaught. Although the Sioux under Chiefs Sitting Bull and Crazy Horse had a famous victory against the U.S. Army at Little Big Horn in 1876, the Plains Indians were the ultimate losers in the many armed conflicts and skirmishes that occurred from the end of the Civil War to 1890.

The Great Plains Indians were defeated for the very same reasons that earlier Indians had lost to the whites. First, and foremost, was the impact of the Old World diseases of small pox, measles, and influenza which vastly undermined the Indians' ability to resist white encroachment. The Indian, secondly, was technologically inferior. White access to technologically superior weaponry meant that in armed conflict the Indian was never equal to his adversary's fire power. Finally, the tribal structure and strength of the Great Plains Indians were fatally weakened by the destruction of the buffalo, which declined from an estimated 15 million in 1865 to the verge of extinction in 1885. With the disappearance of the buffalo from the Great Plains, the Indian's whole pattern of life was thereby destroyed.

With their cultural life shattered, the remnants of the various Indian tribes were placed on reservations, where they suffered the indignity of being dependent upon Indian agents for hand-outs of food, blankets, and clothing. However, among many of the Indians a final hope was offered by the appearance of the so-called Ghost Dance movement. A Piute mystic named Wovoka preached that the ghosts of dead Indians would return to earth, drive the whites away, and restore the land to the way it had been before the whites' arrival. Many tribes embraced this belief and performed ritual dances in the desperate hope of regaining their lost world. White reservation agents and soldiers feared the influence and effect of the Ghost Dance movement. Reflecting this fear, the Seventh Cavalry slaughtered approximately 300 unarmed Sioux men, women, and children in December, 1890 at Wounded Knee Creek in South Dakota.

This "Battle of Wounded Knee" became known as the final armed conflict between whites and Indians in U.S. history.

POST CONQUEST: THE POLICY OF ASSIMILATION

Those Indians who survived the whites' military conquest and diseases went to live on their shrunken tribal lands where many hoped to be left alone to continue their cultural life in isolation far from the mainstream of the dominant culture of white America. However, that was not to be their fate, for Indians soon discovered new challenges to their cultural and ethnic survival.

Many white Americans, for quite a long time, felt that the only lasting solution to the Indian "problem" lay in assimilation. White policy makers, reaching back as early as Thomas Jefferson, argued that the Indian should be encouraged to discard his unique ethnic identity and adopt instead the cultural standards of White America. In other words, the Indian should be persuaded to surrender his "Indianness" into the supposed greater melting-pot of America. Since it exercised control over reservation Indians, the U.S. government held the means to try and force the Indian to assimilate.

With this goal in sight, Congress passed in 1887 the General Allotment or Dawes Act, which empowered the President to transfer tribal lands to individual allotments of 160 acres for each Indian family head on reservations or in Indian territory. The white hope was that this law would destroy the Indian concept of tribal communism and replace it with individualism. It was further anticipated that the Indian owners of each 160 acres would readily take up farming or ranching and thereby enter into the dominant economic pattern of late nineteenth-century white culture.

Another feature of the Dawes Act called for the government to sell unalloted, or "undistributed," tribal lands, of which there was a considerable amount because many Indians rejected the concept of individual ownership of land. This, in turn, resulted in a loss of more Indian lands to whites. After the allotment experiment ended in 1934, tribal lands had been reduced from 138 million to 48 million acres. Indians found that they had to survive on far smaller amounts of land than ever before. The white man's dream had become a nightmare for the red man.

Education of Indian children was another instance of an assimilationist policy adopted by the U.S. government. Although the use of public education as a means of instilling the dominant white Anglo-Saxon American values has long been a valuable means of absorbing various ethnic groups into U.S. culture, the education of Indian youth had many cruel aspects to it. For example, despite parental objections, Indian children were often physically removed to distant boarding schools which taught a limited curriculum of rudimentary English, basic math, farming, and industrial arts. The worthlessness of Indian education was described by the Hopi Don C. Talayesva, who recalled how in his first school year of 1891 all that he had learned were "bright boy," "smart boy," "yes," "no," "nail," and "candy."[4] Indian children, in other words, were given a curriculum which implied that simple basics were the most that they could hope to master.

Moreover, Indian children found it difficult to respect teachers and administrators who could not pronounce Indian names, who insisted on giving Indians English names which the teachers constantly changed or forgot, and who were ignorant of and disrespectful towards the Indians' cultural heritage. Needless to say, education for the Indians failed to hasten their assimilation.

THE INDIAN: 1900-1950

Although they were often the objects of movies, cartoons, radio dramas, popular home-decorative prints, and wooden advertising art, living Indians were all but forgotten by the majority of white Americans. By the 1920s the Indian had successfully defied assimilation and had persisted in remaining an Indian despite the various governmental programs and policies designed to end Indian culture. Indians had stoically turned inward and found the strength to survive by eking out subsistence on small marginal tribal lands.

However, during the Harding administration, renewed efforts were made to remove the remaining Indian resources. The villain of this drama was the notorious Albert Fall, Secretary of the Interior, who later went to jail for malfeasance in office. Fall sponsored the Indian Omnibus Bill to end tribal ownership of Indian lands. He also supported legislation to legitimatize white squatters' ownership of Pueblo Indian lands and made a concerted effort to take oil lands away from the Navajos. The coordinated political and legal opposition of Indians and sympathetic whites, coupled with the scandals associated with the Harding presidency, discredited and halted these new assaults on Indian cultural existence. In 1924, perhaps partially as an act of atonement, Congress recognized all

Indians as legal U.S. citizens. By the end of that decade, these new citizens faced yet another grave threat—the Great Depression.

The presidency of Franklin Roosevelt provided relief and reform for the majority of Depression-weary Americans. Minorities such as the Indian also benefited from the New Deal. The principal reform for the Indian was the Indian Reorganization Bill. This law's most important features were to end the allotment policy, to grant to tribes the right of democratically elected self-government, and to provide the tribes with funds for economic development. As a result, Indians could look to a more optimistic future, being insured self-determination in tribal, political, and economic decisions. The promise of funds for agricultural and industrial development filled many Indians with a new hope for the tribe's continued existence and, possibly, greater opportunities for its young. Although not specifically adopted with the Indian in mind, tribes might also benefit from other New Deal reforms such as the WPA, CCC, or Social Security. In addition, the U.S. Commissioner of Indian Affairs, John Collier, was sympathetic to, and a staunch champion of, Indian rights.

The policies of the New Deal may partially explain the overwhelming Indian support for the U.S. during World War II. Approximately 25,000 Indians served in the armed forces during this conflict and their contribution to the war was often unique. For instance, Indians speaking in their native tongues over walkie-talkies made it impossible for the enemy to eavesdrop on vital American battlefield communications. The war also produced an American Indian hero. It was a Pima Indian, Ira Hayes, who participated in the famous flag-raising on Iwo Jima.

THE "NEW INDIAN": 1950-PRESENT

The generation of Indians that has emerged since the end of World War II may be characterized as "New Indians." Since the 1960s the media have focused on dramatic Indian-white confrontations such as the Indian occupation of Alcatraz Island in 1969-71 or the conflict between young Indians and authorities at the site of the Wounded Knee massacre in 1973. From incidents such as these, one might think that the "New Indian" is a revolutionary militant. Of course, younger Indians, like their ethnic counterparts, are impatient for improvements and less willing to endure injustice as perhaps previous generations were. This younger generation of Indians has presented the white establishment with ongoing challenges over such issues as hunting, fishing, and land-use rights and has even successfully obtained the return of ancestral skeletons from museums. Indian pressures also partially explain the passage by Congress of the Indian Self-Determination and Education Assistance Act of 1975 and the Indian Education Act of 1978, which insured that Indian authorities will be paramount in the areas of social and educational services to the Indian communities.

As shown by demographics, quieter changes have occurred within the Indian community of the United States. For example, between 1945 and 1970, over 300,000 left their reservations for urban centers. By 1980, approximately 50 percent of all Indians resided in towns and cities. Like other Americans, the Indian has felt the magnetic pull of California opportunities. Not only does this state have the largest Indian population (201,311, according to the 1980 census), but the Los Angeles metropolitan areas has the single largest concentration (over 61,000) of Indians in the United States.

Living in an urban landscape subjects the Indian to the wider American cultural environment and its attending shocks and adjustments. Like other earlier, ethnic urban migrants, the Indian has sought out his fellow Indians for companionship and camaraderie. In 1968, the American Indian Movement (AIM) was established in Minneapolis by Indians to aid Indians in urban adjustment. Organizations such as AIM have exposed urban Indians to Indians from other tribes and the incidence of inter-tribal marriages has increased. These factors have contributed to the growth of a Pan-Indian consciousness that has allowed many individuals to transcend mere tribal identity. Consequently, this consciousness has enabled Indians to identify common Indian experiences and difficulties which many realize may only be resolved by all Indians coordinating their efforts.

Throughout most of American history, the failure of Indians to present a common front against white encroachment greatly contributed to their defeat. Pan-Indianism can prevent the practice of "divide and rule" and, therefore, the emergence of this concept may well be of lasting significance for the Indians of the United States.

Demographic trends indicate other positive signs for the American Indian. There are now more Indians (or, at least, more who are willing to identify themselves as Indians) than ever before in recent history. Statistics show a steady increase in the Indian population. The 1950 census numbered 357,499 Indians; 1960: 523,591; 1970: 792,730; and 1980: 1,418,195. Whereas in 1970 Indians formed .4% of the U.S. population, their numbers had increased so that by 1980 they were .6%

of the American population. Since Indians have one of the highest birthrates in the United States, their population is increasing at three percent per annum. The rise in Indian population may also be explained in medical terms, for the Indian death rate decreased 70 percent from 1955 to 1974. For better or ill, the United States will have to cope with more and more Indians.

As one might suspect, not all statistics on Indians are so positive. The population rise has placed great strains on the economies of the reservations, never particularly bountiful spots, to try and find the means of feeding more and more hungry mouths. Although some reservations have attempted innovative methods, such as the Mescalero Apaches' expensive resort-hotel or the Morongos' large bingo-parlor near Palm Springs, the unemployment rate remains shockingly high. An estimated unemployment rate of over 29 percent exists on reservations nationally. Since the median income of a reservation Indian male is lower than his urban counterpart, it is no wonder that the reservation Indian is leaving to seek opportunities elsewhere.

Although a grim economic reality faces the reservation Indian, it should be remembered that the Indian has had difficult times ever since the whites' arrival. Buffeted by disease, defeat, humiliation, and hunger in the past, the Indian survived—albeit slightly battered and perhaps psychically scarred—to confront the consciences of American citizens today. ✦

NOTES

1. J. Terrell, *Land Grab: The Truth About the "Winning of the West"* (New York, 1972), p. 57.
2. As quoted in D. Brown, *Bury My Heart at Wounded Knee: An Indian History of the American West* (New York, 1970), p. 418.
3. As quoted in W.A. Beck and D. A. Williams, *California: A History of the Golden State* (Garden City, N.Y., 1972), p. 231.
4. W. Moquin, ed., with C. Van Doren, *Great Documents in American Indian History* (New York, 1973), p. 280.

SELECTED BIBLIOGRAPHY

Beck, Warren A. and David A. Williams. *California: A History of the Golden State*. Garden City, N.Y., 1972.

Brandon, William. *The Last Americans: the Indian in American Culture*. New York, 1974.

Brown, Dee. *Bury My Heart at Wounded Knee: An Indian History of the American West*. New York, 1970.

Collier, John. *Indians of the Americans: The Long Hope*. New York, 1947. Heizer, R.F. and M.A. Whipple, eds. *The California Indians: A Source Book*. Berkeley, 1970.

Jacobs, Wilbur R. *Dispossessing the American Indian: Indians and Whites on the Colonial Frontier*. New York, 1972.

Moquin, Wayne, ed. with Charles Van Doren. *Great Documents in American Indian History*. New York, 1973.

Report on Indian Education, Task Force Five: Indian Education. Washington, D.C., 1976.

Silverberg, Robert. *The Mound Builders*. Greenwich, Conn., 1970.

Terrel, John U. *Land Grab: The Truth about "The Winning of the West."* New York, 1972.

Washburn, Wilcomb E. *Red Man's Land/White Man's Law: A Study of the Past and Present Status of the American Indian*. New York, 1971.

Yinger, J. Milton and George E. Simpson, eds. *The Annals: American Indians Today*. Philadelphia, 1978.

THE ANGLOS

DONALD HAYDU

THE ANGLOS*

It is not by coincidence that it was in that long, peaceful healing period, following the divisive War of 1812, that Americans created their symbols of nationality. After the name calling and sectional divisions aroused by an unpopular war, the American people were instinctively reaching out for what they could affirm rather than deny. In the 1820s, a new and more graceful capitol was rising from the ruins of a Washington, D.C. that was so recently burned to the ground by invading British soldiers. Less concretely, but just as significantly, a wave of popular nationalistic sentiment was sweeping over the country. A new respect was shown to the American flag. Fourth of July celebrations with attendant parades and "spread eagle" oratory became part of the American way of life. In short, traditions, within the cult of nationalism, were being formulated. Forty

*The term Anglo is currently in a state of great flux. In the common usage of the United States today, Anglo has come to stand for any non-Latino white. In the recent historical past, Anglo has designated whites of a Northwestern European extraction. However, in its strictly etymological meaning, Anglo refers to the Anglo-Saxon peoples who originated in Germany but conquered Roman-Celtic Britain in the 5th Century. They, along with their later Norman conquerors, laid the foundation for the major stock of England. The very name England is derived from Angle's land. In this sense Anglo should be used only to refer to the English people. To complicate the matter, the English became the dominant people in the British Isles, inasmuch as they conquered Wales and Ireland and incorporated Scotland. Ultimately they formed a great world empire that reached its peak in the late 19th Century. With the exception of the Catholic Irish, the other peoples of the British Isles, such as the Celtic Welsh, Scotch, and Scotch-Irish, shared in English power and absorbed much of the English values, such as the dominant Protestantism. Following in this line the word Anglo will be used in this essay to mean the peoples and heritage of the generally Protestant British Isles.

to fifty years after the Revolution, the Founding Father's generation was being romanticized by those who needed heroes for the purpose of national unification within their own generation. Significantly, two slogans from 1776 found official as well as commonplace acceptance in these heady years, "In God We Trust," and "E Pluribus Unum." The latter Latin phase means "Out of Many, One." Some trace the expression back to the Epistles of Horace. Whatever its origins, it has a particularly happy application to the American scene.

Then, as now, this national motto has indicated the process as well as the goal of American nationality. Out of a diversity of peoples, we hope for unity. As late as these 1990s, we must admit, however, the unity hoped for is as much an ideal as it is an accomplished fact. Moreover, because of continual immigration into this country and internal social change, the components of what make an American are continually changing. Statistical tables from the Department of Immigration can give one a fairly accurate picture of the numbers and places of origin of immigrants. However, they cannot describe the process that transforms these immigrants into a new American nationality. For that, the social scientist must join hands with the psychologist and the philosopher to describe when and if our historical diversity has developed into unity.

What is so fascinating about this process of American nationalization is that it has taken place and is taking place in observable historical times. Most modern nations have sprung from peoples whose origin and development took place thousands of years ago. Demographers tell us there are no pure races and ethnic groups. But the amalgamation periods for present nationalities, which were produced by migrations, intermarriage, and war, have sometimes taken place as far back as prehistoric times or at least so long ago that we cannot scientifically test and evaluate the process. What we see now is the finished product of a Chinese, an Armenian, a Greek, or a German who appear as a constant, at least in the last several hundred years.

We are, as a nation, only a little more than 200 years old. Before independence, our colonial period extends back just another 169 more years. What is that compared to the Japanese, Egyptian, or Persian of today whose formulation into a distinct nationality came over thousands of years? Yet if our pedigree is not quantitatively a long one, it is qualitatively a very rich one. More to the point, it can be traced with some degree of accuracy. We have a front row seat at an ongoing historic phenomenon.

The purpose of this article is to explore a moment of self consciousness in the historic process of becoming an American. Ensuing essays have been organized to describe the groups of people who have formed the physical foundations of the American population of today. Their contributions are pointed out and the method by which they blended and created a nationality have been indicated. "Blended" may be too homely a term to describe the involved process of combining many peoples into one nationality. But until a more sophisticated metaphor is found, "blended" will have to do.

What of the American blend? Is the American nationality the homogenized product of a melting pot or is it a tapestry? Does the tapestry still display the distinctive threads of its component people's "parts?" Would not a symphony be an even better comparison for emerging Americanhood? Tapestries are two dimensional, but time is a factor in the definition of nationality. Just as certain sounds predominate or recede at one time or another through a continuing melody, so, too, certain racial, ethnic and national groups dominate or decline through the years of American development. Where are we, then, in the 1990s?

In these racially sensitive and ethnically conscious days, a certain motif has established itself, the dominant idea being that Americans are "Beyond the Melting Pot," if, indeed, they were ever in it. Many contemporary analysts maintain that the parts and pieces of the ethnic-national-racial puzzle of American nationality have never really fit or melded. To use the title of an important contemporary book, we are witnessing the rise of the "Unmeltable Ethnics."

However, we always were, and still are, hyphenated Americans with a pecking order of importance. As to the hyphenation, there are many who would disagree with this judgment. They argue that many ethnics have become so thoroughly Americanized that not only is the hyphen not needed, but additionally, there is no such thing any more as a German-American or a Scotch-Irish-American or a Scandinavian-American, and just barely a Polish-American or an Italian-American. Give them another generation or two, and their ethnicity also will have disappeared. The reader of this book will make his/her judgments. What we as writers of this text have attempted to do is to place the ethnic or racial minority in historical context.

"What is an American?" has been asked from virtually the beginning of our history. As early as the 18th century, the French intellectual and expatriate Hector de Crevecour posed the question:

> What then is the American, this new man? He is either a European or a descendant of a European, hence that strange mixture of blood which you will find in no other country. I can point out to you a family whose grand-father was an Englishman, whose wife was Dutch, whose son married a Frenchwoman, and whose present four sons have four wives of different nations. He is an American who, leaving behind him all his ancient preju-dices and manners, receives new ones from the new mode of life he has embraced, the new government he obeys, and the new rank he holds. He becomes an American by being received in the broad lap of our great Alma Mater. Here individuals of all nations are melted into a new race of men, whose labors and posterity will one day cause great changes in the world.

Both the optimism and European bias of de Crevecour's remarks persisted through a century of self-analysis and foreign opinions.

Among the most important interpretations of America's development from within was that of the late 19th century historian, Frederick Jackson Turner. In the challenges of an unsettled frontier, he saw the genesis of American nationality. It wasn't so much what the immigrant groups left behind in the old country as what they faced in the new land that was the key to the making of an American.

> In the crucible of the frontier the immigrants were Americanized, liberated and fused into a mixed race, English in neither nationality nor characteristics. The process has gone on from the early days to our own.
>
> The frontier is the line of most rapid and effective Americanization. The wilderness masters the colonist. It finds him a European in dress, industries, tools, modes of travel, and thought. It takes him from the railroad car and puts him in the birch canoe. It strips off the garments of civilization and arrays him in the hunting shirt and the moccasin. It puts him in the log cabin of the Cherokee and Iroquois and runs an Indian palisade around him. Before long, he has gone to planting Indian corn and plowing with a sharp stick. He shouts the war cry and takes the scalp in orthodox Indian fashion. In short, at the frontier the environment is at first too strong for the man. He must accept the conditions which it furnishes or perish—the outcome is not the Old Europe, not simply the development of Germanic germs. The fact is, that here is a new product that is American.

Turner had his eye on the rural frontier of the 18th and 19th centuries. For the most part, he was studying the responses of the Western European pioneer to this frontier. However, there can be an urban frontier as well. In our time, it is commonplace to describe the city as a dangerous jungle. Indeed, the most romantic description of the making of an American comes from a play with turn-of-the-century New York City as its setting. In 1898, Israel Zangwill, himself an immigrant English

Jew, coined the expression "The Melting Pot" in his drama of that title. As a playwright, Zangwill was fascinated with Eastern Europeans becoming Americans in a decidedly industrial atmosphere. In the florid prose so dear to our grandfathers, Zangwill places the following speech in his central character's mouth:

> . . . America is God's crucible, the great Melting Pot where all the races of Europe are melting and reforming. Here you stand, good folk, think I when I see them at Ellis Island, here you stand in your fifty groups, with your fifty languages and histories, and your fifty blood hates and rivalries. But you won't be long like that, brothers, for these are the fires of God, you've come to . . . these are the fires of God. A fig for your feuds and vendettas! Germans and Frenchmen, Irishmen and Englishmen, Jews and Russians—into the Crucible with you all! God is making the American.

The problem for the modern student of immigration history is that the fusion of races and nationalities spoken of so surely and positively in the previous quotations has worked in different ways to different peoples in different times. The current joke that all are equal in America but some are more equal than others has some truth in it. As we probe and then analyze this fusion process, it will be our intention to isolate the constants and variables as they apply to some distinctive peoples. To use metaphors already introduced: is there warp and woof to the tapestry, a leit-motif to the symphony, a thickening agent for the stew in the melting pot?

To these questions, I would answer yes—but it is a yes that takes some explaining and some caution. It is this writer's belief that the pattern, however hazy and incomplete, for an American emerges from that movement of people called by Marcus Hansen, "the Atlantic Migration of 1607-1860," a period which covers our colonial and early national history. It was a formative stage for American life in many ways, not the least of which is demographic. During this period, millions of people moved to the English colonies and what came from them, the new United States.

Within this exodus, there were hundreds of thousands of Africans, but all except a small percentage of them were destined for slavery. In contrast, within the white community, multitudes more came with the hope of personal advancement into a land that offered some degree of freedom. Through freedom comes power, and it was that power that was able to define a free colonial and later a citizen.

Throughout these formative years, the whites principally came from the British Isles and the German states, though there was a minor flow from France, the Netherlands, and Scandinavia, and even a few from southern Europe. From the start, there was intermarriage among these groups. The scarcity of mates in the New World and the possession of a common Protestantism, whatever their particular churches, speeded the mixing process. Before the end of the colonial period, there emerged a type that is now somewhat derisively called the WASP—the White Anglo-Saxon Protestant.

If there is a constant to the ethnic-racial history of America, it is this WASP who has served as a dominant and dominating element. To be an American certainly does not mean that one has to be a WASP. However, it does mean in some way to have been influenced by WASP values and power. This is true even if that influence has been expressed by a *rejection* of it. The last 30 years, for example, have witnessed conscious repudiation of the WASP mentality by sizeable sections of the American population. Especially was this true of the counter-culturalists of the 1960s. However, even that exaggerated rejection of some years past was formed by WASP ideas and attests to their importance. To reject or to hate means to be deeply engaged in what one is rejecting or hating.

Of all the ethnic components that formed the WASP, the English, the Scotch, and the Scotch-Irish were by far the most important. After all, it was the Englishman's empire. His language, law, literature, political institutions, mores, and manners—and eventually revolutionary ideas—permeated those 13 colonies and the people who settled there. English social elites set the style and standards. One is struck, for example, by John Adams bragging about the greater English quotient of the inhabitants of his native Boston as compared to Philadelphia, a boast which came on the eve of the Revolutionary War. Benjamin Franklin, appearing before Parliament to ask for repeal of the Stamp Act, emphasized how the colonists had prided themselves on being "Englishmen" before the infamous Act had been passed. It is hard to overestimate the Englishman's influence on American nationality.

Within our society, the Anglo-American has been the measuring rod of acceptance and success for so long that we sometimes forget upon what that eminence is based. Fundamentally, the power of the English, in particular, and other peoples from the British Isles, in general, is based on the following foundations:

1) *Numbers.* From the start of the colonies, people from the British Isles came over in larger numbers than those from other areas of the world. That preponderance was maintained surprisingly well after Independence and into the 1840s of the National Period. At the time of

the first official census in 1790, the percentage distribution of the white population by nationality reads as follows: 60.0% English, 8.3% Scotch, 6.1% Scotch-Irish (Ulster). Therefore, at that time, three-fourths of the American population either were, or were descended from Protestants from the British Isles. Immigration statistics indicate that English immigration continued to be heavy all through the 19th century. From 1820 to 1870, the English were always within the top three positions as suppliers of people for America.

2) A second foundation for Anglo influence is *mother country identification.* The Atlantic seaboard colonies were the nursery of the United States. From English, rather than from Spanish or French America, came the Revolution and evolved the new nation. These colonies were, after all, part of the world-wide British Empire. England, for them, was the seat of political power and social prestige. Although, with the coming of the 18th century, other nationalities were welcomed into these mainland colonies, the English people could still feel more at home than any other group. They could be comfortable with their easy identification with the transplanted English language, law, and political and social structures. And undoubtedly, the English were favored over other groups by the imperial administration, at least until the Revolution. However, even after independence, the English origin of an immigrant could still be a prestige factor. For many years, although politically independent, the United States was a cultural satellite of England. As late as the 1830s, 70 percent of the books read in America were printed in England. It has been noted by many sociologists that as a result of just such factors as language and culture, the English were the most quickly assimilated of all immigrant groups. The bonding of American with Englishman was intensified by the power and glory of 19th century Victorian England and by the close cooperation in foreign policy in the 20th Century's two world wars.

3) *Firstness* and *thickness* of the English settlements in the colonial period. The English were almost always the first white settlers in the Atlantic seaboard areas and they were, by far, the largest. Therefore, subsequent immigrants had to adjust to the English, rather than the other way around. English precedents of pioneering as well as structures of local and provincial governmental power became the models. It is true that small Swedish settlements were present in Delaware and New Jersey before the 1640s. Then, too, before the British conquest of New York, it was called New Netherland with thriving Dutch communities in the Hudson Valley, culminating in the great port city on Manhattan Island.

But whereas the Dutch and the Swedes settled in the hundreds, the English and then the Scotch-Irish migrated in the tens of thousands. For example, in the Great Migration of the 1640s, it is estimated that between 40,000 to 60,000 English came over and peopled New England. There they reproduced the English countryside of close knit towns and provincial cities.

After the British took over New Netherland, which had already absorbed New Sweden, the original inhabitants began the pattern process of adopting English ways. Because the Swedes were smaller in numbers and thinly scattered over a relatively large area, the process of amalgamation started immediately and was completed by the Revolution. The Dutch were somewhat more concentrated geographically. They could present for a while a rival density to the English. Moreover, they had backup institutions which preserved their language and culture into well past independence. Little wonder that Franklin D. Roosevelt, a descendant from Dutch America, could tease the Daughters of the American Revolution at one of their conventions in the 1930s with an address that opened with the salutation, "Fellow Immigrants."

Even with powerful families, the Dutch Reformed Church, parochial schools, and charitable organizations, it was a losing battle for the Dutch in their efforts to preserve their ethnic-cultural distinctiveness. There were just too many English speaking neighbors as time went by. In a move that would be repeated many times in the future among other ethnics, between 1764 and 1803 the English supplanted the Dutch in the services of the Dutch Reformed Church as a result of popular pressure particularly coming from the younger generation.

This factor of density of settlement also played a role in the outcome of the colonial struggles for control of North America between the British and the French. Only on maps did the French Empire rival the British in the 18th century. Though geographically extensive, the French population in Canada and the Mississippi Valley numbered only about 80,000. Often the French settlements were little more than fur trapping stations and trading posts. The French did not really occupy the land so much as they wanted the products of the area. By contrast, the English population was concentrated along the Atlantic seaboard and numbered about two million by 1750. Such concentration and numbers stimulated a more varied and intensive economy. The British colonial victory during the Great War for Empire (our French and Indian War) was in no small way assured by numbers and the pattern of settlement.

4) Finally, the *representative Protestantism* of the English and Scotch-Irish provided an ideological framework for the long dominance of Western European Protestants in America. At the time of colony founding, the English were still enthusiastic for their Reformation faith, now about 75 years old. At least officially, part of the motivation for founding English colonies in the New World was to offset the missionary gains of Catholic Spain. Protestantism and patriotism appeared synonymous as the English began to look upon themselves as the defenders of the Protestant world in the 17th and 18th centuries. The ramifications of this connection between national loyalty and a specific religious solidarity would reach into 20th century America. The 100% American crusade of the 1920s taught that to be fully American one had to be Protestant. Catholics and Jews bore the brunt of discrimination.

At the time of the Revolution, only one percent of the English colonies was Catholic, half of one percent was Jewish, and all the rest could at least generically be classified Protestant. More significant is the fact that within this overwhelmingly Protestant society, it was the Calvinistic interpretation of the Protestant Reformation that dominated. In a survey done on the numbers and nature of churches in newly independent America, over half of the congregations were Calvinist, be they in the form of the English Puritan, the Dutch Reformed, the French Huguenot, or the Scotch-Irish Presbyterian persuasions. English Calvinism was thus more than a religion; it was a way of life.

Furthermore, the "package deal" of Puritanism reenforced the English dominance of American morality. The core ideas and values espoused by these pioneer English Calvinists who are called Puritans and Pilgrims triggered the mainsprings of much of the spiritual heritage of an America that was in the process of defining itself both psychically and physically. In specific terms, this Puritanism grafted on to the colonies, and then the new nation, a sense of mission and supreme self-confidence. Basing their sense of superiority on the Calvinist theological concept of predestination, the English Puritans came to America feeling they were God's Chosen People. This feeling of superiority, together with an emerging English nationalism, created a people who felt they had "an errand in the wilderness" to build a "New Jerusalem" which would be "a light on the mountain" to sinful mankind.

What was English, what was middle class, and what was Calvinist is often hard to disentangle from one another. Puritanism, especially in the 17th century, was such a dynamic movement that even the official Church of England, as well as many of the dissenting sects—such as the

Baptists—were much influenced by it. This is particularly true in colonial America. One of the great historians of American intellectual and cultural life has maintained that Puritanism (English Calvinism) is the longest lasting system of values in our history.

Edward Johnson, cofounder of Woburn, Massachusetts, wrote about the sense of messianic mission his co-religionists had when they embarked on their voyage to New England:

> All you the people of Christ that are here oppressed and scurrilously derided, gather yourselfs together, your wives and your little ones and answer to your several names as you shall be shipped for his service, in the western world and more especially for planting the united colonies of New England . . . you may not delay the voyage intended for your full satisfaction . . . know this is the place where the Lord will create a new heaven and a new earth in new churches and a new commonwealth together. Your Christ hath commanded the seas they shall not swallow you, nor pirates imprison your person or possess your goods.

The melody of this refrain has lingered for a long time. Only in the last 30 years has the moral superiority that it implies been deeply and popularly questioned. Vietnam and Watergate, particularly, spurred the questioning. Still, the "sense of mission" was the foundation of Anglo-American ethno-centrism. The people who shared this religious heritage of predestination and "election of God" also shared a common racial-ethnic stock of Northwestern Europe. There were many variations, to be sure, among English Puritan, Scotch-Irish Presbyterian, and Dutch Reformed, but a common theme.

Therefore, one can see how ethnic superiority and religious superiority could become interchangeable. One of the justifications of American imperialism in the 1840s and again in the 1890s was that it was "the Manifest Destiny" of Anglo-Americans to bring the blessings of the pure religion, better government, and civil liberties to the lesser breeds of people. If one were unfortunate enough to be an Indian, Spaniard, Mexican, or Filipino, one should get out of the way and stop holding up progress. America, directed by the *right* people, had a divine commission to civilize our "little brown brothers." As President McKinley remarked in the Spanish-American War: "If this is imperialism, for God's sake, let's have imperialism."

One of the signs of Puritan Predestination in the religious sense is also an integral part of the economic legacy of England to America's material development. It is commonly called the Protestant Work Ethic. No nation or group of people has a monopoly on the practice of hard work. But few have seen a more spiritual dimension to "the curse of Adam" than the founding English Puritans. Taking their cue from John Calvin's teachings, they stressed what came to be called the Yankee virtues of hard work, frugality, self-discipline, honesty, sobriety, and shrewdness. A person defined his worth in his work.

These very virtues, transferred from the personal realm to that of practical economic life, are the very qualities that make for a successful capitalist. Economic success as a sign of moral success is something definitely not universally taught. In fact, it is quite alien to some cultures and religions. However, it is the distinguishing hallmark of American character formation.

Historically, the Anglo male showed off his virility by being a good economic provider for wife and children rather than by being an object of romantic admiration. As has been pointed out by many scholars, this idea of the intrinsic value of work, this desire to be a "provider," went hand in hand with the rising middle class of England, and England's America. This middle class became the arbiters of American nationality. They pointed to their economic success in assuming leadership in the social and moral worlds. In turn, that leadership opened the door to continued economic advancement, to an emphasis upon the value of education, and to the preservation of power.

However, just as our "sense of mission" seemed to fail in the jungles and rice paddies of Vietnam and our political righteousness in the Watergate scandal, so the superiority of the WASP has begun to be questioned. Peter Schrag, for example, while affirming the historical importance of the WASP, has pointed out:

> They (the Anglos) invented the country and its values, shaped the institutions and organizations and tried to teach the newcomers, lest they become uncouth boors, how to join and behave. But when technology, depression, and the uncertainties of the post World War II frightened them, they drew the institutions around themselves, moved to the suburbs and talked prudence.

Especially since the Second World War, peoples with work ethics of their own, such as the Irish, the Jews, the Japanese, and the Armenians, are all challenging Anglo economic superiority. It remains to be seen whether these rising, materially successful groups can move into the Anglos' place and significantly define Americanhood for the future. But for now, the preeminent position of Protestant peoples from the British Isles has been that they are the constant ingredient and the power element in the making of an American. Their influence has been achieved through numbers, density, and primacy of settlement in the original colonies and has been preserved through political and religious institutional force. The white Anglo-Saxon Protestant American has been the living embodiment of power. Even his or her physical characteristics became standards of excellence. For generations, Anglo values have served as the disciplining and integrating criteria for other ethnic and minority groups who have come to the United States.

For example, one is reminded of all those old World War II movies in which John Wayne, as the super-WASP commander, leads a group of soldiers into battle. His platoon or squad, with all its ethnic diversity, is the microcosm of the nation. It usually contains one Iowa farm boy, an Italian or Irish urban Catholic, a Jew, an Indian or a Mexican, and, most probably, a Texas bigot or a smart-alec Ivy League educated boor from a "Mainline" family. They all fight among themselves until a battle crisis. Then they all become blood brothers. Through the skill of our Anglo commander, the men are led to victory. Two morals apply: 1) if we can act as brothers when facing death, why not during the whole course of our national life; 2) if this ethnic pluralism can be orchestrated, we need an orchestra leader—the WASP, of course. Because of the relatively high percentage of English and Scotch-Irish descendants in the United States, up to now, their values have been the stabilizing factor in an evolving nationality. "At least, one used to know when one had made it," complained an upwardly rising white (Eastern European) ethnic of the 1970s. One looked and acted like an Anglo.

In addition to the Anglos' power base, there is the uniqueness of their contributions. Among the most prominent are: 1) their development of representative institutions. This development provided the structural environment for American democracy to evolve; 2) their rich legal tradition of the common law of England. Anglo-Saxon jurisprudence has served as the foundation of American law; 3) their emphasis on individualism that opened the way to much personal accomplishment and fulfillment. It also bolstered a tradition of civil rights; 4) their openness to education and technology that kept alive the intellectual life of the English humanist tradition in the wilderness of a New World while providing for the popular, mechanical skills that made life easier and, in some cases, even possible. These same skills laid the foundations of American industrialization. Each of these points is worthy of an essay in itself; we must be content with some amplification.

Much of the Anglo inheritance is of a political nature. This is rightfully so. The English colonies were distinguished from other imperial dependencies by their degree of local participation in government. Not only did each of the English colonies have a charter outlining their basic rights, but they had physical institutions to express the popular will. Behind the colonial governmental experience was the English parliamentary tradition which in itself was evolving and influencing America. "An Englishman can have no laws or taxes made over him except with his own consent, given personally or through his own representatives in parliament." This was not just a legal abstraction; it was taken as reality in town meetings in New England and in township councils and county governments elsewhere. Each of the colonies had a provincial assembly, one of whose houses (or both) was elected by the people.

The concept of government resting on the consent of the governed was reenforced by the prevalent congregational-presbyterial form of church government. Puritan congregations chose their ministers, deacons, and elders. Covenant theology maintained that the true church rested on a contract between "the Elect of God" and God Himself. Little wonder that a sense of personal freedom grew up in English America that in no small way brought on the Revolution. Clinton Rossiter, the noted 20th century historian, contends that within this seedbedding of representative institutions, there was a system of law. In no small way, this possession of a common legal structure helped provide the basis for a later national legal structure which, in turn, provided the basis for national unity. The principles of English Common Law had evolved over the centuries in the homeland and America was to be one of its chief beneficiaries. English Common Law developed certain safeguards for the rights of the individual such as trial by jury, freedom from arbitrary arrest and imprisonment, the right of private property, and the sacredness of contract to property that were not as emphasized in other national traditions. By building on this English foundation, they became core values in America's own legal system. Then, too, there was the idea that there was a tradition of law superior to the individual enactments of legislatures, and to which these enactments must be in harmony. For many, English Common Law (Anglo-Saxon jurisprudence) seemed to embody, or at least maintain, natural law principles that governments themselves must respect if politics is to be just and people free. The idea of a basic constitution that superseded individual laws became part of the American system from its Anglo inheritance. It is most concretely expressed in the United States Supreme Court's power of judicial review.

The psychological expression of this political and legal development was a sense of individualism. It, in turn, led to a desire to safeguard personal freedom throughout a very large portion of the colonial population. If the English intended to express freedom through an ongoing tradition of charters and institutions that limited arbitrary government and made central authority more representative, then the Scotch-Irish took a more earthy approach. "Doing your own thing" is a modern bit of advice on social behavior. Yet it could have been the slogan of the nearly 300,000 Scotch-Irishmen who came to America in the 18th century. Even more were to follow in the next 100 years. Feistiness, physical mobility, and a desire for space and privacy are about as basic a way as liberty can be expressed. Significantly for the development of an independent America, this sense of individual worth was for them completely divorced from the English parliament and law. As far as the Scotch-Irish were concerned, freedom was to be achieved with the least government rather than through government. Their peculiar history had made them resent anything connected with the British government. In the 17th Century England had resettled thousands of these Scotch-Protestants in Ulster county in Ireland. The lands they were given had been taken away from the native Catholic Irish. The Scots thus became pawns in an effort to subdue Ireland. The pawns, however, prospered. Within a century, the British parliament was placing economic restrictions on them. Their dairy and textile industries competed with similar interests in England. Because of the English restrictions, their economy collapsed. The Scotch-Irish left Ireland by the thousands with English America as their usual destination. Often penniless, they frequently sold themselves into indentured service. Needless to say, wherever they settled, they brought a seething hatred of Great Britain. When they could, they left the British power bases in America and went to the frontier. They became the scouts, pathfinders, and sod-busters. They became the foot soldiers and cadres of the Revolution; indeed, they fought and hated the British and American Tory with equal fervor and delight. Their sense of adventure, their common sense, their reverence of social equality and individualism all contributed greatly to America's tradition. Andrew Jackson stands as a monument to the Scotch-Irish.

A further word needs to be said about pioneering, in other than the political sense. Though, to be historically accurate, it was the Spaniards and Frenchmen who explored and first settled many sections of our country, the WASP definition of the pioneer image is the one that has lived longest in the popular imagination. From the *Leather-stocking Tales* of James Fenimore Cooper through western dime novels to contemporary Clint Eastwood movies, the tall, rangy, blue-eyed Anglo embodies the frontiersman. "Westward, the course of Empire" always beckoned the British Islers, for whatever reasons. Certainly, thousands went West simply to feel freer. They, like the Scotch-Irish, just moved out. But it was the Scotch-Irish, particularly, who left an indelible imprint on the Western common-man hero. They came not as part of a corporate enterprise, not as governmental agents, and not as religious missionaries. They came as individuals, or at least individual families. They were the poor man's odyssey, for their epic pits the common man against the world. The end result was that the Scotch-Irish helped transform the wilderness into a powerful modern nation. In the process, they intensified the individualism of the Anglos' heritage.

The Anglos' survival on the frontier, however, created both virtues and vices which have become part of the American character. Aggressiveness, social mobility, democracy, egalitarianism, nationalism, violence, genocidal racism involving the Indians, escapism, and materialism have all been seen as patterns of behavior which resulted from the Anglos' peculiar contact with the wilderness. In the past, the positive side of the WASP Western experience has been stressed. Now there are negative views. Consider, for example, these words from Phillip Slater's *The Pursuit of Loneliness:*

> The avoiding tendency lies at the very root of American character. The nation was settled and continuously repopulated by people who were not personally successful in confronting the social conditions obtaining in their mother country, but fled these conditions in the hope of a better life. This series of choices (reproduced in the westward movement) provided a complex selection process—populating America disproportionately with a certain kind of person.
>
> In the past we have always, explicitly, or implicit]y, stressed the positive side of this selection, implying that America thereby found itself blessed with an unusual number of energetic, mobile, ambitious, daring and optimistic persons. . . . But very little attention has been paid to the more negative aspects of the selection. If we gained the energetic and daring we also gained the lion's share of the rootless, the unscrupulous, those who value money over relationships and those who put self aggrandizement ahead of love and loyalty and most of all, we gained a critically undue proportion of persons who, when faced with a difficult situation, tended to chuck the whole thing and flee to a new environment. Escaping, evading and avoiding are responses which lie at the base of much that is peculiarly American—the suburb, the automobile, the self-service store and so on.[3]

Among the advance agents of Anglo civilization in the settlement of the country were the sheriff, the minister, and the teacher. The teacher, be she ever so humble a Yankee school "marm," is one of the key people in the perpetuation of WASP values. Appreciation of education was an important part of both the English Puritan and Scotch-Irish Presbyterian mentality. John Calvin taught that people should be able to read the Scriptures in order to be saved. His Scotch disciple, John Knox, emphasized an educated clergy. Thus it is not surprising that the beginnings of a public school system took place only 17 years after the founding of the Massachusetts Bay Colony. The "Old Deluder" Law of 1647 stipulated that every community that reached 50 households had to tax itself to support an elementary school teacher. Every community that attained 100 households had to support a Latin Grammar School (secondary) teacher. Most of the New England colonies and some of the townships in the Mid-Atlantic areas followed this pattern.

When one considers how early in colonial history this law was passed, the sacrifices made for education are nothing short of phenomenal. Barely convinced that they could even survive, the colonists, nevertheless, put education among their top priorities. Much of this education and this love of learning came from Puritan clergy trained at Cambridge and Oxford. These ministers instilled the desire to learn that was part of the great English humanist tradition. Only six years after the founding of the Massachusetts Bay Colony, a college called Harvard was established for the purpose of training a learned ministry and magistry. Scotch-Irish Presbyterians also revered education. Even as they tamed the frontier, they constructed grammar schools and sometime "log colleges." Of the 207 colleges established before the Civil War, 49 were founded under the auspices of the Presbyterian Church. Among them is prestigious Princeton University.

A commitment to education became an integral value in the new American Republic. As far back as 1787, Jefferson had successfully urged the Articles of Confederation Congress to set aside part of the revenues derived from the sale of public lands for the support of public schools in the Northwest territories. In that wave of political and social reform called Jacksonian Democracy, most of the states inaugurated or expanded or reformed their public school systems. Horace Mann, one of the great educational reformers of the 1830s and 1840s, pointed out the close connection between an educated electorate and a functioning democracy.

Furthermore, it was realized that the school was truly the nursery of a common nationality. The shared experiences of childhood and adolescence might be as important as governmental institutions in the moulding of many people into one. Henry Steele Commager, a historian who has influenced generations of 20th-century college students through his textbooks, wrote this about the 19th century public schools: "Education mirrored society and the public school was the great leveler. The playing field, which was equally important, had its own standards. Like the frontier and the school, it was leveling."[4]

What Commager did not describe was what level. The thrust of this essay is that it was, and, for the most part still is, a distinctly Anglo-Saxon level. The Puritan Work Ethic, the Gospel of Success, competitiveness (especially for males), the superiority of Western Civilization, English historical, constitutional, and literary models, Protestant morality and even Anglo social decorum and manners were taught with and through the A.B.C.s. Those who could best assimilate these values of the British Islers were those who had the greater promise of success both in the classroom and, more importantly, in general life.

After the 18th century, most of the English and Scotch-Irish coming to America were literate. Their command of the language enhanced their acculturation at school as elsewhere. Language, after all generates or at least clarifies the very categories of thought by which we understand as well as communicate. This is probably why the bilingualism proposed for schools in the Southwestern states seems such a threat to some of the Anglo heritage. They are afraid that any supposed challenge to the dominance of the English language is a challenge to the worth of their values. They fear that their children in particular and the next generation in general will be thinking and feeling differently. As of the 1990s, it is still an open question as to whether it will be the tolerant, positive and open side or the defensive, self-righteous and discriminatory aspects of the Anglo heritage that will predominate.

A true pluralism, like a real humility, must be based on an honest appraisal of worth. The virtues as well as the vices of the ethnic group careers in America must be evaluated as to their intensity and relative weight. The problem in past understanding of American character formation has not been so much an overestimation of English and Scotch-Irish accomplishments as it has been an under-estimation or even non-recognition of the contributions of other ethnic and racial groups. This imbalance created for so many years a lopsided view of our history. The fact that most American historians, until the 20th century, were WASPs themselves certainly contributed to this view. Today, however, there is a danger that in an attempt to right past wrongs, the pendulum may swing too far in the other direction. It is an irony of our times that with the exception of the much heard Polish jokes, the only "safe" subject to ridicule racially and ethnically in the popular media or in the halls of academe is a white Anglo-Saxon Protestant male. Two wrongs never made a right. The position taken in this essay confronts this new prejudice. The role of the Anglo must be accurately gauged and appreciated if we are to have a good shot at knowing what an American is. ✦

NOTES

1. U.S. Department of Commerce, Bureau of the Census, *Historical Statistics of the United States* (Washington, D.C.), 1975, pp. 1; 168.
2. Peter Schrag, *The Decline of the Wasp* (New York, 1970), pp. 64-65.
3. Philip Slater, *The Pursuit of Loneliness* (Boston, 1970), pp. 13-14.
4. Quoted in Schrag, p. 25.

SELECTED BIBLIOGRAPHY

Ballzell, E. Digby. *The Protestant Establishment: Aristocracy and Caste in America* New York, 1966.

Brogan, D. W. *The American Character.* New York, 1962.

Dinnerstein, Leonard; Reimers, David M. *A History of Immigration and Assimilation.* New York, 1975.

Dinnerstein, Leonard, Nichols, Roger, and Reimers, David M. *Natives and Strangers.* New York, 1979.

Gordon, Milton. *Assimilations in American Life: The Role of Race, Religion and National Origins.* New York, 1964.

Graham, Ian Charles Cargill. *Colonists from Scotland: Emigration to North America, 1707-1783.* Ithaca: N.Y., 1956.

Greeley, Andrew. *The Denominational Society.* Glenview, Illinois, 1972. Handlin, Oscar. *The Uprooted.* Boston, 1973.

Hansen, Marcus Lee. *The Atlantic Migration,* 1607-1860: *A History of the Continuing Settlement of the United States.* New York, 1961. Jones, Maldwyn Allen. *American Immigration.* Chicago, 1960.

Leyburn, James G. *The Scotch-Irish: A Social History.* Chapel Hill, 1962.

Novak, Michael. *The Rise of the Unmeltable Ethnics.* New York, 1972.

Olson, James Stuart. *The Ethnic Dimension in American History.* New York, 1979.

Schrag, Peter. *The Decline of the Wasp.* New York, 1971.

Silk, Leonard, and Silk, Mark. *The American Establishment.* New York, 1980.

Slater, Philip. *The Pursuit of Loneliness: American Culture at the Breaking Point.* Boston, 1970.

AFRICAN AMERICAN HISTORY

MARIA A. BROWN

WHO THEN IS THE AFRICAN AMERICAN?

He is Hannibal of the Alps, Mansa Musa, King of Mali. He is Cinque, an African prince. He is the slave trader, the involuntary immigrant to the western hemisphere, Africa, Europe. He is the American Revolution, the Cotton Gin, the source that produces the wealth for the American Industrial Revolution. He is Frederick Douglass, Sojourner Truth, Harriet Tubman, the abolitionists, Tom in *Uncle Tom's Cabin*, the Civil War, Reconstruction, Brer Rabbit, Booker T. Washington, George Washington Carver, a horticulturist—pursuer of the American Dream, the Progressive Movement, the National Association for the Advancement of Colored People, the Urban League, Ida B. Wells, a women's and Civil Rights activist. He is the minstrel man, the cake walk, the flapper, Bessie Smith, Ethel Waters, Josephine Baker, Eubie Blake, Paul Robeson, an artist. He is Marcus Garvey, the Harlem Renaissance, the Cotton Club, a poet, a sculptor, a novelist—Langston Hughes, Zora Neil Hurston, Rudolph Fisher, Jessie Fauset, Sterling Brown, Augusta Savage, James Baldwin, Ralph Ellison. He is an historian, an intellectual, a scholar, an internationalist—W.E.B. DuBois, Carter G. Woodson, John Hope Franklin, E. Franklin Fraizer, Ralph Bunche. He is not the *invisible man* but rather, he is the Depression, World War II, Korea, Lorraine Hansberry, a "Raisin in the Sun," a "Soldier's Play." Who then is the African American? He is the Civil Rights Movement, Viet Nam—Martin Luther King, Jr. with a dream—Malcolm X by any means necessary, Angela Davis, Andrew Young, Ron Dellums, Maxine Waters, Jessie Jackson, a minister, political and Civil Rights defender, an astronaut from M.I.T., Denzel Washington, Maya Angelou, the poet laureate of the 1993 Presidential Inauguration of William Jefferson Clinton, Bill Cosby, Toni

Morrison, the Nobel Prize winner in Literature, Eddie Murphy, Angela Basset, Lawrence Fishburne, Ossie Davis, John Singleton, Ruby Dee, Spike Lee, all doing the right thing! Michael Jordan, O. J., Charles Barkley and Magic.

He is beautiful, ugly, right—wrong. He is love—hate, warm —cold. He is funny—sad. He is soul— jive. He gets up and he gets down. He is rich and he is poor. He has eaten "in sorrow's kitchen and licked out all the pots." He know "why the cage bird sings." He "wears the mask" and yet he is "My country 'tis of thee, land of liberty—of three I sing." He is black, but as Ralph Ellison so eloquently wrote:

> It is not the skin color that makes a (Black) American, but rather the cultural heritage as shaped by the American experience, the social and political predicament . . . the memory of slavery and the hope for emancipation and the betrayal by allies and the revenge and contempt inflicted by . . . former "masters" after the Reconstruction and the myths, both Northern and Southern, which are propagated in the justification of that betrayal.[1]

Ellison's statement captures what it means to be black in America. It speaks to the fact that the African American is an authentic American and yet he is still suspect, misunderstood, and the object of racial contempt. Most unfortunately, the African American must live forever with the reality that he, a native son, has always been viewed as an intruder, not because of who he was as a person, but because of the color of his skin.

In spite of the fact that America, after more than 200 years of existence, has yet to become the harmonious society it at least theoretically strives to be, the African American still seems to be optimistic about the future and believes that one day the nation will defeat the overpowering forces of racism, hatred, and fear. Then, perhaps, he will be recognized for who he is as opposed to what he is. This sentiment is not new. It is one that has been nurtured in the historical experiences of America and in the belief that the "American Dream need not forever be deferred . . ."

In 1607, when the English North American colonies were founded, it was assumed that no one had the intentions of establishing a system of slavery. Even in 1619, when a Dutch frigate arrived in Jamestown, Virginia, and upon its departure left approximately 25 Africans in the colony, there is no indication that the desire to create such an institution existed. However, by the end of the 17th-century, such a system did become firmly entrenched in American life.

Ironically, it was in this society that Thomas Jefferson, a slave owner, could and did write the Enlightenment article of faith: "We hold truths to be self-evident, that all men are created equal. . . ." It was in this society that emerged an institution that would not only become an important tool in the development of an economy, but would also draw a demarcation line between the white and black races. Slavery would play a significant role in the development of racial attitudes that would become a traditional part of American social thought and behavior. Thus, slavery stripped the African American of his humanity while denying him access to the opportunities the American society had to offer.

No one knows what actually happened to the first Africans who arrived in Jamestown, Virginia. The evidence concerning their status is scanty. Whether or not they were slaves or indentured servants is difficult to ascertain. However, by the 1640s and 1660s, the status of the black man in the colonies was dearly defined. He was chattel property. He was subject to the complete domination of another, with no will, no power, and no privileges. He was forced to accept an unnatural condition that gave the appearance of a natural inferiority.

In 1641 Massachusetts, though it did not establish slavery in the New England colonies, sanctioned involuntary servitude.[2] In the same year, Virginia became the first to condemn blacks to perpetual slavery and subsequently stipulated that the condition of the slave would be inherited by his children. Between 1662 and 1702, similar laws were passed in the colonies of Maryland, Massachusetts, and South Carolina. These laws were know as slave codes.

Between 1682 and 1739, additional slave laws were adopted by the colonies. These codes were designed to regulate and control the mobility of the slave. In most colonies, the slave could not appeal or testify in civil or criminal cases involving whites; he could not participate in the trading or the buying or selling of goods; he was prohibited from lifting a hand against a white person, even in self-defense. In some colonies, the slave was denied religious or educational instruction, for he might use such knowledge in an attempt to attain freedom. Often, at the hands of his owner, the slave would suffer public ridicule, maiming, and possibly even death for stealing or attempting to run away. Naturally, slaves were forbidden to carry arms or participate in military exercises.

The laws sanctioning slavery and the slave codes relegated the black man to the bottom of a color-class caste system in colonial America. By the mid-19th century, blacks, totally separated from society, were doomed to a color-caste that perpetually denied them both human and civil rights.

Slave codes, laws, court decisions, and religious belief sanctioning slavery gave validity to the formation of a racially stratified society. They reinforced colonial notions held about those of African descent. Accordingly, the colonists viewed the slave as a savage—a descendant of a primitive race who lacked self-direction and a sense of will. Adhering to the Elizabethan concepts of the colors black and white, colonists associated the blackness of the slave's skin with all that was evil and degraded, while maintaining that they were God's chosen people because of their whiteness. It is fair to conclude that the blackness of the slave's skin served as a frightening contrast for the colonists in that it reminded them of all the things that they were not supposed to be.[3] As the demand for labor increased and the influx of African immigrants became greater, the fear the colonists had of the slave intensified as blacks now became an economic and social menace. Given the alleged inferiority of the slave and the belief that he could only be driven by force and could never be accepted as an equal, the colonists rationalized that social as well as physical distance had to be maintained and proceeded to take every precaution to classify and separate the races.

The free black population was also affected as racial fears, segregation, and discrimination laws were passed to deny them the rights to common liberty and to keep them separate from and inferior to the increasingly mobile white population. In no Southern colony could free blacks testify against whites. They did not have the right to vote. Laws were passed to prevent interracial marriage and racial mixing. Manumission, particularly in Southern colonies, was next to impossible, even though evidence demonstrates that prior to 1740, some slaves were freed by their owners. The colonists felt that the public interest was a stake—the public had to be protected. If an owner freed a slave, it was believed that the slave, given his supposed docile and childlike character, would become a public ward.

The desire to reduce the growth of the free black population is clearly indicated in the legislation passed in Virginia in 1691. If a slave was freed by his "master," the "master" had to make provisions for the freed man to leave the colony. Whites believed it would be impossible to control a large free black population that might ultimately consume the white community through miscegenation and amalgamation. It would also be difficult to control a populace that constantly reminded colonists that all blacks were not slaves and that to equate blackness with slavery was fallacious. Also, the existence of the free blacks contradicted the notion that blacks could not aspire to or handle the responsibility of freedom in white America, and the success of free blacks challenged the theory that blacks were inferior to white. Thus, free blacks were a thorn in the side of whites. They were also a constant source of racial tension, as well as a source of inspiration for those confined to slavery.

The contradiction between an economic system of slavery and an intellectual notion of racial inferiority on the one hand, and the increasingly rationalistic and democratic view of English settlers on the other, became especially bothersome as the Ace of Revolution moved closer to the American experience. As the patriots mobilized themselves and challenged British authority, the call for freedom intensified and spiraled throughout the colonies. Blacks, too, responded to the call for freedom. They listened to the patriotic slogans that proclaimed the right of man—and took these slogans seriously. Indeed, they were among the first Americans who died in the Boston Massacre of March 1770. Crispus Attucks, a black longshoreman yearned for freedom; a position not new for blacks, for they had resisted slavery from the beginning and had attempted to regain their freedom long before the colonies called for independence from England.

As early as 1712, a slave conspiracy was uncovered in York. Subsequent to this, a group of slaves on a plantation near Charleston, South Carolina, succeeded in escaping. They were apprehended, but not before they had resisted every effort to re-enslave them, and the Stono Rebellion became a tragic blot in American history. In 1740, a slave conspiracy was uncovered in South Carolina in which an estimated 200 slaves were involved. Slave conspiracies were also uncovered in Louisiana in 1763 and again in 1777. Slaves and free blacks on more than one occasion were even known to make common cause with poor whites and Native Americans in an attempt to attain freedom. Although most North American slave insurrections and revolts were unsuccessful, they indicated that the black man's love for freedom had not been destroyed by his enslavement.[4]

Immediately before and during the American Revolution, blacks bent on testing the sincerity of the American theories of equal rights intensified efforts for emancipation. Many blacks filed suits and petitioned for freedom, but to no avail. In 1777, a group of slaves filed suit in Massachusetts, proclaiming that: "We have no property, we have no children, no city, no country."[5] In 1779, 19 slaves petitioned for their rights as men in New Hampshire on the grounds that slavery was contradictory to the American principles of humanity and justice. The New Hampshire legislature, like most colonial legislatures in such cases, took no action.

Other slaves became openly insubordinate and increasingly rebellious. Many, aware of the consequences, risked their lives and fled. According to Thomas Jefferson, over 30,000 slaves had fled plantations in Virginia by 1779. Many of these runaways found employment in the Continental Army and Navy. In the crucial years of the war, by voluntarily enlisting, many blacks exchanged military service for freedom. When George Washington, a large slave owner himself, took command of the Continental army after the battle of Bunker Hill, he officially barred blacks from further military participation. This was done in spite of the fact that Peter Salem became a hero in that battle when he shot the British Major Pitcairn, and Salem Poor was awarded an official commendation as a brave and gallant soldier. However, when the British offered freedom to all slaves who joined their ranks, the colonies quickly responded by adopting policies that included blacks. In 1776, New York passed a law providing for the enlistment of free blacks. The result was that 50,000 slaves from both colonies escaped to the British lines of General Cornwallis.

Black soldiers participated in every capacity during the war from spy to infantryman. The French Marquis de Lafayette, who aided the cause of the colonists, commended the courage of black soldiers and defeat of Cornwallis. Fugitive slaves from South Carolina accompanied the "Swamp Fox," Francis Marion, on his campaign. In desperation at Valley Forge, George Washington enlisted the aid of a black battalion from Rhode Island. About 5,000 blacks, both slave and free, fought for American independence. Perhaps an equal number served behind the British lines.

The participation of black soldiers in the War of 1776 had a dual meaning, for they not only fought as slaves seeking freedom, but also as Americans. Yet, their efforts were in vain. At the close of the war, the majority of blacks who had fought on both sides, American and British, were re-enslaved. This action would later prompt Frederick Douglass to challenge American liberty and the reality of slavery as "a gross injustice and cruelty" to which the black man was a perpetual victim.[6]

The creation of a total and mature system of chattel slavery perhaps could have been reversed following the War of 1776. Philosophers of the Age of Reason recognized the intrinsic evil of slavery. Politicians of the Confederation Congress forbade the institution north of the Ohio River in the Northwest Ordinance of 1787. And, perhaps most importantly, due to the depressed nation economy resulting from the war, slavery was temporarily unprofitable. Slaver owner John Randolph of Roanoke, Virginia, joked that slaves should advertise for runaway masters rather than the other way around. But the possibility of the peaceful abolition of the slavery system withered away as the framers of the Constitution gathered to give birth to a new nation.

Being of conservative mind, the delegates to the Constitutional Convention of 1787 firmly believed in the philosophy of Adam Smith—that it was the responsibility of government to provide the legal framework for the marketplace, defining and protecting property rights. These men, like Smith, viewed economic freedom without government interference as the prerequisite to political freedom. They supported the creation of a new government and the move to the new constitution, for they had a personal stake in it. With very few exceptions, the members of the Constitutional convention were directly and personally interested in the anticipated economic benefits from the new system. These interests, in the end, pushed ratification of the constitution through state conventions. Thus, the Constitution became an economic document based on the belief that private property rights were to be protected by government.

And what is property? That which generates income or wealth. Land, capital, and labor. And what was the Black man? As a human being, the black man was invisible. But as a slave, he was chattel labor, owned by his "master." He was an investment, a means to an economic end. The planters who made this investment demanded and got, at the Constitutional convention, recognition and protection for that extraordinary investment.

The delegates who attended the convention in 1787 struck a compromise, and the conflict of economic and political interest was resolved. A strong federal government had been created and property rights were acknowledged and protected. Through compromise, the slave was counted as three-fifths of a human being for the purpose of southern white representation in Congress. Yet, the slave owner had to pay a tax on his human property. As the question of the end of the Trans-Atlantic Slave haunted the 18th-century international community, the American Congress agreed to end its participation in the trafficking of slaves in 1808. Thus, economic and political interests took precedence over the moral question of slavery.

There were those enlightened rationalists and humanitarians who believed that the moral question of slavery would resolve itself by economic disincentive. But that hope was dashed in a single afternoon in 1793 when Eli Whitney built a small hand-driven machine that revolutionized the cotton industry. With this simple machine that, unfortunately for Whitney and his patent hopes, any skilled blacksmith could duplicate, one slave could do the work of fifty. Smooth, soft cotton which, because of its expense had been the preferred cloth of kings, would become available, mass-produced by slaves, for the world. In a decade, the South moved toward wholesale production of that vital raw material which fed the looms of textile manufacturers and launched the Industrial Revolution. And the institution of slavery burgeoned into a "brutal, exploitative economic and social system."[7]

By 1860, one-half million slaves estimated to have been in country by the first national census of 1790, had grown to almost four million—most of them confined to living and working on plantations in the cotton-producing South. Cotton accounted for more export dollars than all other American exports combined. Almost the entire capital of the South was invested in slave labor and the land upon which that labor toiled. Planters found that not only were they the benefactors of what their slaves sowed and reaped, but they also found themselves in the midst of the most controversial issue of the 19th-century—the abolition of slavery.

The existence of slavery in America had always been controversial. In response to white resistance of change, free blacks had no alternative but to turn inward and to rely upon themselves to being about improvement in their social, economic, and political conditions. As early as 1798, blacks began to formulate mutual aid societies such as the Sons of the African Society and the Dorcas Society to give aid and support to the beleaguered free black population and the fugitive slave. In the struggle for freedom, other African Americans served as the primary conductors on the Underground Railroad. In 1827, the first black newspaper, *Freedom's Journal*, was published in New York. The purpose of the paper was to articulate African Americans' grievance against America's refusal to live up to its stated principles and values of liberty and equality. However, the grievances of African Americans did not generate much interest in the greater American society. In both the North and South, African Americans continuously fought against slavery, racial discrimination and alienation from the mainstream of American life. It is noteworthy that because of the undaunted effort of the black community, Boston became the first city to integrate its public schools in 1855.

In September, 1830, after some months of planning, the first National Negro Convention assembled at Bethel Church in Philadelphia. This convention marked the beginning of a movement that lasted for more than twenty-five years and became an increasingly important part of the Abolitionist crusade. The movement protested against and demanded the end of slavery, segregation and discrimination against free blacks. It also aimed to instill in the minds of African Americans racial pride and the belief that they could obtain respectability and wealth through mechanical and agricultural trades and the cultivation of American virtues and character.

However, the moral, legal and political methods employed by the Convention movement yielded little tangible results other than as a training ground for 19th century black leadership and perhaps laying the foundation for future black nationalism. The failure to achieve more positive results led to frustration and disillusionment. This disenchantment with the American society caused such leaders as Martin Delany and Henry Highland Garnett to call for the emigration of blacks to Canada, the West Indies, and ultimately Africa in hopes of finding a better life. Meanwhile, slaves continued their own desperate and obviously illegal action to break out of the hated bondage. In 1800, the slave Gabriel Posner, having organized what could have been thousands of blacks in eastern Virginia, failed in a planned uprising as a result of his last minute betrayal, coupled with a raging tropical storm that drowned all the hopes of freedom. Gabriel and about 35 other slaves were executed, but terror gripped the slave masters. In 1822, Denmark Vesey organized another widespread conspiracy uprising. Vesey and 37 other black men and women were hanged. Four white sympathizers were jailed and heavily fined.

Other blacks relentlessly continued the struggle. Nat Turner of Southhampton County, Virginia, led an uprising in 1831 in which 60 whites were killed. White suppression of the Turner revolt cost at least 100 black lives. The moral issue of slavery or freedom for blacks could no longer be ignored.

Early in the 19th century, white planters and their spokesmen in political office used a rather apologetic rationale for holding slaves. Admitting the undesirability or even the evil of slavery, they complained of seeing no way to end it; or, even if it were ended, no way that whites and blacks could live in and share equal rights in the same society.

Besides, slavery was undeniably profitable to the plantation economy. It was nothing more than a political evil. But after the Missouri Compromise of 1820, when it became painfully obvious to the South that it was to have a declining influence in Congress, the defense of slavery changed. Senator John C. Calhoun of South Carolina was the first major Southern leader to stand on the floor of the Senate and proclaim that slavery was not an unfortunate economic accident of the British colonial period but was a positive good. Reacting to the legalistic appeals of northern free black conventions, to the hopeless fury of rebellious slaves, and to the growing anti-slavery sentiment being fanned by William Lloyd Garrison and other white abolitionists, the defenders of slavery took their stand.

Slavery, Southern white ministers claimed, had been instituted by God. Ham had sinned against his father Noah. God, in his righteous wrath, had cursed Canaan, son of Ham, and all his descendants to eternal servitude. Southern intellectuals pointed to glorious antiquity, arguing that Greek and Roman civilizations were able to achieve power and strength on the firm bedrock of slavery. They argued democracy was suitable only for enlightened and educated people, not for undeveloped minds or character. Hence, whites had to deal with black people as they really were—as children, savage and inferior beings. Slavery, according to the view of its advocates, helped uplift and protect those who were not capable of taking care of themselves. Even before Charles Darwin published his theory of evolution, Dr. Josiah Nott of Alabama, in 1852, concluded the Africans and Europeans had evolved from entirely different species. The African was and would always be inferior.

The shrill tone taken by defenders of slavery was matched by an equally acrimonious assault by incensed abolitionists. Slavery was an unmitigated evil, a "barbarous" custom, a stain upon American civilization. Harriet Tubman divided her time between speaking at abolitionists' meetings in the North and making her solitary voyages back into the slave South, as she did 19 times, guiding to freedom some 300 runaway slaves. Frederick Douglass, the most eloquent black abolitionist and himself an escaped slave, indicted American principles and justice on July 4, 1852, when he charged that to the slave, the American celebration of Independence was a "thin veil to cover up crimes that would disgrace a nation of savages."[8] Harriet Beecher Stowe, a gentle lady, descendant of generations of conservative ministers, decided to put into words her feelings about the moral evils of slavery. Her book, *Uncle Tom's Cabin*, was first published serially in "National Era" during 1851- 1852, and in one year sold more than 300,000 copies, helped crystallize anti-slavery sentiment in the North. Topsy, Eliza, Little Eva, Simon Legree and Uncle Tom became common nouns in many households. Yet at the same time, Stowe's characters reinforced popular negative stereotype images of the African American.

As the conflict over slavery became more acute, the government attempted once again to conciliate the opposing forces. The Compromise of 1850 upset the balance of power in the United States Senate in favor of free states, but placated the South by passing a stringent Fugitive Slave Act. This portion of the compromise compelled all citizens to aid in the capture and return of all fugitive slaves. As soon as the compromise went into effect, it was assumed by most of the parties concerned that the slavery question had been resolved. But such was not the case.

Between 1852 and 1856, the tempers of pro-slavery and anti-slavery forces continued to flare as they struggled for control over the territory of Kansas-Nebraska. In the climate of this hostility, Stephen A. Douglas introduced the doctrine of popular sovereignty in hopes of preserving the harmony between the sections. Douglas concluded that the only way to solve the issue of slavery was to let the people decide and to get it out of the hands of Congress. By the end of 1856, armed conflict in Kansas had done much to sectionalize the nation and the Supreme Court decision of 1857 declared that popular sovereignty was not the answer to the question of slavery when it rendered its decision in the case Dred Scott v. Sanford.

Dred Scott, a slave, had been taken by his owner to Minnesota, a free territory, and then returned to Missouri, a slave state. Abolitionists convinced Scott to demand his freedom, based on the premise that his temporary residence in Minnesota had made him free. The Supreme Court decision stated that slaves were property wherever they were, and that Congress had no power to prohibit slavery in any territory. This decision, although a victory for the South, inflamed anti-slavery feelings, negated the spirit of compromise, and was a major factor in escalation toward Civil War.

On October 16, 1859, the abolitionists' crusade was brought clearly into focus. John Brown and a biracial army of 17 followers captured the United States military arsenal at Harper's Ferry, Virginia, and called for a general slave uprising. Although Brown and his followers were quickly killed or apprehended, the raid and Brown's trial and execution continued to polarize the nation on the issue of slavery.

The result of the Civil War brought an end to slavery, but an ambivalence about the status of the newly freed slave. By December of 1865, when Congress convened, it was obvious that the South had no intention of recognizing the new status of former slaves. In an attempt to secure the real freedom of ex-slaves as well as the Republican Party's control of the government, military rule was established in the states of the now defunct Confederacy. However, the problem was not exclusively a Southern one. Long before the Civil War, it was apparent that most white abolitionists were oblivious to what freedom meant to blacks. They were more concerned about the concept of slavery than they were with the status of blacks in the American society. They concerned themselves, honestly and with great courage, with eliminating slavery but foresaw no steps to assimilate the newly freed slave into society. Abolitionists who had found themselves actually uncomfortable at being seated next to a black compatriot, now that slavery was abolished by military force, were uncertain how much further they wished to go toward an egalitarian society. Many whites viewed blacks as inferior and incapable of handling their new freedom and their own destinies.

No such view existed in the radical leadership in the Republican Congress. With the House of Representatives leader, Thaddeus Stevens, and Senate stalwart Charles Sumner, in dominant roles, the Congress enacted and sent to the states the Thirteenth, Fourteenth and Fifteenth amendments to the Constitution. The amendments outlawed slavery, defined and guaranteed citizenship to the freed man and granted him voting rights. Stevens and others of the radical minority were prepared to go even further to implement the promise of the American Dream of equality. But by 1868, it was evident that deep seated social change was hindering the possibility of speedy reconciliation between the North and the South. White hostility had intensified and Southern terrorist groups, like the Knights of the White Camellia and the Ku Klux Klan, suggested the possibility of another outbreak of a Civil War.

The Congressional coalition of radicals, moderate abolitionists, and business-oriented Republicans broke down. In an effort to settle political differences and to preserve national peace, white leadership in the North and South moved toward reconciliation. The election of Republican Rutherford B. Hayes in 1876, with his promise to withdraw federal troops and to restore home rule to the South, brought an official end to Reconstruction in 1877. The Republican Party then abandoned blacks and left the South to establish its own racial policy.

Throughout the decade of the 1880s, the status of blacks in America was ambiguous. However, by the 1890s, racism had taken a more ominous form. Southern states began writing into their constitutions Jim Crow provisions that denied blacks the right to participate in the political arena and deprived them of social and economic opportunities. This institutionalization of Jim Crowism, through discrimination and segregation, reflected the belief that the white man was superior and the natural economic and social and political status of the black man was and should be beneath whites. The concept whites held of themselves provided an ideological basis for the formal institutionalization of racism and the color class caste system. Once the black man was under the control of Jim Crowism, whites felt sure that their supposed superiority would be sustained. The new laws also served to control labor and political competition in favor of whites.

In 1896, the concept of Jim Crowism was reinforced by the Supreme Court decision in the case of Plessy v. Ferguson, which upheld a Louisiana statute requiring segregation of the races in public conveyances. The Court held that states could require separate but equal facilities for black people The decision helped to resolve a moral conflict between America's professed egalitarianism and long practiced racism. Facilities could be separate if they were accepted as equal. In actual fact, the equal facilities were quickly forgotten in the interest of maintaining what W.E.B. Du Bois was to call the veil between the white and black races. The decision made it possible to artificially remove black people from the American society. Segregation was to be the law of the land for the next 58 years.

Between 1890 and 1910, there were over 2,000 lynchings of black people. Both the North and South became scenes of vicious anti-black riots. In the midst of this racial hysteria, Booker T. Washington emerged as a spokesman and leader of blacks in America from 1895 to 1915.

Deeply concerned about the survival of black people, Washington, in a speech commonly referred to as the Atlanta Compromise, delivered in 1895, offered a philosophy and a program he hoped would resolve racial conflict in the American society. Subscribing to the 19th century concepts of liberalism and progress, he preached black accommodation, self-help, economic progress, thrift and racial solidarity—a brand of economic nationalism. Accordingly, if blacks learned how to elevate themselves, acquire land and an agricultural or mechanical education, and saved their money, demonstrating that they were productive citizens, they would generate respect and acceptability in society.

Washington's popularity among whites, including his ability to raise considerable money from white donations for black technical education, may possibly be traced to the Social Darwinian philosophies held by many white Americans at that time. Whites were able to read into Washington's speeches what they perceived to be an admission of black inferiority. At the same time, whites could accept the far distant elevation of black people without abandoning racist attitudes then held. Nothing necessarily precluded the improvement of the inferior race because according to Social Darwinism, all Americans were in an evolving progressive society.

Although Washington's approach to the racial conflict in America was worthwhile and meaningful, it was not strong enough to overcome the continuing violence and aggression directed towards black people. At the beginning of the 20th century, Jim Crow laws made it apparent that whites were not going to make room for blacks in the American society.

A new and more radical leadership surfaced in the North in the person of Dr. W.E.B. Du Bois, a brilliant and highly educated scholar. Du Bois, unlike Washington, had never been a slave or a product of Southern society. He rejected the view that blacks should be forced to earn first class citizenship. Indeed, by encouraging "the talented tenth" of black youth to obtain a classical liberal education and by demanding immediate political and civil rights, black people would earn respect and become a part of the society. Du Bois rejected racial stereotyping and insisted that blacks were inherently equal to whites.

This demand for immediate social, political and economic equality became the philosophy of the Niagara Movement, which was the forerunner of the National Association for the Advancement of Colored People, organized in 1910 by liberal whites and with Du Bois as editor of the Association's paper, "The Crisis." Other organizations concerned with the immediate problems of black people also surfaced. The League for the Protection of Colored Women and the Committee on Urban Conditions Among Negroes were designed to help black people adjust to a changing urban society. The black press rejected the abundance of literature that held that the black was an inferior being and strove valiantly to counterattack articles in white newspapers that referred to blacks as "coons," "darkies," and "pickaninnies." In white newspapers, the achievements of blacks were not newsworthy unless they had committed crimes; that is why black newspapers deemed it important to make note of every black accomplishment. Black journalists such as William Monroe Trotter of the *Boston Guardian* and T. Thomas Fortune of the *New York Age* condemned the government for not making an attempt to protect the constitutional rights of black people—but to no avail.

Discrimination became common practice in Southern and Northern communities and a matter of national policy. In the South, blacks were discriminated against at the ballot box and were subject to the intimidation of the hangman's rope. Blacks who fled from the atrocities of the South to the North, in hopes of a better life, found themselves alienated from almost all aspects of the American mainstream. Pushed into overcrowded and unsanitary urban areas, restricted from both professions and skilled trades, blacks were forced to take menial jobs, thus making impossible their benefiting from the resources and comfort that the society had to offer.

Through blacks were mistreated, they were able to maintain their humanity. They became aware of their self-worth, which provided a spiritual means to resist racial oppression. This was done by finding joy and comfort within the creation of their own cultural and religious organizations. They created fraternal societies and social clubs. These associations, though they catered to upper class blacks, provided the opportunity to express their racial consciousness, a feeling of self-fulfillment and a sense of personal achievement.[9] For the majority of black people who could not find relief from the rituals of such associations, the church became the place of social, economic and political activities as well as of worship.

The role of the 20th century black church differed from that of the pre-Civil War Era. Prior to the War, North black churches were the center of anti-slavery agitation; they were ministered by learned men who were often highly respected in both black and white religious circles. The black church on Southern plantations, however, often served contradictory purposes. Most slave owners believed that Christianity served their ends by turning the slave's attention from his plight towards heavenly salvation. Some slave preachers did, indeed, offer "pie in the sky" and worked to soothe slave anger. Many slaves responded by adopting a pious acquiescence. Yet evidence reveals that other seemingly complacent preachers subverted slavery and instructed their congregation in the possibility of following the "drinking gourd" (the Big Dipper) to Northern freedom.

During the Reconstruction period, black and white clergy and laymen from the North went South to turn black churches into school houses and to teach children and adults, formerly slaves, to learn to read directly from and behave according to the Protestant Bible. Generations of black believers learned to quote verbatim and to take the Scriptures literally. This inclination to absolute spiritual conviction often made it easy for charlatans and fraud to flourish among pious but unsophisticated congregations.

Black religiosity throughout its history appears to be both more spiritual and more literal than its white Protestant counterpart. Whether this phenomena, as some anthropologists have suggested, is due to its shadowy connection with pre-slavery African animism or is merely the unique arena in which black people have been forced to practice religion is unclear. Blacks did not question fine theological points; they accepted the Bible as written, and they composed numerous and moving spiritual songs which both gave testimony to their belief in the Bible and often masked their desire for freedom as they sang about Moses and the Israelites.

By the turn of the century, the black church not only accommodated the unique religious needs of its membership, but also became the center of social activity. It served both as an agency of charity and as an employment bureau. The church promoted education and upon occasion business enterprises, as well as fostering the expression of the black point of view through the leadership of the clergy. Given the role of the church, it is little wonder that it became the single most influential institution in the African American community.

By 1920, the church found its position in jeopardy as unorthodox cults became a vital part of the black experience.[10] Many blacks were attracted to the debonair presence of Daddy Grace and the godlike image of Father Divine. Others became members of the Mt. Sinai Holy Church of America, Inc., Church of God (Black Jews) or the Moorish Science Temple of America. All of these cults promised heaven on earth and/or life eternal. However, they did provide blacks a greater opportunity to experiment in business, politics and social interaction. They fulfilled, more importantly, the need of belonging to a "distinct culture" which, in many cases, was not found in traditional black churches.[11]

Many black people found the need to belong to a "distinct culture" in the Harlem Renaissance, and an outpouring of literary and artistic excellence in the post-World War I period. Black intellectuals "saw art and letters as a bridge across the chasm between the races."[12] For them, the Renaissance was a means by which blacks could bridge the racial chasm, discover and define their culture and make it known that they had contributed to the building of civilization. The poetry of Langston

Hughes and the prose of Claude McKay inspired both blacks and whites on both sides of the Atlantic.

Yet, the powerful verse of Hughes and the stark realism of McKay reached only the tip of the intellectual iceberg. Only the aware, fairly well-educated minority had the time and opportunity for such erudition. For the working masses in the streets of Harlem, for those thousands who suffered every day the deprivation of color, another voice, rich with West Indian dialect, said what they wanted to hear.

Part demagogue, part genius, Marcus Garvey was to have a most profound effect on the poorer strata of black society by his absolute insistence on the brotherhood of all people of African descent, on solidarity with the peoples of the world, and on speaking out manfully and forcefully for all to hear that the day of "colonial oppression" by whites was ending. The Universal Negro Improvement Association was to become during the 1920s the largest black organization ever developed in the United States.[13] Significantly, the UNIA grew to its strength and prominence without help of any of the established black and white churches, pressure groups, or black fraternal lodges. The Garvey Movement was in truth a grass roots coalition demanding black power, African independence, and the end to racial oppression. The African American had come of age.

Financial difficulties and alleged irregularities, plus the world-wide opposition to the spread of Garveyism, plagued the UNIA from 1922 on. Garvey himself was jailed in the Atlanta Federal Penitentiary in 1925 until his deportation as an undesirable alien in 1928. But in spite of harassment (perhaps mismanagement) and the exile of the charismatic Garvey, poor black men and women in the United States would never be quite the same. The cries of "Black Power" and "Black is Beautiful" would be heard again and again.

In October of 1929, the New York stock market crashed. That event meant virtually nothing to black people at the time because almost none of them owned a single share of American industry. Before long, however, the black working men and women of the nation knew all too well what "depression" meant. By 1933, when Franklin D. Roosevelt became President of the United States, black share-croppers in the South had seen their prices for cotton drop to four cents per pound and wheat to thirty cents a bushel. Roosevelt had come to the Presidency promising a "New Deal" to the American people. Blacks waited to see what guarantee they would have of sharing in that New Deal. Generally, but with some exception, they waited in vain.

During the course of the New Deal years, an enormous body of social and economic laws were legislated. The governmental system of the nation is, however, a Federal system and therefore most of the implementation of the New Deal programs was left to the local arm of the government, where prejudice and discrimination could continue to be practiced.

One of the first economic programs was the Agriculture Adjustment Administration, designed to increase the farmers' purchasing power and restore agricultural prosperity. The implementation of the AAA was almost entirely at the county level. There, white county agents saw to it that the Southern black tenant farmers, who made up one of the largest portions of the impoverished, received virtually no relief. Indeed, since farmers were paid to withhold their land from cultivation in order to artificially create scarcity, it often made more sense for large white landowners to simply evict their tenants altogether and let the land lie fallow and collect the government checks.

Congress passed the Federal Housing Act to enable poor people to secure federally guaranteed home purchase loans. Adhering to written and unwritten codes of segregation, loans were not made to blacks if they had intentions of moving or building in white neighborhoods.

Under the Social Security Act of 1935, aid was granted to the elderly and to certain categories of the unemployed. Agricultural and domestic workers were not included. These two job classifications stifled the overwhelming majority of Southern black labor. These people did not qualify for Social Security benefits.

The examples were depressing. Organizations such as the Urban League and the NAACP repeatedly emphasized that blacks needed special consideration because they were demonstrably the most impoverished group in America. But they spoke to deaf ears. It was largely in those programs which were directly administered from Washington, such as the Public Works Administration and the Works Progress Administration, that black workers got the most nearly equal treatment.

Indirectly, but of great importance, the National Labor Relations Act did assist black workers as well as whites in the heavy basic industries. The N.L.R.A. not only legalized labor unions, but mandated that employers must recognize and bargain fairly with those unions freely chosen by the workers. Black workers, already employed in the automobile, rubber, steel and other mass production industries, were able to benefit through contracts negotiated for them by the various industrial unions of the newly formed Congress of Industrial Organizations. Despite the continued exclusion from most of the skilled trade unions of the American Federation of Labor, about one and one half million black workers were covered by union contracts by 1940.

Although the actual help to black people as a result of New Deal programs was questionable, the great majority seemed to believe that Mr. Roosevelt and especially Mrs. Roosevelt meant well and gave the Democratic Party their overwhelming support; a support for many African Americans that has not wavered to the present day. Ordinary black people continued to demonstrate their faith in the conventional political processes and in the eventual realization of the American Dream.

During World War II, the irony of the United States engaged in a life-and death struggle with an avowed racist Nazi regime in Germany while practicing racism at home became too blatant to be overlooked. Immediately before the war, blacks were excluded from the Air Corps, the Marine Corps, and most of the specialized departments of the Army. Even in the regular Army and the Navy, they were restricted to largely menial jobs. As the war progressed, black insistence on the right to fully participate in the defense of the country led to some minor changes. As early as 1940, the War Department decided to accept black enlistees in the Air Corps to train at a special school set up at Tuskegee Institute, the school founded by Booker T. Washington in Alabama. Before the war's end, black men were being commissioned as officers in the Army, Navy and Marines, but continued to serve their country in segregated units. Not until 1948 did President Truman yield to the pressure of A. Phillip Randolph, president of the Brotherhood of Sleeping Car Porters, and other black leaders to order the complete desegregation of the armed forces.

On the home front, it also seemed in the beginning that black workers were not to be considered suitable for employment in the burgeoning defense industry. Randolph threatened to lead thousands of black workers through the streets of Washington if the government did not halt job discrimination. President Roosevelt responded with an Executive Order prohibiting such discrimination and established the Fair Employment Practices Commission to monitor all companies with United States government contracts.

In the popular culture of America, changes, small as they may have seemed at the time, were being made. In the 1936 Olympics, held in Berlin with Adolph Hitler in the audience, Jesse Owens, a black

American, won three gold medals. In 1938, Joe Louis, proudly ignoring the invariable introduction as a "credit to his race," knocked out German Max Schmeling in two minutes of the first round to the cheers of most Americans. The magnificent contralto voice of Marian Anderson, the virtuoso stage and film performances of Paul Robeson, the innovating jazz trumpet of Louis Armstrong, the bitter but brilliant writing of Richard Wright—all were known and admired by educated and sensitive Americans, black and white. In 1947, when Jackie Robinson became the first black baseball player to be permitted in the major leagues, he had to tolerate racial slurs and jeers from hundred of baseball fans. Robinson soon would hear the cheers of thousands. All of these individuals made tremendous contributions to American life and culture, and did so with the hope that the doors of opportunity would be opened for all black people.

With the end of World War II, blacks became more aggressive in their demands for a place in America, with full civic and political equality. The Congress of Racial Equality, founded during the war, sent out its first freedom rides against segregation in interstate travel. Ms. Irene Morgan carried her arrest for refusing to move to the back of a bus all the way to the Supreme Court. The case had little or no effect, the challenge was on. In the cases McLaurin v. Oklahoma and Sweatt v. Painter, the Supreme Court had ruled by 1950 that a qualified black student must be admitted to previously all-white professional and graduate schools.[14] The climax of the legal and constitutional approach was reached in 1954 when the NAACP legal fund carried five identical cases to the Supreme Court. The Court ruled in alphabetical order on the first of these—Brown v. the Board of Education of Topeka, Kansas. Chief Justice Earl Warren, speaking for the unanimous Court, declared that segregation of the races in public school violated the equal protection clause of the Fourteenth Amendment. The court overruled the "separate but equal" doctrine sanctioned in the Plessy v. Ferguson case of 1896.

The decision made by the high court immediately met opposition. Angry Southern congressmen vowed that they would overturn the ruling by all legal means. There was massive resistance in most Southern towns, and with the aid of local white citizens' councils, racial tension reached a dangerous height. By 1955, it had become apparent that Southern States were not going to abide the Supreme Court ruling, for not one black child attended school with white children. In response to the resistance, the Court ordered the desegregation of public schools with all deliberate speed.

However, in 1957, the governor of Arkansas, Orval Faubas, yielded to white opposition to desegregation and threats of violence when he called out the National Guard to bar the entrance of nine black children to one of the public schools. A court order was issued to remove guards from the scene. Riots broke out. President Dwight Eisenhower, who had not previously taken a firm stand on Civil Rights for blacks, sent Federal paratroopers to escort the black children to school. Meanwhile, other public schools in the South were closed to avoid integration.

On December 1, 1955, Mrs. Rosa Parks, a black seamstress in Montgomery, Alabama, riding the Cleveland Avenue bus, refused to give up her seat to a white passenger on the demands of the bus driver. Mrs. Parks was arrested. In protest to Mrs. Parks' arrest, leaders of the black community persuaded 17,000 black citizens to boycott the Montgomery bus line. For 381 days, blacks organized carpools and walked to work rather than continue to accept second-class citizenship. Withstanding the bombing of homes, legal harassment, massive arrests and civil suits, their action produced positive results, for on December 13, 1956, the United States Supreme Court declared that segregation on public transportation in Montgomery was illegal. The success of the Montgomery Bus Boycott added a new dimension to the African American crusade for social and equal justice. It gave birth to the Civil Rights Movement and a brand of black radicalism based on love and inspired by Dr. Martin Luther King, Jr.

Influenced by the doctrine and philosophy of Christian passiveness, the writings of Henry David Thoreau, and the Leadership of India's Mahatma Gandhi, King molded old and new hopes and dreams into a comprehensive and cohesive mass movement in which King would become a symbolic leader for black people throughout the decades of the 1950s and 1960s.

Never before had black people been asked to sacrifice so much; they were asked to accept suffering without retaliation. Black people were encouraged to cling to the belief they had in themselves, in the American judicial system, and in their faith in God, for God and justice were on their side.[15] Through non-violent protest, persistent and unyielding, black people could transform the American society into a just and equal one. King institutionalized his vision for a finer America in the founding of the Southern Christian Leadership Conference. Through this organization, black people appealed to the moral and social consciousness of America in a solid unified front.

The spirit of the movement captured the imagination and the ears of thousands of young people seeking a better tomorrow. In 1960, four black students in Greensboro, North Carolina, refused to leave the lunch counter at an all-white restaurant. The refusal touched off a full scale protest demonstration that spread throughout the South and into some places in the North. It had become evident that no longer would the enemy, racism, go unchallenged—the revolution was on.

The Student Non-Violent Coordinating Committee (SNCC) grew out of the sit-in movement in Raleigh, North Carolina, in the fall of 1960. The following year, black and white students from all over the country, formed a ragged incorruptible front line and dedicated themselves to destroying the sickness that pervaded the lives of the people in the furrows of the Deep South. Characterized by their spirit of commitment and determination to change the country, these young people challenged age-old traditions through non-violent direct action.

The presence of SNCC in what was considered the most hard core racist section of the South met hostile and bitter opposition from those who were bent on preserving the status quo. Yet, the opposition failed to suppress the optimism and determination of the members of SNCC. In 1962, the organization began a voter registration campaign, which led to the formation of the biracial Mississippi Freedom Democratic Party. In the meantime, the Civil Rights forces stepped up their attack in massive marches that led them to Birmingham and Sheriff Bull Connors and Company on April 3, 1963.

When the marchers reached Birmingham, they were totally unprepared for their reception. Sheriff Connors led a vicious attack on the marchers with night sticks, dogs, and high-powered water hoses. This act of repression, seen by millions on television, not only generated national and international public opinion which would compel President John F. Kennedy to propose Civil Rights legislation to Congress, but it also augmented a growing feeling of frustration and belief that racism would not relinquish its stranglehold on African Americans.

Protectors of traditionalism continued to lash out at civil right activists. Riots and demonstrations occurred throughout the country. Medgar Evers, NAACP field secretary in Mississippi, was assassinated by a sniper and his alleged assailant was acquitted. Congress refused to take on the civil rights proposal presented by President Kennedy. Pressure in the rank and file of the civil rights forces began to build for more radical and militant action. Responding to the turmoil and tension that filled the nation's air and to the dissipating hopes of the movement, Dr. King and other black leaders, young and old, made preparations to march on Washington.

On August 28,1963, 250,00 black and white Americans gathered at the Lincoln Monument in Washington, D.C. to lobby for the passage of a comprehensive civil rights bill by Congress. At this historic gathering, Dr. King delivered one of the most famous and inspiring speeches in the history of American oratory. He reaffirmed the hopes and dreams of black people that America would indeed became a land of equal justice. Although the march on Washington did eventually prompt Congress to take legal action, it did not take many blacks long to realize that old beliefs die hard.

One month following the march, a black church in Birmingham, Alabama, was bombed and four young children lost their lives. Black radicals saw this action was a typical white response to religiously oriented non-violence. They began to reject what they considered to be accommodating and conciliatory approach to the problem. Too long, black radicals rationalized, had black people attempted to prove they were equal and that white Americans had nothing to be afraid of.

In the initial stages of his flamboyant yet tragic career, Malcolm X, the dynamic spokesman for the Nation of Islam (Black Muslims), articulated this loss of faith in the American system. Before large black audiences in the urban North, Malcolm indicated American intentions concerning the plight of black people. He charged that American Christianity was a fraud. He preached that it was time for black people to face reality and become the instrument of their own liberation. He argued that black people could attain liberation through black pride, unity, solidarity, self-determination, and the creation of a separate black nation.

Malcolm X's brand of black nationalism had a psychological effect on the American society as a whole. It frightened white Americans still clinging to the concept of their racial superiority. They could not grasp the idea of black people rejecting them. It also frightened blacks who had spent their lives attempting to assimilate into the American society. It challenged their faith in the American dream and their relentless belief that somehow white America would change. Although his brand of nationalism while he was still a member of the Nation was narrow and sectarian, Malcolm X became a symbol of freedom in perhaps the most critical years of the Black Revolution.[16]

In 1964, after his official withdrawal from the Nation, Malcolm X made several trips to Mecca and Africa. These trips had a profound impact on his thinking. He was no longer opposed to progressive whites united with revolutionary blacks. But he felt that the role of progressive whites was in their own communities, educating whose who had not been converted to the black cause. He felt that before racial solidarity could be achieved between blacks and whites, unity had to be achieved among black people. Malcolm X so made it clear that no compromises between blacks and whites would be made. Blacks would establish their own voting blocs, organize their own communities, and protect their rights by any means necessary.[17]

After the founding of the Organization of Afro-American Unity, Malcolm X became more convinced that cause of African Americans should be internationalized. He believed that if African Americans linked their cause with other oppressed black people of the world,they would achieve the first step toward freedom. Once the black struggle was subject to the scrutiny of the United Nations and the World Court, justice could be served. Malcolm X met his death before he could completely develop a strategy for procuring his objective.[18] But he left behind a spirit of pride and dignity that many black people could identify with.

From the beginning of and through the complete demise of the Mississippi Freedom Democratic Party at the Democratic National Convention in 1964, the mood of the leaders of SNCC shifted toward black nationalism. They had lost faith in conventional American tools used to bring about change. They had become impatient with Southern hostility and resistance. They were inspired by the words of Malcolm X and Franz Fanon. They began to swell with resentment and contempt for white participation in the movement because whites did not really understand the problems of black people. They began to reconsider the feasibility of black-white coalitions and concluded that black people alone would have to take charge of their own destiny.

By June of 1966, the tens of thousands of veterans of the Civil Rights Movement had marched thousands of miles, gone by the thousands to jail, had sweltered in the heat of front of the Lincoln Memorial in Washington, D.C., and listened to Dr. King tell them of his dream. They also had seen the Congress finally enact the Civil Rights Act of 1964, and the Voting Rights Act of 1965.

But in the humid month of June, 1966 James Meredith, the first black student at the University of Mississippi and himself a man of such independent mind as to be a member of no activist organization, decided to take a walk—a Freedom Walk through Mississippi. As he walked along the Southern highway, alone in his insistence on testing whether a black man could safely make such a pilgrimage, the answer came. A shot blast left him sprawled screaming in pain on the side of the road.

Telephone calls flew between Martin Luther King, Floyd McKissick of CORE, and Stokely Carmichael of SNCC, and after a visit to the hospitalized Meredith, the three men decided to commit their organizations and themselves to continuing Meredith's march. It was on that march, in the long warm nights of discussion of tact and overall philosophy, that "Black Power" began to be heard repeatedly. The younger marchers, and especially the black residents of central Mississippi where SNCC had exerted itself in th voter registration drives, found the phrase irresistible. King and most of the older workers of the movement were troubled by the slogan because of fear of alienating white civil right supporters.

Black Power had, and has many meanings. To groups not dedicated to the non-violent passivism of the Southern Christian Leadership Conference, like the Deacons for Defense in Louisiana and the Black Panther Party in California, Black Power seemed to mean that no longer would anyone ever hint that a black man should not defend himself against the brutality and thuggery of cattle-prod wielding Southern sheriffs or Oakland policemen. No more cracked heads, no more German Shepherd dogs ripping clothing and flesh indiscriminately, no more tortured and mutilated corpses found buried in earthen dams in Alabama. Stand up and be a man, a proud black man! To Carmichael, it meant taking control of the political economic institutions of the black ghettos and rural black areas of the South to reverse what he called "the colonial nature of the arrangement" in which businessmen for too long had driven from the suburbs to open their general shops and drove back at the end of the day to those same white suburbs with black ghetto money in their cash boxes.

During the 1970s, older apostles of non-violence lost their hold on what use to be the Civil Rights Movement. The turbulence caused by the riots during the long hot summers of the 1960s seemed to be disparate with the mood of African Americans. Instead, the mood of blacks became more hopeful and more determined without becoming less militant. This sentiment did not advocate violence but rather the development of a systematic group effort using available resources to influence the American political system.

A young and pragmatic generation set the tone for African Americans. In Congress, forceful and practical leaders such Barbara Jordan, Shirley Chisholm, Ron Dellums and John Conyers led the Black Caucus. The mayoralties of Tom Bradley in Los Angeles, Richard Hatcher in Gary, Coleman Young in Detroit, and Maynard Jackson in Atlanta marked the passing of the central city to black political leadership. Julian Bond in Georgia and Willie Brown in California raised the standard of leadership for both black and white members of state legislatures. Jesse Jackson, a protege of Dr. King, became a spokesman for some blacks.

Through the political process, blacks began to assert themselves in their local districts by forming voting blocs, electing politicians they believed would be responsive to them, and advocating control of their communities. White reluctance to recognize black claims to humanity and equality, combined with the failure of both the federal and local governments to respond to basic needs, led to this outburst of political action by blacks.

For well over 300 years, African Americans had been engaged in changing their status—changing from slave to free man, from second to first class citizen, from a despised and oppressed minority to a proud and vigorous people in a pluralistic and hopefully healthy society. In this struggle, they used many tactics. There were revolutionaries and accommodationists, pious Christians and spartan Muslims, men who demanded, pleaded and died for their rights. Undoubtedly, all methods of bringing changes had some effect on both black and white Americans.

The passage of the Civil Rights Act of 1964 and the Voting Rights Act of 1965 brought about some changes in American life. The principle of legal equality was established and voting qualifications had to be applied equally. This legislation also produced positive movement towards equalization of the opportunities in the American society. On the presidential level, Lyndon Johnson issued Executive Order 11246, which give political and social clout to Title VII of the 1964 legislation as he declared that all businesses and universities receiving federal assistance were to take "affirmative action" to insure that applicants were not discriminated against because of race, color, or creed.

Within the last three decades, Affirmative Action programs have been instituted in businesses and universities throughout the country. These programs were designed to help blacks as well as other victims of societal discrimination overcome the obstacles that had so long denied them access to opportunities. To a large extent Affirmative Action programs did and do provide a means for black competition. Yet the programs proved to be socially inconclusive. The remedy produced more resentment in whites toward blacks who, as they perceived it, received preferential treatment which led to the legal charge of reverse discrimination.

In 1976, Allan Bakke filed suit against the Regents of the University of California and Davis Medical School on the grounds that his civil rights, under the equal protection clause of the Fourteenth Amendment of the Constitution, had been violated. He claimed that he was denied admittance to the Medical School in favor of a black student because he was white. The Bakke case made its way to the United States Supreme Court. On June 27,1978, the Court ruled, in a split decision, that Bakke's civil rights had been violated. In its decision, the Court declared that quotas specifying specific places in given programs were unconstitutional. And so the struggle for access to American opportunities continued as black people, perceiving themselves as the underclass, saw the court decision as a possible reinstatement of the practice of "last hired and the first fired."

Progress had been made in the African American community. Blacks, in large part due to Affirmative Action, gained more access to job and educational opportunities than ever before. But only a small percentage of the black populace were able to take advantage of the opportunities. The bulk of the black populace remained subject to the despair of rural and urban slums, poverty, inadequate housing, high unemployment, crime and racial segregation. The Civil Rights legislation and programs of the last three decades did not change these conditions. Nor did legislation change how white Americans viewed their black counterparts.

White Americans still do not understand that black Americans want out of life precisely the same things that they do—good jobs, comfortable housing, peaceful neighborhoods, and a chance for themselves and their families to participate in America's often proclaimed promise of opportunity. White Americans, clinging tenaciously to myths and fears from the past, have difficulty accepting the human wants of African Americans. They insist on maintaining the prescribed social distance based on the historic past of total segregation. Every city has witnessed the complete turn of neighborhoods from white to black within five years after the first black family moves in. Whites have proclaimed their belief in equal education opportunities while in many cities and towns opposing all practical methods to bring it about. Social distance indicators reveal that whites do not oppose vigorously a black man's success as long he does not move within their immediate proximity.

The nation does not seem willing to pay the price to correct the legacy of the past any more than it is willing to create a fair and equal society.

This became evident in the late 1970s as a tax revolt swept the country. The result of that revolt forced states to level a heavy blow to social services and jobs that depended on tax revenues. Without many social services and jobs, a large number of blacks faced more devastating despair.

In 1980, a charming movie actor and Republican, Ronald Reagan of California, was elected President and took with him Republican control of the United States Senate. This was accompanied by the Federal Reserve Board's decision to "squeeze inflation" out of the economy by a policy of extremely tight money controls and high interest rates. The effect was to create a devastating recession, the worst since the 1930s, with a resulting massive unemployment of 10 plus percent among black and white workers who were unable to buy anything, let alone get credit. Prices did go down but at a great cost to both black and white workers.

By 1983, Reagan's polices of enormous tax reductions for upper income groups, combined with equally huge increases in military spending, broke the back of recession and launched an economic recovery accomplished by unprecedented government borrowing to the point that the nation debt tripled. A three trillion dollar debt legacy was bequeathed to the future.

The economic recovery benefited relatively few African Americans. A crisis has erupted in the black community. The most prevalent cause of death among African American men under the age of 25 is murder at the hands of other African American men. Drugs are slowly but surely killing the youth. The second highest school drop out rate among any identifiable group is young black teenagers. Over half of all black children today are born to unwed mothers. Black workers constitute a large proportion of the permanently unemployed. And the unemployment rate among African American men under the age of 21 is between thirty and forty percent. Newspapers are constantly reporting that 25 percent of young black men under the age of 25 are presently incarcerated in penal institutions, on parole, or in other ways under the jurisdiction of the criminal justice system. Meanwhile, in blighted urban areas, the black community is being held hostage by street gangs and drive-by shootings.

A permanent "underclass" was created as Reagan's policies ignored the problems of African Americans by refusing to acknowledge that they existed. The Reagan Administration implemented a national policy which, in effect said that the nation could no longer afford to accept the responsibility for the injustices of the past, unless of course, it was done on a voluntary basis. In 1988 George Bush, combining the fears of the

Willie Hortons and the most sentimental fantasies of a "Thousand points of light," successfully created in the minds of the voter a "kinder and gentler nation." Bush adopted the Reagan legacy of benign neglect to society's ills, in his response to the riots in South Central Los Angeles following the acquittal of the police officers charged with the beating of Rodney King. It was obvious that Mr. Bush was oblivious to the fact that the riots were symptomatic of a deeply rooted economic problem, the gap between those who have and those who do not have. And for the African American, the struggle continues.

In 1994, it is almost as though the African American's struggle for humanity had taken two steps backward, as Americans do not respond to who the black man is but what he is. This fact has caused a deep cynicism and disillusionment among young black people and compelled them to continue to challenge the hypocrisy of a nation that champions the values of liberty and equality while denying them to its own citizens. However, a feeling of optimism seems to exist in the general black populace. This remarkable optimism has been inspired by the passing of the torch to such political figures United States Senator Carol Moseley-Braun, Secretary of Commerce Ronald H. Brown, and Mayor Sharon Pratt Kelly of Washington D.C.; literary artists such as Alice Walker, August Wilson, and Terry MacMillan, all Pulitzer prize winners; and entertainers such as Harry Belafonte, James Earl Jones, and Denzel Washington, all courageous African Americans operating in the face of overpowering historical opposition. These are among the many African Americans who are determined not to let the dream die. They continue the struggle.

And who then is the African American?

The African American is an authentic American. He evolved out of the American experience—he too is a benefactor of this rich and glorious land. And yet the irony of it all is that he is still, after about 10 generations, viewed as an intruder, undeserving of the opportunities America has to offer. He is a stranger in the "land of the free and home of the brave." He is still searching for identity and acceptance, for "his place in the sun." ✦

NOTES

1. Ralph Ellison, "The World and the Jug," *Shadow and Act* (New York, 1972), p. 131.
2. Lorenzo J. Greene, *The Negro in Colonial New England* (New York, 1971), pp. 63-64.
3. Winthrop D. Jordan, *White Over Black, American Attitudes Toward the Negro 1550-1812* (Balitimore, 1971), pp. 43-44.
4. James H. Dormon and Robert R. Jones, *The Afro-American Experience: A Cultural History Through Emancipation* (New York, 1975), pp. 117-120.
5. Benjamin Quarles, "A Group Portrait: Black America at the Time of the Revolutionary War," *Ebony Magazine*. (August, 1975), p. 46.
6. Frederic Douglass, "What to the Slave is the Fourth of July?" in Herbert Apteker, ed., *A Documentary History of the Negro People in the United States* (New York, 1968), p. 334.
7. Mary Frances Berry and John W. Blassingame, *Long Memory: The Black Experience In America* (New York, 1982), p. 12.
8. Douglass. *Ibid.*
9. Seth M. Scheiner, *Negro Mecca: A History of the Negro in New York City 1865-1920* (New, York, 1965), pp. 92-93.
10. *Ibid.*, p. 87.
11. Arthur Huff Fauset, *Black Gods of the Metropolis: Negro Religious Cults in the Urban North* (Philadelphia, 1971), p. 107.
12. Theodore G. Vincent, *Black Power and the Garvey Movement* (California: Rampart Press, 1971) p. 16
13. Alton Hornsby, Jr., *The Black Almanac: From Involuntary Servitude, (1619-1860) to the Age of Disillusionment (1864-1971)* (New York, 1972) pp. 76-77.
14. Vincent Harding, "Black Radicalism: The Road From Montgomery," in Eric Foner, ed., *America's Black Past* (New York, 1970), p. 465.
15. Nathan Irvin Huggins, *Harlem Renaissance*. (New York, 1971), p. 5.
16. Harding, *Ibid.*, p. 472.
17. *Ibid.*, 475.
18. *Ibid.*

SELECTED BIBLIOGRAPHY

Anderson, Jervis. *This Was Harlem: A Cultural Portrait, 1900-1950*. New York, 1982.

Aptheker, Herbert, ed. *A Documentary History of the Negro People in the United States From Colonial Time Through the Civil War*. Volume I. New York, 1968.

Berry, Mary, and Blassingame, John. *Long Memory: The Black Experience in America*. New York, 1982.

Carrow, David J. *Bearing the Cross*. New York, 1988.

Cose, Ellis. *The Rage of a Privileged Class*. New York, 1993.

Ellison, Ralph. *Shadow and Act*. New York, 1972.

Fauset, Arthur Huff. *Black Gods of the Metropolis: Negro Religious Cults in the Urban North*. Philadelphia, 1971.

Forget, Robert William. *Without Consent or Contract*. New York, 1989.

Foner, Eric, ed. *America's Black Past: A Reader in Afro-American History*. New York, 1970

Glasgow, Douglas G. *The Black Underclass*. New York, 1981.

Greene, Lenzo Jonston. *The Negro in Colonial New England*. New York, 1971.

Harlan, Louis R. *Booker T. Washington in Perspective*. Mississippi, 1988.

Harding, Vincent. *There is a River: The Black Struggle for Freedom in America*. New York, 1981.

Hornsby, Alton. *The Black Almanac: From Involuntary Servitude (1619-1860) to Disillusionment (1864-1971)*. New York, 1972.

Huggins, Nathan I. *The Harlem Renaissance*. New York, 1973.

Jordan, Winthrop D. *White Over Black: American Attitudes Toward the Negro, 1550-1812*. Baltimore, 1971.

King, Martin Luther, Jr. *Where Do We Go From Here, Chaos or Community*. New York, 1968

Lewis, David Levering. *W.E.B. Dubois: Biography of a Race*. New York, 1993.

Lynd, Staughton. *Class Conflict, Slavery, and the United States Constitution*. West, Connect: cut, 1967.

Marable, Manning. *Race, Reform and Rebellion: The Second Reconstruction in Black America, 1945-1982*. Mississippi , 1989.

Northrup, David, ed. *The Atlantic Slave Trade*. Massachusetts, 1994.

Potter, Joan and Claytor, Constance. *African-American Firsts*. New York 1994.

Quarles, Benjamin. *The Negro in the American Revolution*. Chapel Hill, North Carolina, 1961.

____. *Black Abolitionists*. New York, 1969.

____. *Black Mosaic: Essays in Afro-American History and Historiography*. Amherst, 1988.

Scheiner, Seth M. *Negro Mecca: A History of the Negro in New York City, 1865-1920*. New York, 1965.

Shade, Will G. and Roy C. Herrenkol, ed. *Seven on Black Reflections on the Negro Experience in America*. New York, 1969.

Sterling, Dorothy, ed. *The Trouble They Seen: The Story of Reconstruction in the Words of African Americans*. New York,1994.

Stuckey, Sterling. *Slave Culture: Nationalist Theory and the Foundations of Black America*. New York, 1987.

____. *Going Through the Storm: The Influence of American Art in History*. New York, 1994.

West, Cornel West. *Race Matters*. New York, 1993.

Wintz, Cary D. *Black Culture and the Harlem Renaissance*. Texas, 1988.

Wright, Donald R. *African American in the Colonial Era: From African Origins Through the American Revolution*. Illinois, 1990.

THE MEXICAN AMERICANS AND THE AMERICAN WAY OF LIFE

GLORIA E. MIRANDA

The United States Southwest stretches from Texas to California and is the cultural homeland of various native American peoples including Mexican Americans. These Mexican Americans, who also identify themselves today as Chicanos, have had a long and continuous history in the region.[1] Over a period of several centuries that extend back in time before Spain, Mexico and the United States claimed the Southwest, the fore-bears of today's Mexican Americans inhabited the land ancient tribal groups called *Aztlán* (The Bright Land to the Far North).

In the centuries to follow under Spanish and Mexican rule, these indigenous Americans who by then carried Spanish surnames, settled community after community in Texas, New Mexico, Arizona, southern Colorado and California from the sixteenth through the early nineteenth centuries. Towns like Victoria and Laredo, Texas, Albuquerque and Santa Fe, New Mexico, Tucson, Arizona and Los Angeles, California bear the indelible imprint of Mexican American development.

However, when the United States conquered the region in 1848, the Hispano-Mexican heritage of the Southwest lost its privileged place in North American history. Cultural and racial deprecation of these newly incorporated United States citizens continued over the next century as Mexican Americans were demoted to a subservient status in American life and were accorded the rank of foreigners in their native land.

In the 1960s, when the black civil rights movement gained national scope and attention, Chicanos (as Mexican Americans by then preferred to call themselves) joined in to demand equal access to the American way of life. Their struggle for self-determination included a plan aimed at achieving equality and justice and restoring the Mexican American heritage to a place of esteem in the Southwest. In the quest to fulfill their objectives, Chicanos rediscovered and reclaimed *Aztlán* as their homeland. *El Plan Espiritual de Aztlán* (The Spiritual Plan of Aztlán) was enthusiastically proclaimed by civil rights activists: "We are a nation, We are a Union of free pueblos, We are Aztlán."[2]

What that declaration meant to Chicanos eluded the majority of Americans caught up in the national social upheaval of the time. But for Mexican Americans, the symbol of *Aztlán* confirmed and affirmed their right to consider themselves Americans without qualification. Furthermore, Chicanos also realized that by virtue of their historic presence in North America they no longer needed to view themselves as foreign immigrants to this country.

In the decades since that initial self-discovery, Mexican Americans have learned a great deal more about who they are and what they have contributed to the American nationality especially west of the Mississippi. And, it has been a considerable historical role indeed. But, self-study has also taught Americans of Mexican descent that the United States way of life permanently has reshaped and redirected their traditional Hispano-Mexican values. Explaining those dimensions of the Mexican American experience represents a central focus of this essay. Certainly, it is imperative that we familiarize ourselves with the largest ethnic and racial minority of the western United States.

HISTORICAL AND CULTURAL DIMENSIONS UNDER SPAIN AND MEXICO

Americans of Mexican ancestry have influenced immeasurably the history and culture of the American Southwest. They have served as the pioneers of the "Spanish borderlands," the transmitters of rich cultural and religious customs and values, the builders of a vast number of civilian and military communities, surrogates and role models for southwestern indigenous tribal groups as well as the purveyors of the Hispano-Mexican notion of community solidarity. Mexican Americans also promoted and encouraged the growth of the cattle and sheep industries of New Mexico, Texas and California, became the first vaqueros of the United States, mountain men and fur trappers of the Far West and launched the initial successful land rush within the present borders of the United States. Additionally, the cuisine, music, dance and art of the Southwest bears an indelible Hispano-Mexican character as does the legal, mining, irrigation and civil codes and traditions of the border states.

The saga known in North American history as the northward movement served as the genesis for much of these fruitful endeavors. First as Spanish subjects and later as Mexican citizens, the earliest Mexican American settlers of the Southwest accomplished the permanent occupation of the area as they made their way north in the sixteenth century into New Mexico and the remainder of the borderlands in the seventeenth, eighteenth and early nineteenth centuries. In the process, they introduced the Hispano-Mexican culture to their indigenous counterparts in *Aztlán.*

Historians have long credited the Spaniards with the primary role of colonizing this portion of the United States.[3] This claim to fame has deprived the non-Spaniards who shared in the settling of the borderlands from receiving similar recognition for this impressive venture. The distinguished native American historian, Jack D. Forbes, has taken exception to these perceptions.

> The present boundary between the United States and Mexico is an artificial line carved out by Anglo-American expansionists without reference to indigenous boundaries or natural features . . . Understandably then, native groups formerly crossed back and forth across the present line, some going northward and some going southward. In ancient times the ancestors of the Nahuans may have resided within the present United States, perhaps in areas where their relatives within the Uto-Aztecan or Mexicanic language family still exist.[4]

Forbes further contended the northward movement under Spanish auspices was accomplished by tribal Mexicans because "the northward expansion of the Spanish Empire was dependent on their aid, willing and otherwise." Later, mixed-bloods including some who had miscegenated with various tribal groups of central and northern Mexico joined in the migration into the borderlands. By the time the northward movement settlement rush had concluded, "the overwhelming majority of Spanish-speaking people in the northern portions of the empire were of Mexican or indigenous ancestry, or were mixed-bloods."[5]

Part of the problem of accurately identifying the racial heritage of the frontier settlers centers principally on the fact that the majority of indigenous northern pioneers carried Spanish identities. But if we are to accurately understand the Mexican American people, it is important to acknowledge that they overwhelmingly are native American genetically in part or whole. The Spanish names carried by the group today originally were bestowed on their ancestors by Spanish missionaries during the three centuries of Christianization in North America.

> Tribal groups throughout New Spain during three hundred years of colonial rule commonly acquired Spanish names when baptized into the Catholic faith. At that moment missionaries bestowed on new converts Christian first names and Spanish surnames as permanent symbols of their new spiritual and cultural identity.[6]

The identity conferred at baptism also de-tribalized the indigenous Mexicans as they were socially and culturally separated from their former tribal values. However, the genetic commonality of Indian origin remained unaltered. Even race-conscious Americans entering *Aztlán* after 1821 frequently made reference to the fact that Mexicans were Indians in spite of their Spanish surnames.

What observers discovered that was dissimilar between the indigenous tribes and the Spanish-surnamed populace was the Hispano-Mexican religio-philosophical ethos of the latter. Western European and Catholic Christian ideals which originally had been merged in the sixteenth century in central Mexico with the indigenous customs, mores and familial values of the well-developed civilizations that Spain conquered in 1521 were introduced onto the various regional frontier zones by the recruits who enlisted and joined the northward movement. This transplanted Christian culture created lasting influences on the lifestyle practices of both Spanish and Mexican societies that countless sojourners into this region in the nineteenth century recorded in their travel diaries.

Mexican independence from Spain in 1821 brought freedom from colonialism but the deeply embedded Christian ethos introduced into the far north by earlier Spanish subjects remained rooted in the frontier culture of this portion of North America.

Family life, which has always served as the central vehicle in the formation of the Mexican American character, then played an especially significant role in conveying to its members the value of good upbringing and Christian morality, respect for elders and love of duty and service to others. Commitment to cultural education led the then Mexicans to strive to inculcate among the young similar appreciation for religious values. In this setting, religion imbued culture with profound symbols of expression. For example, in California

> religious education was carefully observed in all the houses. Before daybreak it was the custom to pray and sing an alabado (hymn in praise of the sacrament) in chorus; at twelve noon other prayers were recited;

at orizons (about 6 p.m.) and in the night before retiring all joined in a rosary and another alabado, sung in chorus.[7]

So, too, community life nurtured religious cultural education. The great feast days of the Catholic calendar served as a unifying force for community residents. But the most profound Christian celebration was the feast day of the Virgin of Guadalupe. In New Mexico, she was made the patron saint of the territory. One United States official visiting the region in the mid-nineteenth century remarked that "her image is conspicuous in all churches, and is also quite common in the drinking and gambling saloons as are those of General Jackson and Tom Thumb in American barrooms."[8] In California, in the 1840s, Guadalupe attained the status of patroness of community schools. Other similar traditions received widespread enthusiastic involvement by the populace since these events functioned to solidify community life.

Hence, in assessing the pre-Anglo-American character of the Southwest, an awareness of the importance of traditional values rooted in family, faith and community life identifies the significant repositories of the Mexican American historical and cultural past before 1848. When this major chapter in western North American history came to a close after the United States conquest of Mexico, the former lifestyle of the new American Southwest changed forevermore.

THE SOUTHWEST AFTER 1848: FOREIGNERS IN AZTLÁN

At the close of the Mexican-American War in 1848 almost 300,000 Mexicans and southwestern tribal groups came directly under United States rule. The Treaty of Guadalupe Hidalgo, signed on February 2, 1848, formalized the acquisition of the region and granted former Mexican residents absorbed by conquest treaty rights as citizens of the United States. Becoming "American" citizens meant the right to vote, religious liberty, protection of property from confiscation in addition to a promise of fair treatment in all endeavors. Lamentably, over the next half century, the popular nativist and racial supremacist practices of the nineteenth century American way of life forced the abrogation of treaty guarantees made to the Mexican population of the Southwest.

Tragically, these new United States citizens experienced racial and religious bigotry, social ostracism and the greed of land hungry opportunists who coveted their property holdings. Widespread cultural genocide efforts and the segregation of Mexican Americans into

"Mexican towns" (segregated enclaves) symbolized the impossibilities of becoming "Americans." By the end of the nineteenth century, the group had been effectively checked in its search for full American standing. In every region of the Southwest, political powerlessness and ostracism by white Americans was the sad consequence of blatant anti-Mexicanism. Unethical obstacles established to prevent Mexican Americans from exercising the franchise such as grandfather clauses, literacy tests and poll taxes, or bossism proved insurmountable barriers to overcome to achieve full-fledged American citizenship recognition in every state and territory in the region. The political end result for these new Americans was underrepresentation in assemblies, town and national government. Horrendous racial violence directed at Mexican Americans in concert with the blatant confiscation of their lands compounded the lot of the group and entrenched them in a colonized-like condition from Texas to California.

Why brown-skinned Spanish-surnamed Mexicans received such un-American treatment in this period can best be summed up as the consequence of the centuries old irrational Anglo-Saxon contempt for Spanish-speaking Catholic peoples which was coupled with the popular frontier notion of the age that Mexicans and Indians were the national enemies of Anglo-Saxon civilization.[9] The sad scenario evoked a mindset among nineteenth century Caucasians that included a strong contempt for the Hispano-Mexican culture of the Southwest. The majority of Americans perceived the Mexican American way of life to be not only inferior, but un-American, foreign and alien to the more secular and individualistic Anglo-Saxon heritage of their forefathers. To brown-skinned Mexican Americans, it was inconceivable how they had been ascribed such a lowly status as Americans. After all, when travelers from the United States ventured before 1848 into Aztlán, had they not been graciously welcomed?

Yet, in spite of the extensive racial and cultural ostracism and deprecation of these people in their historic homeland, many civic leaders surfaced among Mexican Americans to demand that the Treaty of Guadalupe Hidalgo be truly honored so that civil rights be extended to every citizen and resident of the American Southwest. The extensive Spanish and bilingual community newspaper network established by men like Francisco Ramirez in Los Angeles or Carlos Velasco in Tucson served as community vehicles to convey displeasure of Mexican American citizens to their colonized condition.

And when all legitimate avenues of redress and protest were exhausted, social justice activists, often labeled bandits by ethnocentric Caucasians, were formed to challenge the Establishment of that era. In most cases, intolerable discrimination forced men like Tiburcio Vasquez in California and Juan Cortina of Texas to resort to so-called banditry to demand the end to the blatant and deplorable mistreatment of Mexican Americans. As a consequence, history has bestowed the status of villains on these individuals for attempting to insure that the American process of democracy extend to Mexican Americans. Men like Vasquez and Cortina came face to face with the most extreme and hostile manifestations of the frontier Anglo-American character. Exaggerated individualism, racially charged ethnocentric nationalism and coarse religious bigotry clashed violently with the Mexican American character of community, family, faith and cultural pride.

As the century drew to a close, a popular literary and folkloric tradition surfaced to reinforce the historical Anglo-Saxon assessment of Mexicans as greasers, bandits and thieves. So profound were these images that they served as effective evidence of why Americans had conquered Mexico a half century before. After all, the Mexicans had contributed nothing of real value to the development of the area was the underlying message of many a western tale.

The unsavory images conjured up in this period were fueled further by the first written histories of the West. In these amateurish chronicles of the westward movement and the conquest of the Southwest, the Mexican place in history had been systematically relegated to insignificance. Instead, the Spaniards received singular recognition for the settlement, colonization, political and and economic development of the pre-1848 west. Spaniards, as fellow Europeans, made noble substitutes for Anglo-Saxons in preparing the west for the superior American way of life. For decades, the majority of historians followed this school of interpretation. Consequently, until the emergence of the Chicano civil rights movement, the history of the Southwest was principally the story of Spanish colonizers and Anglo-American conquerors.

How much of this distorted reconstruction of the Mexican role in United States history was absorbed and accepted by the Spanish-surnamed Mexican Americans in the latter half of the nineteenth century remains yet to be fully studied. But apparently, the Mexican American needed little inducement to participate in the community life of the region. A tradition of activism dating back to the Mexican era thrived in this period in towns like Tucson, Arizona, Laredo, Texas, and throughout other communities in New Mexico and California. The town builders and powerbrokers of the Southwest included names like Benavides, Carrillo, Ochoa, Otero, Samaniego and countless others who served as politicians, merchants, educators, financiers and philanthropists to their respective communities.

But as the century drew to a close, the preeminent Mexican American place in these southwestern communities where this type of activism functioned to bond the group's members, had noticeably deteriorated in all but a few areas. The building of the railroads brought increasing scores of non-Mexicans from the east who were to reshape the heritage of the Southwest into their own image.

From the 1880s increasing numbers of "Mexican towns" emerged as segregated enclaves because the newcomers considered these town sections as too un-American and foreign in customs for them to reside in. In New Mexico, where Mexican Americans succeeded to some extent in averting the rapid decline of political power and prestige felt in other areas of the Southwest, little progress had been made in achieving statehood status. As late as the 1890s, the United States Congress denied the territory admission to the Union as a state because New Mexicans were too un-American in language, religion and mores. The Spanish-surnamed residents of the area could only lament the fact that half a century after the Treaty of Guadalupe Hidalgo had set forth the constitutional criteria citizenship, that little progress had actually been made in realizing full acceptance and status as Americans. Democracy and freedom were hollow guarantees in this part of the United States.

MEXICAN IMMIGRATION AND THE CHALLENGE OF AMERICANIZATION

In the initial decades of the twentieth century, over one million Mexicans migrated north across the border as they mainly fled civil strife and social upheaval engendered by rebellion in Mexico. To these immigrants, the cultural affinity of the Southwest appealed to their social needs and circumstances. More importantly, widespread de facto segregation made it impossible for either immigrants or Mexican Americans to reside in Caucasian enclaves. After all, to the majority of Americans they were a foreign entity.

The hostility of the initial Anglo-American response to Mexican immigration produced a new wave of discord in the region. By the 1920s, a general resentment to Mexican resettlement in this country had given birth to a popular national immigration restriction campaign that called for the repatriation of these immigrants to their homeland. Social scientists, educators, geneticists, politicians and evangelists, too, denounced the steady flow and relocation of Mexicans in the United States. As a rule, most opponents of Mexican immigration feared the effects on United States life of the Mexican ethos. One local southern California Protestant minister who was then working among the immigrants poignantly identified for Americans the root of the Mexican problem as he understood the issue.

> Fifty and one hundred years ago Uncle Sam accomplished some remarkable digestive feats. Gastronomically he was a marvel. He was not particularly choosy! Dark meat from the borders of the Mediterranean, or light meat from the Baltic, equally suited him, for promptly he was able to assimilate both, turning them into bone of his bone, and flesh of his flesh—But this *chili con carne*! Always it seems to give Uncle Samuel the heartburn; and the older he gets, the less he seems to be able to assimilate it. Indeed, it is a question whether *chili* is not a condiment to be taken in small quantities rather than a regular article of diet. And upon this conviction ought to stand all the law and the prophets so far as the Mexican immigrant is concerned.[10]

As the Reverend Robert McLean perceived the situation, culture conflict was inevitable so long as Mexicans remained in the United States. Worse, the American way of life was threatened by so contradictory a cultural value system as that of the Mexicans. Thus, the urgency of the repatriation program of the 1930s that deported close to half a million immigrants as well as American citizens of Mexican descent south across the border.

But some Caucasian Americans responded in a less acrimonious manner towards the immigrants. In particular, a minority of social workers and educators insisted that a program of instruction to teach Mexican vocational skills and the essentials of the American way of life would convert them into useful workers. Americanization, however, was never intended to build future group leadership so that the offspring of immigrants could compete on an equal footing with white Americans. Staunch neo-nativism in the years after World War I in concert with the rise of a triumphant social Darwinist thought surmised that Mexicans were culturally and racially unacceptable to be considered part of the W.A.S.P. society of the United States.

As the rest of the world drew closer and closer to global confrontation in the 1930s, in the United States Southwest, the sons and daughters of immigrants reached maturity and become significantly socialized to understand American values. By then, too, they had grown up amidst a cultural renaissance in the isolated barrios of the region which were home for the majority of the three million Americans of Mexican descent in the United States. Celebrations like Mexican independence and Cinco de Mayo, pro-active community self-help units, political and labor activism and unionization efforts in rural and urban areas were but a few of the major thrusts of barrio life even under the most deplorable of conditions. Quite energetically, immigrants reinvigorated and revitalized the Mexican cultural legacy of the Southwest in spite of the forced segregation still rampant in this part of the United States.

At the center of this activity was the family. Traditionally, the principal purveyor of cultural values, the immigrant family in particular felt obligated to preserve the heritage for their offspring. Most parents, understandably, feared some of the consequences of the more liberal and individualistic United States social customs and mores of pre-World War II times. In many ways, their predicament mirrored similar painful experiences shared by other immigrants to the United States in this period.

The distinguished sociologist, Emory Bogardus, worked extensively among Mexican immigrants and their offspring in southern California in this era. Bogardus discovered almost universal concern by immigrant parents about the affect of Anglo-American independence and individualism on their youngsters. One mother interviewed by Bogardus effectively described her cultural fears.

> The thing that shocked me most about the United States was the lack of solidarity in the home. The American children do not have much regard for their parents. I was renting in an American home where there were four daughters from nine to sixteen years of age and every one of them was out until three o'clock at night. Their parents had no control over them. In Mexico I had to be in by eight o'clock with my father and mother. But here it is different. Of course it makes for individuality and independence. They learn to think for themselves, but experiences teach wonderful lessons, and they refuse to accept the lesson which the broader experiences of their parents have taught them. The freedom and independence in this country bring the children into conflict with their parents. They learn nicer ways, learn about the outside world, learn how to speak English, and then they become ashamed of their parents who brought them up here that they might haves better advantages.[11]

Another mother voiced similar fears. "I can never get used to it . . . the freedom which our women enjoy" in the United States. "What can Mexican mothers do?"[12]

Exercising parental authority, reinvigorating traditional customs and inculcating expected behavior among youngsters seemed to these parents the most effective way of avoiding deculturation for their children. But it must be understood that the cultural nationalist posture of the immigrant was not rooted in a total anti-American sentiment in other areas. In particular, these parents expected their children to attend school and receive an education that would afford them every opportunity to succeed in American society.

While many educators have long assumed that a tradition of indifference towards education exists in Mexican and Mexican American culture, the opposite sentiment prevails. In Los Angeles during the pre-war era, many a city and county school experienced overcrowding because Mexican and Mexican American parents insisted that their children attend classes. A city school board member explained the group's enthusiasm:

> So great is the hunger of these Mexican children and so great is the zeal of their parents for them, that they are liable to outdistance our on boys and girls in their school work. So often American parents insist that they do not want their children to avail themselves of certain privileges which are offered, while the Mexican parent frankly declares that he wants his child to have an opportunity which is provided.[13]

Unfortunately, southwestern schools hardly provided the sons and daughters of immigrants the same educational opportunities Caucasian youngsters in more affluent communities received. After all, as minority children, they were entitled at best to attend "Mexican schools" where the vast majority of educators felt they belonged. In these segregated classrooms and schools the majority of Mexican American youngsters indeed learned a great deal about the American way of life. Lamentably, they also discovered that their Mexican heritage received no similar glorification in spite of the historical linkage of the Southwest. Worse yet, punishment for speaking Spanish on school playgrounds, callous reidentification of their names to Anglo-sounding ones and a general plan to prevent children of Mexican ancestry the opportunity to enter high school indicated the obstructive role of the schools. Understandably, the Mexican origin population had the highest drop out rate in the 1930s among all groups in southwestern schools.

Mexican American youngsters fully understood the futility of continued school attendance in such a classroom setting. Those who remained, attended segregated schools and learned that they were expected to prepare themselves for a subservient station in American life: landless, leaderless, powerless. Yet, having been socialized in this country, this particular generation refused to forfeit the fact that they were Americans. So, when the United States entered World War II, among the first citizens eager to express their loyalty were Mexican Americans. During the war, the exploits of this generation garnered the most decorations of any minority group in the armed forces. Eleven Congressional Medal of Honor winners were also included in the total with names like Jose Lopez, Macario Garcia, Jose Martinez and Silvestre Herrera added to the roll call of American heroes of World War II.

The war represented a significant watershed in the Mexican American experience since the global holocaust marked the end of the exclusively Mexican cultural and intellectual influence on southwestern Brown Americans and the emergence of the bicultural Mexican American and Chicano experience of the post-war age. In the two decades after the war ended, tremendous social change in this region ushered in an era of self-awareness that formed the basis for the hyphenated Mexican-American socialization to postwar life.

FROM MEXICAN-AMERICANS TO CHICANOS

Considerable re-definition by Mexican Americans of what it meant to be American generated in the postwar era a psychological, sociological and cultural metamorphosis in the Southwest unlike any the group had experienced since becoming citizens in 1848.

As we have already seen, most Americans chose to accord these Mexican Americans a foreign status in social and formal interaction during their first century of formal United States citizenship. But Mexican Americans also continued adherence to the traditional Mexican mode of life that had existed in the region before 1848. The geographical isolation of the Southwest from the rest of the country for much of this period of history contributed to this cultural insularity. In turn, limited exposure to the American ethos impeded Mexican Americans from gaining first hand knowledge of the mores, customs and social patterns of this country in the nineteenth century.

However, Mexican immigration at the turn of the twentieth century made possible some reduction in the social distance that had existed between Caucasian and Mexican Americans. This was particularly noticeable in urban areas like Los Angeles and San Antonio. Nonetheless, social interaction in these urban centers while exposing the immigrant and Mexican American to the technological, material and secular mode of national life, generated very little alteration in the cultural and social status quo of the group. Monolingualism and the retention of traditional values seemed outwardly immune to change.

Continued segregation in barrio enclaves along with the arrival of large numbers of Mexican immigrants also rejuvenated and reinforced the Mexican intellectual mind set of the Southwest. More importantly, American society in the pre-World War II era of resurgent nativism and restrictionist thinking generally refused to consider allowing full cultural and social Americanization for the immigrant Mexican or Mexican American citizens. However, the World War II effort of brown Americans gave Caucasians an opportunity to rethink their attitude toward the "Mexicans," at least as hyphenated Americans.

A more humanitarian and democratic sentiment toward the Mexican American resulted not only from their heroic role in the war, but from the influx of Americans from other regions of the country during this time who harbored little perceivable anti-Mexicanism. The relaxation of traditional social distancing between the two groups similarly elicited a positive response to this generation of Mexican Americans.

This catalyst for change symbolized to war veterans in particular, that Americans were willing to allow them to seek to homogenize into the mainstream. A mass exodus from the barrios of the Southwest by the war veteran generation facilitated new residential and social patterns for Mexican Americans that were impossible beforehand. The demographic realignment accelerated social interaction with other Americans on an intimate level. Mexican-Americanization, therefore, was directed, first, at achieving full-fledged American status and, secondly, at escaping the anti-Mexican discrimination experienced by barrio residents for several decades.

To achieve full Americanization, the postwar Mexican American came to the conclusion that de-Mexicanization was an essential first step criteria for acceptance into the mainstream society. This led many of them to resort dramatically to redirecting their identities by altering their names to Anglo-sounding ones, speaking only English and fraternizing exclusively with non-Mexicans (i.e., Caucasians). More significantly, Mexican Americans concluded and thus realized that to be considered full-fledged American in this period meant being Caucasian. However impossible it is to alter one's racial heritage, postwar Mexican Americans who wholeheartedly endeavored to attain American ranking, also claimed racial whiteness through identification as Spanish or Spanish American. The expectation of first class citizenship like that enjoyed by whites underscores the reason for the denial of their native American indigenous identities.

After two decades, Mexican-Americanization had led many who embraced deculturation as the road to successful Americanization and societal assimilation to drift away from the heritage of their forefathers. Indeed, many who aspired to realize the American dream were no longer in touch with the community focus, cultural fraternity and Catholic Christian ideals of their parents' generation who had remained behind in the various barrio enclaves of the Southwest prevented by de facto traditions from assimilating into mainstream society. Most certainly, these aspiring Americans had internalized the mores, social customs, expectations, credos and canons of the American way of life. But, the Mexican American was still politically, socially and economically an outsider in American life. Worse yet, even as hyphenated Americans, they were still considered Mexican by the majority of whites with whom they came in contact in these two postwar decades.

Embittered by the fact that racial and cultural self-denial had achieved little more than alienation from their heritage, many Mexican Americans found expression for their frustration in the civil rights struggles of the 1960s.

> Urbanization and direct exposure by the first generation removed from the barrios to the dominant society begot a unique marginal product. And it was members from this group that contributed most of the militant leadership that sprung forth the Chicano movement.[15]

As angry personalities, they denounced white Americans for having dispossessed them of their self-identity, dignity and self-worth.

> Our ideals, our way of looking at life, our traditions, our sense of brotherhood and human dignity, and the deep love and trust among our own are truths and principles which have prevailed in spite of the gringo, who would rather have us remade in his image and likeness: materialistic, cultureless, colorless, monolingual and racist.[16]

This militancy among Mexican Americans psychologically represented a longing for the suppressed native culture they had scorned in their Mexican-Americanism efforts aimed at achieving assimilation. The nostalgic search for cultural rebirth in the 1960s also included a re-identification as "Chicanos" even though very few knew much about the barrio lifestyle of this distinctive behavioral typology of the Southwest. Most militant types, born-again Chicanos at best, assumed that barrio Chicanos possessed a non-Anglo self-image and were also probably anti-

American in thinking. In truth, the Chicano type was an individual who had emerged alongside the Mexican American in the postwar era but was barrio born and reared and preferred not to leave the traditional enclave which was home for so long to his ancestors in order to gain acceptance as an American.

Barrio Chicanos had also undergone cultural modification of the Mexican value system and ethos since World War II times. What emerged in the postwar period was a bicultural synthesis that blended traditional Mexican religious and cultural ideals with the most positive dimensions of the American way of life. The more harmonious biculturalism of the Chicano was devoid of the racial and cultural alienation of the hyphenated Mexican-American mind set of the same generation. Having been socialized in the United States and exposed to the culture of this nation by way of work, movies and television, the Chicano was astute enough to understand the pitfalls of deculturation which at best marginalized one from the traditional heritage. For the barrio resident, American status meant democracy, good citizenship, patriotic love of country and the right to a culturally pluralistic lifestyle. However, the obstacles to acquisition of these privileges rested on the same premise as the one which denied the non-barrio Mexican-American complete emancipation from an inferior and foreign status. Abject poverty, social ostracism, limited upward mobility and inferior educational opportunities compounded the lives of the majority of these brown Americans in the 1950s and 1960s living in the Southwest.

But, the barrio-raised Chicano had little experience in the American mainstream to organize and direct a civil rights campaign within an Anglo-American context which was aimed at achieving full self-determination. This is one major reason why militant reborn Chicanos (actually neo-Chicanos) spearheaded the group's struggle for liberation from over a century of limited access to the fruits of the American system. Most of these Mexican Americans were better educated, sophisticated and more savvy about the United States way of life than their barrio counterparts. Their articulate leadership won over barrio support for the general cause of Chicano self-determination since few community figures of similar style and ability could be found who appealed to non-barrio types.

Hence, the rediscovery of Aztlán as the Chicano homeland and the subsequent Spiritual Plan of Aztlán declaration mentioned at the beginning of this essay, stirred both barrio and non-barrio converts to a cultural nationalism that included an awareness of the group's native

American heritage. What the homeland idea also meant was that what it took to be considered American in the 1960s had been sharply redefined by the Mexican and Chicano generation of that era. The Anglo-American was the foreigner, not them.

THE CHICANO AND MEXICAN AMERICAN EXPERIENCE TODAY

In the last quarter of a century some strides have been made by Chicanos and Mexican Americans in their quest for equal access to the American dream in spite of the limited permanent societal changes wrought by the civil rights era. The Chicano movement nevertheless is singularly responsible for opening doors, often forcibly, to educational and political institutions heretofore closed to Mexican Americans. The emergence and establishment of ethnic studies programs at colleges and universities and the election of public officials represent crucial arenas for much needed change.

Certainly the rise of political figures like Henry Cisneros, Secretary of Housing and Urban Development for the Clinton administration and former mayor of San Antonio, Federico Pena, Secretary of Transportation, former New Mexico governors Tony Anaya and Jerry Apodaca or Gloria Molina and Richard Alatorre, Los Angeles county and city officials, can be directly attributed to the impact of the Chicano movement as a vehicle for inspiring Mexican Americans to seek empowerment. Additionally, resurgent community activism involving church-based organizations like Communities Organized for Public Service (COPS) in San Antonio and United Neighborhoods Organization (UNO) in East Los Angeles have injected a vibrant grassroots element to Chicano politics that has redefined Chicano efforts to gain power. Furthermore, the rise of the militant *La Raza Unida Party* (The United Peoples' Party) in south Texas during the civil rights era for a brief period introduced Americans to the possibilities of third political party organizations as vehicles for local self-determination among minorities. Certainly, the success of Mexican Americans in the 1980s in gaining control of rural and urban local government in various southwestern communities signifies that the Chicano movement has spawned a generation of forceful activism and gritty determination.

The impact of the 1960s has been felt in other and varied ways including a popular resurgence of cultural activity formerly and publicly suppressed in the Southwest because of past anti-Mexicanism Today, celebrations like Cinco de Mayo, *El dia de los muertos* (The Day of the Dead) on November 2nd and Posadas nativity processions have gained widespread popularity beyond the barrio enclaves of the Southwest.

Similarly, a preponderance of artists, writers and even playwrights like Luis Valdez have stimulated considerable interest and pride in being Mexican American or Chicano. Valdez, for one, who began his career with Cesar Chavez's Farmworkers Theatre gained fame with his play *Zootsuit* which dramatized the Anglo's racial bigotry towards Mexican American adolescents in Los Angeles during World War II. The play also raised the Chicano experience to a level of interpretation that extended beyond the traditional southwestern enclaves and created a forum for Caucasians to view the Mexican American tragedy of the war years from a non-white perspective.

Sports figures, too, have benefited from the civil rights movement. Nancy Lopez in golf, Jim Plunkett and Tom Flores in football and Fernando Valenzuela in baseball are but a few of the most recognizable role models young Mexican Americans can emulate and identify as examples of success. They are heroes for all Americans as well.

But, in spite of the numerous strides Chicanos and Mexican Americans have made in the last two decades, much remains unchanged that the earlier Chicano movement failed to permanently transform. Educationally, the average years of school attendance has not improved at all since 1970 when ten years of education was the norm for Mexican American youngsters. The attainment levels are worse for Mexican and Central American immigrants who average eight years of schooling and have additional linguistic barriers to overcome in their educational experiences.

The recent emphasis on bicultural-bilingual educational programs has stirred much emotionally charged debate but some public school districts at least seem predisposed to implement these types of programs as alternative solutions to the longstanding instructional challenges posed by the presence of Spanish-surnamed youngsters who today predominate in most southwestern school districts. The culturally pluralistic model incorporates and encourages appreciation of the self-worth, self-esteem and value of the Mexican American heritage to *American* society alongside the traditional curricular regimen of public instruction. Thus, a student who has a healthy self-esteem need not worry about being accepted as an American in this institutional setting. Other schools, however, remain reluctant to alter traditional curricular patterns and continue to focus largely on deculturating Spanish-surnamed children as part of their educational mission while placing less emphasis on substantive pedagogical goals such as nurturing the necessary skills needed for success as adults. Conversely, Catholic parochial schools have succeeded with Mexican Americans who are among the large number of these private school graduates who enter colleges and universities each year. Parochial schools succeed because they de-emphasize deculturation-Americanization issues and concentrate on the development of the skills these pupils will need to compete in American society.

Since Americans have long cherished the classroom as the central vehicle for socializing, unifying and nationalizing children under an American umbrella, then, it is imperative that redefinition of what nationalism, ethnicity and Americanism means in today's world of the 1990s must be part of the mission of the nation's educational policymakers. In particular, instruction that prepares minority youngsters to compete fairly with their Caucasian counterparts in the sciences, mathematics, the arts and humanities should be an overriding consideration in future matriculation assessment of Mexican American pupils.

It is indeed a lofty ideal to wish to uplift and improve the lot of the disadvantaged in order to teach them to appreciate the American way of life. In the past, however, conformity to the ideal of Americanism meant instruction that demeaned the self-worth and cultural pride of those whose ethnicity was not Anglo-Saxon. Mexican youngsters in the early decades of this century discovered how traumatizing such an educational policy was to them. The Pachuco generation of the 1930s and 1940s represented a severely marginalized group of youngsters who were psychologically suspended and divorced from both Mexican and American cultures. This subcultural typology produced the initial gang conditions in the urban Southwest among Mexican Americans which have reappeared each subsequent generation since that time.

The United States has benefited greatly from the contributions of Mexican Americans and Chicanos. There is no need to continue to view them as foreigners or to demean and resent the cultural values they cherish and refuse to completely discard. America has been well served by their loyalty and patriotism in peacetime and in periods of war. This country has also been greatly enriched by the culture—language, folklore, music, dance, art, diet, faith—that clearly identifies this ethnicity as Mexican American.

In turn, Mexican Americans and barrio Chicanos have embraced and identify intimately with the institutions and democratic principles of this nation. They also aspire to achieve material success, to excel and to serve as their communities' leaders just as other Americans. But, the major onus for the future political, social and economic well-being of the group rests with the majority society of the United States which influences political and social changes as well as public policy. The willingness of Anglo-Americans to agree to the fact that the definition of an American is indeed more diversified today than ever before will go a long way to help Mexican Americans and Chicanos achieve self-determination. Only then will Aztlán be recognized as the southwestern cradle of American cultural diversity. ✦

NOTES

1. Both terms, Chicano and Mexican American, have been used as self-referent appellations by the group. In a general sense, Chicano identifies a Mexican American. More accurately, it describes a Mexican American born and reared in a barrio. Mexican-American with a hyphenated spelling symbolized the self-identity of Chicanos in transition from their former Mexican heritage in the post-World War II era. It also has been applied as a general designation for Chicanos. Of the two terms, Chicano has more specific cultural value while Mexican American indicates the transitional condition of those who seek majority group approbation. As a rule, non-barrio residents have preferred to call themselves Mexican Americans while barrio dwellers prefer the Chicano designation.

   The labels Hispanic and Latino have gained widespread attention in the media in recent years. But both terms lack a specific definition of the ethnicity of Chicanos and Mexican Americans and in particular are devoid of the indigenous cultural or racial basis of the group's heritage. The federal government coined the expression in the 1970s to lump together all Spanish-surnamed groups in American society without concern for the racial and ethnic diversity of the various "Hispanic" peoples of the United States. On the other hand, Latino has gained growing acceptance by Spanish-surnamed groups and others as a generic substitute for categorizing citizens and immigrants of Latin American background. Of course, the Latin focus again points only to the European dimension of the culture of these peoples but not their native indigenous roots.

   Chicanos and Mexican Americans are neither Hispanics nor Latinos because of their indigenous racial and cultural origins and their United States socio-psychological upbringing. Mexican, Central and South American immigrants to this country fit the designation of Latinos due to their formative years socialization in Latin American society.

2. Jack D. Forbes, *Aztecas del Norte*, (Greenwich, Conn., 1973), p. 174.
3. The distinguished historian, Herbert Eugene Bolton, was the first scholar to promote and emphasize the Spanish role in North American history.
4. Forbes *Op. cit.*, p. 70.

5. *Ibid.*, p. 71.
6. Gloria E. Miranda, "Racial and Cultural Dimensions of Gente de Razon Status in Spanish and Mexican California," *Southern California Quarterly*, LXX (Fall, 1988), 265.
7. Nellie Van de Grift Sanchez, trans., "Things Past," *Touring Topics*, XXII (September, 1929), 19.
8. W.W.H. Davis, *El Gringo, or New Mexico and Her People*, (New York, 1857), p. 118.
9. E. C. Orozco, *Republican Protestantism in Aztlán*, (Glendale, Calif. 1980), p. 86.
10. Orozco, p. 162.
11. Emory S. Bogardus, *The Mexican Immigrant in the United States*, (New York, 1970), p. 28.
12. *Ibid.*
13. Robert McLean, *That Mexican! As He is, North and South of the Rio Grande*, (New York; 1928), p. 25.
14. Raul Morin, *Mexican-Americans in World War II and Korea*, (Alhambra, Calif., 1966), is the only study on this subject to date.
15. Orozco, *Supra*, p. 219.
16. Armando Rendon, *Chicano Manifesto*, (New York, 1971), p. 46.

SELECTED BIBLIOGRAPHY

Acuña, Rodolfo. *Occupied America*. New York, 1981.

De Leon, Arnoldo. *They Called Them Greasers*. Austin, 1983.

Forbes, Jack D. *Aztecas del Norte*. Greenwich, Conn., 1973.

Galarza, Ernesto. *Merchants of Labor: The Mexican Bracero Story*. Santa Barbara, 1964.

Griswold del Castillo, Richard. *La Familia: Chicano Families in the Urban Southwest, 1848 to the Present*. Notre Dame, 1983.

Hinojosa, Gilberto. *A Borderlands Town in Transition, Laredo 1755-1870*. College Station, Texas, 1983.

Lamar, Howard. *The Far Southwest, 1846-1912: A Territorial History*. New York, 1970.

McWilliams, Carey. *North From Mexico, The Spanish-Speaking People of the United States*. New York, 1968.

Morin, Raul, *Among the Valiant: Mexican-Americans in World War II and Korea*. Alhambra, Calif., 1966.

Orozco, E. C. *Republican Protestantism in Aztlán*. Glendale, Calif., 1980.

Petit, Arthur G. *Images of the Mexican American in Fiction and Film*. College Station, Texas 1980.

Reisler, Mark. *By the Sweat of Their Brow, Mexican Immigrant Labor in the United States, 1900-1940*. Westport, Conn., 1976.

Robinson, Cecil. *Mexico and the Hispanic Southwest in American Literature*. Tucson, 1977.

Sheridan, Thomas E. *Los Tucsonenses, The Mexican Community in Tucson, 1854-1941*. Tucson, 1986.

Servin, Manuel P. *An Awakened Minority: The Mexican-Americans*, 2nd ed. Beverly Hills, 1974.

✦✦✦

THE GERMAN AMERICANS

✦

JOSEPH COLLIER

> John and Regina Pferrer left Bavaria in 1880 primarily because John, a military officer, was to be conscripted again for an unknown period of service by the Prussian command. However, later, in the security of his ample farm in Brownstown, Indiana, he would often proudly display his uniform. Emma Pferrer was six years old when her parents emigrated. When she was 26 years old, she left the farm and went to Indianapolis where she could practice as a practical nurse. There she met Eugene Christian, of French-Canadian descent, who had joined the westward movement from his home in Massachusetts. Eugene and Emma were married in 1901. In 1905, Josephine was born, my mother, the second of three daughters. My paternal grandfather came from England, my paternal grandmother from Ireland.

This ancestry fits neatly into the assimilation pattern of Germans. "The typical German-American is often part English, Irish, French, Scandinavian, Polish or Italian, with perhaps a Cherokee great-grandmother. No other minority has so vigorously spanned the ethnic rainbow."[1] It is now, too, generally recognized that more Americans have some German heritage than that of any other ethnic.

THE BEGINNING

Although at least three Germans, known only as Unger, Keffer, and Valday, helped settle the colony at Jamestown in 1607, there was only a scattered number of Germans in the colonies during most of the 17th century.

October 6, 1683, is the date celebrated by Germans as the beginning of their history as settlers in this country. Led by Franz Pastorious, after having been encouraged by William Penn who had invited him and his followers to settle in his Quaker colony, families of Mennonites sailed on the *Concord*, the "German Mayflower." Penn welcomed them to his "City of Brotherly Love." They settled on a 43,000 acre tract bordering Philadelphia; the tract fittingly was called Germantown. Pastorious was elected the town's first Bürgermeister (mayor). In their little town, these "plain people" settlers flourished an ocean away from Lutheran, Catholic, and Calvinist magistrates and clergy who had refused to let them practice their faith in peace. There, they also, in 1688, condemned the practice of Black slavery, a condemnation which characterized German feelings throughout the period of slavery.

A large migration of Germans to England from the Palatinate region in southwestern Germany began in the early 1700s. For a variety of reasons, over 13,000 Palatines left their land: overpopulation, ruin from yet another war of the seemingly endless wars among European powers, burdensome taxation, unusually harsh winters. The British ultimately sent 2,800 of these refugees to New York to manufacture naval stores along the Hudson River. When the naval stores plan failed, some of the Germans stayed along the Hudson, but most went to Pennsylvania.

The Palatine migration signaled an outburst of interest by Germans who became desperate to get to America. Probably half to two-thirds of them came as redemptioners under a plan that allowed them either to pay for their voyage within a fixed time (usually two weeks) after they arrived or to be sold into servitude for a period to cover the cost of their passage. The ship was often the market where the buyers and the immigrants bargained the redemptioners' future: the price or servitude time normally depended upon the amount demanded by the captain of the ship or by the person who had paid for the transportation. Four years became a common period of servitude.

That is, for those who made it. The death rate during passage was astoundingly high. In 1745 a ship left Germany with 400 passengers and arrived in America with only 50 still alive. It was not uncommon for as many as half the men, women, and children to die in passage. Packed into vessels almost as tightly as African slaves were, they died from starvation, disease, or shipwreck. For those who did not die, they survived a horrible trip, much like the one described by Gottlieb Mittelberger, a German organist who emigrated to Pennsylvania. Mittelberger wrote that, besides inedible food:

> During the journey the ship is full of pitiful signs of distress, smells, fumes, horrors, vomiting, various kinds of sea sickness, fever, dysentery, headache, heat, constipation, boils, scurvy, cancer, mouth rot. . . . Add to all that, shortage of food, hunger, thirst, frost, heat, dampness, fear, misery, vexation . . . there are so many lice, especially on the sick

> people, that they have to be scraped off the bodies. All this misery reaches its climax when, in addition to everything else, one must also suffer through two or three days and nights of storm; with everyone convinced that the ship with all aboard is bound to sink. . . .
>
> Misery and malice are readily associated, so that people begin to cheat and steal from one another. And then one always blames the other for having undertaken the voyage. . . .
>
> One can scarcely conceive what happens at sea to women in childbirth and to their innocent offspring. Very few escape with their lives, and mother and child, as soon as they have died, are thrown into the water. . . . Children between the ages of one and seven seldom survive the sea voyage.

The most famous of these servants was to be John Peter Zenger. At the age of 13 he arrived in New York City in 1710, with his mother, sister, and brother—the father had died of fever during the voyage. At first, Zenger was apprenticed to a city printer; a few years later he began publication of his own *New-York Weekly Journal* in which he decried the "corruption" of the Royal Governor William Cosby and his supporters. Cosby had Zenger arrested and tried on the charge of publishing seditious libels, which then meant anything likely to bring the government into disrepute. Zenger's lawyer convinced the jury that truth ought to be a sufficient defense. The verdict was instrumental in establishing freedom of the press in America. The life and trial of Zenger are bright lights in the history of American journalism.

What were these people, these Germans like *generally*? Where did they go? What were their customs?

1. Some were artisans and merchants who went to the cities, but most were and remained farmers who settled in heavily wooded areas, where they raised livestock, grew flax, grain, and vegetables as they had in Germany. They concentrated in the middle colonies, Pennsylvania in particular.
2. They invariably settled as groups and hung tenaciously to their "old country" way of life, including language, religion, and education. Their families were large. They had a reputation of being industrious, frugal, and skilled farmers who cared more for their land and livestock than for their own comfort. Family and community ties were strong and lasting. Children usually settled on farms adjoining those of their parents. When they did move, almost always West, they moved as groups. Wherever they went, they settled, cleared, and developed the earth. Mostly they are the unknowns who helped

make the West, especially the Midwest, the agricultural wonder of the world.

3. They retained their language as much as possible, both spoken and written. Between 1732 and 1774, more than 35 German newspapers were published.
4. They were deeply religious, whether Lutheran, Catholic, Calvinist, or one of the several sects for whom religion was *all* encompassing, such as the Moravians and Mennonites.
5. They were highly literate and believed firmly in education; for most of the 18th and 19th centuries, this meant parochial education. They saw education as a means of teaching their children reading, religion, and manners, and schools as vehicles for retaining their children's ethnic heritage.
6. They, or a significant majority, objected strenuously to that part of the Puritan ethic which would deny them the right to enjoy the Sabbath as they wished, and what they wished was a day of rest and leisure after the Sunday services, a day to enjoy their family and their beer. The Germans opened every major brewery in America.

THE AMERICAN REVOLUTION

Although the German-Americans were mostly uninvolved in colonial affairs during the 17th and part of the 18th centuries, the French and Indian War (1756-63) drew not only Germans but other ethnics into the life of the general community.

"For many German-Americans the war was their first close and sustained contact with their non-German countrymen. After the war the use of the English language, English dress, even English manners noticeably increased in areas of German settlement. Participation in colonial politics increased, too. For the first time, Germans began to protest the necessity of paying taxes to support the established Anglican church in Virginia. When Indian problems reappeared with Pontiac's Rebellion (1763-65), many Germans joined the Scotch-lrish 'Paxton Boys' march on Philadelphia to demand—and to get—better protection."[2]

However, it is the American Revolution which dramatically united ethnics, although all groups, even the Scotch-Irish who hated the British with a passion, produced its Tories as well as its Patriots. The Germans, with their ethnic roots in continental Europe, were never as friendly toward the British as the British subjects.

Consequently, when the revolutionary war began, several German regiments were raised with ease, the first in Pennsylvania and Maryland. Later thousands of Germans served both in their own regiments, where German was spoken, and subsequently in other units, which included men of various national origins. Along with the Irish, the Germans proved to be among the toughest troops in the line whenever gritty engagements with the British regulars occurred.[3]

The most famous of the German-Americans was Peter Muhlenberg of Virginia. An ordained minister of the Evangelical Lutheran Church, in 1774 he presided at a meeting in which the citizens went on record as supporting their "suffering brethren of Boston." When Virginia recruited six new regiments, Muhlenberg became a colonel and leader of one.

Although Muhlenberg was to be promoted to a Brigadier General and lead his men into several battles, very possibly his most dramatic moment occurred in January, 1776, when after finishing a sermon, he removed his clerical garb to reveal a military uniform. Saying that there is a time to preach and a time to fight, he ordered drums to beat at the church door for recruits; more than 300 men mustered.

For much of the war, General Washington's personal bodyguard troops were German-speaking Continentals. Among the many German colonists who died were Brigadier General Nicholas Herkimer of New York, who had earlier fought valiantly during the French and Indian War and who had organized several largely German battalions, and Major General Johann Kolb, who died while leading a Maryland unit in the disastrous attack on Camden, South Carolina.

However, the most famous German during the War was not a German-American, but one of many European adventurers who came to join the American cause—Frederick William Augustus Henry Ferdinand, Baron von Steuben. It seems that von Steuben gave himself the title of Baron and that he had never been a lieutenant general in the service of the King of Prussia. Nevertheless, Benjamin Franklin wrote for him letters of introduction to Washington and the Continental Congress. What a fortuitous move! Steuben joined Washington during the darkest days of the Continental Army at Valley Forge in 1778 and proceeded to teach the generally unorganized troops the principles of drill and other military maneuvers.

Steuben's lack of English posed both a handicap and a sense of relief.

Once he gave an order which, because of his pronunciation, was misunderstood. Some of the men went one way, some another. He shouted it in French, then in German, but the model company was in

> complete confusion. He tried the sign language with no success. Then he blew up and cursed them vigorously in French and German, with an occasional "Goddam" for emphasis. Everybody laughed uproariously. A young American officer, Captain Benjamin Walker of New York, came to his aid, addressed him in French, and offered to interpret the command to the troops. Steuben said later that he was like an angel from heaven. The company was re-formed, the command given, and the maneuver executed. It needed only such a bit of comedy, which was repeated more than once, to make the baron one of the most popular officers in the camp.[4]

Before Steuben died in 1794, he had been made an honorary citizen of New York and of Albany, Congress had bestowed upon him a good pension, and New York State had given him 16,000 acres of land in Oneida County. Steuben Day, featuring a parade and other festivities, is held annually by the German-American community of New York City.

On the darker side from the Patriots' standpoint was the role of the German Hessians, the mercenaries who fought with the British. The practice of using mercenaries, people paid to fight for a particular country, is as old as history and is still common. Some German mercenaries also served with the French troops fighting with the Americans. Many historians agree that the Hessians were not especially effective or reliable soldiers; many defected to the American cause, and at the close of the war, about 12,000 of the original 30,000 remained in America.

1800-1861

For almost 50 years after the Revolutionary War, German immigration came virtually to a halt, primarily because of the Napoleonic Wars, including our War of 1812. During this period, the Germans were assimilated rapidly, both in the cities and the frontier areas. Only in rural Pennsylvania did the process of acculturation and assimilation not occur; these were communities of original German settlers, communities which grew as other non-German settlers moved away.

The resumption of large-scale, non-English immigration began about 1815, and it was a remarkable resumption. Between that year and 1861, about five million immigrants came to the United States, a number equal to the entire population of the nation in 1790. After the Irish, the Germans constituted the largest number of immigrants. In 1854 215,009 Germans came; in 1882 over a quarter of a million; between 1830 and 1890 Germans were consistently at least a fourth of all arrivals.

The Germans, like other Europeans, came primarily in the hope of finding a better life. Overpopulation, eviction of tenant farmers by landlords, failure of the potato crop in parts of Germany, tragically like the more overwhelming disaster in Ireland, various personal reasons—all combined to create this torrent of immigrants. Newspapers, also, written for prospective emigrants, and numerous associations formed to advise or direct emigrants played important roles in convincing many Germans to come to the United States. Private letters, however, remained the greatest stimulus to emigration, especially when they contained passage money from relatives and friends in America.

Two movements prior to the Civil War are important in German-American history: 1) the attempt to create a German nation in America; 2) the migration of those who came to be known as the "Forty-Eighters."

The concept of a German nation within our borders was born in the early 1800s, a reaction, in part, to the Napoleonic Wars and political suppression. Romantic bearers of this concept knew that America was a huge land, and the West, particularly, sparsely settled, and subject to practically no authoritarian control. Known as the Giessener colonists, from their origin in Giessen in 1834, their spirit is reflected in the following passage by Paul Follenius, one of their idealistic leaders:

> We ought not to depart from here . . . without first giving expression to a national idea. The foundation of a new and free Germany in the great North American Republic can be laid by us, so we must take with us in our own migration as many as possible of the most worthy of our countrymen, and at the same time make the necessary arrangements to ensure that each year a considerable group shall follow us. Thus we may in at least one of the American territories, create a state that is German from its foundations up, in which all those to whom in the future the situation here at home may seem, as it does to us now, intolerable, can find refuge, and which my develop to be a model state for the whole commonwealth of men.

Although no new German nation was ever created, the Giesseners and many other Germans who had come a few years earlier, inspired by the poetic praises of America by the writer Gottfried Duden, made a significant impact on the American West. In Missouri, the influence of the Giesseners attracted hundreds of Germans, especially Lutherans from Saxony who made St. Louis a center of German Lutheranism in the United States. Other "Little Germanies" appeared as efforts to found the new German nation were made. In Texas, German colonists founded New Braunfels and Fredericksburg, but the most German of all the states was to be Wisconsin, with the city of Milwaukee becoming the "German

Athens." All ideas, however, for a New Germany died in the outrages of the nativist movement of the 1850s, when the hostility of American nationalists convinced the new immigrants that a separate state would be impossible. Many Germans refused to lose their Germanness, the essence of *German*-American; this holding out for old world ethnic culture would not be seriously questioned until the First World War.

The Forty-Eighters were a group, primarily of intellectual radicals, who left Germany when the democratic revolution of 1848 failed, resulting in even greater authoritarian suppression. Although only a fraction of German immigration before the Civil War, they came to have an influence on the status of German-Americans, for good or for bad. The good is that they brought a revolutionary fever which bestirred some German-Americans, noted for their "stockade mentality," a "let us alone" mentality, into political and social ferment. They also produced a Carl Schurz, who arrived in 1852 and became in the 19th century the greatest political leader produced by Germany. Possibly as important in the long run, at least to those who love fine California wines, was the emigration of Charles Krug. A free-thinking Prussian, Krug settled near Sonoma, California. Upon marrying the niece of General Mariano Vallejo, whose name is linked inextricably with California history, he and his wife acquired a 540-acre vineyard. Krug's label became the most famous of all California wines, and although the winery passed into the hands of others when he died, these others, especially his employees, Carl Wente and the Beringer brothers, continued to produce outstanding wines. Today, a tour of Napa Valley wineries invariably includes those of Krug, Wente, and especially Beringer, whose wine aging takes place in cavernous cellars built by Chinese coolies. The wines of Krug, Wente, and Beringer are still acclaimed as among the finest in the world.

The bad is simple: the Forty-Eighters, in current parlance, rocked the boat. Many of them were not at all concerned with bettering the social and economic problems of German-Americans who had been in this country for several years; they were concerned only with arousing a revolutionary fever or soliciting funds for which they hoped to use on their return to Germany and attempt an overthrow of the government. They were, thus, not interested in becoming German-Americans; they were revolutionaries in exile, awaiting the right moment to return to their native country. As such, many became an embarrassment to those German-Americans who did not have the slightest desire to go back to the old country, but who were being harassed by the nativist Americans because of these radicals.

THE CIVIL WAR

The role of the German-Americans in the Civil War is not dramatic. As with all other ethnics, some fought for the North, some for the South. This is from a scene described by a Confederate officer after a battle in West Virginia.

> And when the firing was over, as night came on, nothing was to be heard but the roaring of the waters, intermingled now and then with snatches of a song from some of the German soldiers on either side, which produced a touching effect at such an hour. Ofttimes one of our Germans could be seen leaning on his rifle, listening to the sounds of his mother tongue as they wafted over from the enemy's camp. At times, one of the sentinels would shout across "From what part do you come, countryman?" "I am a Bavarian. From whence art thou?"

However, because Germans in the North far outnumbered those in the South, the Union Army was much better represented. Richard O'Connor, using figures from a 1869 study by Benjamin A. Gould, states that "the Germans supplied a larger proportionate share of volunteers for the Union army than either the native Americans— many of whom hired substitutes under the bounty system—or the Irish."[5] The Germans, also were the least inclined of the ethnics to protest government actions, including the Conscription Act of 1863 which made it no longer possible to claim exemption from the draft because a man was the sole support of his family. This Act provoked the worst rioting in American history; in New York City alone over 2,000 persons were killed, eight to ten thousand injured, and property damage soared to over five million dollars.

Many German-Americans fought in divisions of the XI corps. Several of the officers, including Carl Schurz, were Forty-Eighters. Others had had military experience in Germany. During the war, the best-known general was Franz Sigel; "I fights mit Sigel" was a proud claim of many German soldiers. Responding to President Lincoln's call for volunteers were many members of the Turnvereine—gymnastic clubs. Such men played a decisive role in keeping St. Louis, hence, Missouri, in the Union. The general, ultimately, who would receive the most attention and fame (or infamy) was George Armstrong Custer, a great-grandson of a Hessian deserter who had settled in Michigan. A man of tremendous ego and courage, Custer became a brigadier general at the age of 23; this same ego, unfortunately, would lead to his death and those of his men on a Montana plain a few years later.

The Civil War did enable the Germans to strike hard at two elements they most hated in American life—nativism and all it implied, and slavery. Nativism would continue, especially during World War I, but with the victory of the North, slavery would end.

ASTOR AND SCHURZ

Through the lives of John Jacob Astor and Carl Schurz can be traced an outline of the entire 19th century. Quite possibly the two best known German immigrants of the 18th and 19th centuries, they also are an interesting study in differing attitudes toward wealth and society. Astor was a confirmed and ruthless capitalist; Schurz was a reformer who tried tirelessly from his student days at the University of Bonn to his death in New York City to make as much of the world as he could a better place.

Born in Waldorf, Germany, Astor came to New York City in April, 1784 and began work at a small fur store. Within two years he had his own fur and musical instruments business. By 1800 his fortune was estimated at $25 million, made principally by trading furs on the western frontier and as far north as Montreal, where he worked through the powerful British North West Fur Company. Astor also imported necessities from Europe for the American market, such as cutlery, ammunition, and dry goods. He bought New York real estate and in 1800 he began trading with China.

Shrewd, close-fisted, and ruthless, Astor accomplished his purpose of becoming one of the richest and one of the most powerful men in America.

> Astor was a looter on the imperial scale. His method of trading with the Indians who supplied most of the furs at his trading posts was to debauch them with whiskey and cheat them out of a fair price for their goods. He compounded the profits from this villainous trade by slippery maneuvers in shipping and high finance. Walter Barrett, in *The Merchants of Old New York*, described one of Astor's operations: "John Jacob Astor at one period of his life had several vessels operating in this way. They would go to the Pacific and carry furs from thence to Canton. These would be sold at large profits. Then the cargoes of tea (picked up in Chinese ports) would be sold for good four and six months' paper, or perhaps cash."[6]

After the War of 1812, Astor rapidly assumed monopoly control of all U.S. fur trading. He bought up rivals and took over the entire upper Missouri valley. "His friendships at high government levels helped—he knew Thomas Jefferson well and was a personal friend of James

Monroe. Astor did not go to places he traded with, but lived mainly in New York or Europe, so he never came in contact with the thousands of frontiersmen and little people who worked for him. In this he was a model capitalist, who treated his workers like commodities. The bulk of his fortune was made in shrewd land and property purchases in Manhattan. Astor realized that the transportation revolution would make New York a great city, and he bought the land when it was cheap."[7]

By 1835 Astor was reported to be the richest man in America. O'Connor contends that Astor's "methods of exploitation set the pattern for the material conquest of the West. His manner of extracting every last penny from the bloodstained and whiskey-reeking fur trade served as the real fable, as opposed to Horatio Alger's homilies, for his time and the time that followed."[8]

Carl Schurz was not only the most famous of the 48'ers, but one of the most respected figures in 19th century American history. O'Connor called his chapter "The Great Good Schurz." The "good" appeared early in his life. A leader of the student revolutionary movement at the University of Bonn, at the age of 20 he was fighting as a lieutenant in the revolutionary army against Prussian tyranny. Barely escaping capture, he fled to Switzerland but returned to Germany to plan and execute the rescue of his mentor and friend, Gottfried Kinkel, who had been sentenced to life imprisonment at the Spandau fortress jail. Schurz's daring escapade on the night of November 6, 1850, won him plaudits around the world.

Schurz came to America in August, 1852, settling in Wisconsin. He became an ardent spokesman for the anti-slavery cause and was drawn into Republican party politics. An able orator in both German and English, he gave what is considered his most important speech in September, 1860, a merciless criticism of Stephen A. Douglas, the Democratic party's nominee for president. When Abraham Lincoln was elected, he rewarded Schurz with an appointment as minister to Spain. Diplomatic service did not interest him, and he returned to the United States, where he urged immediate emancipation of slaves as a means of securing European sympathy for the North.

With the outbreak of the Civil War, Schurz immediately volunteered; at the second battle of Bull Run, August, 1862, and at Chancellorsville, he served as a division commander. He led the XI Corps at Gettysburg, where there were charges that his German troops had failed to stand their ground during a Confederate charge. However, his courage was never questioned; he was promoted to major-general, and he and his corps were transferred to the western front. At the end of the war he was with General William Sherman's army.

Schurz returned immediately to journalism and the political wars. As a journalist, he defined as fourfold the purposes of the German press which, in 1876, printed 74 German dailies with a circulation of almost 300,000: 1) to explain America to the German immigrant; 2) to promote cooperation among the Germans in America; 3) to inform the Germans living in the United States about Germany; 4) to teach the German immigrant about the open-handed generosity of the United States.[9]

Politically, Schurz received the high honor of being asked to deliver the keynote address at the Republican National Convention in 1868. General Ulysses S. Grant, the Civil War hero and Republican nominee, went on to win the presidency, and Schurz was elected United States senator from Missouri. He very soon became an outspoken member of the anti-Grant Congressional contingent. He opposed the President's favorable endorsement of the spoils system; he introduced a bill to create a permanent civil service merit system; he made incessant attacks upon public corruption. Infuriated Grant partisans successfully led the fight to keep Schurz from being reelected as senator. Because, however, of Schurz's support of Rutherford B. Hayes in 1876, a support bolstered by his speeches and by respect of thousands of German-Americans, he was nominated to the Cabinet as Secretary of the Interior by the new president.

Upon his appointment, Schurz took over the most notoriously corrupt, inefficient, and mismanaged department of the executive branch. For years the Department of the Interior had been plagued by scandals over the bribery of Indian agents, the mistreatment of the tribesmen for whose welfare it was responsible, the theft of timber and mineral lands by powerful and politically protected interests, and the various evils of the spoils system he was to fight. He proceeded to fire Indian agents who had been diverting for their own profit supplies supposed to go to the Indians, and he brought a humanitarian attitude toward the Indian, in opposition to the feeling of many War Department officials and army men, that the only good Indian was a dead Indian. "He pressed so vigorously for conservation that opponents of Schurz in the Senate attacked the Secretary, claiming that 'a Native of the Kingdom of Prussia . . . was applying to the territory of Montana the land laws of Prussia, not the land laws of the settled territories of the United States.'"[10]

Carl Schurz was, indeed, a man for all seasons: military general, editor, politician, diplomat, a lifelong supporter of civil rights, and patron of the arts. Long after he had died in 1906, some words of Schurz were used to blunt anti-German malice during World War I. Speaking at the October 6, 1904, celebration of German Day in St. Louis, he said: "We German-Americans are the hyphen between Germany and America; we present the living demonstration of the fact that a large population may be transplanted from one to another country and may be devoted to the new fatherland for life and death. . . ."[11]

Another German-American whom some consider as memorable as Schurz was John Peter Altgeld, although his basic claim to fame rests primarily with his four years as governor of Illinois, 1893-97. But in those four years he managed to outrage public opinion by pardoning three German-born anarchists who had been convicted of complicity in the Haymarket Square explosion of 1886, in which seven policemen died, and to anger conservatives by opposing on constitutional grounds President Grover Cleveland's use of regular army troops in the Pullman strike of 1894. Predictably, he was defeated in his attempt for reelection in 1896. However, his courageous decisions as governor has placed him among the 56 greatest American statesmen, according to a listing by historian Richard B. Morris. (*Encyclopedia of American History*, 1965, pp. 668-669).

Other German-Americans, of course, were to leave their imprint upon America of the 19th century. Among some of the most important were these:

1. Frederick Weyerhauser: acquired almost a million acres of western lumber land. When he died in 1914, his fortune was estimated at 300 million dollars; the Weyerhauser Company is still one of the largest corporations in America.
2. John D. Rockefeller, Sr: patriarch of the richest family in America.
3. Ottmar Mergenthaler: inventor of the Linotype, a tremendous technological breakthrough for printing.
4. Albert Bierstadt: one of the three great painters of the Old West; the other two are Frederick Remington and Charles M. Russell.
5. Thomas Nast: famous political cartoonist who, through his blistering cartoon attacks, was vitally responsible for the downfall of Boss Tweed and the corrupt Tammany Hall machine of New York.

6. Henry Villard: president and later chairman of the Northern Pacific Railroad; he helped merge several utility companies into what eventually became General Electric.

EDUCATION

German education in America is divided into two segments: 1) the schools to which German children and/or adults went, and 2) the influence German universities had on American higher education in the 19th century.

As with all ethnics, most German children went to parochial schools. The preponderance of these schools were bilingual; they taught religion and other ethnic subjects in the traditional language while "American" subjects, such as American history, geography, and bookkeeping were taught in English.

Although some Americans were deeply suspicious of these parochial institutions, Maxine Seller contends that

> . . . ethnic schools transmitted a great love of the United States to their young pupils. Parochial schools taught American history and geography with great enthusiasm and held elaborate pageants to celebrate national holidays. Members of religious orders whose English was poor brought in special American born teachers to give the children to the public schools for high school or for vocational courses when this education was not available in the parochial system. The English part of the curriculum was the most successful part taught in the parochial schools because parents and children both saw its relevance to American life. Bilingual education of the parochial school was especially valuable to the child who had just immigrated or who had had little or no opportunity to learn English. These children were frequently able to transfer to the public school system at their appropriate grade level after a few years of parochial school education.[12]

These schools, therefore, served the very functional purposes of not only giving the child a good education (arguing that most ethnic schools were good), but also providing the children with a better understanding of their foreign born parents and in building the strength of the ethnic community—understanding and strength that were critical before the immigrant even tentatively lowered himself into the "melting pot."

Actually, the German influence on the American school has been an enveloping one. "From the idea of the *Kindergarten*, first established in Wisconsin by Margaretha Schurz (wife of 'The Great Good Schurz'), to the concept of the university as a center for primary research, begun at

Johns Hopkins, the whole range of American education was transformed."[13]

Apparently, it was "the symmetry, exactitude and discipline of a German university education," which in the 19th century, particularly, convinced many upper-class Americans to gain a higher education at German institutions. "Ten thousand Americans, it has been estimated, were educated in German universities up to 1900. The old-country educational and cultural magnificence contributed to an impression that German-Americans must come of a superior stock, and they were not slow to accept the second-hand tribute, undeserved as it was."[14]

The Johns Hopkins transplantation of the German model resulted in what most American graduate schools are still like today: Ph.D. candidates write their dissertations in a severely restricted area of research; secondary sources are almost universally used; originality of expression is frowned upon; and no one can attempt a graduate degree until attainment of the bachelor's degree.

POPULAR CULTURE, ARTS, AND SCIENCE

For the German, a vague distinction exists between what is popular culture and what is art. For example, the Germans through their Turner clubs introduced gymnastics to America, but gymnastics is a form of art—the artistry of the fine athlete, amateur or professional. To the German, a healthy body was, indeed, the necessity for a healthy mind. Francis Lieber, editor of the *Encyclopaedia Americana* and author of several books on political philosophy, began his work in America by teaching swimming at the first pool built in Boston. Physical education programs, appearing in almost every school in America, are an outgrowth of the Germans' emphasis on health of the body; one can argue that his emphasis, in turn, led to the connection in American schools made between the development of citizenship and enthusiasm for sports.

The Germans, too, could appreciate the polka and Beethoven and Bach at the same time. In drama, they could love both Schiller and amateur theatrical plays. *Mannerchors,* local singing societies, proliferated in every Germantown around the country, often in conjunction with colorful operatic extravaganzas. They could spend many Sundays, to the chagrin of non-German churchgoers, in carousal: bands blaring, steins banging, and customers singing, while at the same time organizing symphonic orchestras in every major city. The influence of the Germans in development of orchestras is exemplified in the following:

> Thanks to its German heritage, Philadelphia was the first American city to support an orchestra. Organizational talent for an orchestra came from the city's Musical Fund Society, begun in 1820. It arranged both sacred and secular programs and combined instrumental and vocal musical renditions for its concerts. Later, the society founded a school, built a music hall, and gave concerts until 1857. New York's Philharmonic Society also had the benefit of German leaders. The Philharmonic Society gave its first concert in December, 1842, with about 60 performers, 22 of whom were Germans. Subsequently, under the baton of distinguished conductors, Leopold Damrosch, Theodore Thomas, Adolph Neuendorff, Anton Seidl, Walter Damrosch, and Emil Paur, membership in the orchestra increased to 81 musicians in 1865, of whom 70 were Germans. A quarter century later, there were 94 players, only five of whom were non-Germans.[15]

Oscar Hammerstein, whose grandson collaborated with Richard Rogers to write such perennially favorite musicals as "Showboat," "Carousel," "Oklahoma," and "The Sound of Music," contributed greatly to the development of American opera. And German names practically encompass the instrument makers: Steinway, Wurlitzer, Knabe, Gemünder, and Schwab.

On a more pedestrian level, German-Americans excelled in baseball. O'Connor suggests why: "Baseball, the 'Great American Pastime,' with its geometric order, its requirement of technical skills as well as brute strength and quick reflexes, its disciplined pattern, appealed to something in the German psyche."[16] A lineup of just some of the great German-American baseball players verifies O'Connor's suggestion:

- Lou Gehrig, first base
- Frankie Frisch, second base
- Honus Wagner, shortstop
- Heinie Groh, third base
- Heinie Manush, left field
- Bob Meusel, center field
- Babe Ruth, right field (Born George Herman Erhardt in Baltimore, Babe Ruth is considered the man who did the most in the history of the game to make baseball the Great National Pastime.)
- Ray Schalk, catcher
- Rube Waddell, pitcher

The impact of Germans on science in America is almost incalculable. The most prominent name remains Albert Einstein, a giant in theoretical physics, whose signature on a letter to Franklin D. Roosevelt helped convince the President to initiate the Manhattan Project. This Project ultimately developed the atomic bomb, allowed the United States to defeat Nazi Germany in the race for the bomb, and bring the war against Japan to a sudden conclusion. An American citizen since 1941, Hans Bethe served as chief of theoretical physics at the Manhattan Project. Other major contributors to the bomb and nuclear energy were not born in Germany, but spent many years studying in German universities: J. Robert Oppenheimer, an American and head of the entire Project; and Edward Teller and Leo Szilard, born in Hungary. Szilard, also, was one of four pioneers in the discovery of DNA, the carrier of heredity, the "secret of life." Wernher von Braun, often called the "Father of Rocketry," is, according to *Newsweek* "the German-born engineering genius who made the U.S. space program possible.[17] German-Americans, many now in the second and third generation, continue to excel in mathematics and other sciences and hold key positions in the Research and Development areas of major corporations. Undoubtedly much of this is due to the Germans' love of logic and precision, along with patience and attention to detail.

In political science, the most outstanding German-American name of this century and possibly in all of American history is Henry Kissinger. First, National Security Adviser, then Secretary of State in President Richard Nixon's administration, Kissinger advised or participated in virtually every major foreign policy decision for six years. For his role in ending the Vietnam War, he received the Nobel Peace Prize. Not without critics, however, Kissinger has been condemned for his arrogance even while being praised for his intellectual brilliance. He and the other "Germans" in the White House, Robert Haldeman, John Erlichman, and Ronald Ziegler, had significant influence on Nixon, standing as a "Berlin Wall, isolating the president from other elites. . . ."[18] These men, however, according to Rippley did not elicit any particular pride from the German element in American—"nor were they disillusioned in the slightest when some of these men were convicted for their Watergate crimes. For that matter, while Americans generally laud German-born former Secretary of State Henry Kissinger, one seldom hears German-Americans express ethnic pride or a sense of cultural identity with him. In Kissinger's native Germany, however, nearly every citizen hastens to remind one that Kissinger is German-born."[19]

The period of 1900-1914 may well be considered the high point of German-American history, although forces were operating which would hasten the decline of "Germanness" by 1914 when Germany and her allies went to war against Great Britain, France, and their allies. Still, in 1900, there were over 1,000 national religious parishes (the Germans created their own parishes to escape Irish-dominated congregations), and a press to propagate these parishes, which in 1900 produced 61 dailies and weeklies; there were an additional 613 general German-language publications; and in 1901 the German-American Alliance was formed.

> The Alliance was a federation of existing organizations and claimed more than two million members by 1914, though perhaps no more than one-tenth were active. Leaders were mainly middle-class businessmen, journalists, clergymen, and professors. Prohibited by its charter from direct political action, the Alliance sought to promote cultural interests, particularly the teaching of German; to encourage citizenship and participation in public affairs; to promote amicable relations between the United States and Germany; and to fend off nativist attacks. By 1914 German America confronted the war in Europe with a strong organization, well-financed by brewing and liquor interests and with high public visibility and assurance.[20]

Until America's entry into World War I in April, 1917, on the side of England and France, German-Americans were preponderately for American neutrality. They applauded President Woodrow Wilson's appeal for impartiality. "The German-American Alliance and other German organization sponsored press bureaus, mass demonstrations, collections for war relief, lobbying for arms and loan embargoes, and as Wilson's pro-British bias strengthened, a massive campaign for his defeat in the 1916 presidential Election."[21] The editor of the New York *Staats-Zeitung* flew the German flag over his building, and when the mayor of New York ordered it removed, he hung it inside.[22]

However, strict neutrality was virtually impossible. Although Americans had won their independence by fighting the English, pro-English sentiment remained strong, excepting the Irish; also, the "clannishness" of Germans—in their schools, in their churches, in their clubs—either raised suspicion or infuriated many Americans.

The German government proclaimed, in February, 1915, that the waters around the British Isles were a war zone and announced that neutral craft entering this zone would do so at their own risk. Our government's response was that in the event American vessels or the lives of American citizens were destroyed by Germany on the high seas, the United States would view the act as an indefensible violation of neutral rights and hold Germany strictly answerable. The sinking of the *Lusitania* on May 7, 1915, caused a revulsion of American public opinion and stern notes from our government. The *Lusitania*, a British transatlantic steamer, was sunk off the Irish coast without warning by a submarine, with the loss of 1,198 lives, including 128 Americans. Germany then complied with American demands. It promised not to attack unresisting belligerent merchant and passenger vessels without warning and without providing for the safety of those on board. However, when President Wilson's efforts to end the war through mediation failed, Germany resumed unrestricted submarine warfare in February, 1917. The United States responded first by breaking diplomatic relations and then by declaring war in April.

Treatment of German-Americans during World War I is succinctly summarized by Kathleen Conzen:

> The real purgatory followed U.S. entry into the war in April 1917. Most German-American newspapers and associations quickly declared their loyalty; there was minimal protest against conscription of Liberty bond campaigns. Nevertheless, a storm of anti-Germanism raged between the fall of 1917 and spring 1918. A government-sponsored structure of local defense committees, the national propaganda machine of George Creel's Committee on Public Information, and the civilian watchdogs of the American Protective League all fostered a climate of harassment, including a ban on German-composed music, the renaming of persons, foods, and towns, vandalism, tarring and feathering, arrests for unpatriotic utterances, and even a lynching in Collinsville, Ill., in April 1918. Public burnings of German books were frequent. By summer 1918 about half of the state had restricted or eliminated German language instruction, and several had curtailed freedom to speak German in public. The German press suffered under the censorship powers of local postmasters, and pacifist Mennonites endured harsh attempts to force conscription on them.[23]

Examples: hamburger became salisbury steak, sauerkraut—liberty cabbage; Brooklyn's Hamburg Avenue was renamed Wilson Avenue; pinochle, a card game closely associated with Germans, became "liberty"; German shepherd dogs became Alsatian shepherds. But even when German-Americans tried to conform to whatever the majority expected of them, there often were cries of sham. A cartoon in *Life* magazine, August 8, 1918, pictures a dachshund addressing a court composed of three obviously "American" dogs: the caption read, "More Camouflage: 'Please, Your Honor, I would like to change my name from

Teckelheim von Limburger to Silas Saltonstall.'"[24] In California, "the state board of education directed that all pages in music textbooks that contained German folk songs were to be cut out."[25] Hollywood, too, did its part in fomenting hate toward the Germans, which had to affect German-Americans. This selection from Daniel J. Leab's essay captures the approach:

> In the First World War a highly effective Allied propaganda campaign made 'Hun' a common and derogatory synonym for German, and upon America's entry into the war, the movie industry in the United States became a very active part of the Hate-the-Hun campaign. The Hun behaved with unbelievable brutality on screen. In the 1917 melodrama *Bitter Sweet*, characterized by one critic as a 'typical account of Belgium's distress,' a 14-year-old girl suffers dreadful hardships at the hands of the Germans before finding refuge in America. In other such melodramas a French mother is humbled by the Prussians, Belgian children are shipped to the Fatherland to work as whipped and starved laborers in war industries, and an American nurse who goes to France is captured by Germans and raped.[26]

Kaiser Wilhelm, ruler of Germany, became the focal point for anti-German propaganda, the personification of the hated Hun. "The Kaiser perfectly fit the stereotypes of the German in American eyes, with his arrogant stare, upturned moustache, and arched eyebrows." In movie after movie, the Kaiser was punished, and in the movie, "*The Kaiser—The Beast of Berlin*, 1918, he was at war's end 'stripped of all his glory' and 'handed over to the people of Belgium. . . .'"[27]

1918-1992

World War I ended on November 11, 1918. Germany surrendered and later would feel "humiliated" by the terms of the Treaty of Versailles, terms dictated by England, France, Italy, and the United States. This "humiliation" would be one of the springboards to German acceptance of Adolph Hitler and the Nazi party in the 1920s and 1930s.

In America, the war resulted in a dramatic decrease in the German-American associational structure.

> The total number of German-language publications declined from 554 in 1910 to 234 in 1920; daily newspaper circulation in 1920 was only about a quarter of its 1910 level. Language shift accelerated rapidly in the churches as elsewhere; in 1917 only one-sixth of the Missouri Synod Lutheran churches held at least one English service a month, while at the end of the war, three-quarters were doing so.[28]

A bill sponsored by Senator William King of Utah abrogating the 1907 charter of the German-American Alliance had been overwhelmingly approved by Congress in July, 1918.

Conzen states that "for most German Americans, ethnic culture had been a means to social, religious, or economic ends and was not valued for its own sake. When it jeopardized their status as Americans, their otherwise rapid assimilation permitted most to abandon its formal trappings with minimal difficulty."[29]

Reviewing the war years, Frederick Luebke writes that the "church Germans" suffered the most. "There was an inverse relationship, it seemed between the degree of persecution endured by a German-American group and the threat it posed to American security. Erstwhile champions of German imperialism . . . escaped unscathed, while at the opposite extreme harmless German-speaking Mennonites and Hutterites from the Plains states—rural, separatistic, pacifistic, non-resisting, apolitical, most of them immigrants from Russia rather than Germany—were ridiculed, harassed, beaten, painted, tarred, robbed, and betrayed in the name of American democratic ideals."[30]

After the Armistice, suspicion and/or hate toward the German-American quickly faded, partly because of their contribution to the war effort, partly to the fact that Americans now were confronted with what they considered a new menace, "the Red Scare." This "Scare" implied a Bolshevik attempt to subvert the United States government, led by Communist or Socialist "dupes" from eastern and southern Europe. Now, as solid citizens from northwestern Europe, heavily WASP, the German-Americans were almost forgotten in the new Nativist movement, which contributed to such things as restrictive immigration quotas and a dramatic revival of the Ku Klux Klan in the 1920s. And although many would continue their love for the Fatherland, to take a keen interest in how American politics affected Germany, and to support, at least on a limited basis, their associations, German-Americans "were determined never again to be publicly isolated from the main stream on emotional issues."[31]

In the 1920s, however, another force arose which would again trouble some German-Americans—the Bund movement. Based on Hitler's pronouncement that a German is first of all a German regardless of the country in which he lives, Bund leaders in America began recruiting their ethnic brethren to the Nazi cause. The German Nazis had concluded "that an estimated six to seven million German-Americans still spoke German as their primary language in 1930 and that about a fourth of the

American population was German extraction, "and that the children of the millions of German settlers who had arrived in America in the 18th and 19th centuries could be unified into a viable political force."[32] The Bundists' "ideology included widely varying aims from the elimination of Jews and Communists to the unification of the German folk throughout the world. Since racial ties were emphasized over the bonds of citizenship, the concept of the 'melting pot' was ridiculed as a 'Jewish' invention."[33]

The influence of the Bund (different groups coalesced in 1936 to become one—the German-American Bund) is difficult to assess. In his lengthy study, Sander Diamond states that the Bund, led by Fritz Julius Kuhn, never attracted more than 25,000 followers,[34] whereas O'Connor writes:

> During its peak of influence and noise-making, in 1937, the *Boston Globe* assigned the star investigative reporter, Joseph F. Dinneen, to look into the coast-to-coast network of Nazi organizations. He found that their boasts of having around 200,000 members were probably justified. Seventy-eight different units had been organized. Among the largest were those in Los Angeles and San Francisco.[35]

As with any organization, people joined and people left. Whatever the number, it is virtually negligent against the fact that there were approximately 1,600,000 German-born in the United States when Hitler came to power in 1933.

Indeed, historians agree that the overwhelming number of German-Americans not only never became involved with the Bund, but viewed the "Brown Shirts" as an embarrassment. There is also agreement that those who were active in the Bund were primarily immigrants who had come to America after World War I, many of them veterans of the war who believed defeat of Germany had been caused by Jews and Communists. Finally, from a publicity standpoint, the Bund's best and worst year was 1939. On February 20, 22,000 people jammed Madison Square Garden in New York City for a Nazi rally. Kuhn, "a forceful speaker who possessed an undeniable magnetism on the platform," and other Bund leaders "compared Hitler to George Washington, called for a united fascist front, denounced President Roosevelt, and predicted that the Bund would have a million members by 1940."[36] Yet in December of that year Fritz Kuhn was sent to Sing Sing prison to serve a two-and-a-half to five-year sentence; he had been convicted of forgery and larceny, involving Bund funds. From that date

> no one, including the Bundists, considered the Amerikadeutscher Volksbund effective. Its formal, that is, officially declared, death came five days before the surprise Japanese attack on Pearl Harbor. The eventual destruction of the Bund was predictable; the causes of its destruction were not very complex and, by now, were quite obvious. Cast off by the Germans, under constant pressure from Federal and local authorities, financially desperate, depleted in numbers, and with its members openly expressing doubt about a duplication of the Hitler feat in America the Bund could no longer sustain itself in its adopted environment.[37]

Hollywood's treatment of the Nazis was very muted until Europe stood on the brink of war in 1939. A good German market for American movies provided one reason; another was the strength of isolationist sentiment in the 1930s.

Confessions of a Nazi Spy, released in the spring of 1939, was outspokenly anti-Nazi. "It attacked the Bund as a nest of subversives and spies, asserted that German consulates in the United States served as command posts for espionage, and declared that the Nazis waged a clandestine war against America."[38]

Most of Europe went to war in September, 1939. Although America remained officially neutral, President Franklin Roosevelt's sympathy, as well as a majority of Americans', lay quite clearly with England, who stood alone against the German military machine after the defeat of France in the spring of 1940. Japan's attack on Pearl Harbor led to a declaration of war against us by Germany and Italy, partners in the Axis pact.

As Hollywood went to war, dozens of anti-Nazi movies poured out of the studios.

> As might be expected, these propaganda vehicles presented a highly negative image of Germans and relied heavily on certain kinds of stock characterizations. Is there a viewer of such movies on television who does not know that World War II Germans spoke with guttural accents, heiled Hitler. shouted "Schweinhund" at the slightest provocation, and enjoyed tormenting old people and pretty young women? The officers and upper class were presented as cultured swine willing to bleed Russian children to obtain plasma for German troops, or to shoot innocent hostages; German noncoms and middle-echelon types were presented as libidinous, sadistic bullies given to rape and torture.[39]

Yet Leab emphasizes that the "nasty Nazi" theme of World War II never approximated the vicious proportions of the Hate-the-Hun campaign of World War I.[40] He ascribes this change to guidelines laid down by the Bureau of Motion Pictures of the Office of War Information which emphasized that America did not view the German people as enemies, only their leaders, or "don't hate the Nazis because they are German, hate those Germans who are Nazis." Obviously, too, the rapid decline of "Germanness" after World War I, the German-American assimilation into the mainstream of American society, the absence of fear that people of German descent owed a divided allegiance, all that a generational difference implies—combined to create the more sane approach.

Many movies following World War II portrayed Nazi soldiers in a more favorable light; particularly memorable are *The Desert Fox* and *The Young Lions*. In the former, Field Marshal Erwin Rommel is shown as an aristocrat who deplored Nazi excesses, fought for country, not ideology, and participated in the unsuccessful attempt to assassinate Hitler. In *The Young Lions*, the main German character is a patriotic idealist who becomes disillusioned and dies needlessly. On the other hand, films, such as *Judgment at Nuremberg* and *The Boys from Brazil* show the total evil of Nazi thinking. The very popular television series, "Hogan's Heroes," stands by itself—a ridiculous farce making the German officers and non-coms appear as fools.

As to the fighting in World War II itself, there is practically nothing to say as far as German-Americans are concerned. O'Connor summarizes it all in one paragraph:

> Unlike World War I, pro-Germanism was a dead issue in the United States by the time the country went to war with the Axis. No hysteria this time. How could there have been with an Eisenhower leading the second American expeditionary force against Germany, a Spaatz commanding the bombers which were pulverizing Germany, a Nimitz in command of the Pacific Fleet, an Eichelberger and a Kreuger commanding the two armies under General MacArthur?[41]

Post World War II years also saw the German-American rapidly become the German American; only traces of the hyphen linger. To some extent this was due to the new immigrants from West Germany, the DP's—Displaced Persons'—desire to disassociate themselves from Old World culture and enter quickly into the mainstream of American professional and labor careers; partly, it is simply another generational gap. As one German immigrant worker in New York in 1954 told an interviewer his attitude about the German Americans who still were enthusiastic about their clubs: ". . . they keep wishing for a Germany that doesn't exist any more. I can't understand all that gush of theirs. Forever singing about the Rhine, the Main, the Neckar—they live in a vacuum. My sons are married, my grandchildren don't know a word of German except for Christmas songs. I'm satisfied, no regrets."[42]

According to Rippley, the German vote, which had once been feared or curried by candidates, disappeared during the 1950s.

> There are no longer any German political candidates, no German component in the ethnic structure of any American city's political machine, and seemingly there was no German-American backlash to the desegregation movement during the 1960s. When Nathan Glazer, Andrew Greeley, Michael Novak and others write about American ethnics, they rarely include references to the German element. Today there is only the Anglo-Teutonic white stock, which makes up a segment of America's silent majority.[43]

Of course, the historical and widespread intermarriage of Germans with other ethnics has played a dominant role. Quoting O'Connor again, "No other minority has so vigorously spanned the ethnic rainbow." And for those German Americans who still pursue the German culture in America, they "remind the observer of a great Gatsby. They are marvelous courtly lovers who seek the affection of their lady *Deutschtum* with a passion that is old, less than ardent, and quite out of date. And besides the ladylove has already passed away."[44]

In terms of population movements, a relative shift has occurred in the last 20 years as persons of German ancestry have moved away from farms and small towns into cities—a shift common to many other ethnic groups and caused by rural depopulations and immigrant preferences for cities. Many German Americans moved to Chicago, smaller midwestern cities, and California. The largest centers now for people of German ancestry are, in order: Los Angeles, Chicago, and New York City.[45] Reflecting the numbers of German Americans in Los Angeles is a circulation of over 25,000 for the *California Statts-Zeitung*, a German language weekly newspaper.

The fact that there is no longer a West and East Germany (the symbolic Berlin Wall is long gone) will have some effect on German Americans living here and on migration from the unified Germany. The extent of that effect will take years to be seen.

NOTES

1. Richard O'Connor, *The German Americans* (Boston, 1968), p. 5.
2. Maxine Seller, *To Seek America* (Englewood, New Jersey, 1977), pp. 48-49.
3. La Vern G. Rippley, *The German-Americans* (Boston, 1976), p. 33.
4. Christopher Ward, *The War of the Revolution* (New York, 1952), Vol. 11, p. 553.
5. O'Connor, p. 130.
6. *Ibid,* pp. 161-163.
7. Peter d'A Jones, in *The Encyclopedia of American History* (Guilford, Connecticut, 1973). p. 21.
8. O'Connor, p. 208.
9. Rippley, pp. 162-163.
10. *Ibid*, p. 155. For Schurz's close relationship with President Hayes, a relationship which included a long correspondence between the two men that ended only when Hayes died in 1893, see Claude Moore Fuess, *Carl Schurz Reformer* (New York, 1932); Carl Wittke, "Carl Schurz and Rutherford B. Hayes," *The Ohio Historical Quarterly* 65 (October 1956), pp. 337-355; and Kenneth E. Davison, *The Presidency of Rutherford B. Hayes* (Westport, Connecticut, 1972).
11. *Ibid*, p. 188.
12. Seller, p. 163.
13. Bernard Eisenberg, "The German American," in Joseph Collier, ed., *American Ethnics and Minorities* (Los Alamitos, Califomia, 1978), p. 185.
14. O'Connor, p. 268.
15. Rippley, pp. 133-134.
16. O'Connor, pp. 309-310.
17. Quoted in Rippley, p. 159.
18. Thomas R. Dye and L. Harmon Ziegler, *The Irony of Democracy* (Monterey, California, 1981), p. 302.
19. Rippley, p. 217.
20. Kathleen Neils Conzen, "Germans," in Stephan Thernstrom, ed., *Harvard Encyclopedia of American Ethnic Groups* (Cambridge, Massachusetts, 1980), p. 422.
21. *Ibid.*
22. Rippley, p. 165.
23. Conzen, pp. 422-423.
24. Frederick C. Luebke, *Bonds of Loyalty: German-Americans and World War I* (Dekalb, Illinois, 1974), p. 283. This is an excellent and thorough study of the topic, covering not only the war years, but 1870-1920.
25. *Ibid*, p. 249.

26. Daniel J. Leab, "Deutschland, USA: German Images in American Film," in Randall M. Miller, ed., *The Kaleidoscopic Lens: How Hollywood Views Ethnic Groups* (Englewood, New Jersey, 1980), p. 164.
27. *Ibid*, p. 165
28. Conzen, p. 423.
29. *Ibid.*
30. Luebke, pp. 311-312.
31. Eisenberg, p. 196.
32. Sander A. Diamond, *The Nazi Movement in the United States: 1924-1941* (Ithaca, 1974), p. 29.
33. Eisenberg, pp. 196-197.
34. Diamond, p. 21.
35. O'Connor, pp. 441-442.
36. Diamond, p. 326.
37. *Ibid*, p. 322.
38. Leab, p. 171.
39. *Ibid*, p. 172.
40. *Ibid*, p. 173.
41. O'Connor, p. 452.
42. Rippley, p. 216.
43. *Ibid*, p. 217.
44. *Ibid*, p. 222.
45. James Paul Allen and Eugene James Turner, *We the People: An Atlas of America's Ethnic Diversity* (New York, 1988), p. 140.

SELECTED BIBLIOGRAPHY

Allen, James Paul and Eugene James Turner, *We the People: An Atlas of America's Ethnic Diversity*. New York, 1988.

Conzen, Kathleen Neils, "Germans," in Stephan Thernstrom, ed., *Harvard Encyclopedia of American Ethnic Groups*. Cambridge, Massachusetts, 1980.

Diamond, Sander A., *The Nazi Movement in the United States: 1924-1941*. Ithaca, 1974.

Dye, Thomas R. and L. Harmon Ziegler, *The Irony of Democracy*. Monterey, California, 1981.

Eisenberg, Bernard, "The German American," in Joseph Collier, ed., *American Ethnics and Minorities*, Los Alamitos, California, 1978.

Jones, Peter d'A in *The Encyclopedia of American History*. Guilford, Connecticut: 1973.

Hawgood, John A., *The Tragedy of German America*. New York, 1940.

Leab, Daniel J., "Deutschland, USA: German Images in American Film," in Randall M. Miller, ed., *The Kaleidoscopic Lens: How Hollywood Views Ethnic Groups*. Englewood, New Jersey. 1980.

Luebke, Frederick C., *Bonds of Loyalty, German-Americans and World War I*. Dekalb, 1974.

O'Connor, Richard, *The German Americans*. Boston, 1968.

Rippley, Lavern J., *The German-Americans*. Boston, 1976.

Seller, Maxine, *To Seek America*. Englewood, New Jersey, 1977.

THE SCANDINAVIAN AMERICANS

ARTHUR VERGE

One of the most profound impacts on both European and American history is the mass emigration of European immigrants to America during the nineteenth and early twentieth centuries. While academic scholarship has carefully detailed the immigrant experiences of such European groups as the Irish, the Italians, and the Germans, the Scandinavians, in contrast, have not received similar attention. Nonetheless, the Scandinavians played an integral role in shaping what we know today as the American experience.

From the frontier to urban cities Scandinavians have aided America's emergence as a world power. On the frontier, the Scandinavians were responsible for the introduction of the now legendary American icon, the log cabin. The Scandinavians, too, helped to tame the American wilderness and turned much of it into productive farm land. Their subsequent foray into farming helped to feed a growing American population, much of which lived in rapidly growing urban areas. And as urban America grew more and more congested, polluted, and physically unsafe, it was immigrant Scandinavian reformers who helped to lead the call for urban social reform. Thus, from the frontier—to the farm—and to the city—the Scandinavian presence in America, while at times neglected, has nonetheless been a very important one. Who then are the Scandinavians?

Scandinavia refers to the three kingdoms of Denmark, Sweden, and Norway. Once briefly united under one crown in the 15th and 16th centuries, these three nations today share, much like New England, a background which is similar in economic, political, and cultural make-up. While each of the three nations speak different languages—Danish, Swedish, and Norwegian—citizens of the three have little difficulty in communicating with one another given the common Germanic root of their languages. These ties also distinguish the three kingdoms from the two nations of Finland and Iceland which are popularly associated with Scandinavia. Although "Nordic" or Northern European, both Finland and Iceland have such unique historical and cultural differences as to merit separate consideration.

Despite their similarities and a relatively common background, the peoples of Denmark, Sweden, and Norway proudly remain distinct from one another. Thus, just as a Scot is different from an Irishman, so too is a Dane different from a Swede. Therefore, while generalizations can be made about the Scandinavian experience in America, it is also necessary to explain the different patterns of immigration and assimilation among the three groups.

COMING TO AMERICA: THE PUSH AND PULL FACTORS

Historians who study patterns of immigration continually focus on what they call the "push and pull" factors. Quite simply, the "push" factor means the causes that made people leave their homeland. Undoubtedly the "causes" were quite serious given that people were willing to leave their friends, oftentimes their families, their culture and traditions in search of a better life. In contrast, the "pull" factor means the things that attracted immigrants to a new land. The peak period of Scandinavian immigration to the United States took place between the American Civil War and World War I. During this same period the countries of Scandinavia were wrecked by serious internal problems that forced or caused many people to emigrate abroad. At the very same time the United States was undergoing an unprecedented period of industrial growth and economic prosperity. Therefore, both "push" and "pull" factors had roles in bringing record numbers of Scandinavians to America.

A driving force behind emigration from Scandinavia was overpopulation. Dramatic advances in medical science, such as the introduction of vaccines and the use of surgical sterilization techniques substantially increased life expectancies which, in turn, furthered population growth. The growth at times was explosive. In Denmark, for example, the population grew by an incredible 39 percent between 1800 and 1839. Quite simply, the population of Scandinavia began to outstrip available resources. Intensifying the problem were economic and natural calamities. Recessions and depressions were numerous throughout

Scandinavia in the nineteenth century. Economic difficulties were due in large part to increased international competition in such traditional Scandinavian industries as agriculture, fishing, and ship building. Foreign competition resulted in reduced profits which in turn cost many workers their jobs. Adding to the difficult situation were natural calamities such as harsh winters and dry summers that caused crop failure and famine. In Sweden and Norway, where only ten percent of the land is suitable for farming, one bad harvest would have a devastating impact on the whole burgeoning population. An example of the effect of a poor harvest is an 1868 Swedish rural newsletter's account which stated, "this past week the church bells rang here for ten corpses. Of these two had starved to death and one froze to death." In a nearby rural area it was reported "Several farmers' children are going around and begging." In the very next sentence the paper wrote, "More than four hundred people from this parish have emigrated to America in the most recent years."

Overpopulation and poor farm production were not the only factors that "pushed" Scandinavians out of their homelands. Dissatisfaction with the home government was another leading cause. Many Scandinavians were angered at government policies that continued to enforce a rigid social class structure. "Upward mobility" through the class structure was simply unheard of. Therefore many embarking Scandinavians felt that their governments were completely out of touch with the new ideals of "liberty and equality" that were emerging world-wide from the successful American and French Revolutions. Still other Scandinavians left due to government restrictions on religious freedom. Dominant throughout the nations of Scandinavia was the Lutheran Church. Religious dissent from the church was punished with lawful imprisonment, fines, or banishment of the dissenters from the home country. Alternative faiths were not allowed until a tide of toleration and liberalization of policies swept over Scandinavia in the 1860s. By then, however, Scandinavian members of such faiths as the Mormons, Quakers, and Methodists had established strong beachheads in America that served to attract similarly minded faithful.

The factors that "pushed" Scandinavians out of their homelands were closely related to those that "pulled" them to America. Those leaving Scandinavia often justified their departure by commenting on what America had to offer work opportunities, inexpensive land, political and religious freedom. Further, many pointed out that America was free from a rigid class structure and therefore offered everyone equal opportunity. These feelings were repeatedly echoed in the "America Letters," which were the letters sent by Scandinavian emigrants to their relatives and friends back in the homeland. These letters had a strong impact and served to persuade hundreds of thousands of other Scandinavians to come to America.

In spite of promises of a better life, Scandinavians, like other immigrant groups, faced great difficulties in coming to and assimilating into America. The journey across the Atlantic was both arduous and expensive. Many sold their life's possessions to finance the five-week-plus journey only to find themselves crammed aboard an unsafe ship. If the voyage was successful, and sometimes it was not, the newly arrived immigrant was overcome by the language and cultural differences of the new homeland. Fortunately, most of the three million Scandinavians who emigrated to America arrived between 1865 and 1914. During this period the United States emerged as the world's leading industrial power. Jobs and economic opportunities were plentiful but newly arrived Scandinavians were hindered by sharp language difficulties. Many found themselves in low paying, dangerous factory work. Jobs such as these did not require language skills but instead relied on brute manual strength. Still, many made the adaption to urban life and worked very hard in the hopes that their sons and daughters would assimilate better than they had into the American mainstream. Many other Scandinavians tended to avoid the urban cities and instead migrated to the nation's rural areas. Farming for them was an excellent choice given that language was not a barrier to success, and because many Scandinavians were farmers before embarking to America. The passage of the Homestead Act in 1862, which provided up to 160 acres of land for settlers who lived on and improved that land, acted as an additional incentive. Further, living out in the rural areas was thought to better preserve the traditions and culture of the motherland.

Life in "North Amerika," as the early Scandinavian settlers called it, proved to be a mixed blessing. On the beneficial side, freedom and opportunity abounded. In contrast, life in "Amerika" was often dangerous and harsh. Nature remained her capricious self. Immigrant Scandinavian farmers suffered droughts and flooding just as their countrymen did back home. Often farmers in America fell prey to disease, Indians, and wildlife. Other Scandinavians died early deaths in America's factories and mines. Still others died harvesting the new nation's forests and others building America's railroads.

Scandinavian immigration slowly diminished after World War One. After 1930, it was reduced to a trickle. Still, many Americans today proudly point out their Scandinavian heritage. They do so in part because of the Scandinavian legacy that connotes hard work, success, and assimilation into the American dream. What is often forgotten are the great difficulties that were conquered in accomplishing this. To better understand the Scandinavian experience in America, a separate discussion of each nation's experience will now be given.

THE DANISH EXPERIENCE

In American immigrant history few groups have assimilated as quickly as the Danes. By 1911, ninety-seven percent of Danish immigrants in the United States spoke English as compared to fifty-three percent for other ethnic groups. Further, by 1930 seventy-five percent of the 179,474 Danish immigrants living in the United States had become naturalized Americans which, at the time, was the highest percentage of any national group in the United States.

Although the Danes did not come to America in large numbers when compared to other ethnic groups, they nonetheless have had a considerable impact on American history. Early Danish exploration led to the acquisition of what is today the U.S. Virgin Islands. Early Danish settlers there followed the pattern of the American South and introduced slavery into the islands. The subsequent large-scale importation of slaves to the islands raised the ire of the Danish government and, in 1792, Denmark became the first nation to outlaw the slave trade. Although slave importation was outlawed, slavery in the islands continued. Inroads were made by religious organizations to aid the plight of the slaves but it wasn't until 1848 that the slaves were legally set free by the Danish government.

While the islands were a source of pride and natural beauty for the people of Denmark, they remained a source of temptation to belligerent foreign powers. Continual wars with Bismarck's Prussia revolved around the desire to turn the islands over to a strong, friendly power. In 1917 Denmark, reacting to the horrors of the First World War, sold the island chain to United States for the bargain price of twenty-five million dollars. Although the islands today are American, both the flags of Denmark and the United States fly over them, thus symbolizing the historic and friendly ties of the two nations.

Danish possession of the islands for more than two hundred years brought significant trade and contact between the two countries. Many Danes in the Danish West Indies enjoyed visiting the nearby mainland of the United States. Many in fact were so impressed with the apparent freedom and economic opportunities there that they decided to remain. One such Dane was Christian Febiger, who arrived from the Danish West Indies in 1772. Traveling throughout the American colonies for the purpose of studying business and economic developments, he decided during his visit to remain. Within a short period he established himself in the city of Boston and traded in a wide variety of commercial goods. Quickly assimilating himself into the American way of life, it was not long before Febiger joined the growing chorus in Boston demanding independence from Britain. As the British sailed into Boston Harbor, Febiger, who had military experience, volunteered to serve the American cause and subsequently fought alongside his fellow Bostonians in the famous battle of Bunker Hill. Not content with being a sunshine patriot, Febiger remained with the American continental army, and commanded troops in such major battles as Brandywine, Monmouth, and Yorktown. Helping to lead his adopted country to victory earned him the affectionate nickname "Old Denmark."

The Danish presence in early America was not limited to visits from the Danish West Indies. Small numbers of Danes migrated directly across the Atlantic in search of a better life. Most who came to the early republic were involved in seafaring or business. One notable Danish immigrant during this period was the artist Christian Guldager. A noted painter in his homeland by the age of seventeen, he originally came to America to study art. Instead, Guldager married an American woman and established himself as a portrait painter. Guldager, who made a very good living from his work, is best known for the now famous portrait of George Washington that adorns every American dollar bill. Tradition has it that Guldager also designed the national seal, which depicts a proud eagle clutching the olive branch of peace in one talon, and three arrows for war in the other. This symbolizes America's primary desire for peace, but additionally, its willingness to fight to ensure the nation's survival.

While Danes did make inroads into early America their numbers were small and their arrival patterns sporadic. The first large-scale movement of Danes came in the 1850s when Danish Mormons began migrating to America. Their migration was based on the earlier conversion of two Danes that had been living in America. From this small base the Mormon faith was able to send missionaries back to Denmark and they were successful in converting thousands of Danes to their faith. Their success was in large part due to the new 1849 Danish constitution, which among many other things, granted an easing of religious restrictions.

Despite constitutional guarantees, Mormons in Denmark suffered large-scale harassment from people not sensitive to their faith. In response, like the Puritans of England and Holland, growing numbers of Danish Mormons came to America in search of religious freedom.

One of the most interesting things about the Danish Mormon migration was the rapid assimilation of the converts into a completely new way of life. Arriving at the new Zion, which today is located in the state of Utah, the new Danes did not separate themselves out from the American Mormons. Rather, the Danes blended in and acted as full participants in the experience. They overcame cultural differences and language difficulties and were instrumental in helping the fledgling colony to prosper.

Between the 1850s and 1860s nearly eight thousand Danes migrated to Utah. Although the number appears inconsequential it is nonetheless significant. Many Danes were not converted to Mormonism but the churches's efforts in Denmark stimulated interest in America. The Mormon church in Denmark began publishing in 1851 a biweekly periodical, *Skandinaviens Stjerne*, that talked not only about their church activities in America but also about land prices, farm conditions, and the construction of the transcontinental railroad. Many Danes that were not interested in the church nonetheless read the paper because of their interest in America. Events such as the great California Gold Rush, which gained strong momentum in 1849, and news of the Homestead Act in 1862, brought increasing numbers of non-Mormon Danes to America. In fact, the vast majority of the Danish immigrants arriving after the American Civil War were not connected to the Mormon church. Further, between 1868 and 1900, in contrast to the earlier movement of Danish Mormon families, more than 60 percent of the newly arrived Danes were young, single males.

The large proportion of single male immigrants helps to explain the rapid assimilation of Danes into the American experience. Letters from these young men back to their homeland often expressed loneliness and a desire for a special woman in their lives. While some of them even went as so far to travel back to Denmark in search of a wife, most remained and ended up marrying non-Danes. In doing so, these Danes found themselves slowly adapting to the American culture at large.

Aiding the Danish assimilation process was the fact that the Danish emigrants came from the cities as well as the rural districts. While the majority were farmers, there were substantial numbers that had work experience in urban-related employment. Thus, upon arriving, the Danes seemed to fan out, with the farmers searching areas of the Mid-west for work as farm hands and the Danes from the cities searching the urban areas for employment.

Aiding Danish assimilation was their ability to surmount hurdles in gaining acceptance in their new homeland. The language barrier in particular was difficult for most Danes. However, since the majority were young, many were able to successfully adapt to the English language. The Danes also faced difficulties in adjusting to American cultural differences. But through marriage and their penchant for hard work they eventually adjusted and were accepted. Also aiding their assimilation was the fact that unlike many other ethnic immigrant groups, who faced blatant discrimination based on race and religion, the Danes often quickly blended into the American mainstream aided by their fair skin and Protestant faith. Further, the difficulties overcome by earlier arrived immigrants helped to pave the way of acceptance for the relatively late arriving Danes.

Once in America, Danes who settled together in groups fared better at retaining their Danish cultural ties than their single male counterparts. Although these groups of Danes were usually a small minority in nearly every American community they settled in, they nonetheless worked hard to retain their sense of ethnic identity. In the rural areas, several groups of Danes founded high schools and tiny colleges whose purpose was to educate the immigrant's offspring in both the ways of Denmark and America. In the urban areas, Danish assistance organizations were founded. Such groups as the Dania Society helped to ease fellow Danes into new surroundings while encouraging the retention of the Danish ethnic identity. Newspapers too promoted ties between the homeland and Danes in America. While these efforts worked early on, the spreading geographic distribution of Danes and their own tendency of marriage to non-Danes contributed to a loss of ethnic identity. As time progressed most of the schools founded by the early Danish farmers closed due to lack of students. The ones that did survive such as Dana college in Blair, Nebraska, and Grand View College in Des Moines, Iowa, today only show small interest in preserving the Danish ethnic heritage.

Immigration to America attracted nearly 300,000 Danes between the end of the Civil War and the beginning of the First World War. Following the pattern of early American settlers, the Danes upon arrival tended to settle into rural areas. Then, over time, the Danes commonly married into other ethnic groups. Subsequently, their offspring usually followed the typical American pattern of movement from the farm to the cities. This in turn would aid in the assimilation process but would also hinder the retention of Danish ethnic identity.

Although their numbers were relatively small, as compared to literally millions of peoples of various other ethnic groups, the Danes left their mark. Small towns such as Dannebrog, Nebraska; West Denmark, Wisconsin; Ringsted and St. Ansgar, Iowa give testimony to their early presence and impact. By 1900, Danish immigrants could be found in every county of California, Connecticut, Idaho, Iowa, Maine, Montana, Nevada, New Jersey, South Dakota, Utah and Wyoming. Solvang, California, an original Danish farming community settled in 1911, is now the site of a replica Danish village. Although the city's population is less than five thousand people, it draws more than two million tourists a year who come to enjoy and celebrate the successful Danish-American connection.

THE SWEDISH EXPERIENCE

A story is told of a Swedish farmer who sadly approaches his local minister. The distressed farmer explains that he has just received news that one of his young sons has died in America. He then goes on to ask the minister if he would be kind enough to hold final rites for his son. The minister declines by stating that the farmer's son was no longer considered a member of the local congregation since he had died in his new place of residence, that of a foreign country. The farmer, it is said, replied in amazement, "But he lived in America! Since when is America a foreign country?"

The above story is reminiscent of a parable. It contains several messages regarding Swedish immigration to America. The first is the death of a young man. The clear message is that America is a dangerous place even for a healthy young man. Second, is the minister's refusal to conduct final services on the grounds that the son died a resident of a foreign country. Clearly, the minister, who represents the establishment, feels that those who emigrate should be considered "foreigners." Last, is the farmer's response of "since when is America a foreign country?" America, where the farmer has several sons living, is accepted by him as an extension of Sweden.

This story helps to explain the great conflict tearing at the Swedish fabric during peak periods of immigration to America. Nearly one-fifth of the Swedish population migrated to America between 1841 and 1914. This substantial loss of population raised such cries of protest and threats of government intervention to stop it. Yet, Swedes continued to migrate to America, often writing back home telling others to come to the "New Sweden."

Prior to 1830, most Swedes had never heard of America. In truth, an early Swedish colony was established along the Delaware River in 1638. The colony, which was illegally settled on Dutch land, only lasted till 1655. Unfortunately, for Sweden, the colony was operated on a shoe string budget and therefore when Dutch troops showed up in 1655, the Swedes peacefully agreed to end the settlement. News of America, though, continued to make its way back to Sweden due in large part through the visits by Swedish sailors. Through the subsequent decades, many of these sailors returned to their homes and told interested friends and neighbors about the new land and the opportunities it offered. Prior to 1840 Swedish law prohibited Swedes from emigrating abroad. But as the Swedish population grew and the country's economic conditions worsened the laws were eased to allow foreign migration.

The first substantial migration to America was undertaken shortly after the new law was in place. One man that quickly took advantage of the opportunity was Gustav Unonius, a young government bureaucrat. Unonius had read at length about the American and French Revolutions. Impressed with their ideals, he began to question Sweden's firm social class system and its relative lack of political freedom. Dissatisfied with the possibilities of change in Sweden, Unonius left his village with some of his friends, and emigrated to America in 1841. Unonius and his friends purchased a farm at Pine Lake, Wisconsin and it would become the first Swedish colony of the nineteenth century established in the United States.

Unonius was very impressed with the new country and all that it had to offer. Discussing the new country with Swedes back home, he wrote, "Every workman has there the same right of citizenship as the nobles. Conventional judgments, class interest and narrow-mindness do not hang to your coat tail nor trample on your heels." Others seeking political and religious freedom quickly followed. Per Cassel, leading a group of immigrants that originally planned to settle in Pine Lake, instead founded New Sweden, Iowa in 1845. Like their countrymen in Pine Lake, the Swedish settlers built the colony with the expressed ideal of political liberty for all of its residents. In 1846, a group of Swedish immigrants, dissatisfied with the practices of the Lutheran church in Sweden, set up an alternative religious colony in what is today Bishop's Hill, Illinois.

Despite the colonists' raw idealism, which often fails to match the reality humans encounter with one another in daily living, the new colonies nonetheless survived and often prospered. Pine Lake, even at its lowest point, served as inspiration to Swedes back home. Despite weather and soil problems, letters from Pine Lake to Sweden enthusiastically spoke of the new country's freedom and abundant natural beauty. And when things were good, as they often were in fertile farmlands of places like Iowa, the enthusiasm could hardly be contained. The "America" letters served as an important inducement in bringing other Swedes to America.

Swedish immigration to America usually followed the pattern of its Scandinavian neighbors, Denmark and Norway. When things were going poorly in the homeland, emigration increased. Concurrently when things went well in the homeland the rates of emigration decreased. The pattern of Swedish immigration in the 1840s was somewhat of an aberration. Most of the immigrants during this period left Sweden not for economic but rather for political and religious reasons. While their numbers were smaller than during other peaks of Swedish immigration, these "rebellious" immigrants were important in furthering the cause of American democracy. As one university commentator remarked to a visiting Swedish national, "Every time a new tyrant has appeared among you in Europe, we have gotten a portion of the Old World's best people over here in America: the insurgents, the revolutionaries, the rebels, the freedom fighters. And they have been of valuable aid to us Americans: they have helped us to uphold and develop our traditions of freedom. We truly have a lot to thank Europe's tyrants for!"

The arrival of politically and religiously dissatisfied Swedes slowed in the late 1850s. The subsequent onset of the American Civil War further reduced immigration to a trickle. Many of the same Swedes that came to America earlier in search of their own freedom subsequently joined the Union cause in hopes of helping to secure the freedom of several million enslaved Africans. The colony at Bishop's Hill, Illinois, for example, quickly organized a Union military unit in 1861. This Swedish unit saw heavy action at the Battle of Shiloh. When the state of Illinois decided to form a regiment of Illinois Volunteers, the award winning Swedish unit was proudly listed as the first company. Other groups of Swedes joined in the Union cause. Estimates calculate that nearly one-sixth of the Swedish population living in the Mid-West served in the Union forces. For these new Americans the war was being waged to preserve the Union and to end the despised institution of slavery.

Echoing this is the letter of a young Swede who wrote home asking for his family to understand his enlistment, "I feel my peace made with God. I think this cause is just and a righteous war and should I meet my death on the battlefield I feel I shall die in a glorious cause." Unfortunately the young man died in service to his new country at the Battle of Lexington, Missouri, September, 1861.

At the war's conclusion in 1865, Sweden was in the midst of economic chaos. Repeated poor harvests, a rapidly growing population, and delayed industrialization caused large numbers of Swedes to be unemployed and hungry. Large numbers of Swedes made their way to America hoping what earlier emigrants had told them was true, that jobs and food were plentiful. Since most of the "America letters" were written by relatives and close neighbors many were willing to take the gamble. The early settlers after the American Civil War then wrote back to Sweden to confirm what had been written in the 1840s and 1850s. America, for them, was a land of dreams. Rapid industrial growth meant plenty of work in the cities while the rural areas offered cheap, fertile land.

Large-scale Swedish immigration would continue up until the First World War. Nearly two million Swedes would make the treacherous journey across the Atlantic during this period. Those who came with families tended to be farmers and most of them settled in the Scandinavian Triangle. The triangle whose apex begins in Illinois extends through America's farm belt included the states of Wisconsin, Minnesota, Iowa, North Dakota, South Dakota, Nebraska, and Montana. It should be pointed out that not all of the Swedes settling in the triangle were farmers. Many worked in the mining and logging industries. Single Swedish immigrants tended to migrate to the cities where work in American industry was readily available. A substantial percentage of these men were known as "birds of passage" which meant the men planned to earn substantial money and then return home. Most, however, stayed and their growing numbers made the city of Chicago, the world's largest Swedish speaking city outside of Stockholm.

Swedish immigrants soon earned an enviable reputation as hard workers. One railroad magnate boasted, "give me Swedes, snuff and whiskey, and I'll build a railroad to hell." In the cities, fellow Swedes created informal job networks to help their newly arriving countrymen to obtain work. Many employers encouraged this and promised jobs to the workers' friends and relatives.

Swedes in both the cities and on the farms were also known for their adaptability to American culture and beliefs. Most Swedes were pragmatic and goal oriented. They worked hard to overcome the language barrier and expected other immigrant groups to do the same. The Swedes also put great value on moving up the economic ladder and therefore put great value on education for their children. In fact, some visiting Swedish nationals complained at the rapidity at which immigrant Swedes and their off-spring Americanized. This criticism would often fall on deaf ears as the immigrant Swedes continued on the fast track into the cherished American mainstream.

THE NORWEGIAN EXPERIENCE

Next to Ireland no other nation, between 1840-1920, had a higher rate of immigration to America than Norway. Between 1825 and 1920, this relatively small nation would lose more than one million of its citizens to America. Coming in five distinct waves of immigration, the Norwegians mostly settled and remained together. As late as 1890, nearly eighty percent of Norwegian immigrants were living in primarily distinct Norwegian settlements. In the same year, it was found that more than one-half of Norwegian immigrants had settled in the two states of Wisconsin and Minnesota.

The tendency of the Norwegian immigrants to remain together did not mean that they didn't acculturate to the American way of life. Quite to the contrary. Norwegians became actively involved in American politics and publishing and found substantial success in both. Further, in the new sports craze sweeping the nation, the Norwegians would introduce the sport of skiing and produce America's greatest collegiate football coach, Notre Dame's Knute Rockne.

The first wave of Norwegian immigration began in 1825. The sailing sloop, *Restauration*, brought fifty-three persons to America. Like their earlier immigrant counterparts, the Danes and Swedes, most of the early Norwegian immigrants came to America for religious and political freedom. After the end of the American Civil War, this changed as increasing numbers of Norwegians arrived in search of economic stability. As the homeland grew increasingly plagued by poor harvests, these new Norwegian arrivals added to the conviction of the early settlers that they had done the right thing in leaving the homeland years before.

The tendency of the Norwegians to settle together made for an interesting combination between the two groups. The early settlers put great value on the concept of liberty and toleration whereas the latter arrivals tended to put high value on economic prosperity. Put together, the two groups evoked the American ideals of freedom and capitalism.

The early Norwegian settlers were in part responsible for the large immigrant waves that took place after the Civil War. The early settlers often wrote glowing letters about life in the new land and sent them to friends and neighbors back in Norway. These letters in turn helped to bring about "America fever" in their former home villages. Although increasing numbers left, the Norwegian government took no formal action against those wanting to emigrate. Rather, it was hoped that returning Norwegians would tell their friends and relatives of the difficulties that awaited those going to America.

The positive reports about America in the settlers' letters often contradicted the reality of immigrant life. Most Norwegians settled on the frontier and faced a multitude of dangers. Chief among them were Indian attacks. The Norwegians were particularly vulnerable because they had a greater tendency than other immigrant groups to seek land on the farthest edge of newly opened lands. The Sioux Indian tribe in Minnesota, for example, fighting the continued takeover of their lands, took to the warpath in the summer of 1862. In the battles that followed nearly 500 settlers were killed. Disease, too, wrecked havoc on the Norwegian settlements. Cholera, typhoid, tuberculosis, and malaria were particularly treacherous. Even today one can still see such things as "cholera graveyards" in the open fields in what used to be the early Norwegian settlements.

The tenacity of the Norwegians on the frontier helped them to escape large-scale discrimination. Many Americans saw Norwegian settlement in the wilderness as a sign of progress in the battle to conquer the expansive American frontier. The frontier, in turn, had great impact in shaping the beliefs and ideologies of the Norwegians themselves. The frontier fostered a democratic spirit. The long held social class divisions of Norway, for example, fell by the wayside as the new immigrants worked together to survive.

As their population grew, from new births and immigration, the Norwegians took increasing interest in the governmental affairs around them. Given their tendency to settle and live together, the Norwegians were well experienced in organization. As their settlements gave way to townships, the Norwegians became increasingly familiar with participatory democracy. While they wanted to assimilate into the American mainstream, the Norwegians also wanted to maintain their ethnic heritage. Thus it was not uncommon for the community to elect fellow Norwegians to such positions as mayors and sheriffs. As the emphasis turned to state and county offices the Norwegians again retained their ties to fellow Norwegian office seekers. Often this created problems, as in the case of Winnebago County, Iowa in 1870. The dispute began when locals, fearing a dominance of Norwegian immigrant candidates, began disrupting the nominating convention. The breaking point came when a rotten apple hit the face of "Kjaefte" (Big-mouth) Hans Petersen, a leading spokesperson of the Norwegian cause. While no one was killed in the subsequent riot, many were injured. Outraged Norwegians retaliated by going to the polls in record numbers. They won by a substantial margin and continued to literally control the county government all the way up to World War I.

At the state level, the Norwegians learned the value of uniting with other groups to wrest political control. A natural ally were fellow Scandinavians. In the predominant Scandinavian states of Minnesota and Wisconsin, the negotiated candidates often won election. One particularly significant win was the election of Knute Nelson, a Norwegian, to the Minnesota governorship in 1892. Very successful and popular, Nelson was able to successfully pave the way for the other ethnic Scandinavian candidates. In fact, to the present day, the vast majority who have obtained the Minnesota governorship have been of Scandinavian extraction. While opponents criticized the Norwegians for being "special interest oriented," and "un-American," the truth was that politics helped to assimilate Norwegians into the American mainstream. Successful Norwegian politicians learned to branch out and form alliances and loyalties with other groups. Further, the election of ethnic candidates helped to more firmly tie the immigrants to American society.

The Norwegians also played an important role in tying Scandinavian immigrants to the new land through the publishing of newspapers. One important one was the *Scandinaven*. Begun by two Norwegians in 1866, the paper was first distributed free of charge by newsboys at the railroad station in Chicago. For arriving Scandinavian immigrants the paper proved to be of great help. It contained information on jobs, prices, assistance agencies, and things newcomers should watch out for. For other readers, the paper contained pertinent information about local and homeland affairs. Politically oriented, the paper encouraged Americanization while retaining ethnic identity. It consistently preached the values of hard work, perseverance and patriotism to the new country. At its peak in 1912, the paper had a wide distribution and totaled nearly 54,000 subscribers. Two other well distributed and popular Norwegian papers were the *Minneapolis Tidende* and the *Decorah-Posten*. Like the Danish and Swedish immigrant press, these papers kept readers informed about important new events from the homeland. But as important were stories relating to the successful adaptation of Norwegian immigrants to America. Thus, the papers contained lengthy profiles of successful business and education leaders. Also the careers of Scandinavian-American entertainment and sports stars were closely monitored. As a result these papers served as a important motivating force for Scandinavians to become Americans while retaining their native heritage.

The Norwegians also sought to retain their ethnic ties through the Lutheran Church. Although the church at times was faced with internal division among competing Norwegian synods, it still acted as an important cultural unifier. And unlike the Danes who adapted to worship services in English, the Norwegians have continued to present day to conduct religious services in their native tongue. The Norwegians, though, were acutely aware of the much larger non-Norwegian world around them. Thus, the early settlers put a great emphasis on the development of educational institutions that would help the immigrants adapt to American life. As late as World War II, nearly seventy-five Norwegian-American schools remained in the United States and Canada. Today, the well known St. Olaf College in Northfield, Minnesota, continues as a living testament to the Norwegian community's desire to assimilate into the American mainstream while retaining a sense of ethnic identity.

By the onset of World War I, Norwegian settlement has spread across the Mid-west and the Great Plains. While most remained farmers, substantial numbers had become lumber jacks, miners, and factory workers. And while Norwegian settlement remained predominately rural, increasing numbers had moved to urban areas. In time, such cities as Minneapolis, Chicago, New York, and Seattle had substantial Norwegian populations. In these cities, the Norwegians followed their rural pattern and settled together. These urban colonies often prospered. On both the east and west coasts, for example, the Norwegians were particularly successful in the shipbuilding and fishing industries.

The onset of World War I marked the end of large-scale Scandinavian immigration to the United States. When hostilities ended in late 1917, the United States slowly turned inward and began passage of legislation that restricted immigration. Norwegian farmers wishing to emigrate were further discouraged by an agricultural recession which swept the United

States in the 1920s. In contrast, Norway, which gained its independence from Sweden in 1905, had continued on a path towards economic prosperity. The large numbers that left for America had opened up opportunities for those left behind. More land became available and the growing impact of industrial technology allowed the remaining Norwegians to better harness their abundant natural resources.

CONCLUSION

From the frontier, to farms, to urban cities, Scandinavians have played an integral role in fostering America's prosperous development. Their ability to overcome difficult language and cultural barriers have made them a model ethnic group. While it is true that their assimilation was aided by their fair skin and Protestant faith, the Scandi-navian immigrants have nonetheless earned the praise that many give to them today. It can be pointed out that the Scandinavians helped to conquer the American frontier. The Scandinavians, too, aided in the development of America's great farm belt and also substantially contributed to the country's great industrial growth. And in the hour of the country's greatest crisis, the American Civil War, Scandinavians fought and died in large numbers for the preservation of their new nation.

The legacy of the Scandinavian immigrant remains alive today through the written word. Pioneer life on the American frontier is powerfully described by Norwegian author, Ole Rolvaag, in the novel classic, *Giants in the Earth*. Focusing on a Norwegian family's desperate struggle to survive on the South Dakota frontier, the book gives an important psychological interpretation to American westward movement. In relation to the problems of late nineteenth century urban America, the work of Danish immigrant Jacob Riis stands out. His 1890 work, *How the Other Half Lives*, served to focus national attention on the plight of America's urban poor. As important to the Scandinavian legacy are the letters from the immigrants themselves. Their written record gives testament to the hope for a better life. Expressing that view was a letter that extolled the virtues of the new land for all Scandinavians. "Here the Swede would find again his clear romantic lakes, the plains of Skane rich in corn, and the valleys of Norrland; here the Norwegian would find his rapid rivers, his lofty mountains, for I include the Rocky Mountains and Oregon in the new kingdom; and both nations, their hunting-fields and their fisheries. The Danes might here pasture their flocks and herds, and lay out their farms on richer and less misty coasts than those of Denmark."

Although the Scandinavian community in America continues to diminish in number, many Americans with Scandinavian ethnic heritage are rediscovering their roots. Since the 1970s there has been a strong growth in Scandinavian-American social and historical societies. The American-Scandinavian Foundation, for example, publishes historical works on such topics as the effects of immigration and assimilation. The foundation, too, arranges student exchanges and helps to promote the offering of Scandinavian language courses at American universities. The Danish American Heritage Society, the Swedish Pioneer Historical Society, and the Norwegian-American Historical Society all serve to promote their respective histories. ✦

SELECTED BIBLIOGRAPHY

Barton, Arnold H. *Clipper Ship and Covered Wagon: Essays from the Swedish Pioneer Historical Quarterly*. New York, 1979.

Benson, Adolph B.; and Naboth Hedin. *Americans From Sweden*. New York, 1950.

Blegen, Theodore C. *Norwegian Migration to America, 1825-1860*. Northfield, Minnesota, 1931.

Hale, Frederick. *Danes in North America* 1984.

Hvidt, Kristian. *Flight to America: The Social Background of 300,000 Danish Emigrants*. New York, 1975.

Janson, Florence Edith. *The Background of Swedish Immigration, 1840-1930*. Chicago, 1931.

Lass, William E. *Minnesota: A Bicentennial History*. New York, 1977

Lovall, Odd S. *The Promise of America: A History of the Norwegian-American People*. Minneapolis, 1984.

Moberg, Vilhelm. *The Unknown Swedes: A Book About Swedes and America, Past and Present*. Carbondale, 1988.

Mulder, William. *Homeward to Zion: The Mormon Migration From Scandinavia*. Minneapolis, 1957.

Nielsen, George R. *The Danish Americans*. Boston, 1981.

Norman, Hans and Harald Runblom. *From Sweden to America: A History of the Migration*. Minneapolis, 1976.

Ostergren, Robert C. *A Community Transplanted: The Trans-Atlantic Experience of a Swedish Immigrant Settlement in the Upper Middle West, 1835-1915*. Madison, 1988.

Scott, Franklin D. *Trans-Atlantica: Essays on Scandinavian Migration and Culture*. New York, 1979.

The Irish

Robert D. Cross

Whether or not Irish sailors reached St. Brendan's Isle, and so established an irrefutable claim to being the first Europeans to reach the New World and the real founding fathers of what was to be the United States, there were undoubtedly Irish Catholics in the British colonies from a very early time.[1] By comparison with immigrants speaking German and with the large numbers of Irish Protestants who would later insist on being called Scotch Irish, the numbers of Irish Catholics were not substantial. The prevailing anti-Catholic temper of the colonies would have in any case prevented any important Irish ethnic life. even if their numbers had been larger. Even those Catholics like the Carrolls of Maryland, whose faith was not covert, were not Irish and do not seem to have been any more notable in their interest in the well-being of the Irish than were the Catholic gentry of eighteenth century England. Too few to be singled out for opprobrium, the Irish Catholics experienced the mixed blessings of insignificance.

During the years when the new nation was being established, the Irish continued to be largely inconspicuous. If they were notably combative—a trait regularly attributed to them subsequently, and a source of reproach and obloquy in the next generation—the militance of a Commodore John Barry was, in Revolutionary years, highly welcome. George Washington's prohibition of traditional expressions of anti-Catholic feeling and festivity in the Continental army may have been calculated to prevent the alienation from patriot ranks of Irish Catholics as well as of Catholics of other stock. Certainly there was no disposition among the rebels to inhibit the deep-rooted hostility Irish felt toward British power. Similarly,

---

the tentative efforts of patriot statesmen to develop a working alliance with those in Ireland resentful of the tyrannies of George III could not have failed to soften attitudes toward the Irish in America; probably, however, the connection between the righteousness of the Irish cause in Ireland and the well-being of the Irish in America was seldom made.

In the years after the Peace of Paris, and especially in the 1790s, however, the position of the Irish in America was more problematic. The Federalists, like the leaders of most new nations, were paranoid about any expressions of dissent or even any appearances of difference. Whether or not the Irish in America were disproportionately "Jeffersonian" in thought or affiliation and whether or not there was much connection between the Irish rising in 1798 and the hydra head of the French Revolution, Federalist guardians of America were terrified by the sight of hordes of "wild Irishmen" in America.[2] The Naturalization Act of 1795 and the Alien and Sedition Acts of 1798 certainly had the Irish in view—as well as dangerous Frenchmen, Englishmen, and treacherous natives. This flurry of legislative animus, though malevolent in intention and frightening in prospect, proved to be largely impotent. In any event, the Irish had neither the numbers nor the status to mount an effective protest. Native-born Jeffersonians, on coming to power, quickly obviated the need for Irish concern or action.

Irish Catholics continued to migrate to America in the early years of the nineteenth century, but still not in numbers suffficient to cause much alarm or to enable them to foster a vigorous ethnic life. With the progressive deterioration of American party organizations, political affiliation seemed less portentous. Anti-Catholic feeling was at a low ebb, and the creation of Catholic parishes in many cities did not provoke alarm. Irishmen were now more conspicuous, and Matthew Carey may be taken as a typical Irish-American leader.[3] Born in Dublin in 1760 and migrating to Philadelphia in 1784, he readily won, by his energy and manifest in intellectual abilities, a prominent role as a publisher of classical and English writings, as an original economist, and as a spokesman for such causes of general interest as Greek independence. But he did not cease to be an "Irishman." As early as 1790, he helped organize the Hibernian Society in Philadelphia to aid emigrants from the old country. In his *Ireland Vindicated*, published in 1819, he was arguing not just for the rights of Ireland, as all Irish, then and later, were bound to do; he was also, however consciously, providing a rationale for the self-respect that the Irish, like every other ethnic group in America, would require and seek. This caused little controversy, if one came from an established home country. Unless there was a prospect of war with the United States, English immigrants could vaunt the achievement of Britain and French immigrants celebrate *la gloire* of France. But in a nationalist epoch like the nineteenth and twentieth centuries, emigrants from a weak or nonexistent state understandably felt inferior. Many Irish felt they would be denigrated as "slavish" just as long as Ireland was "enslaved." (Generations later, Poles, Czechs, and Serbs would have similar feelings.) German Americans supported Bismarck; Italian Americans would be proud of Mussolini.[4] Certainly, for Carey, and probably for most Irish nationalists in subsequent years, there was no felt conflict between a strenuous Irish nationalism and a whole-hearted Americanism. Unhappily, many native Americans would never be able to conceive of a benign double loyalty.

As the numbers of Irish immigrating to America rose from a trickle to a flood in the 1830s and remained at high tide until late in the century, the "leadership" of a Matthew Carey was no longer sufficient. Not one, but many, emigrant aid societies were desperately needed. Concern for bleeding Ireland, though in no way slackening, yielded preeminence and importunacy to concern for the well-being of the Irish in America. Appeals to the fair-minded in the western world were supplanted by demands for power in this country. The increasing totals of Irish immigrants, though frightening to native Americans and a source of despair to aid societies, gave these demands for power and respectful attention more than mere poignancy.

More than numbers buttressed the Irish claim. Unlike most immigrants, almost all the Irish spoke English, even if with a mockable accent. They could not, therefore, be quite so easily ignored, quite so readily exploited, quite so simply shunted aside from jobs or positions of status; enough Irish immigrants could read English, so that it was necessary (as it was not for Italians and Slavs later) for the prejudiced to write up signs "No Irish Need Apply."

Furthermore, they brought with them familiarity with techniques of representative government. For most, no doubt, this amounted to little more than a sorrowful experience of the ways in which a "democratic" political system could be manipulated to injure them. But however little the Irish had gained in Ireland by the 1830s and however few of them had actually worked with, or even seen, Daniel O'Connell, few probably were unaware of the tactics available to the resourceful: the formulation and publication of grievances; the organization of rallies; the inspiriting oratory; the dissemination of newspapers and pamphlets. Many immigrant laymen and most immigrant priests had learned what "O'Connellism" could do, even if Catholic Emancipation had brought little practical benefit to them. Equally important, many of the immigrants had learned the political importance of violence. The "Establishment" in Ireland had never mobilized such overwhelming counterterror as to make "Whiteboyism" seem counterproductive. Politically minded at the same time that they were as a group open minded about the kind of methods to be employed, the mass of Irish immigrants arrived in the United States at a propitious time. Restrictions on adult white male suffrage were disappearning fast; the founding fathers' aversion to party organization seemed increasingly anachronistic; and William Marcy could believe he was only being candid in declaring that to the victors belong the spoils. Such a scene was congenial to the Irish, who had a clear notion of the spoils of office and of how they had been deprived of them; ironically, the scene made more sense to an Irish immigrant than it did to nostalgic native Americans, typified by a Philip Hone or a George Templeton Strong.[5]

At first, the Irish were content to follow the many who volunteered to lead them. But even at an early date they demonstrated a certain ornery fractiousness. In 1817 a group departed from Dooley's Long Room in New York City to express their severe displeasure at the unwillingness of Tammany to nominate the Irish Protestant, Thomas Addis Emmett, for Congress.[6] Though it took several years and several subsequent riots to be persuasive, by the 1840s, Tammany, like Democratic organizations in most cities, had learned to defer, if not surrender, to Irish Americans. Mike Walsh was probably the first immigrant to make the full hegira, reaching Congress in the 1850s after years as leader of New York's "Spartan Band."[7] His upward progress in American politics was paralleled by John O'Sullivan's editorship of *The Democratic Review* and mimicked by the Whigs' feeble attempt to create in 1852 *The Irishman*, edited by Patrick O'Dea.

Irish immigrants soon gave their special tone to American politics. Whether as leaders or followers, they placed extraordinary emphasis upon the virtues of loyalty. This trait, hardly surprising in those who had suffered so much from those who had purported to "represent" them in Ireland, at once enhanced the strength of the leader in his often difficult negotiations with non-Irish America and infuriated those native citizens to whom "independence" politically—not loyalty—was the supreme virtue. "Gratitude is the finest word I know," Richard Croker, boss of Tammany Hall at the close of the century, declared. "I would much prefer a man to steal from me than to display ingratitude. All there is in life is loyalty to one's family and friends."[8] Of course, Irish Americans were capable of deserting a leader; the history of Tammany Hall makes an account of fifteenth century Florence read like a Boy Scout narrative. But when a Curley deserted a Honey Fitz, he did so not to manifest his independence but to support a Martin Lomasney.

Irish Americans did not want their leaders to amend the Constitution or to reform in other ways the body politic. Indeed, "reform" was a suspicious notion, connoting all too often the subversion of traditional institutions like the state, the church, and the family. The Irish hoped their governors would neither succumb to such an ideology as led that generous man, Lord John Russell, to acquiesce, in the name of laissez-faire, to the shipment of food out of Ireland during the Great Hunger, nor wipe out saloons in the name of temperance, nor destroy the state in the interests of the emancipation of Negroes.[9] The Irish *did* expect of their political leaders uncalculated acts of kindness and sympathy—the visit to the wake, the basket of food at Christmas, the off-the-record word to the district attorney in extenuation of a son's petty violation of the law. To the reformer, such services were not trivial; they were disgusting and patronizing payoffs for a license to loot the treasury and to betray the public interest. When the Tammany district leader, George Washington Plunkitt, distinguished "honest graft"—the willingness of a political insider to benefit from advance knowledge of contracts to bid on or land to be confiscated—from the blatant shakedown of helpless prostitutes, criminals, and innocent businessmen—reformers grumbled that no higher ethic could be expected of the Irish. In fact, Plunkitt and his spokesman, William Riordan, did less than justice to Irish-American political attitudes.[10] It was true enough that few Irish immigrants or their children shared the fantasies of the popular Social Gospeler, W. T. Stead, about the wonderful things that would happen "if Christ came to Chicago."[11] They did not suppose that political leaders would be Godlike. They were neither surprised nor dismayed if the men they elected saw their opportunities unities for self-enrichment—and took them. They may even have indulged in private satisfaction that fellow Irishmen could lead expansively prosperous lives in a culture where they themselves were obliged to endure grinding hardship. What they could *not* endure, or tolerate, was the political leader who lost "touch" with them—who by word or deed denied a common humanity with them. They supported a politics and a set of politicians who did not make them feel alien or excluded. With no high opinion of mankind, they gloried in outrageous expressions of hate for their "enemies." They did not boggle at the chicanery of Tammany leaders like "Honest John Kelly"; the buffoonery of James Michael Curley; or the aloofness of Richard Croker. They admired these worthies, and for nothing more than for their ability to get and to use power. They were not much concerned about the ways in which this power was exercised or the goals toward which it was applied, for they were viscerally sure that the result would be good for the Irish. Still, it would misrepresent their convictions to impute to them a belief that politicians, any more than priests or businessmen, would win either for themselves or their followers lasting success. To the Irish American, life in this world was a losing proposition. But the ends for which one fought, and even more the style with which one comported oneself, were the criteria of grandness, the prerequisites for loyalty.

In the nineteenth century political prowess was of great importance not just in bestowing psychological satisfaction and in warding off the forays of an unsympathetic political system but also in enabling the immigrant to make his way economically. Aside from the relatively few who could be awarded a job in the street-cleaning department, or on the "force," or in municipal construction, or in the political machine itself, there remained a large mass of immigrants who needed help in finding a way to earn a living. Arriving in America as "unconditioned labor," the Irish inadvertently demonstrated all too dramatically the illusionary character of the myth of the self-made man. In both factory and construction work, the decision as to whom to employ rested with a foreman or boss. Where that foreman or boss was an Irishman—especially an Irishman from one's own neighborhood in Ireland—the prospect of employment was fair. Failing that, if the employer could be subjected to the importunities of an economic or political leader benignly disposed toward the Irish, the immigrant had a chance. By and large, however, it was only late in the century that an Irish immigrant could hope for intercession in his behalf from an Irish American magnate—a Grace or a Cuddahy—or, more reliably, from a labor union dominated by Irishmen. Until then, he usually needed assistance from the "personal friend" of a friend.

With increasing frequency, that friendly figure would be a priest. Irish-American experience has been so intertwined with Catholic-American experience that almost until the post-World War II period it has been possible to regard the two as virtually indistinguishable. Certainly that was the way in which most Irish immigrants thought—and with justice. For centuries in Ireland, Catholicism was the sign and seal of being Irish.[12] The Roman Catholic Church, beleaguered as it was, organized the life of the Irish peasant and gave meaning to it. Immigration to America changed little. To the Irishman, birth, marriage, and death were meaningless apart from the theology and the ceremonies of Catholicism. The hardship of daily life, the apparent prosperity of non-Catholics, and—perhaps most egregious of all—the opprobrium bestowed on them by enemies of the Faith—all such incongruities were explained by the Catholic plan of salvation, which reiterated that whatever the appearances of this world, there was salvation for no one outside the Church; colloquially, Irishmen were assured that God in His inscrutability had ordained that non-Catholics were allowed to fatten in this world so that they would fry the hotter in the next. Sunday mass, Easter duty, confession and penance, and the last rites made it possible for an Irishman to endure in a non-Irish world.

All such consolations depended on the presence of a Catholic clergy, preferably an Irish Catholic clergy. And, in contrast to the predicament of many Catholic immigrants, there was never any real shortage of Irish clerics in America. Many had come to America early; a surprisingly large number accompanied the famine migrants; the Church in Ireland took special steps to ensure a steady flow of priests to America; and American bishops found a gratifying response to their regular pleas for more priests and nuns for the missions in America.[13] Furthermore, Irish-American families gave strong support to their offspring who undertook lives dedicated to the Church. Whether born in Ireland or, like James Gibbons, born in America but receiving his education in Ireland, the Irish clergy presented Irish immigrants in America with a special kind of leadership. It was largely uncomplicated. Priestly deference to bishops was pretty much unquestioned; few immigrants—until late in the century—ever had to choose between loyalty to parish priest or loyalty to bishop, or to Pope, or to a remembered Church back home. In Ireland, where the parish priest was frequently the only authority to summon up against a Protestant landlord, a "political representative," or, for that matter, an unsympathetic neighbor or father, the priest could assume virtual infallibility. In an era when Catholics in other lands were troubled over questions of papal infallibility, it was a commonplace that no problem existed for the Irish; no good Catholic questioned that the priest, and so the Pope, and so the Church, was infallible. There was no need to indulge in theological or historical quibbles.

In America Irish priests in the nineteenth century were, even more effectively and spectacularly than in Ireland, the real leaders of the Irish. Given their backgrounds and the needs of their people, it is scarcely surprising that they were conservative. Few of them were innovators in theological speculation; even fewer gave much attention to the growing debate elsewhere in the Catholic world over liturgical "reform"; probably still fewer devoted much attention to the problematic relations of the Irish to those non-Irish non-Catholics of seeming good will.[14] The Irish American priest, like the Irish American politician, concentrated on being *available* to the immigrants, in bad times as well as good. A friendly critic could complain that the layman regarded the priest not just as "teacher, father and friend, but boss-teacher, boss-father, boss-friend, perhaps boss-politician.[15] For most immigrants in the nineteenth century, such worries were nonexistent. Enough that the Irish priest was willing to help in every way conceivable.

When, for example, the Presbyterian John Breckenridge of Philadelphia began to publish a series of insulting attacks on Catholics and Catholicism, the Irish Catholic priest John Hughes was willing to answer charge with charge, billingsgate with billingsgate.[16] When states threatened to intensify discriminations against Catholic schools, or against the religious life of Catholics in public schools or caring institutions, priests like Hughes were more than ready to take up the cudgels. Later in the century, when employers exercised undue force against all workers, or against Catholic workers particularly, "labor-priests" like Peter Yorke were quick and sturdy in their intervention.[17] Even in the twentieth century, Father William Dorney of Chicago was popularly and affectionately known as "king of the Yards" because of his ability to help his parishioners to get jobs, to keep them, and to improve their wage rates.[18]

Given both the ability of and the deference granted to the Irish priesthood and given also the steady if slow evolution of an American Irish lay leadership in politics, in business, and in society, it is understandable that eventually the Irish in America at times suffered not from a lack of leadership but from a surfeit. A dramatic example early in the nineteenth century was the series of sporadic contests over control of the property of Catholic parishes: should control be exercised by bishops, by priests, by the laymen who had contributed most of the money, or by some combination of these? Occasionally the "trusteeship" controversy extended even to the prerogative of selecting an appropriate priest for the parish. American civil law tended to assign control of property to those persons, usually laymen, who had provided it. It did not seem implausible, furthermore, that laymen with demonstrated skills and accomplishments in the world of business should have the decisive voice in deciding business options confronting a parish. But it seldom proved the case that matters of worldly moment could be neatly separated from matters of felt spiritual significance. Anyway, priests and bishops were not disposed to defer to, or even to cooperate as equals with, lay "leaders." A large number of the conflicts which ensued involved Irish priests and non-Irish congregations, but quite enough conflicts pitted Irish clergy against Irish laity to make the very word "trusteeism" a bugaboo. In the upshot, partly because of the abilities, determination, and persistence of the clergy and partly because most American states eventually made it legally possible to vest control of all church property in the bishop as a "corporation sole," by the end of the century "trusteeism" was for the Irish little more than an unpleasant memory of a time when they were sorting out which leaders to follow. Henceforth, among Irish Catholics the clergy would be the unquestioned leaders in all matters remotely involving the Church.[19] When the Catholic University of America was established with a board of trustees that included wealthy Catholic laymen along with a preponderance of bishops, it was tacitly understood that the laymen would withdraw whenever "sensitive" measures were under discussion.[20] It was the duty of the faithful to be faithful—just as it was the duty of the precinct worker to follow the direction of the district leader.

By the time of the Civil War, therefore, with at least two million Irish-born or children of Irish parents in America, patterns of leadership highly suitable to the Irish past and present had developed. In a deeply politicized society, Irishmen had established their usefulness as leaders of street gangs, as "shoulder-hitters," as district leaders and ward bosses who could turn out the vote—through friendship, through rational persuasion, through "hurrah," through not very seriously disguised techniques of coercion and violence. Only a few had yet achieved the prestige of being aldermen; most Irish political leaders were still outside the civics textbook table of formal political organization. The Irish, therefore, could satisfy only imperfectly the natural desire of an immigrant group for "recognition." They were reasonably suspicious of appeals made to them, they felt, out of necessity rather than shared sympathies, such as that of General Winfield Scott in 1852: "I think I hear again that rich brogue that betokens a son of old Ireland. I love to hear it! I heard it on the Niagara in '14, and again in the Valley of Mexico. . . ." To which, not unfairly, the *Irish American* replied, "Gineral, Gineral, you are a big delulherer!"[21]

The predicament of the Irish, possessed of very considerable but not decisive political power (except in local elections), was painfully demonstrated by the unmistakably anti-Irish elements in the Know-Nothing surge in the 1850s. Though nativists of that type were unable to carry through any permanent legislative proscription of ethnic political or social activity, they were able to exclude for a time Irish Americans from most political offices in states like Massachusetts. At least as galling, they were able to harass the Church by authorizing "sniffing" investigations of churches and convents, as well as making life miserable for prominent Catholic clergymen, especially Gaetano Cardinal Bedini, sent by the Pope to assess the progress of Catholicism in America.[22] From the perspective of later generations, Know-Nothingism was really "the last hurrah" of overt, nationwide, anti-Irish politics.[23] Even in the 1850s it helped strengthen the hand of defenders of the faith like Archbishop Hughes, whose militant leadership seemed entirely appropriate. Nearly a century later, an Irish politician like James Michael Curley found it useful in consolidating Irish American support to invoke the memory of the preposterous and often obscene antics of the Know-Nothings.[24]

By about 1860, too, the Irish had also succeeded in gaining effective control of the Roman Catholic Church in America. Not only had trusteeism been squelched; even more, though non-Catholics continued to proselytize, the clergy was in a position to take vigorous and confident steps to prevent "leakage." Men like Hughes devoted only a small part of their time to exchanging apostolic blows and knocks with Protestant seducers; they devoted even less effort to putting down such articulate non-Irish Catholics as Orestes Brownson, who dared to question Irish hegemony within the Church; most of the energy of the clergy could be devoted to building the churches, schools, and charitable institutions which, staffed by Irish priests and nuns, would serve and safeguard the Irish immigrant and his family.[25] To describe Catholicism as the church of the immigrants was to speak of the present and the future with confidence, not with apprehension.

In firm control of the Church and with a good grasp on the lower rungs of the political system, Irish Americans in the latter half of the nineteenth century were confronted with new problems requiring new types and new techniques of leadership, not so much to supplant as to supplement the old. An enormously absorbing issue was the possibility that the Irish who had fled to America might be the key figures in securing the redemption of the old country from British misrule. From the ignominious failure of Young Ireland in 1848 to the establishment of an independent Ireland in 1921, Irish in America were intimately involved in virtually every effort to expel British soldiery, to secure a juster representation in Westminster, or to reform the system of land tenures.[26] One of the earliest, most straightforward, and most completely unsuccessful enterprises was the series of Fenian adventures. Sinn Fein, and its parallel organization, the Irish Revolutionary Brotherhood, were founded before the American Civil War; American membership burgeoned during the War, when Irish Americans, north and south, imagined that their hard-earned military skills would serve them well against Britain. Sinn Fein, rent with factionalism from the beginning, did manage to establish a headquarters in Union Square in New York, from which the Fenian flag was conspicuously hung and from which the organization issued letters of marque and reprisal and in other ways conducted itself as a sovereign nation—until President Grant finally balked. No doubt his decision stemmed partly from the smashing of the Irish rising in 1867, in which a few "Americans" took part, and even more from the pathetically inept invasions of Canada from St. Albans, Vermont, in 1866 and 1870. At its height, the Brotherhood may have counted 45,000 members; yet over 100,000 persons attended a picnic in Yorkville in 1866. Years later, Finley Peter Dunne was to wisecrack that if Ireland "cud be freed by a picnic, it'd not only be free today, but an empire."[27] But such turnouts of Irish Americans were important. Their presence affirmed the solidarity they felt in America; the oratory they heard demonstrated that even if Canada or Westminster or Dublin was beyond their reach, they were no hapless, feckless, insignificant peasant immigrants, but independent Americans to be reckoned with; they were affirming their right to a full measure of self-respect. The point was not lost on either Irish American or native American leaders.

Still, throughout the long, shifting struggle—replete with New Departures, preoccupation with Home Rule, or Land Leagues, or the reform of the land system—and despite the huge popularity in America of such striking figures as O'Donovan Rossa, John Devoy, Alexander Sullivan, and Michael Davitt—leadership in Irish America remained pretty firmly in the hands of those unmistakably committed to life in America. The increasingly prosperous businessmen tended to grumble that Irish nationalist endeavors were "a waste of time"; the clergy were obliged to condemn all calls for violence and to reproach as "socialism" some of the proposals for land distribution or nonpayment of rents; those New York Irish, now in control of Tammany, while yielding to no one in the bitterness of their vituperation of the English, were unwilling to ask their supporters to follow Henry George when he campaigned for the mayoralty of New York on a platform of justice to Irish and American farmers; Tammany had nominated Abram Hewitt who was safely Democratic and (it was hoped) more unqualifiedly committed to American interests.

Incarnating the proper balance of Irish and American interests was Patrick Ford. Born in Ireland in 1837 and brought to America at the age of seven, he served an apprenticeship with Garrison on *The Liberator*. Probably more important, as editor for many years of *The Irish World*, he rallied Irish Americans to a wide variety of causes and indignations, but he always stopped short of demanding that they choose, irrevocably, between support of change in Ireland and their dearly won gains in economic, religious, and political status in America. Better than most Irish American nationalists, he recognized the precariousness of the Irish achievements; they lacked, for example, the wealth of the German Jews, and they needed, unlike British immigrants, to prove that Gaelic interests were as "legitimate" as Anglo-Saxon ones. Under Ford's leadership, *The Irish World* managed to tread the narrow line between "despair and enthusiasm, jealousy and cynicism."[28] If Ford was obliged to forego the gratification of leading a gloriously noble lost cause, he never forfeited the respect of American priests, politicians, and businessmen, nor the affection of the Irish American masses.

By the late nineteenth century, an increasing number of Irish Americans had scrambled their way up to middle-class amenity. Looking through the lace curtains they could afford at the newcomers from Ireland and at the "shanty Irish" who still considered themselves fortunate to have a hod to carry or a wheelbarrow to shove, these "successful" Irish Americans were all too painfully aware that their curtains were necessary to shield *them* from the not generally friendly gaze of non-Catholics. All too easily lampooned by Harrigan and Hart in plays like "O Reilly and the Four Hundred" and too frequently reproached by such social arbiters as Lelia Hardin Bugg, who deplored the "low manners" of the "people of our parish," the lace-curtain Irish required a different kind of spokesman.[29] One such was John Boyle O'Reilly. His "Irish" credentials were unchallengable. Born in the old country to a middle-class family, he had early laid to rest any suspicion of being a member of the establishment, by being sentenced to death and exiled to Australia on his conviction of treason against the British Army which he had, with conscious duplicity, joined.[30] Escaping to America, he helped edit *The*

Boston Pilot, from 1870 to 1890, at the same time publishing a large amount of poetry and prose. He publicly sympathized with the plight of the black freedmen, hoping that many would some day become Catholics and intermarry with whites. He certainly incurred no shame, and yet avoided suicide, in boxing with John L. Sullivan. He wanted good done, but he effectively ridiculed "do-gooders." He was not terrified by the epithet of "socialism" which he saw flung at those working, admirably he thought, to improve the conditions of the working class. Yet his own political science was "Jeffersonian" enough to reassure the Catholic and non-Catholic bourgeoisie.

He was the premier figure among an increasing number of writers, many of them women, who in poetry, prose, and drama helped the Irish to see themselves as they wanted to be seen. His aesthetic was conventionally Victorian, though he no doubt pleased his compatriots with his contention that Anglo-Saxons were preoccupied with facts while Irish poets reached toward Truth. Most of his writing is eminently forgettable. but he wrote one sharp-edged couplet about

> the organized charity, scrimped and iced
> In the name of a cautious, statistical Christ.

It was characteristic of him that he wanted "pride without bitterness," and he succeeded remarkably, and not only with the Irish; he became, also, in the patronizing phrase of the Brahmins, Boston's favorite Irishman. He was asked to deliver poetic tributes on the death of Wendell Phillips and at the dedication of the monument to Crispus Attucks. Strikingly, he was asked to write the poem for the dedication of Plymouth Rock in 1887. O'Reilly's life in America was a continuously troubled one. Irish nationalists and socialists, lace-curtain and shanty Irish, condescending Brahmins and close friends like William Dean Howells, rabid anti-Catholics and the Catholic hierarchy to whom he sedulously deferred, rebellious priests—all these and others looked constantly over his shoulder. He deeply felt his marginality, suffered desperately from insomnia, and died at the age of forty-six, probably from an overdose of sleeping pills. He felt more of the pains than the exhilarations of leadership.

By the late nineteenth century, a substantial number of Catholic workers had acquired the skills and the time-in-rank to regard themselves, and to be regarded as, more than casual labor. On the industrial and mining frontier, this was not always the case; in the coal fields of Pennsylvania, the "Molly Maguires" responded to what they regarded as soulless oppression by American and British employers and supervisors with a movement that combined inarticulate rage, the rhetoric and primitive organization of the Ancient Order of the Hibernians, an embryonic trade-unionism, and a ready recourse to violence. Overwhelmed by economic and political power and driven to secrecy by the brutal tactics, legal or tacitly sanctioned, of the standing order, the Molly Maguires produced no important leaders; their legacy was the need for more careful organization, more prudent tactics, and concentration in areas where Irish workers had achieved a more commanding position. All these conditions were met in the American Federation of Labor. Except in the needle trades, most of the workers in the federation were Irish; they were completely in sympathy with the aspirations of Gompers for "more and more" and with his predilection for working "within the system."[31]

The Knights of Labor from its beginnings in 1869 had less clearly defined notions about membership or goals. Terence V. Powderly, born in Pennsylvania in 1849, became Master in 1879. He was well aware that the order's rituals seemed quasi-Masonic (and so intolerable) to many Catholic clergy and that its commitment to secrecy—even if, as he arranged, it could be breached in the confessional—appeared to jeopardize the clergy's exclusive responsibility for the care of souls.[32] "Between the men who love God and the men who don't believe in God," he lamented, "I have a hard time of it."[33] Threatened with condemnation by papal authorities, the Knights were cautiously but effectively supported by James Cardinal Gibbons and other "Americanist" prelates; after years of maneuvering. Rome declared in 1886 that the order "can be tolerated." Whatever relief this brought Powderly was vitiated by a series of defeats the Knights suffered in the next few years in the economic arena. In the 1890s Powderly abandoned the labor movement when he was appointed Commissioner of Immigration by President McKinley; later he left the Church. His own travails and those of his clerical supporters were not without meaning, however, for the Irish in America. They benefited from the prominence of an Irish labor leader, even one more gifted in flamboyant rhetoric than in ability or willingness to foster labor militancy. The existence of the Knights—and Gibbons' deft defense of them in Rome—made it possible for Irish workers to seek to improve their lot without confining themselves to the all-Irish or all-Catholic unions which conservative Catholics in America and Rome considered the only appropriate modality. If Powderly was condemned to be a marginal man because of the times in which he lived, William Green and George Meany were confronted with no such predicament.

Meanwhile, Irish power increased steadily, especially in the cities. Tweed was the last non-Irish Catholic to be the leader of Tammany until the 1950s, and though it was necessary at first—in the 1880s—in order to win mayority elections in New York or Boston to nominate lace-curtain Irish like Hugh O'Brien and William Grace, by the turn of the century the Irish-dominated machines could be defeated only by a precarious "fusion" of Republicans, "renegade" Irishmen, independents, and other ethnic groups.[34] Control of city politics meant not only that Irish in need could receive aid more regularly, and on a larger scale, than had been the case when it was necessary to depend on a sympathetic Irish alderman. It also ensured that such key instrumentalities of civil power as the police were now firmly in Irish hands. It was strikingly different from the 1850s, when, after considerable effort, Barney McGinniskillen, twenty-two years in the United States, could win appointment to the Boston force only to be dismissed shortly afterward as an unworthy cop, too "fresh from the bogs of Ireland."[35] Whatever the intentions of Americans in developing a "professional" police force in the major cities, the result was that by the end of the century Irish Americans had adquired a near monopoly of the police power. This power was large by statute and enormous in fact because of the great discretion entrusted to officials whose theoretical obligations to preserve law and order were limited only by the occasional, usually ineffectual, protest against excesses or willful obliviousnesses. As a result, the Irish cop became a more effective and ubiquitous leader than either the local political leader or the parish priest.[36]

Many Irish Americans had, by the end of the century, also won positions of prominence on the managing boards of public asylums, prisons, and schools. The Third Plenary Council of the Church, meeting in Baltimore in 1884, had adjured priests to establish parochial schools, and, where these were created, they rested—like the Catholic high schools which also began to be built—firmly in the hands of clerical, usually Irish, leaders.[37] But at no point were more than one-half of the Catholic children attending school able or willing to attend church schools, so the ability of Irish laymen to ensure that most public schools would not be blatantly anti-Catholic was an important gain. In addition, many young Irish American women became teachers in the public schools. If they were regarded as less omniscient than the nuns in parochial schools, they did enjoy prestige; and their presence rendered it unlikely that Catholic children would have to choose between the injunctions of Catholic priests, Catholic parents, and Protestant public school teachers.

Precisely because the Irish leaders of city machines no longer faced effective challenges from native Americans, they were able, and often willing, to abandon a narrow tribalism. They could solicit support from newer ethnic groups. For example, the large number of Jews in New York were induced not to elect a Jewish Socialist to Congress because Tammany under Charley Murphy had secured the election of Henry Goldfogle.[38] Murphy also recognized that second- and third-generation Irish, like Al Smith, favored a kind of state action which earlier Irish leaders would have rejected out-of-hand. Jane Addams, in Chicago, received crucial, if unexpected, support from Boss Tim Sullivan.

An increasing number of Irish Americans came to realize that the traditional near-automatic identification of Irishmen with the Democratic party was deleterious to Irish interests; many simply found the somewhat more bourgeois commitments of the Republican party more congenial to their ideals than were the compromises of the Democratic party. The most striking illustration of this trend was Archbishop John Ireland of St. Paul.[39] Born in Ireland and migrating at an early age with his family to the midwest, Ireland rose rapidly in the Church and in the estimation of non-Catholic America. A much-revered chaplain with the northern armies in the Civil War, a lionized figure in Minnesota political and economic circles, he came to believe deeply that the well-being of the Irish and of the Church was inextricably tied to the well-being and progress of the United States. He could not conceive that any real conflict of interest could exist. A vigorous supporter of parochial schools, he was quite willing to affirm to the National Education Association his support of the public school system; "withered be the hand," he declared melodramatically in 1890, "raised in sign of its destruction!" Though his attempts to work out compromises by which schools with Catholic students and Catholic teachers could be absorbed, financially, within the Minnesota public school system were frustrated by the protests of militant Catholics and non-Catholics, he was not dismayed. He also supported "total abstinence"—to the consternation of visiting French Catholic friends—and was an advocate of anti-saloon legislation and, at least in rural areas, of state prohibition legislation. He disliked Irish nationalist agitation, fearing that such enterprises would persuade Americans that Catholics were unpatriotic. He persuaded his friend, Cushman Davis, Republican Senator from Minnesota, to attack in Congress the efforts of German Catholics and others to persuade Rome to appoint prelates of German, Polish, and Italian origin. He refused to heed the not very subtle requests from Rome that he declare himself an unqualified supporter of the rights of the Pope to be a temporal ruler of part of Italy. He was an outspoken Republican; his pamphlet attacking Bryan's notions on free silver was circulated throughout the United States. He was probably the key man in persuading McKinley to appoint Joseph as Attorney General and later to elevate him to the Supreme Court. His offices were decisive in securing an effective Catholic voice in the commission which negotiated the disposition of the Friars' Lands in the Philippines after the American occupation. If to many Irish Catholics he was too much the sycophant to non-Catholic power, he was undeniably effective in modifying the total identification of Catholics and Irish Americans and Democrats the dangers attendant on such an identification. No man was more influential than Ireland in precluding any real successes by the American Protective Association (APA), that ominously anti-Catholic organization of the 1890s. If he could not persuade McKinley to denounce APA explicitly, he was effective behind the scenes. Many Irish Catholics in New York wanted a show-down with the APA at that state's constitutional convention; Ireland's allies effectively maneuvered to block APA initiatives, with the result that though state aid to parochial schools was outlawed, a constitutional provision safeguarded the right of Catholic clergy to visit Catholics in state asylums and penitentiaries. No doubt the APA was an anachronism, given the growth of Catholic power in America. But men like Ireland played a crucial role in denying it more attention than it deserved and in hastening its passage into oblivion.[40]

Ireland's willingness to work with non-Catholics and his conspicuous lack of charity toward German Catholics and the more militant Irish Catholics—Bishop Bernard McQuaid of Rochester for example, and Archbishop Michael Corrigan of New York—prevented Ireland from ever being the leader he wanted to be in the Church. Even James Cardinal Gibbons of Baltimore, the most dulcet of men, did not escape the accusations of McQuaid and Corrigan of truckling to non-Catholic America. As Irish Americans achieved diverse positions, they needed and sought out diverse leaders and supported diverse strategies. It was inevitable, therefore, that conflict among Irish leaders would occasionally break out.

Perhaps the most poignant example of such conflict was the career of Edward McGlynn, pastor of St. Stephen's in New York City, a man characterized by an admiring biographer as "rebel, priest, and prophet."[41] His vigorous support of social reform, and especially of the ideals and campaigns of Henry George, won him a wide following among his large, lower middle-class parish and also among many other Catholics and non-

Catholics. It did not endear him to Tammany, nor to diocesan leaders. A Democratic politician inquired of Thomas Preston, Archbishop Corrigan's vicar-general, whether McGlynn spoke for the Church. In an open letter, Preston replied that "the great majority of the Catholic Church in this city are opposed to the candidacy of Mr. George," believing his principles unsafe and "contrary to the teachings of the Church." Solemnly disavowing any attempt to intervene in a civil election, Preston continued that the Church "would not wish to be misunderstood at a time when the best interests of society may be in danger."[42] After George's defeat, Archbishop Corrigan issued a pastoral letter condemning George's theories, and McGlynn countered with such a vigorous defense both of George and of his own rights to speak out, that he was suspended from the priesthood. When he refused to go to Rome, he was excommunicated for his contumacy. Somewhat later, Ireland and his allies, worried about the public reaction to this treatment of a popular priest, paved the way for the restoration of McGlynn; "this will break Corrigan's heart," Ireland uncharitably added.[43]

Though only handfuls of Irish immigrated to America in the twentieth century, the Irish Americans have not disappeared from sight, nor have distinctively Irish-American leaders. Andrew Greeley, growing up in Chicago in the 1930s, would recollect forty years later that the Irishness of his family was real if "unself-conscious."[44] In his parish and in the resort in Wisconsin to which his family was able to migrate in summertimes, he encountered few non-Catholics. In Chicago he was more aware of his neighborhood than of his parish. His father was a stalwart member of the Knights of Columbus. Moderately prosperous, his family was on easy, but not especially deferential, terms with priests and with politicians, Irish and non-Irish alike.

In a less heterogeneous metropolis like Boston, the lines between the Irish and "the others" were both more real and more self-conscious. There, a professional Irishman like James Michael Curley could carry on a generally successful political career on the old bases of Christmas baskets for the Irish poor and of mellifluous attacks on both blatant anti-Catholics like the second Ku Klux Klan and the sense of superiority shown the Irish by the Lodges, Cabots, and Saltonstalls.[45] Elsewhere in the country, Irish city leaders retained for a time their control over political machines by their sensitivity to the wants of newer arrivals and by their skill in forging electoral coalitions. Ultimately, such leaders were rendered largely superfluous by the activities of the welfare state and the welfare nation. But a highly skillful and able commander like Mayor

Daley of Chicago not only weathered this competition, and the obloquy of liberal critics. but with exquisite timing delivered the crucial delegates to the presidential candidacy of Jimmy Carter in June, 1976.

Nationally, a steadily increasing number of Irish Americans won positions of prominence. It was the "bad luck of the Irish" that one of the ablest of them Governor Al Smith of New York, should seek to be elected president in 1928. In that year, no Democrat, certainly no one so proudly representative of urban America, certainly no one so openly contemptuous of the noble experiment of prohibition, could have defeated Herbert Hoover, the symbol of peace and middle-class prosperity. Smith's Catholicism and his proud Irishness undoubtedly hurt him, and his overwhelming defeat at the polls corroborated Irish Americans' sense of the ineluctable hostility of non-Catholic America. If Smith could not be elected (it was easy to conclude), America was as alien as ever to legitimate Irish demands for "recognition,"[46] The bitter memory of Smith's defeat made all the more glorious the election of John F. Kennedy in 1960. No more than in any election could one scientifically conclude that one attribute was decisive. But, beyond dispute, it was a "great day for the lrish." Ironically enough, the close circle of O'Briens and O'Donnels whom Kennedy brought with him to the White House came to be called the "Irish Mafia." Equally ironically, that epitome of Yankee America, Robert Frost, adjured Kennedy to be more "Irish than Harvard." But such ironies could be ignored. It was enough that the long proscription—the long heritage of "No Irish Need Apply"—was ended in the most dramatic way America could demonstrate.

Irish Americans also achieved in the twentieth century almost complete emancipation from the responsibility of promoting Irish nationhood. President Woodrow Wilson, though speaking feelingly of the right of national self-determination for peoples, maintained, like many Americans, some reservations about separatist movements from Great Britain. And his relations with outspoken Irish-American nationalists like Daniel Cohalan were openly hostile. But if Wilson did little in America, or at the Versailles Peace Conference, to advance the cause of an independent Ireland, other American politicians were more sympathetic.[47] They welcomed in 1921 the formation of the Irish Free State. During World War II, Irish-American leaders were not harassed for the balky neutrality of Eire. Even when, beginning in the late 1960s, some Irishmen proved willing to kill or be killed in order to incorporate Ulster into Eire, only a handful of Irish Americans attempted to act out a dual loyalty, confident that American patriotism *required* a militant support of total Irish independence of Britain. Irreconcilables like Paul O'Dwyer, a prominent Democratic leader in New York, helped raise money to aid the suffering Catholics in Northern Ireland and to provide munitions for tiny groups like the "Provisional" faction of the IRA seeking to advance the cause of unification by blowing up passersby in Ireland and England. But the great majority of Irish Americans, as well as the Irish government in Dublin, openly condemned violence. *Ireland irridenta* was not a fighting faith in America any longer.

The progress of the Irish in America toward psychological autonomy —away from the helplessness and near-destitution that had for generations made necessary special political, religious, and social leadership— was steady but slow, especially when measured, as many Irish Americans did measure it, by the rise of American Jews. The onset of the Great Depression in the 1930s belied the promise of American life. Andrew Greeley's father, for example, lost almost everything he had earned, and he subsided, his son records, into a kind of "somber, serious" mood.[48] It was no doubt similar reversals, occurring just when the achievement of middle-class status seemed certain, that made attractive the demagoguery of Curley in Boston and, nationwide, the spectacular popularity of Father Charles Coughlin, "the radio priest," who preached in reassuring brogue his demands for economic and political reform— demands which he laced with assaults on international Jewish bankers and on the gradualism of New Deal experiments.[49] After Catholic Church leaders had cracked down, and after the boom produced by World War II rendered Couglin's extremism implausible, fears of Russian power abroad and communist subversion in America gave to Senator Joseph McCarthy of Wisconsin a brief moral authority. Both Coughlin and McCarthy sought, and found, a constituency by no means identical with Irish America. Indeed, the influence of each was limited by the outspoken opposition of other Irish Americans; Monsignor John Ryan was Coughlin's most implacable and most effective antagonist, and McCarthy might temporarily silence but he never eliminated the aversion of Irish Americans who, no less opposed to Communism, saw no need to adopt his "rule or ruin" tactics.[50] Each man distracted Irish America; neither was able to command its whole-hearted loyalty. In the long run, the economic power of Joseph Kennedy was more important; the "eldest Kennedy" could obtain the ambassadorship to England for himself, high-status education for his children, senatorships for three of his sons, and the presidency for one of them.

Finally, Irish Americans, remaining loyal to the Roman Catholic Church, no longer needed to look to priests and bishops for the same kind of leadership as in previous years. A rapidly increasing number of men and women brought to Catholic life the higher education and the professional skills which relieved the clergy from providing leadership in every area of life, social and intellectual. Even in specifically religious spheres, Irish Americans increasingly looked to the clergy for enlightenment and persuasion rather than uncomplicated *ipse dixits*.[51] Especially after Vatican II, with its emphasis on "the people of God," the found themselves assigned a far more defined, though no less exigent, leadership. And they could not rely on a united clerical front. With a capable theologian like the Reverend Charles Curran of the faculty of The Catholic University making public his dissent from the encyclical of Paul VI, *Humanae Vitae*; with Jesuits like the Berrigan brothers taking issue with both civil and religious authorities in calling for militant opposition to the Vietnam War; with a persuasive publicist like the Reverend Andrew Greeley regularly censuring not only Curran and the Berrigans but all his ecclesiastical superiors; and with the proliferation of lay journals like the *National Catholic Reporter* joining the hitherto lonely *Commonweal* and *Catholic Worker* in espousing norms for Catholic thought and action; the priest or diocesan still might win a role of leadership, but he had to win it; it was not bestowed upon him by his ordination.

Furthermore, the Church, though still drawing a disproportionate number of its leaders from among Irish-Americans, now responded more generously to the very large numbers of Germans, Italians, Poles, and other European ethnic groups in its constituency, as well as to swelling numbers of emigrants of Catholic denomination from Latin America.[52] By the middle of the twentieth century, the Church in America was moving toward ecumenicism, not just in regard to Catholic immigrants but also to non-Catholics, white and black. The leadership of Robert Lucey, Archbishop of San Antonio, was as important to Irish Americans as that of John Hughes of New York a century earlier, but it was of a very different character. Similar changes affected Catholic educational institutions; parochial schools enrolled many non-Catholics, especially blacks in the inner cities. And Irish Americans saw no anomaly in supporting "the fighting Irish of Notre Dame," coached by Ara Parseghian, an Armenian Protestant, and starring players who were Protestant and Catholic, black and white.

An ethnic group, if it is to survive, finds, or is given, or develops the leaders it needs. Over the long history of the Irish in America, there has been no dearth of Irish needs, and the variety of leaders—charismatic or programmatic, eloquent in voice or effective in achievement, rogues or saints, those anathema to the non-Irish, or favorite Irishmen among the most reluctant Boston Brahmins—is evidence of the variety of Irish Americans and of their resources and resiliency. Hoping for everything in American life, they secretly expected little. The combination of exuberant optimism and mordant pessimism conduced to a proliferation of leaders whose enterprises ensured that Irish Americans would never be ignored. It was characteristic of Irish America that its most prepotent hero, John F. Kennedy, demurred when he was told that his election had finally laid to rest the awful bugaboo of anti-Catholicism (and anti-Irishness). That would depend, he rejoined, on the course of subsequent events.[53] ✦

NOTES

1. I have drawn freely upon a wide variety of excellent general histories of the Irish in America. Among the most useful are: Carl Wittke, *The Irish in America* (Baton Rouge, 1956); William V. Shannon, *The American Irish* (New York, 1963); John B. Duff, *The Irish in the United States* (Belmont, Calif., 1971), Andrew M. Greeley, *That Most Distressful Nation* (Chicago, 1972); Thomas N. Brown, *Irish-American Nationalism, 1870-1890* (Philadelphia, 1966); Nathan Glazer and Daniel P. Moynihan, *Beyond the Melting Pot* (Cambridge, Mass., 1963); and Oscar Handlin, *Boston's Immigrants, 1790-1880* (Cambridge, Mass., 1959). Lawrence McCaffrey's excellent *The Irish Diaspora in America* (Bloomington, Ind., 1976) was published after I had finished this paper.
2. Harrison Gray Otis of Massachusetts, cited in Jones, *American Immigration* (Chicago, 1960), p. 85.
3. Boigraphical details are drawn from Brown, *Irish-American Nationalism*, p. 25.
4. John A. Hawgood, *The Tragedy of German-America* (New York, 1940); John P. Diggins, *Mussolini and Fascism: The View from America* (Princeton, 1972).
5. Moynihan, "The Irish," in Glazer and Moynihan, *Beyond the Melting Pot.*
6. Shannon, *The American Irish*, p. 52.
7. *Ibid.*, pp. 52-54.
8. *Ibid.*, p. 78.
9. Cecil B. Woodham-Smith *The Great Hunger: Ireland,* 1845-1849 (New York, 1962).
10. William L. Riordan, *Plunkitt of Tammany Hall* (New York, paperback ed., 1963).

11. W. T. Stead, *If Christ Came to Chicago* (Chicago, 1894), is a fair example of the Christian perfectionism of many Protestant exponents of the Social Gospel.

12. Emmet Larkin, *The Roman Catholic Church and the Creation of the Modern Irish State,* 1878-1886 (Philadelphia, 1975).

13. In 1852 at least one-third of the 1,500 Roman Catholic priests in the United States were Irish-born or of Irish stock. See T. T. MeAvoy, "The Irish Clergymen," in *The United States*, vol. 6, in *A History of Irish Catholicism*, Patrick J. Corish, ed. (Dublin, 1970), p. 19.

14. The Paulist fathers, whose special mission was to non-Catholic America, were sometimes slightingly referred to as "Protestant priests." Quoted in Robert D. Cross, *The Emergence of Liberal Catholicism in America* (Cambridgc, Mass, 1958), p. 51.

15. Quoted in ibid., p. 168.

16. Ray A. Billington, *The Protestant Crusade, 1800-1860: A Study of The Origins of American Nativism* (New York, 1938).

17. B. C. Cronin, *Father Yorke and the Labor Movement in San Francisco, 1900-1910* (Washington, 1943); A. I. Abell, "The Reception of Leo XIII's Labor Encyclical," *Review of Politics* 7 (October, 1945):486.

18. Gregory Baum, ed., *Journeys: The Impact of Personal Experience on Religious Thought* (New York, 1975), p. 170.

19. R. F. McNamara "Trusteeism in the Atlantic States, 1785-1863," *Catholic Historical* 30 (July, 1944): passim.

20. Quoted in Shannon, F. Egan, *Recollections of a Happy Life* (New York, 1924).

21. Quoted in Shannon, *The American Irish*, p. 51.

22. Billington, *The Protestant Crusade*, passim.

23. John Higham, *Strangers in the Land* (New Brunswick, N.J., 1955).

24. Stanley Coben, "The Assault on Victorianism," *American Quarterly* 27 (December, 1975):621-23.

25. J. P. Dolan, *The Immigrant Church: New York's Irish and German Catholics 1815-1865* (Baltimore, 1975) shows however, that despite the strenuous efforts of priests and laymen to provide "bricks and mortar," immigration continued at such a rate that at no time in the nineteenth century were there more than half the churches and schools needed. Shortages continued in the twentieth century when other Catholic immigrant groups surpassed in numbers those from Ireland.

26. In the section that follows, I have relied especially heavily on Brown, *Irish-American Nationalism*, for both interpretation and specific details.

27. Quoted in ibid., p. xv.

28. *Ibid.* p. xvii.

29. On Harrigan and Hart, see Shannon, *The American Irish*, p. 143; Lelia Hardin Bugg, *The People of Our Parish* (Boston, 1900).

30. On O'Reilly, see Arthur Mann, *Yankee Reformers in the Urban Age: Social Reform in Boston,* 1880 -1900 (Cambridge, Mass., 1954), pp. 24-51.

31. Shannon *The American Irish, p. 140;* Philip Taft, *The AFofL in the Time of Gompers* (New York, 1957), and Taft, *The AFofL from the Death of the Gompers to the Merger* (New York, 1959)

32. Terence V. Powderly, *The Path I Trod* (New York, 1940); Henry J. Browne, *The Catholic Church and the Knights of Labor (*Washington, 1949).

33. Shannon, *The American Irish,* p. 127.

34. See, for example. Edwin R. Lewinson, *John Purroy Mitchel: The Boy Mayor of New York* (New York, 1965).

35. Roger Lane, *Policing the City: Boston, 1822-1885* (Cambridge, Mass., 1967), p. 93. In New York considerable numbers of Irish were on the force in the 1850s; see James F. Richardson, *The New York Police: Colonial Times to 1901* (New York, 1970).

36. Leadership in American localities has always been handicapped by the enormous geographic mobility of the population. A stream of local studies has demonstrated that "persistence rates"—whether in Trempeleau County or Newburyport—have been very low. In such a milieu, longstanding *personal* leadership was seldom possible. Instead, one was more likely to be recognized as a leader because one occupied a recognized position in a recognized institution: the church, the political machine, the police force. Because the Irish early came to dominate such institutions, they were leaders in a way not readily available to outstanding men in other ethnic groups.

37. Robert D. Cross, "Origins of the Catholic Parochial Schools in America," *American Benedictine Review* 16 (June, 1965):194-209.

38. Arthur Gorenstein, "A Portrait of Ethnic Polities: The Socialists and the 1908 and 1910 Congressional Elections on the East Side," *Publication of the American Jewish Historical Society* 50 (March, 1961):202—38. See also Nancy J. Weiss, *Charles Francis Murphy, 1858-1924: Respectability and Responsibility in Tammany Politics* (Northampton, Mass., 1968).

39. Biographical details are to be found in James H. Moynihan, *The Life of Archbishop John Ireland* (New York, 1953). See also Cross, *Emergence of Liberal Catholicism,* passim.

40. Donald Kinzer, *An Episode in Anti-Catholicism* (Seattle, 1963).

41. Stephen Bell, *Rebel, Priest, and Prophet: A Biography of Edward McGlynn* (New York, 1937).

42. Quoted in Cross, *Emergence of Liberal Catholicism*, p. 121.

43. *Ibid.*, p. 123.

44. Quoted in Baum, ed., *Journeys*, p. 171.

45. Shannon, *The American Irish,* pp. 201-32.

46. *Ibid.*, 151-81.

47. Carl Wittke, *The Irish in America* (Baton Rouge, 1956), p. 282; John B. Duff, "The Politics of Revenge: The Ethnic Policies of Woodrow Wilson" (Ann Arbor Microfilms, 1965).

48. Baum, ed., *Journeys*, p. 171; Greeley, *Distressful Nation*, p. 185.

49. Sheldon Marcus, *Father Coughlin: The Tumultuous Life of the Priest of the Little Flower* (Boston, 1973).

50. On Ryan, see Francis L. Broderick, *Right Reverend New Desler: John A. Ryan* (New York, 1963); on Irish Catholic reaction to MeCarthyism, see Shannon, *The American Irish,* pp. 367-91.

51. Daniel Callahan, *The Mind of the Catholic Layman* (New York, 1963).

52. For example, see Victor Greene, *For God and Country: The Rise of Polish and Lithuanian Ethnic Consciousness in America* (Madison, Wise., 1975).

53. Shannon, *The American Irish*, p. 413.

SINCE 1492: THE JEWISH EXPERIENCE IN AMERICA

RICHARD P. SHERMAN

In an 1820 letter Thomas Jefferson wrote that the United States was:

> The first to prove to the world two truths . . . that man can govern himself, and that religious freedom is the most effectual anodyne against religious dissension; the maxim of civil government being reversed in that of religion, where its true form is "divided we stand, united we fall."

American cultivation of religious and political equalitarianism has produced a land of liberty and opportunity for ethnic and religious groups. Jews, as well as others, have responded, have benefited, and have given of themselves in the development of the country.

The story of Jewish involvement in America actually goes back to the year 1492. Columbus mentions in his journal that the year he made his voyage the Jews were expelled from Spain. Since Jews had played a prominent part in the cultural development of the Iberian peninsula and felt at home there, it was to be expected that not all of them took part in the exodus from Spain. Many remained and converted to Christianity. For some the conversion was sincere; for others it was a matter of convenience as they continued secretly to practice Judaism. In either case, these *conversos* or *Nuevos Christianos* were viewed with suspicion by Church authorities.

Eventually these converts and their descendants were to be called "Marranos." The etymology of the term is somewhat obscure but it seems to be derived from an old Spanish word meaning "swine," thereby expressing the contempt and hatred felt by the Spanish population towards this new group. The Inquisition was introduced to try and judge those accused of heresy for Judaizing. Its sentences were announced at an *Auto-da-fe* (Act of Faith), and those who were to be executed were formally condemned by civil authorities and taken by soldiers to the *quemadero* (place of burning).

Some historians have suggested that Columbus himself came from a Marrano family but the evidence is not convincing. However, his expedition was financially supported by Marranos, and a few members of his crew on that famous first voyage have been identified as Marranos.

In 1496 Jews were ordered expelled from Portugal but, paradoxically, forcible conversions, plus restrictions on their leaving, kept most of them in that country. Under the circumstances the Inquisition was extremely active and many of the Marranos tried to emigrate to the New World.

In the Americas many nations were involved in the European scramble for land. For several years the Dutch contested with the Portuguese for control of Brazil. Jews were welcomed into the Dutch areas, and in those places many Marranos openly professed their Judaism. As Portugal turned back the Dutch challenge and became sole master over Brazil, the Jews who had fought valiantly in the Dutch cause, fled. Some settled in Amsterdam; others in various Caribbean islands; and a small group arrived in New Amsterdam (the later New York City) in 1654. It should be pointed out that the first Jews who came to America were the Sephardim (the Hebrew word for Spain is *Sepharad*). These were the Jews from Spain and Portugal and their descendants. Later, the Ashkenazim (in Hebrew, *Ashkenaz* means Germany) began to arrive. This term is used to refer to the Jews from central and eastern Europe.

The Dutch West India Company forced a recalcitrant Peter Stuyvesant to admit the Jews into New Amsterdam with the proviso they support their own poor. The Dutch fight against Portugal in which the Jews lost all possessions, plus the fact that Jews were among the directors of the company, are given as reasons for the company's order.

However, the New Amsterdam government placed restrictions on the Jews so that they were not permitted to engage in certain occupations and were denied full political and civil rights. A hard struggle was waged by the Jews to obtain the right to serve in the militia; later the right to be burghers was granted them. But Stuyvesant never permitted the Jews to establish a synagogue, so religious services were conducted at home.

The English took possession of the colony in 1664 and the Jews received confirmation of the rights won from the Dutch government. At first, the prohibition against public worship remained since England's charter for the colony permitted freedom of worship only for all Christians. The Duke of York widened the religious provision so that

Jews were permitted to establish a house of worship. Over the years other rights were extended to Jews and they lived comfortably in the colony, but they did not receive full equality until the period of the American Revolution.

The treatment of Jews received in English America varied from open toleration to total exclusion. Because the Puritan colonies did not offer a friendly climate for Jews, a wide berth was given that area. In several colonies the Church of England, the established, official church in England, was organized and was the formal religion. Even there, due partly to the wide diversity of religion and dispersal of religious groups in the colonies, many sectarian groups were usually tolerated, although more in some colonies that in others.

The Calvert family established the Maryland colony as a refuge for persecuted Roman Catholics, but disputes soon arose in that colony between Catholics and Protestants. In an effort to resolve those troubles the Maryland Toleration Act granted religious freedom to all Roman Catholics and Protestant Trinitarians, but not to other groups. By contrast, in South Carolina, despite religious controversy and occasionally bigoted government officials, freedom of conscience was guaranteed to include "Jews, heathens, and dissenters" under John Locke's Fundamental Orders of Carolina.

Three colonies were especially known for their tolerant attitudes towards religious choice and contributed mightily to the development of the American principle of religious equalitarianism: these were Rhode Island, Pennsylvania, and Georgia.

Rhode Island, the colony established by Roger Williams on the principle of complete religious toleration, was a place where Jews could settle free of fear and harassment. Although Jews settled in the town of Newport within a few years of the settlement of New York, it was almost a century later before a group of Marrano merchants helped develop the prosperity of the Jewish community and of the city itself. During the colonial period Newport became the home of the largest and most flourishing Jewish community in the English colonies. The affluent members of that community made their living as shipowners and merchants. In the Revolution nearly all of that group took the American side, so that when the British captured Newport in 1776, their ships were confiscated, their businesses ruined, and the community dispersed.

In Pennsylvania William Penn also welcomed those of various religions to this colony. Harry Emerson Wildes, in his biography entitled *William Penn*, has suggested that, in part, Penn's friendly attitude towards the Indians was based on the belief that they were the descendants of the Ten Lost Tribes of Israel. The Jews entering the colony settled not only in Philadelphia but also in other communities, including the frontier trading town of Lancaster.

Georgia was another refuge for Jews. Soon after the start of the colony a group of Sephardic Jews from London arrived in the colony in 1733, hoping to engage in business and viticulture. A year later a group of poor German Jews arrived. Fleeing oppression, they had landed in London, where three members of the Jewish community, commissioned by the Georgia Trustees to raise money for the charter, used the money to send a group of these poor German Jews to the Georgia colony. General James Edward Oglethorpe, the colony's founder, ignored the instructions from the Trustees that the Jews "be given no encouragement" and, instead, welcomed them. Later, John Wesley, one of the founders of Methodism, came to know the Jews of Savannah and was favorably impressed by them.

By the time of the American Revolution there were about 2,500 Jews in the English colonies. Six hundred of these Jews fought for the American cause and some performed distinguished service. Francis Salvador, who had come to America in 1773, was selected a member of the South Carolina Provincial Congress. He rode his horse 28 miles to warn the militia commander of an impending British-instigated Indian attack, an episode that earned him the title of "the Southern Paul Revere." In helping to stem the attack Salvador was killed and scalped by the Indians.

Haym Salomon came to Philadelphia from Poland in 1772. During the Revolution he displayed great personal courage and was condemned to be hanged for revolutionary activities but escaped. Salomon is best remembered for having been instrumental in helping to finance the Revolution.

At the time George Washington was inaugurated as president of the United States, the six Jewish Congregations (Newport, Charleston, Savannah, New York City, Philadelphia, and Richmond) sent letters of congratulations to the first president. Washington's response to the Newport letter, certainly partly inspired by the Jewish role in the war, is a classic of American religious liberty and concludes in the spirit of the prophets Isaiah and Micah:

It is now no more than toleration is spoken of as if it were by the indulgence of one class of people that another enjoyed the exercise of their inherent natural right, for happily, the government of the United States, which gives to bigotry no sanction, to persecution no assistance, requires only that they who live under its protection shall demean themselves as good citizens in giving it on all occasions their effectual support. May the children of the stock of Abraham who dwell in this land continue to merit and enjoy the good will of the other inhabitants, while every one shall sit in safety under his own vine and fig tree, and there shall be none to make him afraid.

In 1852 Henry Wadsworth Longfellow made a visit to Newport. The city, long without Jews, was the setting as he concluded his poem, "The Jewish Cemetery at Newport," with a sad lament.

But ah! what once has been shall be no more!
The groaning earth in travail and in pain
Brings forth its races, but does not restore
And the dead nations never rise again.

While Newport's Jewish community had vanished, other communities continued to exist. By 1800 Charleston, South Carolina, was the home of the largest Jewish community in the United States. Its dominance was based largely on the trade with the West Indies, and as that trade declined, the Charleston Jewish community lost strength.

Between 1815 and 1880 a growing stream of German Jews moved to the United States. In the 1830s, as this immigration increased, many entered the business of peddling. The turn to manufacturing diminished the prominent position of the New England peddler. Others, including Jews, now assumed that role. German Jewish settlement was widespread through the nation. While perhaps a majority settled in the Northeast, other Jews located in Southern towns, up and down the Mississippi River, in the Midwest and Far West, with many taking up residence in California. Relative to the percentage of the population, Jews formed a higher percentage of the population in the West than in the Northwest and, before the Civil War, formed a larger proportion of the white population in the South than in the North.

During the Civil War Jews served both the Union and the Confederate forces. Jewish religious services, like those of their Christian neighbors, offered inspirational support to the patriotism of North and South. President Lincoln was friendly to individual Jews and sympathetic to

Jewish causes, but no Jew in the North achieved the eminence of Judah P. Benjamin in the Confederacy. President Jefferson Davis appointed Benjamin successively to the positions of Attorney General, Secretary of War, and Secretary of State.

Bertram W. Korn, in *American Jewry and the Civil War*, highlights some factors that affected the status of Jews as citizens during the war. An example would be the chaplaincy controversy. While the Confederate Congress provided for chaplains in the military without specifying denomination, the situation was different in the North. The Union Congress in the Volunteer Bill provided for the appointment of chaplains who would be of "some Christian denomination."

Representative Clement L. Vallandigham, the Ohio Democrat later to be known for his Copperhead sympathies, moved to replace the words "Christian denomination" with the term "religious society." Vallandigham attacked the idea of the United States politically being a Christian country and spoke out defending Jewish rights. Vallandigham's amendment failed and the bill passed intact. It would be over a year later before the law would be amended to permit Jewish chaplains.

The German Jews were proud of their German culture and before the Civil War had joined with other German groups to promote German cultural organizations. While this continued after the war, more and more they began to consider themselves part of American society. Dr. Korn has pointed out that the war greatly speeded up the Americanization of Jews and all other immigrants. Spread throughout the nation and making up only a small part of the total population, Jews adjusted well to the American scene and integrated themselves into the American mainstream.

Such an adjustment was partly responsible for the development of Reform Judaism, a major effort to adjust to the American environment while retaining the Jewish religion. While Orthodox Judaism stresses traditionalism, Reform Judaism was a response to the challenge of the Enlightenment and attempted to modernize religious practice on the basis of rationalistic thought. The idea of reform had been brought from Germany by some of the Jews familiar with the Hamburg Temple, but the first American attempt at reform seems to have been an indigenous effort. In the Charleston congregation a petition was offered to reform the service. This petition was rejected but a group of the petitioners formed the "Reformed Society of Israelites."

The successful development of Reform Judaism in America was the work of Rabbi Isaac M. Wise, who became the leading 19th Century spokesman for America's Jews. Besides establishing two newspapers, the

Deborah in German and the *Israelite* in English, Rabbi Wise was responsible for the organization of the Union of American Hebrew Congregations, the Hebrew Union College, and the Central Conference of American Rabbis. Wise's activities were directed towards the preservation of Judaism in America and helping Jews adapt to the American cultural environment.

In the 1880s the immigration of East European Jewry began. The pogroms of 1871, 1881, 1890, 1891, 1903, 1905, and 1906 served as an impetus for Jews to leave the Russian Empire. The Russian government unofficially turned loose the mob in Jewish sectors. Murder, rape, destruction, and looting were the orders of the day. The notorious Kishinev pogrom in 1903 finally aroused public opinion. The distinguished Russian novelist Leo Tolstoy placed the blame squarely on the Russian government. Theodore Herzl, the leader of the modern Zionist movement, traveled to St. Petersburg, asking the Russian government to use its influence on Turkey to permit more Russian Jews to enter Palestine. The Hebrew poet Chaim Nachman Bialik told the story in "The City of Slaughter," in which he criticized the Jews for hiding and running instead of fighting back. But when Jews did try to resist, the police, who stood around watching, would attack the Jews.

Lloyd P. Gartner, however, maintains that pogroms were not the main cause of emigration. More important, he feels, was the large population increase among East European Jews during the 19th Century, combined with a stagnant economy. At the same time, Russian repression not only limited economic opportunity but developed in Jews a sense of hopelessness about the future. In addition, entrance into the United States was open, while Russia did little to prevent hundreds of thousands from departing. Steamship lines and railroads were capable of moving large numbers of people and advertised their services at affordable prices.

The new immigrants, in contrast to the old who had spread across the country, tended to settle in the large cities, especially New York City, Chicago, Philadelphia, Boston, Baltimore, and Cleveland. Efforts made by Jewish groups to spread immigrants, such as the Galveston idea (to disembark newcomers away from eastern ports) and the agricultural projects sponsored by the Baron de Hirsch fund (to settle immigrants on farms rather than in cities), were only moderately successful. Still, it would be a distortion to ignore the impact of Jews who settled in small towns in the South and West, not to mention the Jewish peddler.

Philanthropic organizations, such as the Hebrew Immigrant Aid Society, in trying to help immigrants to become self-supporting, financially aided a number of men so they could peddle housewares and goods in rural areas.

In numerous communities in the South and West Jews were being accepted politically and even socially. For example, in towns and cities where they existed in small numbers, Jews were being elected to public office, something that would only be duplicated later in the Northeast because of a preponderance of Jews.

While the German Jews were generous in their financial and economic support of the new immigrants, and while both groups ultimately realized their common heritage, a deep gulf developed to separate the two groups. Sometimes those who had acclimated to American life were embarrassed by the seeming ignorance and old world ways of the newer immigrants. But the greenhorns were here to stay. Because of the large number of Jews who emigrated from eastern Europe, most of whom came to the United States, and because of their emphasis on education and with their religious fervor, the American Jewish community became culturally an East European community and by tradition remains so today. No more striking demonstration of the differences between the German Jewish community and the East Europeans can be found than by reading two books of recent years: Stephen Birmingham's *Our Crowd*, the story of the very successful, and Ande Manners' *Poor Cousins* about the newcomers.

Similar to other immigrants entering America at the same time from eastern and southern Europe, the East European Jews were attracted by the opportunities and freedoms of America. Like some other immigrant groups, such as the Greeks, they emphasized education for their children, and like most immigrants they were willing to work hard and sacrifice for a better future; if not for themselves, at least for their children. Unlike many other immigrants of the late 19th and early 20th centuries, they came to America to find a new home. Segments of some other groups came to America with the idea of striking it rich and then returning home to Europe, but the Jews (the same had been true of the Irish) came to America to stay. The Jews had no place to which they could return, so success or failure, their future was in America.

Among the newer immigrants some were intense in maintaining their religious zeal, while others were equally intense in rejecting the old values and assimilating into the American mainstream. Abraham Cahan, the editor of the important newspaper, the *Jewish Daily Forward*, wrote in *The Rise of David Levinsky* the story of a young immigrant who found much success in America but without losing his roots. By contrast, Mary Antin in *The Promised Land* placed more emphasis on the "melting pot," the idea that immigrants are "fused" into one American mold.

In religion the new immigrants would strengthen the ranks of traditional Orthodox Judaism, although many joined the Conservative movement. Some of the newcomers found their way to Reform, with the numbers increasing later with their children and grandchildren. Since Judaism seems more a way of life than a dogmatic theology, it is difficult briefly to define various branches. However, Orthodox Judaism adheres to Halakah (law) and practices its ethical and ceremonial teachings. Strictly speaking, this means giving faithful attention to the Torah (the first five books of the Bible) and careful study of Talmudic teachings in an effort to live life within those guidelines.

As previously mentioned, Reform represents an effort to modernize religious ideas and practices in keeping with rationalistic thought. It uses the vernacular along with Hebrew in the weekly Sabbath serice, and Reform stresses the prophetic heritage. Probably most Reform leaders see the message of the prophets as a call in today's world for social improvement and justice, although it does appear to some that the tone of the prophets was a conservative one, calling for a return to the past.

The Conservative branch is not, as it may seem, just an attempt to compromise between Orthodoxy and Reform. Instead, it has a basis all its own. Conservatives try to obey Jewish law, but have changed some practices. For example, although procedures vary among congregations and individuals, at religious service men and women sit together, unlike the separation in Orthodox services. Also, while Orthodox only eat Kosher food, Conservatives may or may not choose to follow that practice.

All segments realized that the survival of Judaism in America depended, in part, on the development of well-educated and trained rabbis and teachers. To further that aim the Orthodox founded several educational institutions, the best known today being Yeshiva University. The Conservatives had set up the Jewish Theological Seminary of America in the late 19th Century, just ten years after Isaac M. Wise (the leader of Reform) established the Hebrew Union College. It was not until after the turn of the century when scholarly Dr. Solomon Schechter became its president that the Jewish Theological Seminary was placed on a sound footing. Early in the 1920s the dynamic Dr. Stephen S. Wise, rabbi of New York's Free Synagogue, formed a second Reform rabbinical college, which later merged with the older institution to form the Hebrew Union College-Jewish Institute of Religion.

In the fields of primary and secondary learning Dr. Samson Benderly helped turn religious education into a Jewish community responsibility. He worked to combine the Jewish heritage and the American environment so as to perpetuate Jewish life in America. Jewish education has been further strengthened by the outstanding textbooks authored by Rabbi Mordecai I. Soloff. Through his writings and leadership Rabbi Soloff has instructed three generations of American Jews on the history of the Jewish people and the meaning of Judaism.

In contrast to the more than two million East European Jews who came to America a small group of German Jews (including a young Henry Kissinger) immigrated to the United States in the 1930s. These desperate people were refugees from Hitler's fury; their brethren were victims of restrictive U.S. Immigration laws (adopted in the 1920s), which permitted only a few thousand to enter the United States. Little was done by the American government to help those who managed to escape the Nazi terror, and the State Department remained adamant in its opposition to relaxing immigration quotas so more Jews could be admitted. During World War II, after it became known in government circles that Hitler's "final solution" was the total extermination of European Jewry, President Franklin Roosevelt seemed unwilling to act. Jewish leaders urged ransom payments to purchase Jewish lives and the bombing of Auschwitz and the railroads to the gas chambers. These and all other proposals were rejected with the argument that the way to stop Nazi atrocities was a rapid winning of the war. Not until 1944 did President Roosevelt establish the War Refugee Board in an effort to save the small remnant of Europe's Jews.

Ethnic groups in the United States, especially if they are European-derived, face the problem of survival. America's emphasis on freedom and equality tends not only sometimes to produce a leveling effect but often cultivates uniformity and sameness. The "melting pot" concept, so popular earlier in the century, has been questioned by some cultural historians who believe America is a "salad bowl" and its salient feature is "cultural pluralism." Still, ethnics have always faced much pressure, both overt and subtle, to join the mainstream. Certainly, Jews have become such a vital part of the American scene, and in the areas of science, medicine, literature, music, and art, they have played a role far out of proportion to their numbers, that ethnicity seems to disappear.

In order for a group to survive and retain its distinctiveness, it must think not just of today but of future generations. So it is necessary to look at cohesive factors that hold the group together as a counterbalance to the centrifugal forces that threaten to fracture the circle.

Just after World War II, two events served to remove distinctions between community. One was the Holocaust, the Nazi murder of six million European Jews, the gruesome details becoming known to the American public after the war. The other event was the formation of the state of Israel. President Harry Truman, ignoring the advice of the State Department, quickly gave U.S. recognition to the new nation. Truman's desire to aid democratic nations and to resist Communist expansion eventually made support of Israel a part of U.S. foreign policy. Today, Israel remains the only democratic nation in the Middle East.

The support of Israel is the single most powerful unifying force among America's Jews. Individuals, leaders, groups, and organizations may differ on many other issues, but they almost all agree on the necessity for supporting Israel, a nation that in its forty years' existence has been required to fight four wars and daily faces the threat of terrorist attack. The Ma'alot massacre, the murder of Israeli athletes at the Munich Olympics, the skyjacking at Entebbe, the bus attack near Tel Aviv are typical of the terror that makes the headlines, but literally thousands of smaller incidents and border incursions have occurred.

The two-year old Arab uprising (*infitada*) has posed a serious problem for the Israeli government. According to the Arabs who call themselves Palestinians nothing short of a state of their own carved out of Israeli territory will be acceptable. As a sovereign nation Israel resists such a solution.

As a democratic nation Israel has permitted virtually unlimited media coverage of its troubles, ironically something none of its Arab neighbors would permit. Israel's handling of the Arab uprising has also eroded support for Israel in the United States, especially by the Bush administration. The president and Secretary of State James Baker seem less friendly to Israel than most previous administrations.

One of the age-old factors that has forced Jews together has been the scourge of anti-Semitism. While there were incidents of anti-Semitism in earlier American history, and "the Jew" was often portrayed unfavorably in the theater, as a rule, Jews had no religious difficulties. Sometimes the Jew was a matter of interest or curiosity but not of hostility. It was an event in 1840 from the Middle East, the Damascus Affair, a false "blood libel" charge, that for the first time mobilized American Jews to concerted action. But the real worry of anti-Semitism developed in the late 19th-early 20th centuries. The large immigration of eastern and southern European peoples to the United States, of which Jews were only a small minority, was accompanied by the development of racial theories stressing the superiority of the older immigrants from northern and western Europe. For Jews these theories were piled on top of traditional, old world anti-Semitism.

Jewish leaders were quick to demonstrate the falsity of accusations against Jews, but denials, no matter how positive and accurate, seldom could repair the damage already done by the original charges. Defense organizations began to grow up to protect Jews against unfair accusations and growing discrimination. The American Jewish Committee (formed by Jews of German descent), the American Jewish Congress (Jews of East European descent), and the Anti-Defamation League (an agency of B'nai B'rith, a fraternal organization) are among the better known such groups.

At the same time, since coming to America, Jews have tried to do the right things. They have served in America's wars in larger proportion than the general population. They became noted as generous contributors to charity and philanthropy. The East European immigrants had struggled to learn English and Americanize themselves and sacrificed to educate their children so they could be better Americans. In the 20th Century, Jews became known as liberal contributors of both time and money to political candidates. They took an active role in the post-World War II Civil Rights Movement. But such is the irrationality of prejudice that anti-Semitism continued to grow and still exists today.

In the 1930s Hitler's persecution of the Jews in Germany seemed to inspire imitation on the part of some Americans. The German-American Bund and the Silver Shirts spewed forth hatred for Jews and tried to imitate Nazi organizations in Germany. Father Charles E. Coughlin, in his magazine, *Social Justice*, and on his radio program, called Jews "a menace to America." Equally malignant were the words and actions of William Dudley Pelley and Gerald L. K. Smith. Smith started his hate-mongering *The Cross and the Flag* just as the United States was beginning the fight against fascism in World War II.

The post-World War II period appeared to offer a diminution of anti-Semitism. Movies were produced which critically examined anti-Jewish prejudice, notably "Crossfire" and "Gentlemen's Agreement." Unfortunately, the respite was partially short-lived as the Radical Right was joined by the New Left, which added to the anti-Semitic lexicon the specter of anti-Zionism in its opposition to support for the state of Israel.

Revelations of Black anti-Semitism sent a shock wave throughout the Jewish community, which, as previously mentioned, had taken an active role in the Civil Rights Movement. Many moderate Black leaders deplored Black anti-Semitism, and many Jewish leaders at first tended to play down the problem, but the phenomenon was real. For example, the Anti-Defamation League reported in the late 1960s that: "Raw, undisguised anti-Semitism is at the crisis level in New York City schools," after "building for more than two years," and was "unchecked by public authority." The Anti-Defamation League accused officials of the Afro-American Teachers Association and other militants of generating hostility against Jewish teachers among school pupils. A Black Writers Conference in Montreal, Canada, openly expressed anti-Semitic feelings, and the National Black Political Convention, meeting in 1972, endorsed an anti-Israel resolution, which appeared to some as a thinly disguised form of anti-Semitism.

In the Williamsburg section of Brooklyn, Rabbi Meir Kahane organized the Jewish Defense League to protect elderly Jews from attack by Black and Puerto Rican youths. Later the J. D. L. spread to other communities to offer active protection to Jews under attack. The J. D. L. has openly resisted marches planned in predominantly Jewish areas by the American Nazi Party. However, establishment Jewish organizations have tried to ignore the J. D. L. Many a rabbi from the pulpit has deplored its activities, but its willingness to stand up for Jews with its slogan of "Never Again," referring to the Holocaust, has made a strong appeal to less affluent Jews and to those who feel threatened.

A promising sign in many cities during the 1980s and into 1990 has been the efforts of many Black and Jewish leaders to work together to try to remove difficulties between the two groups. It so happened that in the latter years of the 1980 decade the United States experienced an increase in hate crimes with Blacks and Jews the most likely targets. For example, in 1989 Los Angeles County reported a significant increase in hate crimes directed against both Jews and Blacks.

A further concern for many Jews has been the specter of anti-Semitism raised in the recent events taking place in Eastern Europe. As the former Soviet satellites try to work out their new destinies, some ultra-rightist groups have revived old-style anti-Semitism, even though there are only small numbers of Jews left in those countries. An additional worry is felt concerning the proposed reunification of Germany.

Another factor which mobilized Jewish consciousness was a shock of a different kind. In 1972/3 the "invisible" poor surfaced when it was revealed that for 400,000 American Jews poverty was a way of life. In recent years the western states have been experiencing the most rapidly growing Jewish communities. In Los Angeles, California, the home of the second largest Jewish community in the United States, and one of the most affluent, it was learned that 55,000 Jews subsisted at, or below, the poverty level, which meant one out of every six households was involved.

The Jewish poor show some of the same characteristics as other poverty-stricken people. The aged lack proper housing, nutrition, and health care. The young cannot find jobs. Broken homes often leave the woman to be both mother and breadwinner. Additional, unique problems include older persons who feel alienated and forgotten, isolated from the mobility of population movements. There is not longer a synagogue within walking distance and no kosher butcher shop is close by. First generation people whose primary language is not English find it difficult to seek help from public welfare agencies, as they often do not understand and cannot cope with bureaucratic red tape. In many places in the Southwest a telephone call to the Social Security Office or some other welfare agency finds first a message in Spanish before one in English. Nothing of that type awaits the Jew whose first language is Yiddish. In addition, there is a cultural feeling, as with some other ethnic groups, of being degraded by having to apply for public assistance when other members of the group are well off.

Jewish community and social service agencies have been trying to alleviate the problems of the poor with a variety of assistance programs. For example, in New York City, the home of the largest American Jewish community, and the largest poverty problem, efforts have been made to permit Jews to take part in electing representatives to the anti-poverty community corporations. However, since these elections are held on Saturdays, the Jewish Sabbath, observant Jews are excluded from participation. In Los Angeles, Project "GELT" (Getting Employment Leads for Teenagers) has been set up to help find jobs for youths from low-income homes. More programs have been started but the problem remains, and may unfortunately be getting worse. In 1972 the poverty level was a household income below $4,000. By 1990 that figure has tripled which means even more people are unable to cope and fall into the poverty classification.

In examining Jews as an ethnic group a unifying force for the Jewish people is religion. While Judaism in the United States is divided into branches, religion seems to remain as the most powerful force for the preservation of Jews as a group. Conversely, many Jews, like other people, are alienated from their religion. Statistics on religious affiliation have not always been accurate, due partly to the difficulties in compiling figures of membership. Using approximations, there are six million Jews in the United States and of that number each of the major branches—Orthodox, Conservative, Reform—has over a million members, possibly even as high as a million and a half. Added to that is a small number of Jews in the Reconstructionist movement, founded by Rabbi Mordecai M. Kaplan, emphasizing Judaism as a civilization, not just a religion. These estimates still leave a large group of unaffiliates. While not members of a synagogue or temple, many unaffiliated Jews do attend religious services once or twice a year, usually on the High Holidays of Rosh Hashanah (the New Year) and Yom Kippur (the Day of Atonement).

Some Jews express their connection with the group only in their support of the state of Israel or through philanthropy, by supporting the United States Welfare Fund, the United Jewish Appeal, or other similar bodies. Some have only a mere form of attachment, such as eating Jewish food (usually of East European origin) and have turned themselves into the "bagel and lox" crowd.

Still it would seem in a pluralistic American society only religion can preserve Jews as a distinct group. After all, today's American Jew blends easily into the American mainstream. There are many worthwhile charities other than Jewish that need support; lots of other fascinating food; and while it does not seem feasible at this time, there might be some future day when there is peace in the Middle East and Israel is self-supporting. If Jews are to remain as Jews, religion seems to be the only force capable of maintaining a distinct group in the future.

✦✦✦

In examining the Jewish experience in America, note should be made of at least some Jews who have significantly contributed to varied facets of American life. In government service Henry Kissinger, the former Secretary of State, Bernard Baruch, "park-bench statesman" and advisor to presidents from Woodrow Wilson to Lyndon Johnson, Henry Morgenthau, Jr., Secretary of the Treasury in Franklin Roosevelt's administration, and Supreme Court Justices Louis D. Brandeis, Benjamin N. Cardozo, Felix Frankfurter, Arthur J. Goldberg, and Abe Fortas. In organized labor Samuel Gompers, Sidney Hillman, and David Dubinsky. In business and finance Jacob Schiff, Julius Rosenwald, and Paul M. Warburg.

Turning to Science outstanding persons include Albert A. Michelson, the first American to be awarded a Nobel prize, Albert Einstein, J. Robert Oppenheimer, and Edward Teller. In medicine Selman A. Waksman, the discoverer of streptomycin, Jonas Salk and Albert Sabin, the conquerors of polio.

Moving to the arts well known personalities include sculptors Jo Davidson, Jacob Epstein, and Victor D. Brenner, the designer of the Lincoln penny. In music, performers such as Jascha Heifetz, Yehudi Menuhin, Mischa Elman, composers Ernest Bloch and George Gershwin and conductor Leonard Bernstein. In literature, novelists Henry Roth, Bernard Malamud, Herman Wouk, Philip Roth, and Nobel-prize winners Saul Bellow and Isaac Bashevis Singer. Mention should also be made of the New York intellectuals (both Jews and non-Jews) of the 1930s, 1940s, and 1950s such as Philip Roth, Lionel Trilling, Delmore Schwartz and the influential *Partisan Review.* Delmore Schwartz's life seemed almost symbolic of the difficulty of being an artist in America.

Many Jews have become known for contributions in popular entertainment. In music Benny Goodman, Barbra Streisand, Neil Diamond, and Barry Manilow. In sports Hank Greenberg, Sid Luckman, Sandy Koufax, and Mark Spitz. In vaudeville, theater, films, radio and television, actors Paul Muni, Kirk Douglas, George Segal, Richard Dreyfuss, and Henry Winkler; entertainers Eddie Cantor, Al Jolson, George Jessel, Fanny Brice, Sophie Tucker, Ted Lewis, Jack Benny, George Burns, and Milton Berle. In fact, Jews have played a leading role in the motion picture industry as producers and directors, as writers and actors. In comedy, from the Marx Brothers, sometimes employing the hilarious scriptwriting of S. J. Perlman and George S. Kaufman, to the movies of Mel Brooks and Woody Allen, Jews have been a vital force. Steven Allen estimates that eighty percent of American comedians are Jewish. Allen points out that Jewish humor often changes a joke into social commentary, since in the past, humor was a way to strike back at tormentors; sometimes the only safe way. In addition, self-criticism is often a characteristic of Jewish comedy, with much of the laughter directed inward. A later generation or two of comedians included Zero Mostel, Sid Caesar, Jack E. Leonard, Sam Levenson, Alan King, Buddy Hackett, Joey Bishop, Don Rickles, Lenny Bruce, David Brenner, Andy Kaufman, Joan Rivers, and Rodney Dangerfield. ✦

SELECTED BIBLIOGRAPHY

Allen, Steve, *Funny People*. New York, 1981.

Atlas, James, *Delmore Schwartz*. New York, 1977.

Birmingham, Stephen, *Our Crowd*. New York, 1967.

Blau, Joseph L. and Baron, Salo W., eds. *The Jews of the United States, 1790-1840: A Documentary History*, 3 vols. New York and Philadelphia, 1963.

Dawidowicz, Lucy. *The Jewish Presence: Essays on Identity and History*. New York, 1977.

Dinnerstein, Leonard and Reimers, David M. *Ethnic Americans*. New York, 1977.

Forster, Arnold and Epstein, Benjamin R., *The New Anti-Semitism*. New York, 1974. Freund, Miriam, K., *Jewish Merchants in Colonial America*. New York, 1939.

Galloway, David, *The Absurd Hero in America Fiction,* 2nd rev. ed. Austin, Texas, 1981.

Glazer, Nathan, *American Judaism*, 2nd ed. Chicago, 1972.

Gordis, Robert, *The Dynamics of Judaism: A Study of Jewish Law*. Bloomington, Indiana, 1989.

Handlin, Oscar, *Adventure in Freedom*. New York, 1954. Howe, Irving, *World of Our Fathers*. New York, 1976.

Joseph, Samuel, *Jewish Immigration to the United States From 1881 to 1910*. New York, 1969.

Kessner, Thomas, *The Golden Door*. New York, 1977. Kohut, Rebekah, *My Portion*. New York, 1927.

Korn, Bertram W., *American Jewry and the Civil War*. Cleveland, 1961.

Kramer, William M., ed. *The Western Journal of Isaac Mayer Wise, 1877*. Berkeley, California, 1974.

Laqueur, Walter, *Terrorism*. Boston, 1977.

Learsi, Rufus, *The Jews in America*. Cleveland, 1954.

Levine, Naomi and Hochbaum, Martin, eds. *Poor Jews: An American Awakening*. New Brunswick, N.J., 1974.

Levinger, Lee J., *A History of the Jews in the United States*. New York, 1970.

Lyman, Darryl, *The Jewish Comedy Catalog*. New York, 1989.

Manners, Ande, *Poor Cousins*. New York, 1972.

Marcus, Jacob R., *The Colonial American Jew, 1492-1776*, 3 vols. Detroit, 1970.

Margolis, Max L. and Marx, Alexander, *A History of the Jewish People*. New York, 1965.

Miller, Randall M., ed. *The Kaleidoscopic Lens: How Hollywood Views Ethnic Groups*. Englewood, 1980.

Mow, Arthur D., *While Six Million Died*. New York, 1968.

Oring, Elliot, *The Jokes of Sigmund Freud: A Study in Humor and Jewish Identity*. Philadelphia, 1984.

Oz. Amos, "Make Peace Not Love," in *Reform Judaism*, Spring 1990.

Parkes, James, *Anti-Semitism*. Chicago, 1969.

Prinz, Joachim, *The Dilemma of the Modern Jew*. Boston, 1962.

Rischen, Moses, *The Promised City: New York's Jews, 1870-1914*. Boston, 1962.

Rosten, Leo, *The Joys of Yiddish*. New York, 1968.

Roth, Cecil, *A History of the Marranos*. New York, 1966.

Roth, Cecil, *The Spanish Inquisition*. New York, 1964.

Roth, Henry, *Call It Sleep*. New York, 1934.

Sanders, Ronald, *The Downtown Jews*. New York, 1976.

Schoenberg, Harris O., *A Mandate for Terror: The United Nations and the PLO*. New York, 1989.

Selznick, Gertrude J. and Steinberg, Stephen, *The Tenacity of Prejudice*. New York, 1969.

Sklare, Marshall, *America's Jews*. New York, 1971.

Soloff, Mordecai I., *The Covenant People*. Middle Village, N.Y., 1973.

Soloff, Mordecai I., *How the Jewish People Lives Today*. New York, 1956.

Soloff, Mordecai I., *When the Jewish People Was Young*. New York, 1934.

Stern, Selma, *Josel of Rosheim*. Philadelphia, 1965.

Taylor, Philip, *The Distant Magnet*. New York, 1971.

Vorspan, Max and Gartner, Lloyd P., *A History of the Jews of Los Angeles*. Philadelphia, 1970.

Werbell, Frederick and Clarke, Thurston, *Lost Hero: The Mystery of Raoul Wallenberg*. New York, 1982.

Winter, Nathan H., *Jewish Education in a Pluralist Society*. New York, 1966.

Yaffe, James, *The American Jews*. New York, 1968.

♦♦♦

From the Mediterranean: Italians, Greeks, Arabs, and Armenians

♦

Roger Daniels

The nature of immigration from the northwestern European countries began to change toward the end of the nineteenth century from largely family groups to single individuals and from immigrants heading for rural economic opportunity to those heading toward urban economic opportunity. Conditions on both sides of the Atlantic caused these changes. In Europe greater and more rapid economic growth—stronger in the West than in the East—attracted migrants from within and emigrants from without to industrializing cities such as Berlin, Stockholm, Paris, and London. In the United States similarly, the cities rather than the prairies drew larger and larger proportions of new Americans. In 1920, when a bare majority of Americans lived in urban areas, three-quarters of the foreign born did. Immigrants from Russia, Ireland, Italy, and Poland were the most urbanized of the larger groups, with rates of urbanization of from 84.4 to 88.6 percent. And the disparity between the urbanization of immigrants and natives is greater than the bare data indicate. The Census Bureau counted places of twenty-five hundred and above as "urban territory." Thirty percent of the urban population—more than sixteen million persons— lived in places with populations between twenty-five hundred and twenty-five thousand. These were overwhelmingly native born, while immigrants tended to live in large cities rather than in the small towns that made up so much of America.

As the steam-powered transportation revolution reached into all but the most remote corners of Europe it provided millions of peasants the practical means of leaving their native villages. The creation of steamships, first of iron, then of steel, intended for the immigrant trade not only reduced the time required for an Atlantic crossing to a matter of days rather than weeks but also made transportation of immigrants into a modern big business. The major European passenger companies—no American line had a significant share—set up vast networks of ticket agencies. The Hamburg-Amerika line, for example, had more than three thousand of them in the United States in the 1890s, most of them sidelines for ethnic entrepreneurs in the process of "making it." Thus the use of prepaid tickets, purchased in America for the use of the immigrant, increased sharply. In the early 1890s perhaps one immigrant ticket in three was prepaid; just after the turn of the century, two in three were.

Emigrant ships still left from dozens of European ports, but by 1907 just four ports—Naples, Bremen, Liverpool, and Hamburg—accounted for more than three European immigrants out of five. Immigration peaked in that year (July 1, 1906-June 30, 1907) as more than a million and a quarter immigrants were recorded entering the United States. Table 7.1 shows the numbers leaving from each of those ports and indicates the main nationalities involved, as these ports, except for Naples, were funnels for much of Europe and exported more foreigners than natives.

Table 7.1

Emigrant Ports, 1907

PORT	NUMBER OF EMIGRANTS	MAJOR ETHNIC GROUPS
Naples	240,000	Largely Italians; also Greeks and "Syrians."
Bremen	203,000	Poles, Czechs, Croats, Slovaks, and other Slavs.
Liverpool	177,000	More than half Irish and other British; many Swedes, Norwegians, and Eastern European Jews.
Hamburg	142,000	Eastern European Jews and Scandinavians predominate, but some from every part of Central and Eastern Europe.

NOTE: Total immigration to the United States: 1,285,349; Europe 1,199,566; Americas——41,762; Asia—40,524; Australasia—1,989; Africa—1,486; other—22.

The great shipping lines, including North-German Lloyd, Cunard, and Hamburg-Amerika, under the pressure of competition and of increasing protective legislation, created modern assembly lines to funnel immigrants onto their ships. Cunard Line representatives met trains in Liverpool and escorted immigrant passengers to its dormitory enclave, where they were housed, fed, and medically examined while waiting for the next ship. Those non-Germans who departed from German ports had a double examination. After the cholera epidemics of 1892—more than nine thousand died in Hamburg alone—the German government subjected migrants from the East to medical examinations, which included baths and fumigation. Those going on to Hamburg, where the shipping magnate Albert Ballin had established a huge immigrant depot, got a second set of baths and fumigations: Men and boys had their heads close cropped and received a chemical shampoo, while women and girls had their hair combed with fine-toothed metal combs. The Amerika village, which could accommodate four thousand persons at a time, was isolated behind brick walls, and emigrants in transit were forbidden to venture beyond them. Inside everything was hygienic. There were even kosher kitchens for observant Jews. Amenities such as daily band concerts and a library were also provided. As regimented as all this sounds—and was—it was a vast improvement on the midcentury conditions, which left immigrants to fend for themselves against those who sought to prey on their inexperience. The ships, too, were cleaner and better run, especially the larger liners, which had begun to substitute "third class" for steerage and actually provided some privacy for immigrant passengers. But even in the twentieth century, not all ships were modern; ships operating out of the Mediterranean—French, Italian, and Greek—probably had the worst conditions. One journalist who traveled as an immigrant from Naples in 1906 reported:

> How can a steerage passenger remember that he is a human being when he must first pick the worms from his food . . . and eat in his stuffy, stinking bunk, or in the hot and fetid atmosphere of a compartment where 150 men sleep, or in juxtaposition to a seasick man?

To similar complaints defenders of the status quo, such as Joseph Chamberlain, the British cabinet officer responsible for overseeing conditions on passenger vessels, had responded a quarter century earlier, that improving bad conditions would cause transatlantic fares to rise beyond the ability of immigrants to pay, and, in addition, argued that immigrants weren't used to any better conditions and that steerage berths were as roomy as peasant cottages or cramped tenements. But, as we have seen, not only did the conditions improve but the price of tickets actually went down, at times of rate wars, to two pounds (ten dollars) from Liverpool, ten days' pay for a common laborer in America.[1]

The immigrants who came to America after 1880 were increasingly from southern and eastern Europe, although, as table 7.2 demonstrates, British, Irish, German, and Scandinavian immigrants continued to come. In the heaviest decade of American immigration, 1901-10, these countries sent more than 1.5 million immigrants; but those sizable numbers were dwarfed by the 6.5 million who came from other parts of Europe: 2 million Italians and very large numbers of Poles and Eastern European Jews, neither of whom can be enumerated with any precision. The obvious lacunae in this table, taken from U.S. immigration statistics, are the absence of Poles and Jews, as well as peoples who came in smaller but still substantial numbers. The Austro-Hungarian and Russian Empires, and, to a lesser degree, Germany, contained subject peoples who did not get recorded in the American data, which listed only national origin, not ethnicity.

Table 7.2

European Immigration to the United States, by Country, 1901-1910

COUNTRY	NUMBER	PERCENTAGE
Austria-Hungary	2,145,266	26.6
Italy	2,045,877	25.4
Russia	1,597,306	19.8
Britain	525,590	6.5
Germany	341,498	4.2
Ireland	339,065	4.2
Sweden	249,534	3.1
Norway	190,605	2.4
Greece	167,519	2.1
Other European	453,780	5.6
Total European	8,056,040	

ITALIANS

Between 1880 and 1920 more than 4.1 million Italians were recorded as entering the United States. No other ethnic group in American history sent so many immigrants in such a short time. Prior to the 1870s only scattered thousands of Italians had come and, unlike most other emigrant groups, large numbers of Italians had ventured outside of Europe—to South America and to North Africa—before and while large numbers were coming to the United States. Up to 1900, perhaps two out of three Italians who crossed the Atlantic did not come to the United States: Most of them went to Argentina and Brazil. Thus the Italians, like the Chinese, had a strong migratory tradition before the major movement, called by one scholar "the Italian emigration of our times," set in.[2] The figures in table 7.3 show only one aspect of the Italian transatlantic migration, that which brought them to the United States. It does *not* show the return migration, which was quite high among Italians, having been estimated at anywhere between 30 percent and nearly half. Thomas Archdeacon has hypothesized that while Italian immigration between 1899 and 1924 was more than twice as heavy as Jewish immigration—3.8 million as opposed to 1.8 million—the number of permanent immigrants from each

Table 7.3

Italian Immigration to the United States, 1820-1920

YEARS	NUMBER
1820-30	439
1831-40	2,253
1841-50	1,870
1851-60	9,231
1861-70	11,725
1871-80	55,759
1881-90	307,309
1891-1900	651,893
1901-10	2,045,877
1911-20	1,109,524
Total	4,195,880

group was more nearly equal—2.1 million as opposed to 1.7 million. This was because perhaps fewer than five percent of Jewish immigrants returned to Europe. In the U.S. Census of 1890, for example, 182,000 persons born in Italy are recorded, even though some 307,000 had immigrated in the previous decade alone. And, of course, many of the returning emigrants—*ritornati* as the Italians say—reemigrated to the United States. We also know that large but unknowable numbers of Italians participated in temporary migration—within Italy, within Europe, or overseas to South America or North Africa—before migrating to the United States.

It was a Genoese who "discovered" America, and many other Italian explorers participated in making it better known to Europeans—the Florentine, Amerigo Vespucci, who gave America its name; the Venetian, Giovanni Caboto, who "discovered" New England and is usually disguised as John Cabot in American history books; and another Florentine navigator, Giovanni da Verrazano, who first sailed into New York Harbor and for whom the magnificent bridge across the Narrows is named. In addition to these seamen, Italian soldiers marched across the American Southeast with De Soto and La Salle, and Italian priests, such as the Franciscan Marco da Nizza and the Jesuit Eusebio Francesco Kino, were among the most important of the mission fathers who explored and established settlements in what became the American Southwest. All told several hundred Italians participated in the exploration and conquest of North America, most of them in the service of either France or Spain. Yet no New Italy was founded to parallel a New Spain, New France, or New England. This was largely because there was no Italy in a national sense until the mid-nineteenth century.

Italy, in some of whose northern cities the civilization of the Renaissance was born in the thirteenth century, became a classic case of uneven development in modern times. The northern cities, although not politically unified, continued to develop culturally and economically. In the center, under papal denomination, a slower but significant modernization evolved. South of Rome—in the Mezzogiorno and Sicily—development was retarded and grinding rural and urban poverty was the lot of the vast majority of the inhabitants. It is no surprise that, eventually, most Italian emigrants came from the south, but initially almost all of them came from the north and center.

During the colonial and early national periods in America, most of the few Italians who came were skilled artisans, like the Venetian glassblowers who were brought to Jamestown in 1622 or relatively well-to-do individuals such as one Peter (surely Pietro) Alberti who is recorded as a landowner in New Amsterdam. As was true for so many other groups, the first large group immigration was impelled by religious motives. In 1656 a party of more than a hundred Waldensians—Italian Protestants—was brought to the colonies by the Dutch who settled them in New York and Delaware.

During the late eighteenth and early nineteenth centuries a surprising number of Italian intellectuals came to the United States. Politically the most significant figure was Philip Mazzei (1730-1816), a physician and scholar who was persuaded by Benjamin Franklin to go to Virginia and attempt to establish some typically Italian agricultural products there: silk culture, wine grapes, and olives. He settled near Thomas Jefferson and is believed to have influenced him and Thomas Paine and, after the Revolution began, served as an American agent and fund-raiser in Europe. (Jefferson had a continuing relationship with Italian immigration. He wrote to Italy to obtain some Italian masons to help in building Monticello and, as president, recruited a number of Italian musicians to form the nucleus of the United States Marine Band.) There were a number of Italian soldiers and soldiers of fortune in the revolutionary armies, one of whom, Colonel Louis Nicola, proposed a throne for Washington. More significant were the activities of the Piedmontese Giuseppe Maria Francesco Vigo (1747-1836) who became one of George Rogers Clark's chief lieutenants in the conquest of the trans-Appalachian West.

Apart from Jefferson's bandsmen, many Italians played an important part in the musical life of the new nation, the most illustrious of whom is Lorenzo da Ponte (1749-1838), Mozart's librettist for *Don Giovanni*, *The Marriage of Figaro*, and *Così fan Tutte*. Born a Venetian Jew, da Ponte converted to Catholicism at age fourteen, became a priest and then renounced his vows, and managed to be expelled from several cities and countries for both political and moral reasons. The United States, where he came in 1805, was the end of the line. He supervised the building of the first American opera house, was a professor of Italian (unpaid) at Columbia University, and engaged in such unmusical activities as running a whiskey distillery in Sunbury, Pennsylvania. Italian performers, impresarios, and even an occasional composer—for example, Pietro Mascagni—ranged all across the nineteenth-century United States, even in such presumably unmusical places as Cheyenne, Wyoming, where an Italian traveler reported hearing an Italian opera company perform *Lucia di Lammermoor*:

> The touching melodies of Donizetti heard in a still wild region where only a few years before ferocious Indians like Sitting Bull and Crazy Horse roamed, left an indelible impression upon my mind.[3]

In the plastic arts, too, Italians made an important contribution. Both the first U.S. Capitol in Washington, which was burned by the British in 1814, and its successor were decorated by Italian painters and sculptors. The most famous and controversial of these was Constantino Brumidi, who has been called, mostly by those with undeveloped esthetic sensibilities, "the Michelangelo of the United States Capitol." Over the protests of American artists who wanted the commission, he painted the huge frescoes in the dome of the Capitol, working 180 feet above the floor when he was more than seventy years old. Other works are in the corridors and on the walls of various parts of the Capitol, notably a fresco of Washington at Yorktown in the dining room of the House of Representatives. More prosaically, the granite quarries of Vermont were exploited with the help of Italian stonecutters who formed one of the first Italian American trade unions.

Among other prominent Italians to come before the great movements of immigrants in the later nineteenth century were priests and political exiles. Most notable among the former were Giuseppe Rosati (1749-1843), who was, for a time, bishop of both New Orleans and Saint Louis, and the Milanese Dominican, Samuele C. Mazzuchelli (1806-64), who organized the Catholic Church in Wisconsin and Iowa and designed many public buildings, including the State Capitol in Des Moines. A different kind of Italian religious leader was Sabato Morais (1823-97), the Livorno-born Sephardic rabbi and friend of Mazzini, who came to the United States in 1851 to serve Philadelphia's Mikveh Israel synagogue and became an abolitionist and a founding father of Conservative Judaism in America. Italian exiles were fairly common during the Risorgimento (1848-1870), and included, for a time, the liberator Giuseppe Garibaldi (1807-82), who supported himself in New York by manufacturing candles. On more than one occasion he used a dubious claim of American citizenship to gain or maintain his freedom. (This ploy was used by a later nationalist patriot, Sun Yat-sen, who sometimes claimed to have been born in Honolulu for the same reason.)

After 1849 there was a regular exile community in New York, large enough to start several newspapers, none of which survived for more than a few years. Nor were all of the political exiles *prominenti* or upper class. From time to time various Italian states simply deported captured or suspected revolutionaries, many of whom took passage on American ships. One such group of exiles from Bologna in 1856 found work in coal mines near Scranton, Pennsylvania. By the time of the American Civil War there were enough exiles and other Italians in New York to form a "Garibaldi Guard," a kind of International Brigade that fought in the Union Army and drew volunteers from many nationalities, although it was officered almost exclusively by Italians and Hungarians.

Most of the Italians who came here were artisans, merchants, businessmen, professional people, musicians, actors, waiters, and seamen. The 1850 census, the first to record foreign born, enumerated 3,645 persons born in Italy. They lived in every state and territory but Delaware and New Hampshire, and almost half of them resided in the South, with the largest concentration *anywhere in Louisiana, in and around New Orleans*. (Ironically, in 1891 New Orleans would be the scene of a lynching of Italians, but the antebellum Italians were well accepted and, when war came, marched off to join the Confederacy along with their American-born neighbors.) It is also interesting to note that, just a year after the California gold rush began, more than two hundred Italians were reported in California, most of them around San Francisco. Settled largely by Genoese, San Francisco remains an important center for Italian Americans, and, as late as 1870 it and New Orleans still rivaled New York as a mecca for Italians. In that year's census New York City (Manhattan) had 2,749 Italians; San Francisco, 1,622; and New Orleans, 1,571. In the latter two the incidence of Italians was much, much higher.

Although most Italians in the United States, then and later, were urban dwellers, there *were* rural colonies, perhaps the earliest of which was a successful enterprise begun in 1868 in Bryan, Texas, comprising chiefly Sicilians who had worked as section hands on a local railroad. By 1900 there were five hundred Italian families there. A Piacenzan, G. F. Secci de Ćasali the proprietor of the first Italian American newspaper, helped organize agricultural colonies of Italians near Vineland, New Jersey, in 1874. The men worked in factories while the women and children did most of the truck farming. By the early twentieth century nearly a thousand Italian families owned land in the vicinity. (Vineland later became the site of a Jewish agricultural colony as well and, during and after World War II, provided agricultural employment for "relocated" Japanese Americans and Japanese Peruvians.)

But most of the Italian presence in agriculture was in the Far West, particularly in California. There Italian immigrants introduced new crops and techniques, and some established businesses that have survived to become some of the major "factories in the field" that dominate California agriculture. From the 1880s immigrants from Genoa, Turin, and Lombardy began to enter California's then small grape-growing, winemaking industry. An early Italian American banker, Andrea Sbarboro (1839-1923) helped establish the cooperative Italian-Swiss Colony vineyard and winery at Asti, California. The vineyard started with five thousand acres. By 1897 it produced more wine than barrels could be supplied for, so the group built a five hundred thousand-gallon cement wine tank that may have been the largest in the world. Its completion was celebrated by a dance for two hundred persons inside the tank. Farther south, in the Central Valley, the Di Giorgio brothers, Joseph (1874-1951) and Rosario founded the Di Giorgio Fruit Corporation, which became the largest shipper of fresh fruit in the state. The Di Giorgios owned more than forty thousand acres, and bought and canned the produce of others under the S & W label. The company became one of the most notorious exploiters of labor in California, as John Steinbeck and others interested in reforming Californian agricultural labor practices often pointed out.

That Italian immigrant farmers were helped by immigrant bankers like Sbarboro is not surprising; in fact, there are consistent patterns of such relationships in most American immigrant groups. Most immigrant and immigrant-oriented bankers were and remained small fry in the banking world. (The German-Jewish bankers mentioned earlier were often bankers before they came here and were not immigrant oriented.) The typical immigrant "banker" of whatever ethnicity was likely to be an entrepreneur who performed all kinds of services for his clientele and was able to do so in their common language. He sent money to the old country, served as a ticket agent, and often went bankrupt, by either mismanagement or outright fraud, as did many nonimmigrant banks in America. The largest and most traumatic such collapse was the bank supervised by Archbishop John B. Purcell (1800-83) of Cincinnati, which failed with a great loss of immigrant's savings. Immigrants, who came to America ignorant and/or distrustful of banks in general, often had their prejudices confirmed by their experience here. The great exception among "immigrant" bankers was Amadeo Pietro Giannini (1870-1949), the son of immigrants from Liguria, who founded the small Bank of Italy in San Francisco's North Beach, a largely Italian enclave, in 1904. Tradition has it that he won the confidence of many by being the first banker to resume payments after the earthquake and fire of 1906.

Whatever the reasons, its growth was phenomenal and, under its later name of Bank of America—adopted in 1928 as Mussolini's unpopularity began to rub off on anything named for Italy—became one of the largest banking empires in the world.

Beginning in the 1880s, the size and character of Italian immigration changed. The three hundred thousand immigrants of the 1880s were more than three times as many as had come in all American history; the six hundred thousand of the 1890s doubled that, and the more than two million of the first decade of the new century represented a further tripling. Put another way, the forty-four thousand Italian born of 1880 represented about six of every thousand foreign born in the nation; by 1920 the more than 1.6 million Italian born represented 117 in every thousand foreign born. (Italians ranked well behind natives of Russia and Germany; the three nationalities comprised two-fifths of the nation's foreign born in 1920.) These Italian immigrants were heavily male—males outnumbered females three to one—and were quite likely to return. Perhaps a majority of all the Italians who came here never intended to stay. What is important is not that fact, but that so many *did* stay.

The settlement patterns for Italians changed with the mass immigration from the Mezzogiorno. Some 97 percent of Italians in the four and a half decades after 1880 migrated through the port of New York, and vast numbers stayed there. By 1920 there were almost four hundred thousand Italian immigrants in New York City, nearly a quarter of all the Italian foreign born. Yet, although some authors persist in writing about New York's Italians as if they all lived below Washington Square, the fact is that as early as 1920 fewer than half lived anywhere in Manhattan; more than a third lived in Brooklyn and a tenth in the Bronx, with some 7 percent in Queens and Richmond. Similarly in Chicago, the neighborhood around Hull-House, habitually referred to as Italian, was in fact only about one-third so. What gave these neighborhoods, and the enclaves of other ethnic groups, their particular flavor were the predominant ethnic businesses in each. Despite much loose talk about ethnic ghettos, only racially segregated neighborhoods, those for blacks and Chinese primarily, came anywhere close to 100 percent uniformity. Counted by region, Italians were concentrated in the Middle Atlantic and New England states; despite a large Italian population in Chicago, they were not heavily represented in the Middle West. In the Far West there was a concentration in California, where in 1920 Italians were the largest foreign-born group, comprising more than a tenth of that population. And although relatively few immigrants now ventured to the South, there was a continuing Italian presence in and around New Orleans.

Counted by occupation, Italians in the United States were found largely in manual labor. As early as the 1890s commentators were noting that the Irish no longer built the railroads and paved the streets; Italians did. This concentration continued into the twentieth century and soon extended into the building trades. Perhaps the classic Italian immigrant novel, Pietro di Donato's *Christ in Concrete* (1939), movingly describes the life of a construction worker and his family as seen through the eyes of his son Paulie, obviously di Donato himself. Other Italian occupations included vending. The pushcart became one of the stereotypes of Italian American life, as did what must have been a relatively rare occupation, that of organ grinder with monkey. So strong was this image that when one showed up in faraway Prescott, Arizona, the young Fiorello La Guardia recalled vividly his embarrassment when his schoolmates noted that both the musician and he were Italians.[4]

Many Italians, especially in the early years of mass migration, got their jobs through ethnic labor contractors, called *padroni.* Similar arrangements were made by other immigrant groups, including Chinese, Japanese, Mexicans, and, as we shall see later in this chapter, Greeks. The labor contractor was most often himself an immigrant, but one who had mastered enough English to mediate for his fellow countrymen. The *padrone,* of course, often exploited the workers shamelessly, and in some industries, such as longshoring and hotel trades, kickbacks of salaries and other practices persisted long after the need for an intermediary translator had passed. (Such practices were not exclusive to immigrant labor contractors, it must be added.) A combination of muckraking exposé, more scientific management in most industries and, perhaps most important of all, increasing chain migration in which relatives and friends already here found jobs for the new immigrant, made the system less important for Italians as the new century progressed. A special and notorious form of the *patrone* system recruited and brought to America large numbers of young boys, mainly Italians and Greeks. The Italian boys were largely street musicians and acrobats, while the Greeks were fruit and candy vendors and, above all, shoeshine boys.

Wages were indeed low, and living conditions in the crowded urban tenements were appalling, but the notion one gets that the Italians were somehow poorer and more disadvantaged than other groups probably has more to do with their number and their exposure during the first age of investigative journalism than with their special plight. The occupants of the lower steps of the American ethnic escalator have always lived in deplorable conditions. Italians tended to send their children to work early: One often-cited study shows that some 90 percent of Italian American girls over fourteen were working in New York City just after World War I, fourteen then being the school-leaving age. Not surprisingly, few Italian youth in those years attended high schools. According to Humbert Nelli fewer than 1 percent of Italian American youth were enrolled in high schools on the eve of World War I.

Unlike most other immigrant groups, Italian Americans founded relatively few communal and fraternal organizations. According to Rudolph J. Vecoli, the leading student of Italian Americans, this is due to their individualism, an individualism that expresses itself as intense attachment to family—especially in South Italian culture and its American offshoots. Along with this went the extreme parochialism that caused Italians to regard themselves as citizens of a village or a town, not a nation. This has been called *campanilismo*, the notion that the true *patria*, native land, extended only as far as the sound of the bells in the local *campanile*, or bell tower. In line with this view of the world, Italian immigrants, even in large American cities, tried to reform village and small town clustering. In an important article Vecoli identified seventeen such clusters within the Italian neighborhoods of Chicago. Nor were such migration chains limited to large cities. William Chazanoff and his students at SUNY, Fredonia, have published a pamphlet tracing the migration of a large number of families from one Sicilian village, Valledolmo, to one western New York village, Fredonia.[5] And similar stories could be written about literally hundreds of pairs of such places.

Although almost all Italian immigrants were and remained Catholics, their Catholicism was of a quite different nature than that of Irish and Polish Catholics on the one hand or German Catholics on the other. Whereas the former groups saw the church and its priests as the preservers of their embattled nationalism, Italian patriots saw priests as agents of the pope and opponents of the risorgimento, and thus opposed to Italian national aspirations. For Italians of the Mezzogiorno, the priest was often the agent of the bishop, who could be the landlord. A strong anticlerical tradition was part of the intellectual baggage that many Italians brought with them. In any event, Southern Italian Catholicism had its own kind of *campanilismo*: the special feast day, of a particular saint or an aspect of the Madonna. (Robert Orsi has described the transportation of one such *festa* to New York in his *Madonna of 115th Street*.)

Such believers often found little comfort in the Irish-dominated Catholic church in America. An outsider, who didn't understand the religious aspects of the *festa* commented, hyperbolically, that Italians went to church only three times—to be hatched, matched, and dispatched—but Italians clearly did not attend church with anything like the regularity of most other Catholic ethnics. Nor did very many, proportionally, find religious vocations. Considering the size of the Italian American community, its representation in the American hierarchy has been amazingly low: Only with the emergence of Joseph Bernardin, the son of Italian immigrants, as cardinal archbishop of Chicago, has an Italian American played a major role in the power structure of the American church. Nor did Italian Americans provide much support for parochial schools, although it is not clear whether this illustrates attitudes toward religion or education. In any event, few Italian immigrants, who slaved at low wages to save twenty-five or fifty cents a day, were going to pay the church for what the state provided free.

The most controversial aspect of the Italian American experience involves crime. Since most incoming immigrants enter American society at its bottom layers and live in decaying, crime-ridden neighborhoods, almost all have intimate contacts with crime and criminals early in their lives in the United States—most often as victims. For a minority of young immigrants, as the sociologist Daniel Bell has written, crime has served as a means of upward social mobility.[6] These immigrants have been of every imaginable ethnic group. Complaints linking ethnicity and crime began in the Colonial Era with talk about the crimes of Irish and German indentured servants and have continued, as witness contemporary stereotyping about Colombian drug dealers, the Chinese Triad Society, Vietnamese street gangs, or Soviet army deserters. It is instructive of the whole process that one of the first major talking pictures on the gangster theme, *Scarface* (1932), based vaguely on the life of Al Capone (1899-1947)—born in Brooklyn of Neapolitan parents—was remade in the 1980s with a Cuban rather than an Italian character as protagonist. (Ironically, a Jewish American actor, Paul Muni, played the Italian gangster, and an Italian American actor, Al Pacino, played the Cuban.)

Yet the persistence of the image of the Italian as criminal, from the Black Hand assassin with a stiletto at the turn of the century, to the Prohibition Era gangsters with machine guns, to the so-called Mafia and Costra Nostra of today, makes it one of the more enduring ethnic stereotypes. The notion of an international Mafia conspiracy centered in

Palermo and dominating all Italian American crime is a foolish one. As students of the very real Italian Mafia point out, its power does not even extend into southern Italy, let alone Brooklyn, Chicago, Las Vegas, or Los Angeles. That there are criminal organizations in the United States with largely Italian American membership and that these and other criminal groups engaged in the drug trade have foreign connections are undeniable statements. But the attempts of some politicians, like Estes Kefauver, John McClellan, and Robert Kennedy, and some district and U.S. attorneys to turn the whole business of crime into an ethnic "conspiracy so vast" have been reprehensible. They are consonant with an American cultural tradition of scapegoating and imagining conspiracies that goes back to the Salem witchcraft trials and has, at one time or another, accused Negro slaves, Catholics, Freemasons, Mormons, and Jews of conspiring at the downfall of the republic.

The changing responses of Italian Americans have been instructive. Some of the earliest were defensive. As early as 1907 some in Chicago organized a White Hand Society devoted to law and order; others have simply denied that there were any such things as Italian American criminal organizations. Recently, however, more ambivalent attitudes have surfaced—attitudes that may be seen most conveniently in reactions to the film *The Godfather*. In Kansas City, for instance, local Italian American groups bought up every seat for the film's premiere but made sure that the house remained empty. On the other hand, some serious scholars have argued that Mario Puzo's book, on which the film is based, is a great immigrant novel about family solidarity. Actually, the Corleone family of the novel resembles real gangsters about as much as Paul Bunyan does real lumberjacks, but the overreaction is understandable. The whole Mafia syndrome is part and parcel of the particularly virulent prejudice that has been heaped on Italian Americans since the late nineteenth century.

As Italians were relatively late to arrive and did not have a great propensity to become naturalized, their political participation was low and few Italian Americans won or were appointed to high political office. Some writers speak of Anthony Caminetti (1854-1923)—a second-generation Italian American who served in the California legislature, was elected to Congress, and then became Woodrow Wilson's commissioner of immigration—as an early ethnic politician, but he was not. Elected from tiny Amador County, which had no sizable Italian population, Caminetti claimed to be the first native son to be elected to Congress from California—thus nicely ignoring a Mexican American congressman,

Romualdo Pacheco (1831-99), elected in the 1870s. Caminetti was not only a leading figure in the state's anti-Japanese movement but was an anti-immigrant commissioner of immigration during the nativist episodes of the World War I era. Fiorello H. La Guardia (1882-1947), initially elected to Congress in 1916 from a partly Italian district on New York's Upper East Side, was the first successful Italian American ethnic politician to occupy a significant position on the national political stage. In the 1930s, as mayor of New York, he became one of the nation's best-known leaders. Less prominent but more typical of Italian American ethnic politics were two New York ward bosses, James March and Paul Kelly. The first, born Antonio Maggio in 1860, came to the United States at age thirteen and was successively a labor agent for the Erie Railroad, a prosperous entrepreneur, and had an interest in an immigrant bank. From 1894 to 1910 he was the Republican leader on the Lower East Side. The second, born Paolo Antonio Vaccarelli in Naples, took his Irish-sounding name when he became a boxer. (In this era and later many boxers of various ethnic cities, including some Jews and blacks, fought under Irish names.) He was the Democratic counterpart to March and later became a vice president of the corrupt International Longshoremen's Association.[7]

Since most Italian Americans in the labor force were in unskilled and semiskilled jobs, relatively few Italian Americans were in the unionized sectors of American industry and even fewer were found in the leadership of the American Federation of Labor in the first quarter of the twentieth century. An exception must be noted for the garment workers' unions. Although the top leadership was largely Jewish, there were Italian vice presidents such as Luigi Antonini (1883-1968) and Salvatore Ninfo (1883-1960) of the International Ladies Garment Workers' Union. Ninfo, who had led a strike of Italian American subway diggers when he was just seventeen, became a vice president of the ILGWU in 1916. In the men's clothing union, the Amalgamated Clothing Workers, Anzuino D. Marimpetri was a longtime vice president. The one AFL union to have Italian presidents in this era was, appropriately, one for the semiskilled—the Hod Carriers and Building Laborers—which had at least two Italian-born presidents, including James Moreschi (1884-1970) of Chicago, who held the office from 1926 to 1948.

In the American radical movement, especially in its anarchist/syndicalist wings, Italians were of increasing importance. Gilded Age American anarchism had been largely German, as exemplified by the anarchists prosecuted and executed after the 1886 Haymarket Riot in Chicago who were mainly German immigrants, despite the *bürgerliche* (middle-class) image that German America presents. But early twentieth-century anarchism in America spoke, and spoke eloquently, with a distinct Italian accent. Brooklyn-born Joseph J. Ettor (1885-1948) and Italian-born Arturo Giovannitti (1884-1959) were key organizers and agitators for the Industrial Workers of the World (IWW) in epic strikes of immigrant workers in Lawrence, Massachusetts (1912), and Paterson, New Jersey (1913). Giovannitti, in addition, is the only American labor leader I can think of who was a serious published poet, as witness his *Arrows in the Gale* (1914), mostly written while he was serving a prison sentence for his radical activities during the Lawrence strike.

It was two other Italian-born immigrants who came to symbolize American anarchism for the world: Nicola Sacco (1891-1927) and Bartolomeo Vanzetti (1888-1927). An obscure fish peddler and an unknown shoemaker, they were arrested, tried, and convicted for a robbery and murder in 1920 and, after a protest campaign that swept the world, were executed by the Commonwealth of Massachusetts in 1927. While a spate of books by historians and pseudohistorians has tried and retried Sacco and Vanzetti with differing verdicts, no one can any longer even pretend that they received a fair trial. These men symbolized, both for patricians like Judge Webster Thayer, who sentenced the men he allegedly referred to as "anarchist bastards," and for millions of ordinary Americans, the dangerous ideas and deeds that foreigners could bring in. Their trial, which took place just before passage of the Emergency Quota Act of 1921, and their execution, which took place three years after Congress all but closed the golden door of immigration, punctuate and symbolize the end of an era—what I have called the century of immigration—for America.

No other Mediterranean groups came in the kinds of numbers that Italians did, but two of them, the Greeks and the largely Christian Arabs of the Levant, will be discussed at some length. Some six hundred thousand Greeks came before 1924, and perhaps one hundred thousand Arabs. The former are discussed in every history of immigration worthy of the name, the latter, until recently, have been largely ignored.

GREEKS

Unlike the Italians, Greeks who immigrated to the United States generally had a fierce sense of their own Greekness, of the glories of the Greek heritage, even though—or more possibly because—that heritage had so long languished under the alien rule of another people of a different faith. This sense of distinctiveness was aided by the fact that they did not have to find a place within a church already well established in America: The Orthodox congregations they founded were ethnically Greek from the very beginning. While it is true that provincial and regional differences and animosities existed—as between Arcadians and Spartans, for example—the general Greek consciousness tended to override them. This is not to suggest that Greek Americans were unified, except in regard to their Turkish oppressors and Balkan enemies. Greek American politics and religion were highly partisan and conflict ridden.[8] Although Greeks came early to the New World, they did so as individuals and not as communities. Numerically significant Greek immigration did not begin until the 1980s. During the era of Greek immigration, more Greeks lived outside Greece—in the Balkans, in Turkey, in Egypt, and all along the Mediterranean littoral—than lived in it. The leading scholar of Greek Americans, Theodore Saloutos, thought it a good rule of thumb to assume that two-thirds of the immigrants from Turkey during this period were ethnic Greeks. The following table, which lists all immigrants from Greece and Turkey recorded by the INS, may be used accordingly. Thus, using the Saloutos formula that two-thirds of Turks are ethnic Greeks, we get a figure of ethnic Greek immigration from Greece and Turkey of 587,970 (370,405 + 2/3 of 326,347, or 217,565). Other parts of the Greek diaspora also sent smaller but still sizable

Table 7.4

Immigrants from Greece and Turkey, 1820-1920

YEARS	GREECE	TURKEY
1820-30	20	21
1831-40	49	7
1841-50	16	59
1851-60	31	83
1861-70	72	131
1871-80	210	404
1881-90	2,308	3,782
1891-1900	15,979	30,425
1901-10	167,519	157,369
1911-20	184,201	134,066
Total	370,405	326,347

numbers to the United States. In 1976, the INS estimated that 640,000 ethnic Greeks had come to the United States between 1820 and 1975. Many experts hold that figure to be too small. By 1975 the Greek American population was at least twice that number.

Although Greece, or some of it, achieved independence from Turkey in 1821, Greece has not been able to sustain its still-burgeoning population, and emigration has been a factor in its demographic history since the late nineteenth century. The Greeks who came to the United States in the era of immigration were very heavily male and were the only fairly large European group of which more than half returned; Archdeacon gives figures of 87.8 percent and 53.7 percent. This was not too different from the Italian American experience—the figures there were 74.5 percent male and 45.6 percent remigration—and, in fact, Greek and Italian immigration are similar in many other ways. But there are important differences.

The settlement patterns of Greeks were quite dispersed, but almost all of them pursued urban occupations. The soil had little attraction for Greek emigrants who associated it with misery and hardship in their native land. The majority during the two heavy decades of immigration of this century came from small villages in the Peloponnesus and elsewhere in Greece proper, but sizable minorities came from the Greek islands and European and Asiatic Turkey. The latter groups were almost all urban, somewhat better educated, and often created small businesses in the United States. Greeks settled primarily in the great immigrant belt of the northeastern and northcentral states, although, as was true for Italians, a large number went to California. A smaller number, almost all of them from the Greek islands, settled on the west coast of Florida, centered around Tarpon Springs, where they pursued, and still pursue, sponge fishing. (One of the American television networks uses a heavily Greek American precinct in Tarpon Springs to inform its viewers how Greek Americans voted, despite the obviously special nature of that area.)

The earliest Greek immigrants took what jobs they could find in both heavy and light industry and were never as concentrated as were Italians and Jews in the clothing industry. Railroad construction gangs, textile mills, meat-packing, and mining occupied significant numbers of immigrants. Others, as we have seen, were employed by *padrone*-organized shoeshine stands, some of which evolved into shoeshine parlors. Relatively large numbers of Greeks became small businessmen and, for reasons that are not at all clear, large numbers of these opened restaurants. These were not restaurants that featured Greek cuisine but were generally modest places that featured inexpensive general food, the kind of place often referred to as a "greasy spoon" restaurant. (Wherever there was a sizable Greek American community one or more coffeehouses where Greek men could meet and talk would be established, but that is a different matter.) The economic niches filled by immigrants in small businesses are not predictable based on what immigrants did in the old country. Few if any emigrating Greeks ran restaurants in Greece, just a few Italians ran barbershops in Italy, and no Chinese ran laundries in China. Yet, early Greek, Italian, and Chinese immigrants established such businesses and hired fellow immigrants who learned the ropes and later went into business for themselves. All three of these dissimilar businesses had common characteristics. None required large amounts of capital, each was labor intensive, and each provided services to the general low-income public. In some instances these businesses could have been interchangeable—Greeks could have specialized in barbershops and Italians in small restaurants—and it was largely historical happenstance that each European group found the niche that it did. (On the West Coast, at about the same time, Japanese immigrants with a little capital often set up small workingmen's restaurants, and, in Seattle, a number of barbershops. And in Lima, Peru, but nowhere else as far as I can discover, Japanese immigrants came to dominate beauty parlors.) Other lightly capitalized lines that attracted large numbers of Greeks were candy stores and confectioneries of various kinds. In addition, there were in the Greek American community, as in any immigrant community of any size, numbers of businesses that catered to the ethnic group—grocery stores (stores that not only stocked large containers of olive oil and resinated wine, but where the shopper could do business in Greek), ticket brokers, and similar enterprises. Most of these were quite small enterprises and the failure rate in immigrant businesses was probably even higher than the general small business failure rate. Few of their owners achieved anything more than a modest competence and many did not even get that.

One line of enterprise in which some Greeks pioneered that did grow into a giant industry was the showing of motion pictures and other cheap amusements for the working public. The first movie houses in immigrant neighborhoods were simply stores in which a few benches, a screen, and a projector were the only equipment. The motion picture industry came to be dominated by immigrants, mostly Jews, but a significant number of Greeks, notably Alexander Pantages (died 1936), who developed one of the largest theater chains showing both films and vaudeville acts, and Spyros Skouras (1893-1971) and his brothers who controlled the 20th Century-Fox studios.

The first Greek immigrants sometimes found existing Orthodox churches—organized Orthodoxy came to North America in 1794 when Russian monks began missionary work among the Aleuts and Tlingit Indians of Alaska—but most Greeks wanted not just Orthodox churches but ones that were Greek in language and culture. The first Greek Orthodox Church in the United States predated the major groups of immigrants by decades: It was founded by Greek cotton merchants in Yankee-occupied New Orleans in 1864. No other churches were established until the 1890s—in New York, Chicago and Lowell, Massachusetts—and by 1909 they were scattered across the country as far as Portland, Oregon; San Francisco; and Los Angeles. There were more in the textile centers of Massachusetts than anywhere else.

Church officials in Greece did not send missionary priests to the United States, since it was technically under the jurisdiction of the Russian Orthodox Church. Thus lay initiative was crucial in the founding of Greek American parishes. Typically, the laypeople would raise money or pledges sufficient to start a parish and then ask the ecumenical patriarchate or the Synod of Greece to send a priest or priests to operate the parish. In such parishes clashes between laity and clergy were all but inevitable. In addition, the governance of all the Greek American churches was quite complex. Initially they were under Russian jurisdiction, as noted. Between 1908 and 1922 they were under the governance of the Church of Greece. But since that church was a state church, and since Greece was torn between monarchist and republican factions, this created confusion and, at times, schisms. At one time, in the early 1920s, there were in the United States the deposed metropolitan of Athens, and two bishops, one appointed by him, one by his successor, each claiming authority over and seeking the loyalty of all Greek American churches. The result was chaotic, and lawsuits and secessions of parishes seemed to be the rule rather than the exception until a general settlement was made in 1930.

These divisions were not over essentially religious matters but over Greek politics and reflected chiefly the disputes between King Constantine I (1868-1923), his supporters, and Eleuthérios Venizélos (1864-1936), head of the Greek Liberal party and his supporters. Greece's two victories in the Balkan Wars of 1912-13, during which some forty-two thousand Greek Americans returned to fight for their mother country, created a wave of Greek patriotism and visions of a new Greek empire with headquarters in Constantinople. But in the early 1920s Greek irredentism suffered a series of disasters at the hands of the troops of Kemal Atatürk. The liberal/royalist split in Greek politics was mirrored by rival post-World War I Greek American organizations—the American Hellenic Educational Progressive Association (AHEPA) and the Greek American Progressive Association (GAPA). Their dispute was not just over Greek politics but over what loyalties Greek Americans should have: issues that arise in every immigrant population in one way or another.

AHEPA preached doctrines of Americanization and nonsectarianism and was accommodationist and aggressively middle class. Its rival accused it of forcing Greek Americans to deny their roots, and many were outraged that it used only English in its proceedings (at least officially), that it sanctioned mixed marriages with non-Orthodox, and that its members needed only to affirm a belief in a Supreme Being, not be members of the Greek Orthodox Church.

GAPA, although it, too, insisted that it was "progressive," was stubbornly anti-assimilationist. GAPA generally thought that all Greek Americans should learn and use Greek, cultivate the Greek heritage, and, above all, adhere to the Orthodox church. AHEPA won the battle hands down. Second- and third-generation Greek Americans are no more likely to have a functional knowledge of the tongue of their ancestors than is any other American ethnic group. And, it should be noted, despite GAPA accusations, AHEPA did stress pride in Greek cultural achievements, particularly those of its classical civilization, about which almost all Greek Americans seem to know a great deal.

The late arrival of most Greek immigrants, and their numbers and relative dispersion, meant that there would be few Greeks of the immigrant generation in American politics, and no Greek Americans played any role on the national political stage in the period under consideration. The most famous Greek in America was clearly Jim Londos (1895-1975), the "golden Greek" who was a world champion wrestler when wrestling in America was still a sport and not an exhibition of sadomasochistic fakery.

ARABS

Although most Americans equate the ethnic term *Arab* with Muslims, the fact of the matter is that until the very recent past almost all Arabs who immigrated to the United States were Christians of several Eastern Rite churches. They came from what was, in the later Turkish Empire, the autonomous administrative district of Mount Lebanon, essentially the area served by the two ports of Beirut and Tripoli. Christianity in that part of the Levant, of course, dates from the beginnings of the Christian Era, centuries before both the rise of Islam and the Christianization of most of Europe. Most of the earlier writing about these immigrants, about one hundred thousand of whom came before World War II, called them Syrians, while many of the immigrants called themselves Lebanese, particularly after the foundation of the republic of Lebanon in 1946. In parts of West Africa and Latin America, where immigrants from this region have also settled, they are known by various names, including Turks, since they were, until after World War I, subjects of the Ottoman Empire. In recent years the umbrella term *Arab Americans* has come to be used to describe a variety of national and religious groups—most of them Muslim—and that usage will be applied retroactively here.

Alixa Naff, the leading student of Arab Americans, believes that the first Arabs "to discover the economic opportunities of the United States" were a group of Christian tradesmen who came under Ottoman sponsorship to exhibit various Syrian wares at the Philadelphia World's Fair celebrating the centennial of American independence in 1876.[9] The enthusiastic reports of these merchants, the activities of recruiting agents, economic pressures at home, and, after 1908, compulsory military service, all combined to create a chain migration from the slopes of Mount Lebanon to the United States.

Although the Arab immigration was initially one of bachelors, women soon began to come, almost always as members of families. Fragmentary records indicate that perhaps 47 percent of the immigration before 1924 was female. The overwhelming majority of early Arabs—as many as 90 percent before 1914—began earning their living in the United States as peddlers. Like other groups this was a specialization they adopted after emigrating: In their homeland peddling was largely confined to minority groups—Greeks, Armenians and Jews. The Arab peddlers covered the entire nation, some of them working a distant territory or route for weeks and even months before returning to their base. Others were city peddlers and slept at home every night. Initially most peddlers sold rosaries, costume jewelry, and notions—the sort of things that would fit into a small suitcase or pack. As they quickly acquired English from dealing with their customers, many learned to stress the "fact" that their religious goods came from "the Holy Land." Later, when they had more capital, some peddlers made their rounds on horseback, with wagons, and eventually automobiles, and were able to vend larger wares including imported rugs and linens.

The supplier, often himself a former peddler who had moved up a rung on the economic ladder, performed the same kinds of functions as did labor contractors and *padroni* for other ethnic groups. He encouraged fellow villagers to emigrate and sometimes financed their passage; he supplied them with goods, usually on credit, assigned routes, banked their money, tried to smooth their conflicts with officials (peddlers were always running afoul of some local ordinance or other), and generally served as mentor during their period of acculturation. As it had been for Jews earlier, peddling was most often a transitory occupation for individuals. The peddler had to acculturate, and acculturate quickly. Unlike the immigrant who spent his life in ethnic enclaves and worked at ethnic job sites, the peddler had an economic stake in learning the language and the folkways of other Americans. Once he—or she, since there were a few women peddlers—had learned the ropes, the economic rewards were greater than those for most contemporary immigrants. Naff, perhaps oversanguine, feels that "relatively few" were failures and that peddlers commonly calculated their annual earnings in thousands. Since in 1907, for example, the average annual wage for all nonfarm employees was $595—and most immigrants made less than the average—the Arab peddlers did quite well. Most peddlers who did well eventually went into business—typically in retail shops—and many of them, of course, became suppliers for other peddlers—often relatives and usually fellow villagers, whom they sponsored.

Not surprisingly New York was the initial center of Arab immigrants, and most of the early suppliers were importers who had settled there. But the expansion of Arab peddling territory meant that suppliers had to move—largely south and west—as well. By 1930 the census—not at its best in identifying small ethnic groups—noted just over seven thousand five hundred "Syrians" in New York City, while Detroit was becoming the Arab American second city, with more than five thousand. By 1970 the motor city would be the undoubted Arab American capital, with more than seventy thousand persons, Christian and Muslim, so identifying themselves. New York was also, in the years before 1914, home to a small group of Arabic-speaking and -writing intellectuals who had little contact with the larger Arab American community. The best known of this group, and the only name known to non-Arabic readers, was the translated poet Kahlil Gibran (1883-1931).

Religious institutions, as among the Greeks, were established by lay initiative after settlement and a certain amount of financial success. Between 1890 and 1895 New York Arabs founded three churches, one for each of the three major sects represented among the immigrants—Melkite, Maronite, and Orthodox—and imported priests to serve them. In the next three decades more than seventy additional Arab American churches were founded, with masses conducted in Arabic or Syriac. As more than half of these were in the East, this meant that many people in the far-flung settlements were not served by any ethnic church. Many of these families, and other Arab Christians, attended "American" churches. both Roman Catholic and Protestant.

For the small Muslim minority the problems were even more difficult. It is hard to be a Muslim in a non-Muslim society. Although Muslims, like Jews, have no priesthood and can pray almost anywhere, the imam and the mosque have become as central to Muslim worship as the rabbi and the synagogue have become to the Jewish. Naff illustrates this by talking about one of the few early Muslim settlements, near Ross, North Dakota, established around the turn of the century. There was no mosque until the 1920s, and prayer and ritual were conducted in private homes. The small community, which received no reinforcement, soon lost the use of Arabic. Many adopted Christian names, married non-Muslims, and others moved away. The ethnically conscious community shrank, and the mosque was abandoned by 1948. Only two other mosques are known to have been built anywhere in the United States before the 1930s.

ARMENIANS

Unlike the other groups discussed in this chapter, Armenians are not a Mediterranean people but originated in northeast Asia Minor. Converted to Christianity early in the Christian Era, the Armenians became in the Later Middle Ages one of the subject peoples of the Ottoman Empire. In the process many Armenians reestablished an Armenian kingdom in Cilicia, in southern Mediterranean Turkey just north of present-day Syria. This, too, was overrun in 1385. While some Armenians achieved high economic status under the Ottomans, becoming bankers, skilled artisans, and at times even advisors to the sultans, most were farmers, and many emigrated in late medieval and early modern times to such places as the Crimea and Poland. A few even came to America: The records show that one Martin the Armenian came to Jamestown in either 1618 or 1619, but nothing more is known of him. Handfuls of other Armenians found their way to America and other parts of the New World in the next two and a half centuries, but it was only in the late 1880s that statistically significant migration began. As is the case with other subject nationalities, it is difficult to differentiate Armenians in the American immigration records. Probably around one hundred thousand came to the United States between the late 1880s and the virtual closing of immigration for them in 1924. The period was punctuated by an awful event few Armenians can forget: the massacres—some would say genocidal massacres—of Armenians by Turks in 1915, which had been preceded by waves of persecution and killings in 1894-96 and again in 1909. Today the Armenian SSR contains more than two million Armenians, while another million live elsewhere in the USSR. The largest non-Soviet Armenian community is in the United States, where perhaps half a million Armenian Americans now live.[10] The fifty thousand Armenians who came in the years before World War I arrived mainly by two distinct routes to establish two very different kinds of communities. Initially most Armenian immigrants came through New York and settled in eastern cities and worked in factories much as did other immigrants of that era. Most of the prewar Armenian migration was of Turkish origin, and, after the 1909 atrocities, it increased rapidly: In 1913 nearly ten thousand came.

Migration from Russian Armenia was much smaller. Only after members of two pacifist sects who lived in and near Russian Armenia—Dukhobors and Molokans—began to migrate to Canada's Prairie Provinces in 1898 did some Russian Armenians follow them. Most did not find Canada to their liking and eventually made their homes in and around Fresno, California, which became and remains the Armenian American capital. Perhaps two thousand five hundred had settled in California by 1914. They were one of the few immigrant groups of this era to settle on the soil, although many worked in factories to save the money necessary to buy land.

Armenian immigrants of the prewar era present a profile both similar to and different from those of other immigrants of that time. They were highly male and had a moderate return migration rate: Archdeacon's table shows 71.3 percent and 18.1 percent. Almost all males over fourteen were literate, about two-fifths had been town dwellers, and there were many artisans, businessmen, and professionals among them, particularly among the Armenians from Turkey. These latter had some of the characteristics of later refugees from the Third Reich. The pre-World War I immigrants, except for a few who had been subsidized by Canada, used their own or community resources to come to America. Most of those in the postwar era were aided by refugee organizations. This immigration presents a vastly different profile: More than thirty thousand persons were involved, just over half of them women and a fifth children.

The Armenians of the Fresno region, made famous by William Saroyan (1908-81), the most celebrated Armenian American author, have a unique history. Their history in this rich farming region, where some thirty thousand foreign-born Armenians lived in 1930 (New York City's seven thousand ranked second and Detroit's three thousand five hundred third) is a story of successful response to special challenge. Only here were there enough Armenians to establish an all-Armenian town—Yettem, which means Eden in Armenian—and only here were there enough Armenians for special discriminatory measures to be used against them. To be sure, all foreigners—especially those who looked and sounded "foreign"—suffered at one time or another in America—but it takes a certain critical mass relative to the general population in an area for special, pointed discrimination to take place; In Fresno the most enduring form of discrimination was the restrictive covenant that kept them, along with Asians, Mexicans, and blacks, from buying homes in Fresno's better neighborhoods. (Elsewhere the most frequent other targets of restrictive covenants were Jews; in some parts of upstate New York, Italians were the target group.) They were also barred from most of Fresno's social organizations, including the YMCA and veterans' groups, and were even expelled from a Congregational Church some of them had helped to fund. More threatening were attempts to have them declared aliens ineligible for citizenship, along with Asians. The federal government began denying Armenian petitions for naturalization in 1909, but a federal court ruling of that year, reinforced by an appellate court decision of 1924 in the *Tateos Cartozian* case prevented such denials. Thus the California Alien Land Acts of 1913 and 1920 affected only Asians. Restrictive covenants, in Fresno and elsewhere, remained legal until struck down by the U.S. Supreme Court in *Shelley v. Kraemer* (1948).

The Armenian Apostolic church in America has had a conflict-ridden history based, as was true for the Greek Orthodox, on Old World problems. The first parish was established in Worcester, Massachusetts, in 1891, and the poor and relatively small community was supporting ten churches and seventeen imported priests by 1916. (Only in 1962 was an institution to train Armenian rite priests opened in the U.S.) The Russian

Revolution caused a severe split in the Armenian church: The crux was not theological but political. Should Armenian Americans recognize the church in Soviet Armenia, which had made its peace, more or less, with the Soviet authorities? One faction, Ramgavars, said yes; the other, Tashnags, said no. Full schism came when Archbishop Levon Tourain was assassinated while he was celebrating mass in New York City on Christmas Eve 1933. Nine members of the Tashnag faction were convicted of the crime. A small minority of Armenian Americans, perhaps 5 percent, are Protestants. There is an even smaller number of Armenian American Roman Catholics, whose few American churches are under the authority of the Armenian Patriarchate in Beirut and use an Eastern-rite mass in Armenian. ✦

NOTES

1. Maldwyn A. Jones, *Destination America* (London, 1976), has a good account of immigrant ships and their disasters. A detailed analysis is in an essay by Günter Moltmann, "Steamship Transport of Emigrants from Europe to the United States, 1850-1914: Social, Commercial, and Legislative Aspects" (in press).
2. Robert F. Forster, *The Italian Emigration of Our Times* (Cambridge, Mass., 1919).
3. Andrew Rolle. *The American Italians* (Wadsworth, Calif., 1972), pp. 23-24. That and his *The Immigrant Upraised* (Norman, Okla., 1968) are particularly good on Italians in the American West. For Italians generally I follow Humbert Nelli, "Italians," *HEAEG**
4. Fiorello La Guardia. *The Making of an Insurgent* (Philadelphia, 1948), pp. 27-28.
5. Rudolph J. Vecoli, "Contadini in Chicago: A Critique of *The Uprooted*," *Journal of American History* 51 (December, 1963): 404-17. William Chazanof, *Valledolmo-Fredonia* (Fredonia, N.Y., 1961).
6. Daniel Bell, *The End of Ideology* (Glencoe, Ill., 1960).
7. The careers of March and Kelly are from Victor R. Greene, *American Immigrant Leaders, 1800-1910* (Baltimore, 1987).
8. Theodore Saloutos's *A History of Greeks in the United States* (Cambridge, Mass., 1964) and his "Greeks," *HEAEG*, are the definitive authorities.
9. Alixa Naff is the author of a pathbreaking monograph, *Becoming American: The Early Arab Immigrant Experience* (Carbondale, Ill., 1985), and the essay "Arabs," *HEAEG*.

---

*Harvard Encyclopedia of American Ethnic Groups

10. Robert Mirak's "Armenians," in *HEAEG* is the source for most of the material on Armenian Americans. For the modern historical background, see Richard G. Hovannisian, *Armenia on the Road to Independence* (Berkeley, 1967).

SELECTED BIBLIOGRAPHY

Amfitheatrof, Erik. *The Enchanted Ground: Americans in Italy, 1760-1980.* Boston, 1980.

Baily, Samuel L. "The Adjustment of Italian Immigrants in Buenos Aires and New York, 1870-1914." *American Historical Review* (April 1983): 281-305.

Bucchioni, Eugene; and Cordasco, Francesco, eds. *The Italians: Social Backgrounds of an American Croup.* Clifton, New Jersey, 1974.

Caroli, Betty B.; Harney, Robert F.; and Tomasi, Lydio F. *The Italian Immigrant Woman in North America.* Toronto, 1978.

Colburn, David R., and Pozzetta, George E. "Crime and Ethnic Minorities in America: A Bibliographic Essay." *The History Teacher* (August 1974): 597-609.

Cordasco, Francesco; and Pitkin, Thomas M. *The Black Hand: A Chapter in Ethnic Crime.* Totowa, New Jersey, 1977.

Covello, Leonard. *The Social Background of the Italo-American School Child: A Study of the Southern Italian Family Mores and Their Effect on the School Situation in Italy and America.* Totowa, New Jersey, 1972.

Egelman, William, and Krase, Jerome, eds. *The Melting Pot and Beyond: Italian Americans in the Year 2000.* Staten Island, New York, 1987.

Gambino, Richard. *Blood Of My Blood: The Dilemma Of The Italian-Americans.* Garden City, New York, 1974.

Gans, Herbert. *The Urban Villagers: Group and Class in the Life of Italian-Americans.* New York, 1972.

Johnson, Colleen L. *Growing Up and Growing Old in Italian-American Families.* New Brunswick, New Jersey, 1985.

Mormino, Gary R. *Immigrants on the Hill: Italian-Americans in St. Louis, 1882-1982.* Chicago, 1986.

Rolle, Andrew. *The Italian Americans: Troubled Roots.* New York, 1980.

Simmons, Donald C. "Anti-Italian American Riddles in New England." *Journal of American Folklore* 79 (1966): 475-78.

Tomasi, Lydio, ed. *Italian Americans: New Perspectives in Italian Immigration and Ethnicity.* Staten Island, New York, 1985.

W SAMO POŁUDNIE
4 CZERWCA 1989

In 1989 President George Bush spoke proudly of sharing "a movement that has touched the imagination of the world. That movement is Solidarnosc."[1] And in a highly symbolic poster, Solidarity blended an historic moment in Polish history with an American movie icon: Gary Cooper at high noon urging voters to come out on election day. **Source:** *New Yorker,* Nov. 13, 1989.

Although President Bush applauded one of Poland's great leaders, Lech Walesa, and spoke of Poland's time of destiny, for many Polish and other Slavic Americans, all of this was a reminder of the traumatic changes in Eastern Europe and the Soviet Union. Who then are these Slavic Americans?

THE SLAVIC HERITAGE

ALFRED J. WROBEL

I

Ancestors of Slavic Americans generally follow three major geographical divisions which by the mid-20th century embraced over 200 million people:

West Slavs: Poles, Czechs (Bohemians and Moravians), Slovaks, Wends (in East Germany).
South Slavs: Serbs, Croats, Slovenes, Macedonians, Montenegrins, and Bulgarians (except for the latter, most South Slavs are in Yugoslavia.).
East Slavs: Great Russians, White Russians, (Byelorussians), Ukrainians, Carpatho-Rusyns (also known as Rusnaks, Ruthenians, Uhro-Rusnyns Carpatho-Russians, or Carpatho-Ukrainians), Cossacks.

Within these geographical distinctions, there is a Slavic heritage deeply rooted in two worlds. Those Slavs in the East were exposed to Byzantine, Mongol, and Turkish influences; whereas, those in the West belatedly shared in some West European developments, such as the Renaissance and the Reformation. Hence, in any survey of the immense complexities of Slavic history, several themes recur:

1. **Super Power Rivalry**: The history of the Slavs and non-Slavs of Eastern Europe is written in the rise and fall of the Ottoman, Jagiellonian, Hapsburg, Hohenzollern, Romanov, and Soviet empires. Harry Schwartz, a specialist on Soviet Affairs, has written that:

> Through two thousand years this region has been the high road for innumerable invasions of Europe and Asia, as well as the battlefield on which rival empires has clashed. Roman, Hun, Mongol, Byzantine, Turkish, Austrian, German, Russian, and Italian armies have marched across Eastern Europe and ruled parts of it for months, years, or centuries. For most of the time since the American Revolution the great

> majority of its people have been the subject of foreign powers, victims of alien oppression. On the eve of World War I the Polish nation was under German, Austro-Hungarian, and Russian rule; the Czechs were subject to Austria and the Slovaks to Hungary; the Albanians had just gained their freedom from Turkey. In 1914, too, there were many Rumanians, Bulgarians, and Serbs who still vividly remembered Turkish rule, which did end until the last third of the nineteenth century.[2]

2. **Nationalism**: Not only has this powerful force been creative (e.g., in Slavic literature), but also, unfortunately, destructive in the sense that it has brought greater division and strife among the various Slavs, each struggling for their own national unity and independence. Even after they left their respective countries, many Slavs very often waged the fight for national survival and liberation of their homelands from American shores.

3. **Religious Differences**: These are reflected in the ethnic groups belonging to the Eastern Orthodox Church (Serbs, Macedonians, Montenegrins, Bulgarians, most Ukrainians, some Carpatho-Rusyns, Russians, Cossacks, and some Byelorussians) and those of the Roman Catholic Church (Croats, Slovenes, some Ukrainians, some Carpatho-Rusyns, most Byelorussians, Poles, Czechs, and Slovaks). There were even Slavic Moslems in some areas of the Balkans. A further distinction may be seen in writing and reading. Eastern Orthodox Slavs use the Cyrillic alphabet; the Roman Catholic Slavs, the Roman or Latin alphabet.[3] Most Slavic emigrants to the United States attempted to maintain their unique religious and cultural differences wherever they settled.

4. **Socioeconomic Backwardness and Instability of Eastern Europe**: Lasting effects of foreign domination, internal crisis, rigid class structure, overpopulation, famine, poverty, and wars—all contributed to the socioeconomic turmoil of this area and provided powerful incentives for emigration. A Croatian newspaper published in the United States, for example, welcomed Croatian immigrants by proclaiming that:

> Here you are your master, you are a gentleman, a real man, you are just as good as the owner of millions, and you have not to bow if you pass somebody in a gilded carriage, someone of a royal family. . . . Do not be afraid, brother. You will efface the black and doleful memories which accompanied you from the Old Country. Do not care what happened abroad. A new man you are now; the Atlantic voyage changed you, from today alone count what you know and what you do.[4]

II

As early as Jamestown, individual Slavs were attracted to America. For the next 150 years, they were a small peripheral group, some of whom, however, made contributions out of proportion to their numbers. Consider these diverse examples:

a. The Virginia Company granted contracts to several Poles for the making of pitch, tar, soap ashes, and glass in Jamestown. On one occasion the Poles helped Captain John Smith in a personal confrontation with one of the "mightiest and strongest Salvadges (sic) that Powhatan had under him."[5]

b. In the mid-17th century, Lord Baltimore of Maryland issued a land grant to the first known Czech immigrant to America, Augustine Herman, who founded Bohemia Manor and named Bohemia River of that colony.[6] The Bohemians with their German and Slavic characteristics also settled in 18th century Pennsylvania and North Carolina and contributed to an important tradition of colonial art and music.

c. In 1639 Russian *promyshlenniks* (fur trappers) reached the Pacific Coast. The Russians, unlike many other Slavic immigrants, settled in Alaska and eventually worked their way down the West Coast, thus setting the stage for a century and a half of big power rivalry with Great Britain, Spain, and the United States for the Pacific Northwest.[7] Today, there are reminders of the Russian Imperial past in such Alaskan names as Pribilof Islands (after a Russian ship's pilot), Baranof Island (after the Russian governor), and Alexander Archipelago (after the Czar);[8] and in California, "Fort Ross, Mount Saint Helena, Russian River, and Russian Gulch."[9]

d. In 18th century Spanish-America, the Croatian missionary, Jesuit Ferdinand Konscak (in Spanish, Fernando Consag) proved that Baja California was a peninsula and not an island.[10]

e. Polish military figures played significant roles in the American Revolution. The brilliant military engineer, Thaddeus Kosciuszko, built fortifications at Saratoga and West Point. His defenses at Saratoga helped to bring about the defeat of General Burgoyne and this stunning American victory changed the course for American independence by making France an open ally.

   After an outstanding wartime career, Kosciuszko—by then a Brigadier General—returned home to wage a similar battle for Polish independence and to become the "Washington" of Poland.

Kosciuszko remained an admirer of the Americans. He once said that "the title of an American will always be sacred to me."[11] And in his will, he named Thomas Jefferson his executor, instructing him to use Kosciuszko's assets for the liberation and education of Negro slaves.[12]

Early in the American Revolution, Kosciuszko's more colorful compatriot, Casimir Pulaski, was commissioned a Brigadier General. He headed an independent cavalry corps—the famous Pulaski Legion. In a trip to Poland, former President Carter noted that "not far from our home in the state of Georgia, a great patriot of both our nations, Casimir Pulaski, was mortally wounded while leading a cavalry legion in the fight for American independence."[13]

Both Pulaski and Kosciuszko helped to insure a permanent place for Polish Americans in the heroic legends of the American Revolution.

f. In the 19th century, a Slovene missionary, Frederic Baraga, prepared a Bible, grammar, and dictionary for the Chippewa-Ojibwa Indians of Upper Michigan and Northern Minnesota.[14]

g. An exile from the Polish Insurrection of 1830-1831, Dr. Felix P. Wierzbicki, after several months in the California Gold Region, authored the first book written *in English* to be published in the state of California: *California As It Is and As It May Be* or *A Guide to the Gold Region.* He was active also in organizing the first medical society in San Francisco.[15]

h. During the American Civil War, the Ukrainian engineer, John B. Turchin (Ivan Vasilevitch Turginoff) achieved considerable fame with the 19th Illinois Volunteers.[16] Likewise, several Polish exiles, among them Vladimir (Wlodzimierz) Krzyzanowski and Joseph Karge, enjoyed reputations as leaders and fighters against the southern forces. By the end of the war, all three had attained the rank of Brigadier General.[17]

III

At the end of the 19th century, there were important changes in the United States immigration which would affect further Slavic contributions to American society. Prior to 1882 most immigrants came from northwestern Europe, especially from Great Britain, Germany, and Scandinavia. After this date, the emphasis was on eastern and southern

Europe: the Slavs from the Austro-Hungarian Empire, the Jews from Russia, and the Italians from their economically poor south.

In the peak period from 1900-1914, some two and a half million East Europeans arrived. Today the second and third generations of these immigrants—the white ethnics—are raising questions about their position in American society. Understandably these white ethnics are taking a new look at the past record of their immigrant ancestors.

Generally of the peasant class, with little sophistication or formal education, the East European immigrants were seeking escape from the suppression of their culture and nationalism, from military authorities (the draft), or generally from unresponsive social and political structures. But above all they came for economic opportunity often expressed in such phrases as *za chlebem* (for bread). Novelist Louis Adamic tells us of the expectations of the Balkan peasants:

> In America one could make pots of money in a short time, acquire immense holdings, wear a white collar, and have polish on one's boots like a "gospod"—one of the gentry—and eat white bread, soup, and meat on week-days as well as on Sundays, even if one were but an ordinary workman to begin with. In Blato no one ate white bread or soup and meat, except on Sundays and holidays and very few then.[18]

There was also the glamour of America. A Slavic immigrant, Stoyan Christowe, who came to the United States alone in 1911 at the age of 13, recalls when he

> . . . was a boy in Macedonia, in my backward mountain village, there was a fascination with America. That's when people were coming in droves—by the millions. There was an obsession with America caused by the people who had been there and returned. They left as peasants, wearing rough clothes. They returned with neckties and collars, and money. The glamour surrounding them was just like the space age—they were Americanauts instead of astronauts. All of us children had never had ambitions to be policemen or firemen—we all wanted to become *komitaji* and fight the Turks. But that was displaced by the fascination with America. America represented this new world. There was no limit to what you could do.[19]

The majority of new Slavic immigrants settled in the northeastern and upper midwestern sections of the United States, with the major urban centers, especially New York and Chicago, providing the initial attraction.

What little job choices the immigrant might have had already would be determined by the location of the heavy manufacturing and mining industries. "Little Russias," "Little Bohemias," and "Little Polands" spread across the mining and heavy industrial areas of Pennsylvania, New York, Ohio, Indiana, Michigan, and Illinois. This heavy work—in the factories, steel mills, mines and slaughterhouses—was the greatest contribution of the pioneer Slavic immigrant to the building of a modern industrial America.

A Slovene immigrant recalled, after many years of hard work, how:

> I—we helped to build these buildings—we Slovenians and Croatians and Slovaks and other people who went to work. We helped to build many other cities, cities of which you never heard, and railroads, and bridges, all made of steel which our people make in the mills. Our men from the Balkans are the best steelworkers in America. And this smoke that you see here—it comes from the coal that we have dug up; we from the Balkans and from Galicia and Bohemia. We have also dug up much ore. I myself worked for a few years in the iron mines of the West. I lost my health in the mines. Miners get asthma and rheumatism. . . .[20]

While many Slavs took pride in being the "best steel workers in America," other Slavic immigrants followed a more traditional farming role. They picked up abandoned New England farms of earlier immigrants and turned them into productive units. Elsewhere, as the first Polish recipient of the Nobel Prize in Literature, Henry Sienkiewicz, reported in the 19th century:

> Polish settlements are to be found at Radom, Illinois; Krakow, Missouri; Polonia, Wisconsin; and Panna Maria, Texas. These are small agricultural towns of several hundred, possessing their own schools, churches, and local government in the American pattern. Their character is so typically Polish that they scarcely differ from similar towns in Poland itself. Even Jews are to be found in these communities but not in the same numbers as in Poland, for here they are attracted to the large commercial centers.[21]

Ukrainians took up homesteads in North Dakota, Montana, and Canada.[22] Wends from Saxony and Prussia settled on Texas farmlands.[23] And Slavic speaking Russian Mennonites—through a Santa Fe Railroad agent—bought 100,000 acres in Kansas and introduced a hardy winter wheat known as "Turkey Red."[24] Many of these immigrants made excellent plains farmers, because they knew, as Ian Frazier observed in the *New Yorker*, "how to build houses from sod, how to use manure and grass for fuel, how to be content on an isolated frontier."[25]

Whether rural or urban, the Slavic immigrant worker was hardly indifferent to his economic plight. The dehumanizing and dangerous working conditions for East Europeans, for example in the Chicago slaughterhouses, is vividly captured in one of America's best known novels, *The Jungle,* by Upton Sinclair. Published in 1906, the novel had a direct influence on the passage of a Meat Inspection Act and the Pure Food and Drug Act.[26]

Low wages and unsafe working conditions naturally led to strikes, some as violent as the 1897 anthracite strike in which 21 Polish and Hungarian immigrants were killed.[27] Other strikes were not so violent. At Lowell, Massachusetts, in 1912, the industrial Workers of the World, a rival union to the American Federation of Labor, led a successful non-violent strike with unskilled immigrant workers along ethnic lines—Italians, French Canadians, Irish, Belgian, and Polish. After eight weeks, the workers gained their demands, and ultimately more than 250,000 New England textile workers benefited in better pay.[28]

For many Slavic immigrants, the trade union might present him with still another opportunity. In 1905, a *Bulletin of the Bureau of Labor* reported that:

> In his trade union the Slav mixes with the Lithuanian, the German, and the Irish, and this is the only place they do mix until, by virtue of this intercourse and this mixing, clannishness is to a degree destroyed, and a social mixing along other lines comes naturally into play. Not only is the Amalgamated Meat Cutters' Union an Americanizing influence in the stock yards, but for the Poles, Lithuanians, and Slovaks it is the only Americanizing influence, so far as could be determined in this investigation.[29]

To Americanize then was to assimilate, but how well did the Slavic immigrant "Americanize?"

IV

The making of an American out of this Slavic immigrant involved adjustments to the pressures of an increasingly industrialized American society. He had come out of a peasant world where "accents, vocabularies, and styles of life varied considerably."[30] All of this added up to a picture of a "foreigner," tolerated by the native American so long as the Slavic immigrant remained a common laborer. After the oppressive foreign rule in their homelands, the Slavs saw freedom here, and they soon began to concentrate their efforts in constructing their own world in America.

Through their own mutual aid societies and immigrant banks, the Slavs sought land and home ownership for its real and symbolic meaning of stability and status. They published their own newspapers to preserve language and culture. Along with cooperative stores, boarding houses, and saloons, they sought medical, legal, and in particular, translating help in communicating with the outside world.

Above all there was the Church. Whether Roman Catholic or Orthodox (or any splinter group of these two), the Church was the initial center for immigrant life. In New Britain, Connecticut,

> . . . a priest first celebrated Mass for Poles in 1894, in an Irish Church. A year later, the Poles had a wooden building of their own. By 1902 this had become the rectory and the school, while a new church had been put up, costing no less than $150,000. By 1920 there were some 9,000 people in the parish, which was equipped with cemetery, orphanage, building societies, and saving banks, cooperative workshop and printing office, as well as a school with an enrollment of 1,700 children and a house for the nuns who taught them. In a larger city, a Catholic parish could show an even greater complexity. At St. Stanislaus Kostka, Chicago, in 1920 there were no fewer than seventy-four organizations, for all ages, some purely local, other branches of nationwide societies.[31]

Out in Cleveland, Ohio, the religious diversity was very pronounced in the founding of the Bohemian's St. Procop Parish (1892), the Slovenian's St. Vitas Parish (1893), the Slovak's SS Cyril and Methodius Parish (1902), the Croatian's St. Paul Parish (1902), and the Ukrainian's SS Peter and Paul Parish (1902).

The importance of this church influence cannot be exaggerated. For many Slavic Americans today, their church and their sense of national identity are closely related. To the Polish American, for example, Polish Catholicism is synonymous with Polish nationalism. For more than a hundred years, Poland was divided among the three partitioning powers of Russia, Prussia, and Austria-Hungary. During this time, the Catholic Church played a crucial role in maintaining Polish cultural traditions through the glorification of the Polish language. Hence, the sense of *polskosc* (Polishness) is firmly wedded to Catholicism. Furthermore, to Polish Americans there is not conflict of national loyalties here; in fact, being American and being Polish strengthen each other.

The visit of the first Polish Pope, John Paul II, to the United States in 1979 confirmed these feelings. Chicago Poles, in a city deemed the "Second Warsaw" because more people of Polish descent live there than in any other city in the world except the capital of Poland, were ecstatic. The Pope, after hearing yet another Polish American group singing the

Polish folk tune, *Sto Lat* (100 years), noted that "If we keep this up, they're going to think this is the Polish national anthem."[32]

This sense of unity among Polish Americans was not always so easily achieved. In the late 19th century, there did develop a serious division of opinion concerning the national and religious aims of Polish Americans. The two most important fraternal organizations for the Polish Americans were the Polish National Alliance (PNA) and the Polish Roman Catholic Union (PRCU), both headquartered in Chicago after 1880. Being nationalistic (for the liberation of Poland) and dominated by prominent laymen, the PNA ran into vociferous opposition of the PRCU which was concerned with the Catholicism of the Polish immigrants under clerical leadership. This division created bitter feelings among the Polish Americans until the First World War when the independence of Poland finally ended their disputes.[33]

Dissension marks the record of other Slavic groups. A majority of the Ukrainian immigrants to the United States were of the Roman Catholic faith—a fact historically determined by their geographical location and domination by Polish landlords. Such Ukrainians became known as Ukrainian Catholics or Uniates. But there were important differences in their type of Catholicism and the western European variety. Because "they enjoy the religious rights, services in the Old Slavonic, and married clergy, they officially call their religion Greek Catholic. This caused some confusion in America and numerous Americans have classed these people as Greeks."[34]

There was much friction between the Ukrainian immigrants and the American Catholic hierarchy, dominated by the Irish and German American bishops who often found the ethnic diversity of the Slavs unacceptable. But unlike other ethnic struggles for church autonomy, the Ukrainians successfully persuaded the Vatican in 1913 to permit their own Bishop an independence of action from the controls of the American bishops. Despite this success, however, many Ukrainians already had joined the Russian Orthodox Church, and after the First World War, continued internecine feuds led to a further proliferation of dissidents into various Ukrainian parishes.[35]

V

As with many other ethnic groups, the Slavic American assimilation into American life has seen a weakening of their cultural traditions. Language may soon disappear, yet the sense of being a Slavic American has not diminished. A pioneer in immigration history, Marcus Lee Hansen, once observed that "what the son wished to forget, the grandson wishes to remember."[36] Hence, some folk patterns have survived.

The Croats celebrate *Tamburitsa* (Tamburica) Day (after a popular musical instrument resembling a mandolin)[37]; the Poles have their *Polka Federation*, and for physical and cultural development, *Falcon* organizations; and the Czechs and Slovaks have their *Sokols* (gymnastics) and choral groups.

Through the Easter season, the Ukrainians display impressive skills in the art of *pysanky,* the colorful decorating of eggs. After a special Easter Sunday morning service, they greet each other with the traditional words *Krystos Voskres* (Christ is Risen). There then follows a special breakfast which includes the twin symbol of this holiday: the *kulich,* a round yeast bread, and the *pashka,* a rich cheese dessert.

Food naturally was a focal point of immigrant life and after the initial exposure to American life, the immigrant was not likely to forget his own food preferences, particularly as they might be indulged in at parish picnics, weddings, or funerals. In Slavic neighborhoods each household had its own vegetable garden as well as an assortment of chickens, rabbits, and pigeons. Much of this helped to keep costs down and to give subsistence during a period of strikes and unemployment. It was also a means to enjoy certain kinds of food. One Polish contribution to American eating has been the garlic-flavored pork sausage, *kielbasa* —what Americans call Polish sausage. Similarly, a third-generation Slovenian recalled that:

> No chicken today tastes like the chickens my mother cleaned and prepared for Sunday dinner. There is no chicken soup in America today like the chicken soup my mother made from our home-grown chickens. Homemade noodles went with homemade soup. My sister and I hung around the kitchen table as my mother floured the cutting board, rolled out the dough and chopped the noodles. The flour clung to our aprons and dusted the floor. Even our eyelashes fluttered flour dust.[38]

Coming from the polyglot area of Eastern Europe, the immigrant groups brought with them a fabulous mixture of cuisines. Gourmet experts have traced how:

> The Italian *gnocchi* (dumplings) have migrated across the Alps to become the Czech *noky* and the Austro-Hungarian *nockerin.* Various veal dishes had found their way from Italy into Central European cuisines as one kind of schnitzel or another. What was called *pierogi* in Poland was called *pirohy* in Slovakia. Hungarian paprika had turned up in the cooking of the Slovaks, Czechs, and southern Slavs.

> A similar intermixture had taken place in the old Ottoman Empire. Turkish shish kabob had become Greek *Souvlaki*, Serbian *raznjici* and the *shahlyk* of the Caucasus. . . . The Ottomans themselves had always applied the old adage that good food knows no boundaries, and had annexed, mixed, modified, and spread the diverse cuisines they had encountered along their paths of conquest.[39]

The Slavic immigrant groups used their food to proudly proclaim their own ethnic identity. Many of today's recipes calling for sour cream can be traced largely to the Polish immigrants. Their popular *barszcz* (Russian, *borscht* or beet soup), once provoked a French chef to say that it "is national in Russia and in Poland, and in Russia, you must swear on your life that it's Russian, but in Poland you must salute it as a symbol of Poland's life blood."[40] For the Ukrainians and Russians *kasha* (buckwheat) is as standard fare as the Irish potato or the Italian pasta. The Czechs will rave about their *kolache* (pastry with different fillings) and the Slovenes, their *potica* (nut roll).

All in all these authentic dishes have been a vivid reminder of a transplanted Eastern European culture and of an enjoyable gastronomic legacy of the Slavic American.

VI

Ethnic contribution to American society is at once so widespread and so complicated that it poses a problem of generalization. If there is any listing of individuals, their uniqueness very often will take away from the commonplace contributions of the many who labored and survived in American industry and agriculture.

Nonetheless, the various ethnic groups in American life have had their share of outstanding intellectual figures, and, understandably, there is considerable pride in their accomplishments. On the other hand, it is admittedly difficult to tell whether, for example, the great Serbian immigrant, Nikola Tesla, and his some 700 American scientific patents can be credited to his Serbian character or to his individuality.

Certainly the refugees both before and after the second World War reveal much about this dilemma. Those fleeing European fascism and communism in the 1930s and 1940s would find in America ample freedom and opportunity to continue their work.

Laura Fermi, in her *Illustrious Immigrants*,[41] tells the story of this multi-ethnic group which made invaluable contributions to American society. Here is a sampling of the Slavic contingent:

Russians:

Serge Koussevitzsky (conductor)
Igor Stravinsky (composer)
Igor Sikorsky (aviation expert)
Vladimir Horowitz (pianist)
Gregor Piatigorsky (cellist)

Ukrainians:

George Kistiakowsky (chemist; special advisor in science and technology to President Eisenhower)
Theodosius Dobzhansky (geneticist)

Poles:

Bronislaw Malinowski (anthropologist)
Alfred Tarski (mathematician)
Stanislaw Ulam (mathematician)
Wanda Landowska (harpsichordist)

Czechs:

Rudolf Serkin (pianist)
George Szell (conductor)
Rene Wellek (literary scholar)
Joseph Schumpeter (economist)
Hans Kohn (historian)

Yugoslavians:

Dragen Plamenac (musicologist)
Dinko Tomasic (sociologist)

All these outstanding individuals and many more from other ethnic groups were a "phenomenon," for in welcoming them, "America did not ask a price for her services, but has been repaid in full from the intellectual migration in a currency compounded of prestige, knowledge, and a general enrichment of culture."[42]

VII

Such a reception for these outstanding individuals was indeed a "phenomenon," because the American response to the late 19th and early 20th century Slavic immigrant was hostile. These Slavs felt the brunt of a rising anti-foreign attitude in American society. By the end of the 19th century, there was apparently no specific Slavic stereotype, as in the case of the Jews or Italians; hence, "Slavic and Magyar laborers impressed public opinion at large simply as foreigners par excellence; uncivilized, unruly, and dangerous."[43]

As a child in the state of Washington, the former Supreme Court Justice, William O. Douglas, recalled that "Poles came to have a connotation of half civilized people in Yakima—an attitude that still brings me a shame whenever I meet a Pole, particularly a distinguished musician, scientist, or diplomat."[44]

The mere number and appearance of southern and eastern Europeans created a fear among the native Americans that somehow the immigrants would not be assimilated and that ultimately they would pose a threat to the predominant Anglo-Saxon race. Such a racial ideology was set forth in *The Passing of the Great Race,* a popular book in 1916. The author, Madison Grant, a well known anthropologist, observed that the "new" immigration:

> . . . contained a large and increasing number of the weak, the broken and the mentally crippled of all races drawn from the lowest stratum of the Mediterranean basin and the Balkans, together with the hordes of the wretched, submerged populations of the Polish Ghettos. Our jails, insane asylums and almshouses are filled with this flotsam and the whole tone of American life, social, moral, and political has been lowered and vulgarized by them.[45]

This unfair judgment gained popularity and added to a growing movement for the restriction of immigrants. Other voices urging limitation also were heard. The president of the American Federation of Labor, Samuel Gompers, had supported a literacy test as early as 1902 as a means of controlling immigration.[46] For a long time, organized labor had complained about the competition of cheap and docile immigrant labor as well as the difficult task of organizing the multilingual immigrant groups.

The first World War and its aftermath produced the climate for crystallizing native American feelings toward the immigrants. Slavic and Magyar men from Johnstown (Pa.), for example, who fought in this conflict were lavishly praised for their bravery and heroism; nonetheless, they were labeled immediately as "foreigners" upon their return.[47]

For diverse reasons—the Bolshevik Revolution of 1917, the Communists' call for worldwide revolution, the disillusionment of peace making, the questioning of the loyalties of so-called hyphenated Americans (e.g., German-Americans, Russian-Americans), the unfavorable Congressional investigations of the new immigration, the domestic strikes, and the high cost of living—many Americans were convinced that a "radical conspiracy" existed which aimed at the overthrowing of democracy and capitalism.

A popular, military figure of this period, General Leonard Wood, former commander of the "Rough Riders" during the Spanish-American War, expressed a common sentiment when he declared: "We do not want to be a dumping ground for radicals, agitators, reds, who do not understand our ideals."[48]

The ensuing "Red Scare" of 1919-1920 developed into a national hysteria not unlike that of the McCarthy era of the 1950s. Attorney General A. Mitchell Palmer's answer to the "Reds" was according to one newspaper, "S. O. S.—Ship or Shoot."[49] Such violent anti-foreign agitation would not be satisfied until some changes in the immigration policy would take place.

In 1924 Congress responded with the National Origins Act which set immigration admissions to two percent of a specific nationality living in the United States in 1890. By using this date, the immigrant flow from southern and eastern Europe was shifted back to northern Europe.

The first United States Senator of Irish extraction, Senator David I. Walsh of Massachusetts, was quick to point out that the "true reason" for the legislation was "social discrimination," because:

> An attempt is being made to slip by this proposal, which is aimed clearly and mercilessly at the Slav, the Latin, and the Jew, under the harmless guise of a change in the date of the census . . . Mr. President, what is the real driving force behind the movement of basing the quota on the census of 1890? The peoples of the world will attribute it to our belief that the "Nordic" is a superior race. The world will assume that our Government considers the Italians, Greeks, Jews, Poles, and the Slavs inferior to the Nordics, congenitally as well as culturally. It is a dangerous assumption. . . . The theories of superior race value and selection that have accompanied the discussion of this question are humiliating and insulting. Do we fancy that the peoples and Governments of Italy, Poland, Hungary, Austria, Greece, or Rumania have no national pride? . . . The liberty-loving Poles, whose sacrifices and struggles for freedom have arrested the admiration of mankind and who saved all Europe from the Turks at Vienna scarcely two centuries ago, were once in the vanguard of culture. . . .[50]

The 1924 law remained in effect until 1952 when the McCarran-Walter Immigration Act was passed over the veto of President Truman. The new law retained the quota system, and, reflecting the cold war atmosphere, added provisions for deportation of "alien subversives." The President, in his veto message, bluntly pointed out that:

> The idea behind this discriminatory policy was, to put it baldly, that Americans with English or Irish names were better people and better citizens that Americans with Italian or Greek or Polish names. It was thought that people of West European origin made better citizens than Rumanians or Yugoslavs or Ukrainians or Balts or Austrians. . . . Today we are "protecting" ourselves, as we were in 1924, against being flooded by immigrants from Eastern Europe. This is fantastic. The countries of Eastern Europe have fallen under the Communist yoke—they are silenced, fenced off by barbed wire and mine fields—no one passes their borders but at the risk of his life. We do not need to be protected against immigrants from these countries—on the contrary we want to stretch out a helping hand, to save those who have managed to flee into Western Europe. . . . But this we cannot do, as we would like to do, because the quota for Poland is only 6,500, as against the 138,000 exiled Poles, all over Europe, who are asking to come to these shores; because the quota for the now subjected Baltic countries is little more than 700—against 23,000 Baltic refugees imploring us to admit them to a new life here. . . .[51]

Finally the quota system was abandoned in the Immigration Act of 1965. By this time an increasingly urbanized society now saw the second and third generation children of the immigrants gaining political power. And the modern welfare state often would help the various ethnic groups turn into pressure groups, each demanding their share of wealth and a place in American society.

VIII

In contrast, the 19th century Slavic immigrant had little success in his political aspiration. Some Polish exiles unsuccessfully tried to form a Slavic block in the election of 1864, but for the most part, the Slavic immigrant lacked political experience; he often succumbed to machine politics in order to simply survive in a hostile American environment. But they were not a passively led voting block. The immigrant, in the words of the ruthless industrialist Henry Clay Frick, "always learns too soon."[52]

The Slavic immigrant quickly learned that his economic interests were with the fortunes of the Democratic Party, rather than with the WASP dominated Republican Party. On occasions, however, when the Democrats might ignore or take for granted the Slavic vote, as in the case of Detroit mayoralty race of the 1890s, the decisive Polish vote went to the Progressive Republican mayor, Hazen S. Pingree.[53] Still later, Republican Theodore Roosevelt "captured the imagination and the loyalty" of many

Slavs and Russian Jews of New York City.[54] Even the distinction of being the first Polish American elected to the U.S. Congress would go to a Republican, John Kleczka of Milwaukee, who made his successful bid in 1918.[55]

In the period before the First World War, Progressive reformers, whether they be Republican or Democrat, might feel sympathy if not compassion toward the immigrant. Nevertheless, they were certain to have misgivings about turning this immigrant into a base for social reform. Many such reformers often saw political bosses manipulating the immigrant "honkytowns" into political machines. As for the immigrant, he was too much occupied with survival to worry about local political corruption.

If the Slavic immigrant showed any political interest, this usually went beyond the political bosses. He was thinking of his homeland and this often embroiled him in foreign issues with an activism similar to today's Jewish Americans and their state of Israel. The First World War and the ensuing breakdown of the Austro-Hungarian empire provided the opportunity for East Europeans to press for the liberation of their homelands. Not surprisingly "the foreign districts of American cities bubbled with agitation and propaganda for such independence movements—a kind of hyphenate activity which served to demonstrate the attachment to American war aims of many technically enemy aliens"[56] Ultimately such enthusiasm would help in the establishment of an independent Czechoslovakia, Poland,and Yugoslavia.

After the First World War, a second and third generation of Slavic American, reaching in varying degrees middle class status, now began to look at domestic politics not only to advance his own interest, but also to provide his own ethnic leadership. The Poles, for example, in 1922 saw one of their own group, Peter C. Jezewski, elected the first mayor of the city of Hamtramck (Detroit).[57] And the Czechs, under Anton "Tony" Cermak, organized the most powerful political machine in Chicago's history. Journalist Mike Royko described him in this manner:

> Uneducated, tough, crude, but politically brilliant, Cermak had the gall to challenge the traditional South Side Irish domination of the Democratic Party. More than gall, he had the sense to count up all the Irish votes, and then counted all the Italians, Jews, Germans, Poles, and Bohemians. The minority Irish domination didn't make sense to him. He organized a city-wide saloon keepers' league, dedicated to fighting closing laws and prohibition. With the saloon keepers behind him, he couldn't be stopped. He became president of the Cook County Board, took over the party machinery, and ran for mayor in 1931.[58]

Cermak won but shortly afterwards on a speaking platform in Miami Beach, Florida, he was killed by an assassin who was attempting to murder Presidential nominee, Franklin D. Roosevelt.

Cermak's political machine ultimately was taken over by Richard J. Daley who remained strongly entrenched until his death in 1976. The two largest groups in the Chicago Democratic Party, the Poles and the blacks, compromised on Michael A. Bilandic, a Croatian, as the new mayor.[59]

In 1940 a Polish American spokesman in Buffalo, New York, told of an increasing political awareness among his constituencies when he noted that "out in ritzy Humboldt Park they get two voters to a family. I get six out of my house. . . ."[60] A few years later, Joseph Mruc became the first Polish American mayor of a major American city.

In Cleveland, Ohio, the son of first-generation Czech parents, Mayor Ralph J. Perk, was introduced as the "Ethnic Mayor" in his bid for re-election in 1973. When he showed up at the Second Annual Czech and Slovak Cotillion Ball, he told an enthusiastic audience that "I am proud to be a Czech. I am proud of my brother Slovaks. I am proud of the nationality movement . . . there is a great upsurge of ethnic power and you're part of it. I'm proud of all of you."[61]

The emergence of the Slavic American as a politician was not only a sign of upward mobility, but also the result of the civil rights movement with its body of anti-discrimination legislation. Over 20 years ago, Political Scientist Samuel Lubell observed that:

> If these statutes (civil rights) have been enacted in recent years, it has not been because there had been more discrimination in the United States than in previous years. Probably there is less. These laws are on the statute books because those who suffered discrimination in the past—the children of the "micks," "wops," "kikes," "niggers," "polacks," and other abused groups—have been in the mood, and at last have gained the political strength to do something about it.[62]

What political strength there was, and is, among the Slavic American has gone generally to the Democratic Party. Mark R. Levy and Michael S. Kramer, in their researches on ethnic voting patterns, have shown, for example, that in the 1960 presidential election:

> . . . John Kennedy won 82 percent of the vote cast in the predominantly Slavic precincts. In Buffalo, where Kennedy campaigned with his wife's brother-in-law, Prince Stanislaus Radziwill, Kennedy took more than five out of every six Slavic votes. In two states—Ohio and Maryland—Kennedy's Slavic vote exceeded 85 percent, and in Michigan, he

won a phenomenal nine out of every ten votes cast in Slavic neighborhoods. New Jersey's Slavic voters gave Kennedy a plurality of 70,000 votes over Nixon and J. F. K. carried New Jersey by only 22,000 votes. Slavic voters also played an important role in Kennedy's victories in Pennsylvania and Illinois. In Pennsylvania, Kennedy came out of Philadelphia and the coal country with a lead of 110,000 Slavic votes, he carried the state by 116,000. The pattern was extended in Illinois, where Kennedy carried the state by only 9,000 votes, but led Nixon in the Slavic precincts of Chicago's "Polish Corridor" by more than 100,000.[63]

The authors concluded that Kennedy's appeal was based on several factors:

. . . the Kennedy family was well known for its interest in Poland and Polish charities, the Senator's economic liberalism appealed to the blue-collar interests of Slavic Americans, and Slavic voters took pleasure in voting for Kennedy because he shared their religion.[64]

Kennedy's appreciation came in the appointment of Wisconsin's Commissioner of Taxation, John A. Granouski, as Postmaster General. In 1968 the Polish Americans found even greater satisfaction in the Vice Presidential candidate of the Democratic Party, Senator Edmund S. Muskie of Maine, who much later in the Carter administration would be the first Polish American to serve as a Secretary of State.

Currently Polish American Congressional influence rests with Dan Rostenkowski (D-Il.), John D. Dingell (D-Mich.), David E. Bonior (D-Mich.), and in the U.S. Senate, Barbara A. Mikulski (D-Md.) and Frank H. Murkowski (R-Alaska). As for Slovak Americans, their first Congressional Representative was Joseph M. Gaydos (D-Pa.). On the state level, California Democrats in 1976 were pleased with the election of the only woman member of the State Senate, Rose Ann Vuich, a first generation Yugoslavian American. In New York, Mary Ann Kupsak became the first Polish American woman to hold a high public office as Lieutenant Governor in the mid-70s. And Bulgarian Americans have been successful in Indiana politics.

Although such examples do indicate a faithful record of Democratic Party support, the Slavic Americans in recent years have at times voted Republican. In the gubernatorial race of 1969, William T. Cahill of New Jersey was the first and only Republican to win a majority of Slavic American votes. Governor Cahill was a moderate politician, and Republicans who planned the campaign in Slavic neighborhoods needed a moderate or liberal stance to compete with the Democratic opponents.

Some pragmatic Republicans have been urging the GOP for many years to get rid of its WASP image.[65]

In any contemporary analysis of the Slavic voter, one thing seems to come through: "The Slavic voter is more discriminating than ever, and the politician who forgets this political axiom does so at his peril."[66]

IX

The political sensitivities of the Slavic Americans is but on indication of recent efforts to upgrade their image in American society. The Polish Americans have been the victims of considerable discrimination in particularly one annoying area: the ethnic joke. In whatever form it may take, ethnic humor is demeaning for the group which is the target of such humor. With the "Polish" joke, for example, such humor represents a kind of respectable bigotry by upper-class Americans. As one prominent sociologist observed:

> . . . bigotry is by no means a lower-class phenomenon and that compassion among the elites is by no means universal. And yet, an attitude of compassion towards one group mixed with bigotry towards another group is, in the final analysis, intolerable on moral grounds because it is hypocritical and intolerable on political grounds because it is self-defeating. The intellectual who "loves" the blacks and the "poor" but has contempt for the Irish or the Italians of the "middle class" is in the final analysis every bit as much a bigot as the blue-collar worker who "hates niggers," for both are asking, "Why Can't They Be Like Us?" And to this . . . there can be but one satisfactory answer: "Because they don't want to be and in the United States of America, they don't have to be."[67]

For a number of years now, the Polish American Congress tried with some success to enhance the image of their people in the communication media. In 1973 this Congress gave its Media Award to NBC-TV because it "rendered the Polish American Community a long overdue recognition for presenting *Banacek* (Mystery Movie Series) as a Polish American, in a positive manner."[68]

As a further reaction to this defamation, articulate voices have risen to defend the character of Polish Americans. A wealthy Philadelphia industrialist, Edward J. Piszek, heads the Copernicus Society to promote the impressive heritage of Copernicus, Chopin, Joseph Conrad, and more recently, Jerzy Kosinski, and the Nobel Prize winner in Literature (1980), Czeslaw Milosz. Similarly U.S. Senator Barbara Mikulski has pursued vigorously the interests of Polish Americans by a strong defense of cultural pluralism.

In the final analysis, the "Polish" joke may have a very beneficial effect upon the Polish Americans by simply united them in their defense of their ethnic community: the Polonia. Such humor may have "thus provided a source of re-vitalization of community efforts, a specific goal and sources of sentiments of peoplehood."[69]

These new ethnic spokesmen have come to symbolize a noticeable upward mobility of Slavic Americans and this movement has brought a sociological interest in whether such gains in the socioeconomic status have diminished the identity of the individuals within such a group. Some recent studies seem to support this view, but Slavic American spokesman, Michael Novak, has defended vigorously Slavic Americans as the "unmeltable ethnics." He would advocate a political radicalism with a new cultural pluralism for those millions of Slavic Americans who "are delighted to discover that they no longer have to pay the price in becoming 'Americanized.'"[70]

The current attention shown to white ethnics reflects a powerful social phenomenon in America. Such interest may be, according to sociologist Andrew Greeley, director of the Center for the Study of American Pluralism in Chicago, "the result of the failure of the liberal establishment to find answers to our problems caused by poverty and racism." So the ethnics have been "rediscovered" and given special attention, especially the black Americans who had shown their impressive ethnic strength since the 1960s. It was now socially acceptable to talk about ethnics.[71]

In the course of this ethnic resurgence, the media often had misunderstood and misrepresented the white ethnics, mainly the Irish, Italian, and Slavic Catholics, as being "anti-liberal" and "racist." But here the data is otherwise:

> In 1967, white ethnic Americans were no less liberal on the war in Vietnam and sometimes more liberal than other Americans. White ethnic Americans were also more liberal and never less liberal on racial questions, and considerably more liberal on issues of economic and social welfare than other Americans.[72]

This is not a defense of the white ethnics as liberals, but rather it is a protest of the image of white ethnics as a bastion of conservatism. In other words, the "alienated, angry, hostile hard hat ethnic is a fiction of liberal journalists and intellectuals."[73]

Furthermore, in matters of race relations, the media again has overlooked important differences in life styles. As sociologist Richard Krickus has observed:

> From the perspective of the Polish resident of the Northwest Side of Chicago who lives in close proximity to an expanding black ghetto, the Italian truck driver who delivers Coca-Cola in the all-black Central Ward of Newark, and the Jewish storekeeper who sells produce in the Bedford-Stuyvesant section of Brooklyn, the black people they come into contact with violate those values they cherish—tightly knit families, a fastidious observance of community mores, hard work, and deference to authority. What they perceive as "black values" are often the product of poverty, racial discrimination, ignorance, and social dislocations common among uprooted people. Were the individuals who cling to these same values to be white, the reaction would be much the same; this is evident in Cleveland and other cities where poor Southern whites constitute the newest source of urban immigration. . . . Clearly it is not the blackness of the newcomers that upsets the Catholic ethnics; it is the perceived differences in socioeconomic status, values, and lifestyles.[74]

It was these "perceived differences" which led the Ford Foundation, in the wake of the turbulent 1960s, to institute white ethnic studies by the American Jewish Committee, and community action programs by the newly founded National Center for Ethnic Affairs, headed by Monsignor Geno C. Baroni. Other efforts were made to diffuse racial conflict on the local (urban) level with such organizations as the North Ward Cultural and Educational Center of Newark and the Black-Polish Conference in Detroit. Such efforts did promote a dialogue between white and non-white ethnics showing that they have more in common than what American society has been willing to acknowledge.

There is much to be discovered about Americans who no longer have to apologize for their background. And as Michael Novak has concluded in his *The Rise of the Unmeltable Ethnics,* millions of Americans of different ethnic origin "are pleased to discover the possibilities and the limits inherent in being who they are; and are openly happy about what heretofore they had disguised in silence. There is creativity and new release, there is liberation, and there is hope."[75]

The Slavic Americans are a part of that liberation, part of that hope. ✦

NOTES

1. New York Times, July 12, 1989, p. A5.
2. Harry Schwartz, *Eastern Europe in the Soviet Shadow* (New York, 1973), p. 6.

3. The Cyrillic alphabet is named after Saint Cyril ("Apostle of the Slavs") (A.D. 827-869); it was adopted for the writing of Russian, Bulgarian, Serbian and other languages of the USSR.
4. Wayne Moquin, ed., *Makers of America, VII* (Encyclopedia Britannica Educational Corporation, 1971), pp. 173-174.
5. Philip L. Barbour, "The Identity of the First Poles in America," *The William and Mary Quarterly,* XXI (Jan. 1964), 79.
6. Thomas Capek, *The Czechs in America* (1920; reprinted New York: Arno Press and The New York Times, 1969), pp. 9-11.
7. James R. Gibson, *Imperial Russia in Frontier America* (New York, 1976), p. vii.
8. George R. Stewart, *Names on the Land* (Boston, 1967), p. 397.
9. *Ibid.*, p. 225.
10. Stephen Thernstrom, ed., *Harvard Encyclopedia of American Ethnic Groups* (Cambridge, Mass., 1980), p. 249.
11. Thomas Fleming, "Kosciuszko—Hero of Two Worlds," *Reader's Digest,* (April 1976), p. 6.
12. Thomas Froncek "Kosciuszko," *American Heritage*, XXVI (June 1975), p. 81.
13. Battle of Savannah (1779), *Los Angeles Times,* December 30, 1977, I. p. 9.
14. Branko Mita Colakovic, *Yogoslav Migrations to America* (San Francisco, 1973), p. 37.
15. Felix p. Wierzbicki, *California As It Is & As It May Be Or A Guide To The Gold Region* (1849; reprinted San Francisco: The Grabhorn Press, 1933).
16. Louis Adamic, *A Nation of Nations* (New York, 1945), p. 148.
17. *Ibid.*, p. 291-292.
18. Louis Adamic, *Laughing in the Jungle* (New York, 1932), p. 6.
19. *Newsweek,* (4 July 1976), p. 51.
20. Colakovic, *op. cit.*, p. 151.
21. Charles Morley, ed., *Portrait of America-Letters of Henry Sienkiewicz* (New York, 1959), p. 279.
22. Wasyl Halich, *Ukrainians in the United States* (1937; reprinted San Francisco: R & E Research Associates, 1969), p. 47.
23. Thernstrom *op. cit.*, pp. 1018-1020.
24. Bernard A. Weisberger, *The American Heritage History of the American People* (New York, 1971), p. 200. See also William Miller, *A New History of the United States,* rev. (New York, 1968), p. 255.
25. *New Yorker,* (March 6, 1989), p. 54.
26. Upton Sinclair, *The Jungle* (New York, 1960).
27. John Higham, *Strangers in the Land* (New York, 1965), p. 90.
28. Peter C. Marzio, ed., *A Nation of Nations* (New York, 1976), p. 378.
29. Stanley Feldstein and Lawrence Costello, eds., *The Ordeal of Assimilation* (New York, 1974), p. 344.

30. Helena Znaniecka Lopata, *Polish Americans: Status Competition in an Ethnic Community* (New Jersey, 1973). p. 45.

31. Philip Taylor, *The Distant Magnet* (New York, 1972), p. 225.

32. *Time,* (October 15, 1979), p. 23.

33. Edward R. Kantowicz, "Polish Chicago: Survival Through Solidarity," *The Ethnic Frontier,* ed. by Melvin G. Holli and Peter d'A. Jones (Grand Rapids, Michigan, 1977), p. 189 ff.

34. Old Slavonic or Old Church Slavic is the oldest attested Slavic (ecclesiastical) language. Halich, *op. cit.*, p. 97.

35. Volodymur Kubijovyc, ed., *Ukraine—A Concise Encyclopedia* (Vol. II) (Toronto, 1971), pp. 1109-1121.

36. Marcus Lee Hansen, "The Third Generation in America," *Commentary,* (Nov. 1952), p. 495.

37. George J. Prpic, *The Croatian Immigrants in American* (New York, 1971), p. 371 ff.

38. Rose Mary Prosen, "Looking Back," in Michael Novak, ed., *Growing Up Slavic in America* (pamphlet), Bayville, New York: EMPAC, 1976), p. 5.

39. James P. Shelton, et. al., *American Cooking: The Melting Pot* (New York, Time Inc., 1971), p. 17.

40. Evan Jones, *American Food* (New York, 1975), p. 124.

41. Laura Fermi, *Illustrious Immigrants: The Intellectual Migration From Europe, 1930-1941* (Chicago, 1968), pp. 125-135.

42. *Ibid., p.* 397.

43. Higham, *loc. cit.*

44. William O. Douglas, *Go East, Young Man* (New York, 1974), p. 67.

45. Madison Grant, *The Passing of the Great Race* (1916; reprinted New York: Arno Press and The New York Times, 1970), pp. 89-90.

46. Oscar Handlin, ed., *Immigration as a Factor in American History* (New Jersey, 1965), pp. 185-187.

47. Ewa Morawska, For Bread with Butter: Life-Worlds of East Central Europeans in Johnstown, Pennsylvania, 1890-1940 (Cambridge, 1985), p. 170.

48. Robert K. Murray, *Red Scare* (New York, 1964), p. 265.

49. SOS is the international call for help. The letters, SOS, do not refer to any specific words; they are simply easy to transmit. Allan L. Damon, "The Great Red Scare," *American Heritage, XIX* (Feb. 1968), p. 27.

50. U.S. Congress, Senate, *Congressional Record,* 68th Cong., 1st sess., 1924, pp. 6355-6357.

51. *The New York Times,* June 26, 1952, p. 14.

52. Alistair Cooke, *Alistair Cooke's America* (New York, 1973), p. 293.

53. Melvin G. Holli, *Reform in Detroit* (New York, 1969), p. 127.

54. Higham, *op. cit., p.* 190.

55. Stephanie Bernardo, *The Ethnic Almanac* (New York, 1981), p. 456.

56. *Ibid., p.* 127.

57. Arthur Evans Wood, *Hamtramck* (1955; reprint, New York: Octagon Books, 1974), p. 48.
58. Mike Royko, *Boss—Richard J. Daley of Chicago* (New York, 1971), p. 42.
59. *Los Angeles Times,* April 20, 1977. I. p. 1, 11.
60. Weisberger, *The American Heritage History of the American People, op. cit.,* p. 305.
61. *Los Angeles Times,* August 22, 1973, I-A, p. 6.
62. Samuel Lubell, *The Future of American Politics* (New York, Colophon, 1965), p. 89.
63. Mark R. Levy and Michael S. Kramer, *The Ethnic Factor* (New York, 1973), p. 144.
64. *Ibid.*, p. 145.
65. Richard Krickus, *Pursuing the American Dream* (New York, 1976), p. 4 ff.
66. Levy and Kramer, *op. cit.*, p. 158.
67. Andrew M. Greeley, *Why Can't They Be Like Us*? (New York, 1971), p. 19.
68. *Daily Pilot* (Huntington Beach) *TV Guide,* June, 1973, p. 18.
69. Lopata, *op. cit.*, p. 77.
70. Michael Novak, *The Rise of the Unmeltable Ethnics* (New York, 1972), p. 291. Compare Neil C. Sandberg, *Ethnic Identity and Assimilation: The Polish-American Community. Case Study of Metropolitan Los Angeles* (New York, 1977), p. 70 ff.
71. Andrew M. Greeley, *Ethnicity in the United States: A Preliminary Reconnaissance* (New York, 1974), pp. 285-286.
72. *Ibid.*, p. 202.
73. *Ibid.*, p. 285.
75. Krickus, *op. cit.*, pp. 297-298.
76. Novak, *op. cit.*, p. 291.

SELECTED BIBLIOGRAPHY

Adamic, Louis. *A Nation of Nations.* New York and London, 1945.

Balch, Emily G. *Our Slavic Fellow Citizens.* 1910 reprinted. New York, Arno Press and the New York Times, 1969.

Bernardo, Stephanie. *The Ethnic Almanac.* New York, 1981.

Bukoski, Anthony. *Children of Strangers*. Dallas, 1993.

Bukowczyk, John l. *And My Children Did Not Know Me: A History of the Polish-Americans.* Bloomington, 1987.

Capek, Thomas. *The Czechs in America.* 1920 reprinted New York: Arno Press and the New York Times, 1969.

Colakovic, Branko Mita. *Yugoslav Migrations to America.* San Francisco, 1973.

Cooke, Alistair. *Alistair Cooke's America.* New York, 1973.

Cross, Samuel Hazard. *Slavic Civilization Through the Ages.* New York, 1948.

Davis, Jerome. *The Russian Immigrant.* 1922 reprinted New York: Arno Press and the New York Times, 1969.

Fermi, Laura, Illustrious Immigrants: The Intellectual Migration from Europe, 1930-1941. Chicago, 1968.

Gladsky, Thomas S. Princes, Peasants, and Other Polish Selves. Ethnicity in American Literature. Amherst, Mass., 1992.

Gordon, Milton M. *Assimilation in American Life.* New York, 1964.

Govorchin, Gerald G. *Americans From Yugoslavia.* Gainesville, Florida, 1961.

Greeley, Andrew M. *Ethnicity in the United States: A Preliminary Reconnaissance.* New York, 1974.

Greeley, Andrew M. *Why Can't They Be Like Us?* New York, 1971.

Greene, Victor R. *The Slavic Community an Strike: Immigrant Labor in Pennsylvania Anthracite.* Notre Dame, 1968.

Handlin, Oscar. *The Uprooted.* 2nd ed. Boston, 1973.

Hansen, Marcus Less. *The Atlantic Migration, 1607-1860.* New York, 1961.

Higham, John. *Strangers in the Land.* New York, 1965.

Jones, Maldwyn Allen. *American Immigration.* Chicago, 1960.

Krickus, Richard. *Pursuing the American Dream.* New York, 1976.

Kubijovyc, Volodymyr (ed.). *Ukraine—A Concise Encyclopedia. Vols.* I-II. Toronto, 1971.

Kuniczak, W. S. My Name is Million: An Illustrated History of the Poles in America. New York, 1978.

Levy, Mark R. and Michael S. Kramer. *The Ethnic Factor.* New York, 1973.

Lopata, Helena Znaniecki. Polish Americans: Status Competition in an Ethnic Community. Englewood Cliffs, New Jersey, 1973.

Morawska, Ewa. For Bread With Butter: Life-Worlds of East Central Europeans in Johnstown, Pennsylvania, 1890-1914. Cambridge, 1985.

Novak, Michael. *The Rise of the Unmeltable Ethnics.* New York, 1972.

Prpic,George J. *The Croatian Immigrants in America.* New York, 1971.

Roucek, Joseph S. *Slavonic Encyclopedia.* New York, 1949.

Shenton, James P., et al. *American Cooking: The Melting Pot.* New York, 1971.

Taylor, Philip. *The Distant Magnet.* New York, 1971.

Thernstrom, Stephen (ed.). Harvard Encyclopedia of American Ethnic Groups. Cambridge, Mass., 1980.

Thomas, William I. and Florian Znaniecki. *The Polish Peasant in Europe and America.* 2 vols., 1927; reprinted New York. Dover Publications, Inc., 1958.

Wittke, Carl. *We Who Built America.* 2nd ed. Cleveland, 1964.

Wrobel, Paul. Our Way: Family, Parish, and Neighborhood in a Polish-American Community. Notre Dame, 1979.

THE ASIAN AMERICANS

DONALD HAYDU

"Oh East is East and West is West and never the twain shall meet till earth and sky stand presently at God's great judgement seat." In 1889, Rudyard Kipling wrote those famous lines. They may be good poetry, but they have proven to be poor history and even poorer sociology. The English spokesman for "the white man's burden" and British imperialism had obviously never visited Gardena, California, or walked through the spectacular annex to the National Gallery of Art in Washington D.C. designed by I.M. Pei, or tuned into television news announced by a nationally famous Chinese-American anchorwoman.[1] A critique of this cliche runs deeper than a few comments about contemporary conditions. East and West have continually interacted, blended, fought, borrowed, and assimilated with one another through the centuries. It is just that with the transportation and technological advances of the modern epoch, the process of mixing and blending peoples of Eastern and Western Civilizations is now more rapid in time and more obvious to see. As a case in point, today, Asian and Pacific-Americans are on a percentage basis America's fastest growing minority. If one measures an ethnic group's growth by births and legal immigration only, they are outdistancing Hispanics (exclusive of undocumented entries). According to census data, the Asian-American population numbered 5,147,900 by 1985.[2] Projecting to the year 2000, this sector of the population should have reached almost 10,000,000 which will make Asians approximately 3% of the total American population.

Before analyzing the historic past, let us stay with the present statistics and their meaning. Two general characteristics do stand out. The first is the great variety of backgrounds represented by the generic term: Asian-American. The second is, ironically, the greater class similarity within this ethnic variety. More of what is called the professional and entrepreneurial middle class is characteristic of those coming into the country as well as descriptive of the status achieved by third and fourth generation Asian-Americans. Since 1965, immigration law has been reformed. This has made possible the expansion in the numbers of Asian Americans. The previous policies, operative since 1921, assigned quotas, based on national origins, as to who could migrate to the United States. These quotas clearly favored Northwestern Europeans. This was done on the theory that they were more easily assimilated into American life. Racist and religious prejudices motivated these policies. Indeed, long standing agitation beginning in the 19th century bore fruit in "Oriental exclusion," in an "Asiatic barred zone" for future immigration and in the restrictive Immigration Acts of 1921, 1924 and 1952.

A more liberal atmosphere prevailed by the 1960s, however. In no small way, it was generated by the Civil Rights movement and the resulting legislation of "The Great Society." Legally and socially, race was and is becoming irrelevant as a criterion for choosing an applicant for a job, housing, education or public accommodations within the country and (more to our point) accepting an immigrant from without. Since the Immigration Act of 1965, ethnic qualitative restrictions have been eliminated but quantitative quotas have remained. An annual ceiling of 270,000 (since 1980) has been stipulated. No more than 20,000 persons are permitted to come from any one single country in a given year. Interestingly enough, "preference categories" have been established under the new system for "skilled workers" needed in the U.S. Labor market (10% of visas).[3] These factors have both made possible Asian immigration on a scale hitherto impossible and stimulated a kind of occupational preponderance within it. The results are literally and symbolically changing the features of America's skilled work force.

Asians and the formerly used "Oriental" are generic terms.[4] They really do not do much to inform one about the specific peoples that come under these umbrella words. How well the Congressional Publications Record puts it when it tries to capture the diversity of the contemporary Asian-American community:

> The Asian American community is a mosaic of cultural, ethnic, national and racial groups, highly educated prosperous third generation Japanese-Americans, impoverished illiterate Hmong tribesmen from Laos, second generation Chinese-American college students attending the top universities, recently emigrated Filipino physicians struggling to learn English, Chinese speaking emigrants from Hong-Kong and Taiwan working long hours for low pay at menial jobs in big city Chinatown restaurants and garment factories, and New Delhi born psychiatrists

opening their own practices. There are Chinese-American street toughs and Nobel Prize winning physicists. There are Christians, Buddhists, Hindus, Shintoists, Taoists, Confucians and Moslems.[5]

The average American is meeting his Asian-American counterpart in a variety of ways and places, from the school classroom to the bank teller's window, to the owner and/or worker of a local franchise store to a shrimp boat off the Texan or California coasts. For the most part, one is struck with their qualities of hard work, ambition, and excellence. These characteristics come from a long historical curve of formation. Three factors which will run as themes through this essay have conditioned the Asian's performance: (1) Racial discrimination by government as well as individuals within the United States have forced Asians to excel in order to be treated with anything approaching acceptance. (2) Long standing traditions of hard work, often based on religious or philosophical systems (i.e., Confucianism) have been brought from the cultures of East Asia. (3) Upwardly mobile, aggressive, and well-educated middle class people have been coming in larger numbers since the easing of immigration restrictions in 1965. Extending this latter point, refugees from repressive regimes in East Asia have a survivors' mentality that intensifies the practice of virtues of a work ethic which creates a middle class. As a survivor of the Cambodian death camps, who has recently prospered in Massachusetts banking and real estate, has put it, "I have to be an American now. But I get my strength from being a Cambodian. If I had been raised here in America, I would not have that kind of strength . . . all that suffering."[6]

By the 1980s, the results have been a spectacular record of achievement by Asian-Americans. Far beyond their proportions in the population, Asians are represented in the student bodies of the top ranking universities. In such prestigious contests as the Westinghouse Talent Search, usually 25% of the semi-finalists are Asian and 50% of the winners over the past ten years are as well.[7] Statistics indicate that Asian American high school students across the country score higher than any other group in mathematics tests. High school graduates from this group are twice as likely as whites to be accepted into the University of California where they comprise 25% of those at the Berkeley campus and 34% at Irvine.[8] Not surprisingly, this results in a higher than national average family median income. According to the 1980 census, this is placed at $23,600—or nearly $400 a year more than all American families.[9] Some of the household statistics must also be viewed with the understanding that Asian families are more likely than whites to have more family members living under the same roof and pooling their individual paychecks. By whatever arrangement, however, the pattern of upward mobility in American society is unmistakable.

Much of the rest of this essay will be devoted to exploring answers to the following question: "Is the Asian-American success pattern a recent phenomenon or is it rooted in the American history of each particular Asian group?" The answer is an unqualified yes to historic patterning. I will illustrate my central thesis by analyzing the group careers of five dominant groups: the Chinese, the Japanese, the Korean, the Vietnamese, and the Filipino. Until recently, when speaking of Asian-Americans or " Orientals," the term usually meant Chinese or Japanese. From 1910 to 1980, the decennial census has listed Japanese-Americans as the largest of all Asian groups within the country. By 1990, the Japanese have dropped to third place behind the Chinese and Filipino-Americans. Since 1965, except for Mexico, the nation that has supplied the largest amount of immigrants has been the Philippines. Demographers calculate that within a thirty year period (from the 1990 census), Filipinos will constitute the largest Asian American group, followed by the Chinese, Koreans and Vietnamese.

THE CHINESE-AMERICANS

The pioneers and patternmakers of all Asian groups in the United States are the Chinese. But how far do the Chinese go back in American history? Was there a Chinese discoverer of America nine hundred years before Columbus? Though never conclusively proven, there may have been a bold voyage at the end of the 5th Century undertaken by several Buddhist missionaries. Perhaps they landed on the Western shores of America by mistake:

> In the year of Yung Yuan during the Ch'i dynasty [in 499 A.D.] a priest by the name of Hui Shen came to Ching Chou. He told of the Kingdom of Fusang [America?] that was 20,000 Li [about 7,000 miles] to the east of Tahan and that country was to the east of China.[10]

This is recorded in the Forty-first Book of Chüan in the two hundred and thirtieth volume of the Great Chinese Encyclopedia which was composed by court historians of the Liang emperors from 502 to 556 A.D.[11] Hui Shen told of a mountain of gold in the lands east of the Sunrise Sea. The legend of Fusang was of course embellished through the centuries. In one of those strange coincidences that occasionally show up in history, the story of the Golden Mountain was to be partly realized in the 1849 Gold Rush to California. More reliable but tantalizing short snippets of information concerning overseas Chinese activity and history in the Americas come from the records of the Spanish Colonial Empire in the New World. The Philippines were Spain's Far Eastern bastion in a world wide empire that was connected by the sailing vessels known as galleons. These heavy rigged ships, used for commerce and war, were often created in Manila. A large colony of "overseas Chinese" resided in that Philippine city and supplied people as well as ships that went to Mexico. One reads of Chinese barbers dominating that profession in the Mexico City of the 18th Century. Acapulco was called the city of the Chinese in the late Spanish Colonial period because of its numerous East-Asian inhabitants. Even on the rim of Christendom, a "Chino" is listed as one of the original pabladores (founders) of the pueblo of Los Angeles in 1781.

Turning from these colonial times of real or imaginary events, historically verified immigration of Chinese to the United States began in the 1850s. News of the discovery of gold in California reached around the world and attracted people from many nations to the American West. The pull of instant fortunes complemented the push caused by problems in each of the countries from which the emigres came. For the Chinese, the problem of overpopulation was coupled with a cycle of typhoons and famines and then intensified by a political catastrophe from 1854 to 1864. The turmoil caused by a popular rebellion called the Tai-Ping Movement created even more unsettled conditions. This revolution originated in Southern China but swept into the north to the very gates of Beijing. However, it failed. Five million people were killed in the reprisals that followed this unsuccessful revolt against Manchu despotism. The people of South China were particularly hard hit. Masses of poor young men, usually farmers and fisherfolk, were ready to get out by any means. The Chinese historian Pyau-Ling has put the appropriate words in the mouths of emigres bound for America: "To be starved or buried at sea are the same, said young adventurers. Why not plunge right into death rather than wait for death." The noted historian added the comment: "Liberty is the star that guides these people to American."[12] Most of the Chinese that came originated in the ninety-eight districts of the province of Kwangtung. Overwhelmingly male and thinking of themselves as sojourners only, they accepted steerage as the price for a passage to riches and adventure. Crossings at their worst could be as long as three months. Thomas Sowell, the noted ethnologist, compared their crossings to conditions on board slave ships and to those that the Irish endured during the years of the Potato Famine exodus. Steerage on a typical ship consisted of three tiers of bunks which were six feet long and thirteen and half inches wide with seventeen to twenty-four inches of headroom. Standees were sometimes taken aboard. They took turns sleeping on the bunks during the voyage. With such causes for emigration and such conditions in transit, a familiar pattern asserts itself. The Chinese fleeing economic hardship reminds one of the English indentured servants that peopled the original thirteen colonies. Their flight from political oppression is no more or less dignified than the Puritan escape from Stuart tyranny in the England of the 1630s and 1640s. No ethnic group that has come to America has a monopoly on hardship, humiliation or dignity. However, the sad fact is that the Chinese participation in the great themes of American history has usually been ignored—and sometimes denied.

The story of the Chinese pioneers of the West diverges from that of other groups who voluntarily came to America in another significant way. Hard work did not usually pay off. For them, the American dream of success and social acceptance through diligent labor was short circuited. In fact, because of the envy and racism of the dominant group, Chinese industriousness often produced the opposite results from what one would normally expect. A reoccurring pattern from the late 19th through the early 20th Century would include Chinese-American successes and contributions, favorable competition with neighbors, a modicum of prosperity and then ostracism and expulsion from the very jobs that the Chinese made their own: mining, railroad building, farming and fishing.

The initial attraction of the Chinese was to the gold fields of California in 1849. Their dream was like that of so many from all over the world. They hoped to make a fortune in the Gold Rush and then return to China with the wealth of a prince and live happily ever after. Ninety-five percent of the Chinese immigrants were male and thought of their trip as a sojourn rather than a one way ticket to a final destination. There had been precedents in recent Chinese history for such an undertaking. From the early 1800s on, at least 30,000 Chinese emigrated to Borneo and developed the tin and goldmining of that primitive region. It was hoped that the California adventure would prove equally successful. According to some experts, it is possible that many of those that developed their expertise in Borneo could have come to California. This may account for the proficiency so many demonstrated early on in their group career in

Western mining operations. Though welcomed at first in the San Francisco region as service and merchandising people, the Chinese were to encounter immediate hostility when staking out gold claims in the field. When vigilante injustice did not intimidate them, there was always the oppressive and cost prohibitive Foreign Miners' Tax to discourage them. The hearty young men of Kwangtung province were more often than not forced to purchase the worked out claims of other miners. With characteristic Chinese thoroughness, they frequently found what the whiteman overlooked. One Yankee miner put it simply, "These little yellow-men were hated by most of the white miners for their ability to grub-out fortunes which they themselves had left for greener pastures."[13] With their experience in hydrology, the Chinese would often divert a river from its bed and then pick out the particles of gold rather than do individual panning. They introduced the Chinese water wheel—a sort of mechanical system of bailing buckets connected by ropes and pulleys to facilitate this method. But what envy this inventiveness aroused. The lines of two contemporary miners songs really reveal more about the psychology of the oppressor rather than that of the Asian oppressed.

John Chinaman, John Chinaman
But five short years ago
I welcomed you from Canton, John
but I wish I hadn't though.
Oh John, I've been deceived in you
And all your thieving clan.
For gold is all your after, John

To get it as you can.[14]
We're working like a swarm of bees
Scarcely making enough to live.
And two hundred thousand Chinese
Are taking home the gold that
We ought to have.[15]

When surface-mining had played itself out by the 1870s, the Chinese proved to be particularly excellent in adapting to hard-rock underground mining. Corporations increasingly controlled the more expensive mining operations of the late 19th Century. With them, the Chinese tended to be hired in favor to that of the general population. However, this proficiency led to being banned from the mines by local and state ordinances. Still . . . as late as the 1870 census, California listed 34,933 Chinese miners in that state, or about 25% of all engaged in that activity, In Oregon, for the same year, the 2,428 Chinese miners represented 61.2% of the mining population. One out of ten people living in Idaho were Chinese at this period of time. The 3,853 Chinese miners there accounted for 58.6% of this occupation.[16] It is clear from these surprising statistics that the Chinese chapter in this part of the saga of the frontier West is yet to be analyzed and given its proper place in both the professional and popular interest.

There is another side to the Chinese presence in the settling of the West. Rather than professional historians, however, it has been literary figures like Mark Twain and Bret Harte who have preserved some intriguing bits of Chinese-Americana. These people of ancient heritage people performed much of the entrepreneurial and service needs of the "Wild West." The legendary Chinese cook, hotel and shop keeper, houseboy and laundryman have their real life counterparts. In no small measure, it was the people of these occupations that kept the frontier from degenerating into complete savagery. It is true that the Chinese had a greater sense of cohesiveness within their community than what could be found among the more individualistic Yankee settlers. Within the Chinese network, there may have been a much larger percentage of skilled and professional people than is usually acknowledged. If so, this accounts for the gift of civility and some remarkable individual contributions made by "the mysterious Orientals" in the Western climes. Few individual names of Chinese pioneers have been preserved but there are some exceptions. Ah-Sang, "the Doc of Yankee Hill Camp," California is a prime example. This remarkable physician created a medical practice that first served his fellow Chinese. His healing fame spread to the white community where he also developed a white clientele. At first operating out of a frontier hotel, he was to build a fifty bed hospital which was to be reputed the best of his time.

From a job description point of view, far more representative were the 12,000 Chinese who worked to build the Central Pacific Railroad. This company received the commission to build east from California in order to meet the westward lines of the Union Pacific Railroad and thus span a continent. Central Pacific had a slow start from 1861 until the day that Charles Crocker, one of "The Big Four" owners of the railroad and the manager of construction, decided to employ "the Celestials" as the Chinese were then called. Much prejudice against "the little yellow monkeys" with their diminutive size and small hands and "effeminate ways" of frequent bathing were used to discourage such a policy. Crocker persisted and summed up his satisfaction years later when he wrote: "Wherever we put them, we found them good and they worked themselves into our favor to such an extent that we found if we were in a hurry for a job of work, it was better to put the Chinese on it at once."[17] The Chinese literally moved the mountains of the West by blasting through the solid rock of the Sierra Nevadas, carving roads thousands of feet high clinging to cliffs and crossing the deserts. In one incredible day, in order to fulfill a wager made by Crocker against the Irish-American gangs building the Union Pacific, the Chinese laid ten miles, fifty-six feet of new track which meant 25,800 wooden ties. After the great transcontinental line was completed, the Chinese worked on the Southern Pacific, the Canadian Pacific, the Oregon Central and innumerable short lines. Yet, in one of the tragic ironies of American history, when the railroad system was completed and the jobs gave out, the Chinese were only permitted to travel on these same railroads in third class segregated cars. How well did Donald and Nadine Hata express the central contradiction of Asian-American History in the title of their essay: "Still Strangers in Their Own Land."

After the end of the railroad building era, Chinese construction prowess was to find another challenge in the making of the levees, dams, and irrigation systems of the San Joaquin and Sacramento River Valleys in the 1870s and 1880s. The Chinese were to reclaim the flooded bottom lands which stretched as much as five to ten miles in either direction of the rivers. A former Surveyor General of California estimated that the labor of the Chinese on the reclamation projects and the railroads was worth at least $289,700,000 to the economy of the state.[18] It should be added that for working on these projects, men were paid between nine and twenty-five cents for each cubic yard of earth they moved. Farming and fishing were to be the next arenas of Chinese employment. They have the dubious distinction of being the first seasonal workers thus starting the tradition of supplying a cheap and efficient labor force on wheat farms and fruit orchards of California.

In 1870 about one-tenth of all farm labor in California was Chinese. Sixteen years later, the California Bureau of Labor estimated that the Chinese percentage had risen to 87.5.[19] No land ownership was allowed to the foreign born Chinese because they were considered "aliens ineligible for citizenship." Leasing and working on the properties of others were the usual conditions. Within these confines, the Chinese pioneered in the setting up of vineyards, orchards, truck gardening and horticulture. Some of the newly developed fruits such as Bing Cherries and Lue Gim Gong Oranges owe their origins to Chinese botanists. Particularly noteworthy is the man who gave his name to the famous variety of citrus just indicated. For this as well as the aggregate accomplishment of his work, he was given the prestigious Wilder award in 1911 by the Department of Agriculture. If ever there was a Chinese variation of the Horatio Alger story, it would belong to this remarkable man. Lue Gim Gong arrived in the United States at the age of twelve after a two month sea voyage from Hong-Kong. He worked as a contract laborer in a shoe factory in Massachusetts and then as a gardener. In the later position, he was befriended by the powerful Burlingame family (one of whom served as an ambassador to China). Through their patronage, he was launched into a career that would move him to Florida where his discoveries helped create the modern citrus industry. He was a master of the cross fertilization process that was the skill that led to his creation of such extraordinary hybrids.

Carey McWilliams, the Los Angeles journalist and historian of Southern California, maintains that by 1895 some four thousand Chinese were producing and distributing nearly all of the vegetables consumed in Los Angeles. The cooks of Chinatown branched out as vegetable peddlers or hucksters pushing their carts from house to house. The retailers, of course, worked in close alliance with the cooks. From this operation base, the Chinese soon acquired a produce monopoly. In 1891 an American conceived of the idea of growing celery in the marshlands of Orange County, California. When his own efforts failed, he fell back on the Chinese market gardeners who promptly agreed to assemble a crew of experienced celery raisers. By 1892, thousands of acres in Southern California were devoted to celery culture which were producing 1,200 carloads of that vegetable annually. The Chinese were used extensively in the vineyards and orchards of Southern California. A visitor to San Gabriel a century ago said he was surprised to find hundreds of Chinese washing, brushing, and sorting oranges "chattering and laughing as they worked under the direction of an American inspector."[20]

If possible, the Chinese made an even greater impact on the development of the fishing industry in the Pacific Coast states. The bean and beef eating white frontiersmen did not sense the possibilities of maritime riches. But the fisherfolk emigres of Kwangtung were quick to introduce their fine mesh nets, fishing gear and, above all, appetites for the delicacies of the seas. Ironically, the Chinese fondness for shellfish was thought of as evidence of the bestial tastes of "the heathen Chinese." They were the first to popularize the merits of abalone. By 1870, they were exporting $1,000,000 of this commodity to China annually. A lucrative abalone jewelry business was developed on the side. By 1880 the yearly value in the Chinese-American shrimp trade was placed at

$3,000,000.[21] Despite efforts to crowd out the Chinese from what now amounted to a prosperous trade, as late as 1897, there were twenty six Chinese shrimping camps in the San Francisco Bay area alone. The years 1860-1880 were the peak of the Chinese involvement in fishing. In this period, Asian-American fishing villages dotted the California coast from San Diego to Monterey. A famous traveler-recorder maintained in 1898 that "Chinamen have large villages, some of them like small cities, along the shore whose inhabitants are wholly engaged in catching, drying and shipping fish to China."[22] Beside the actual fishing, the majority of cannery workers for fish products were Chinese by 1870.

The contemporary successes and contributions of Chinese-Americans are, then, rooted in a long standing tradition. Yet there are no visible reminders or even place names to commemorate their enormously positive role in the development of the western United States. To an incredible degree, these 19th Century Chinese immigrants embodied the American mythic common man hero as farmer, fisherman, construction worker, and miner. However, we don't hear of the "Celestial" Mike Fink or the Kwangtungese Johnny Appleseed. Why then this public amnesia concerning the intriguing persons and events of Chinese-American History? The answer seems to be racism, pure and simple, conscious and unconscious. In the 19th Century, the racism was of the overt and blunt variety. All differences were viewed as signs of inferiority, causes for fear and sources of contention. In the 20th Century, racism has evolved into a more subtle and convoluted kind. Its goal of denying value to the other as other, however, remains the same. By simply ignoring the past, one can bury the successes of the minority as well as forget the now unfashionable oppression by the majority.

Persecution of the Chinese in American began in the 1850s. Much of it was of the simple and direct kind which was the product of a lawless society. Individuals or groups would run the Chinese off of their gold stakes at mid-century, burn out the lands leased in the 1870s and engage in shrimp boat wars in the 1890s. Even the Anglo farmers or growers who employed the Chinese were subject to intimidation by vigilante force. The taunt of "Run Chinaman Run" and "Ching-Chong Chinaman sitting on a fence trying to make a dollar out of fifty cents" were commonplace insults. One of the old time Chinese pioneers reminisced "When I first came here to work on the levees, we were stoned when we got off the ship. We weren't allowed to leave Angel's Island. They fed us like pigs because they thought we were filthy. Finally a group of all men came and led us to Chinatown. But on the way people shouted

'Chink, Chink, Chink' and threw stones at us again."[23] Cutting the queues (pigtails) off the Chinese men was considered a great sport. Sometimes these affronts to personal dignity degenerated into orgies of social violence that a later age would call race riots. In November of 1878, the entire Chinese population of Truckee, California (which numbered almost a thousand) were driven out of their homes. One of the worst of these mob actions occurred in Los Angeles in 1871. When a white man was fatally shot in the crossfire of a Chinatown tong war, a mob gathered for a wholesale attack on the Chinese settlement. As could only happen in a frontier town, one of the city council members resigned his office in order to join in the looting and killing. This disgrace has been described in the following words.

> Trembling, moaning wounded Chinese were hauled from their hiding places; ropes quickly encircled their necks; they were dragged to the nearest improvised gallows. A large wagon close by had four victims hanging from its sides . . . three others dangled from an awning . . . five more were taken to the gateway and lynched . . . Looting every nook, corner, chest, trunk and drawer in Chinatown, the mob even robbed the victims it executed. (Nineteen Chinese were killed.)[24]

"You haven't got a Chinaman's chance" is an expression that originated in this period for obvious reasons. What happened in Los Angeles was representative rather than exceptional. Just about every community with any number of Chinese residents sooner or later witnessed some form of violent persecution. The press did nothing to assuage this mania as it increasingly referred to the Chinese as people of "the Yellow Peril." In 1877, rioters in San Francisco destroyed thirty Chinese laundries. The very peak of such depredations took place in Rock Springs, Wyoming in 1885. Twenty-eight Chinese men were murdered by the local towns-people. Some of the victims were burned alive. The occasion for this horror was that Chinese miners had dissented in a strike vote. The Rock Springs massacre highlights the undertow of competition for jobs which is usually not far from the surface of racial bigotry. One can almost trace the intensity of anti-Chinese violence with the corresponding ups and downs of the business cycle. As mining and railroad jobs declined, the white laborers of the West saw in frugal, disciplined, hard working Chinese, their chief competitors. Indeed, the chief Chinese basher of the nation was Dennis Kearney, the Irish American organizer of the Workingman's Party in San Francisco. It was he who coined the expression, "The Chinese must go." He was not alone among labor leaders. Even so significant a figure as Samuel Gompers as organizer and first president of the American Federation of Labor took up the refrain in a pamphlet he authored. Its title says it all: "Some Reasons for Chinese Exclusion: Meat or Rice, American Manhood against Asiatic Coolieism, Which Shall Survive?" Jack London, known for his political radicalism as well as his literary career, was one of the spearheads for a movement which organized itself in order to prevent any more Chinese from coming to America. A popular song of unemployed workers of this period complained:

O workingmen dear, and did you hear
The news that's goin' round?
Another China steamer
Has been landed here in town
Today I read the papers,
And it grieved my heart full sore
To see upon the title page,
O, just 'Twelve Hundred More'

O Californians coming down,
As you can plainly see
They are hiring all the Chinamen
And Discharging you and me.
But strife will be in every town
throughout the Pacific shore
And the cry of old and young shall be
O, damn, 'Twelve Hundred More'[25]

A parallel legal persecution made the personal failures of decency that much worse. From 1854 to 1872, a California law forbade a Chinese from testifying against a whiteman in court. One of the few newspaper editors sympathetic to the Chinese put it succinctly, "A chinaman apparently has no rights which a white hoodlum, big or little, is bound to respect."[26] Similar policies in practice if not legal theory were operative in other Western States. Some local ordinances prohibited the Chinese from living within city limits or hiring themselves out for certain occupations. This agitation was to culminate in national legislation. In 1882, Congress passed the Chinese Exclusion Act. This law prohibited any future immigration of Chinese workers (skilled or unskilled) into this country for a ten year period. The act did permit the entry of diplomats, merchants and students. Significantly, this is the first law ever passed barring immigration into the United States to a specific people on the basis of race or ethnicity. The Exclusion Act was renewed in 1892 and then again in 1902 for an indefinite period of time. Only in 1943 during World War II was this policy reversed when henceforth one hundred and five Chinese were allowed to come into the United States annually. The victory of the exclusionists in 1882 was followed by two particularly cruel pieces of legislation, considering the overwhelmingly male percentage of the Chinese-American population. The Scott Act of 1888 prohibited Chinese workers temporarily out of the country (usually visiting their families in China) from ever returning. It is said that this law immediately affected 20,000 men. The 1921 Immigration Law denied all foreign born women the right to share their husband's citizenship.

The effect of four decades of intolerance and the above mentioned legislation just about halved the numbers of Chinese living in the United States. From an all time high of 110,000 in 1890, the population was down to approximately 60,000 by 1920.[27] Not only were there quantitative changes but qualitative and geographic locale differences as well for this period. More and more of the Chinese withdrew to the larger cities for mutual protection by the turn of the century. Those that chose to remain and those that were economically stranded in America turned to the areas that offered the only jobs permitted to them. The days of the wide distribution of Chinese settlements in the West were over. The era of the big city San Francisco-New York Chinatowns had begun more by default than by design. Though generally sympathetic to the Chinese, the famed historian, H.H. Bancroft wrote these patronizing lines that just about summed up the job opportunities that were available. "It is not true that the Chinese are filthy in their habits, inefficient in their work or untrustworthy. As cooks, domestic servants, launderers and for orchard and vegetable garden work, they have no superior . . . The American and European are best for high grade work . . . The Chinaman is best for low grade work."[28] The Chinese hand laundry became an American institution because of a lack of alternatives. A minimum of capital investment together with the need of relatively little English proved attractive. These tiny (often one man) operations created *the* stereotype of Chinese-American life. By 1920, over one-fourth of all Chinese men were launderers. In the same year, about 10% were employed in the restaurant business.[29] Chinese cooking establishments proved popular; but were usually centered in Chinatown rather than in the dispersed fashion of today. This avoided the appearance of competition with those of the larger community. Chinese groceries also flourished in Chinatown, supplying the food most preferred by its inhabitants. These holding operations allowed for survival. They should not obscure the sad fact that less than 1% of the Chinese had achieved professional status at this time.

Withdrawal and inconspicuousness became the hallmarks of Chinese-American existence from this era to the post World War II period.

Withdrawal is as much a psychological condition as a physical state. In poignant prose lines that verge on poetry, Stan Steiner summed up this retreat to Chinatown phase by a marvelous use of architecture as metaphor:

> And as demeaned and debased by the land where their families had lived for generations, they turned their eyes not only inward to themselves but backward to history. The buildings of Chinatown began to resemble their nostalgia. Year by year, the facades grew more ornate with replicas of their past. Since they were denied real participation in the life of the West they helped shape, they reshaped the surroundings of their poor ghetto with exaggerated images of their memory. . . .
>
> The facade of Chinatown began to change to fit its new image. It was adorned with a public opulence of design that was as ostentatious as it was exotic more so perhaps to its residents than to its visitors. And yet not even this could quite hide the sorrows that generations of 'menials and servants' had been reduced to. In the dark alleys behind the pomp of the newly ancient papier-mâché dragons, the people had fallen into the deepest poverty.[30]

"The Chinatown after Dark" syndrome and Fu Manchu movies stamped their images and stereotypes into the popular imagination. Thus this period of Chinese-American history has left an indelible mark on the way Chinese are seen both by themselves and by others. Newspaper articles, pulp magazines and the Hollywood of the 1920s-1940s supplied the adjectives which became categories of thought for ways of perceiving the Chinese i.e. inscrutable, secretive, mysterious, clannish, sly, devious, drug-oriented, immoral, murderous, effeminate, patient, overly-polite, traitorous and clever. The lust for the exotic and the deliciously wicked was projected on to the Chinese in their ghetto. They in turn got some financial compensation from it by catering to it. From the early years of the 20th Century, businesses associated with the tourist trade provided, at the least, one more acceptable occupation. They ranged from the legitimate curio shops and tempting restaurants to the illicit opium dens and brothels. Contrasting the present conditions in the 1990s with those of a century ago is worthy of a book rather than a few pages in a chapter. One is really comparing two different Chinese-American worlds. Today most Chinese-Americans do not live in Chinatowns. Those districts are presently most often the homes of the very old or the new refugees "fresh off the boat." Between the present and the past is the successful fight of Chinese-Americans for real equality, social acceptance and educational and professional excellence. Their's has the heroic if not the dramatic quality of the African Americans' similar struggle in these same years of the 20th Century. The advancements of the Chinese have been laboriously piecemeal and gradual but, judging from the results, most effective. Four major stepping stones were used to get Chinese-Americans through the difficult years from 1920 to 1990. They are: (1) the continuing growth in numbers of the American-born Chinese. They are guaranteed the rights of citizenship by birth. (2) the reforming of restrictive anti-Asian immigration legislation. With the doing away of the ethnic quota system in 1965, up to 20,000 immigrants from any nation are permitted to enter America (3) changing attitudes on racial minority rights within the dominant group. This dismantling of segregation from the 1960s on was to be of enormous help for Asian as well as African Americans. The concomitant lessening of common prejudices and habits of discrimination has been partially realized in the America of the 1990s and (4) the shifting power relations of the United States with the People's Republic of China and Nationalist (Taiwan) China. The growth of Chinese political and military power in the second half of the 20th Century has removed the sense of inferiority from being associated with a homeland, once considered on the decline.

In the first few decades of the 20th Century, the isolation of the Chinatown inhabitants from mainstream America generated in the survivors a tough sense of self-reliance. Of course, not everyone survived. The suicide rate of the Chinatown Chinese has been three times that of the national rate.[31] But speaking in general terms, the Chinese developed an infrastructure of self-help groups within their community that produced psychological traits of strength and resilience. When the opportunities would come, especially after 1945, the Chinese had the discipline and capacity to reach out and use them. Even such disasters as the San Francisco Earthquake of 1906 or the Great Depression of the 1930s did not witness many Chinese applying for public assistance. For example, during the unemployment of the 1930s in New York City whereas 9% of the whites went on federal relief, only 1% of the Chinese did so.[32] Business acumen and education were the two lanes of the road out of Chinatown poverty. It was with those few American-born Chinese who had gained an education in the period before World War II that there was the start of something better. Less than 2% of the Chinese community had received a college education as late as 1940 and in that year only about 3% could be considered in professional occupations. Yet twenty years later, professionalization had risen to 18% as compared to 15% among the whites. By 1990, 30% of Chinese males are working in professional or highly technical fields.[33] Some statistics would put these percentages significantly higher. Science, accounting, engineering, drafting and college teaching (in the natural sciences and engineering) comprise the bulk of these positions. Professionalization and business expertise have gone hand in hand. Though the last forty years have been the time that the great Chinese-American businessman has emerged, there were signs of things to come within Chinatown. As early as 1939, Joe Shoong, born in China, created a system of franchise stores that made him a fortune and the possessor of the second highest income in California for that year. C.Y. Tung became in the postwar period one of the largest ship owners of the world. But it is An Wang that is the symbol of a new era. At one time in his life, Wang was a shy engineer from Shangh-hai. He immigrated to America in 1945 and built a $600 investment into a multibillion dollar computer firm. At the time of his death in 1990, Forbes Magazine listed him as the fifth richest man in the world. Wang obtained his advanced degrees at Harvard and, in the late 1940s, became an American citizen and went on to invent the computer core magnetic memory ring. Today every large American city has a Wang skyscraper office advertising not only the brilliance of the man but in no small way the arrival into full participation of the Chinese Americans.

World War II does seem to be the dividing line in Chinese American History. Because the United States and China were allies during this great conflict, it was considered politic to remove the Chinese Exclusion Act. A small number of Chinese were permitted to enter the country thereafter. Special provisions were made for war refugees and the families of Chinese-Americans. Twenty-five thousand Chinese immigrants availed themselves of these new provisions between 1943 and 1950.[34] Perhaps of even greater significance is the fact that the Congressional Act of 1943 removed the legal block that prevented foreign born Chinese from becoming American citizens. The war years generated a public sympathy for the sufferings of China which in its own peculiar way smoothed the ragged edge of anti-Chinese prejudice in this country. Moreover, the labor shortage on the American home front opened up jobs that were hitherto closed to the Chinese-Americans. Refugees fleeing the Communist takeover of mainland China from 1949 on, if anything, intensified the public's sympathy. In the more tolerant post-war society, the growing economic and professional successes usually brought respect instead of the previous envy. This is not to deny that there are still great pockets of poverty in Chinese-America. Particularly is this true of the lot of those called "Fresh off the Boat" (F.O.B.)

Hong Kong Chinese. These refugees from political tyranny had the public's good will but little else. Much of the doubling of the Chinese population from 237,000 to 435,000 in the 1960s was the product of this influx.[35] Though some like An Wang in 1945 were well trained and middle class, the majority were ordinary people who would repeat the old pattern of working long hours at low pay, often in the garment factories and restaurants of Chinatown. In this sense, the 19th Century pattern persisted; but with two important qualifications: (1) The "new" Chinese were usually working for American-born Chinese and (2) hard work could eventually "pay off" in an improvement in one's status within the national society. The possibility of real rewards released enormous amounts of energy that nearly half a century later built the affluent Chinese American community of the 1990s. The Horatio Algers of our time, more often than not, have almond shaped eyes.

THE JAPANESE-AMERICANS

Americans love a winner. They especially love an underdog winner that comes from way behind to gain the triumph of victory. If such a generalization is true, then of all the ethnic groups who compose the American people by 1990, the Japanese should be the favorites. Perhaps this sentiment is partly responsible for the frequent references over the past twenty years to the Japanese-Americans as being "the model minority." This expression, however, cannot but leave a bittersweet aftertaste in the mouths of the people of this heritage. Memories of a whole people's incarceration forty-five years ago are still vivid amid the great educational, entrepreneurial and professional successes of today. Thomas Sowell eloquently encapsulated the grand irony of Japanese-American history with the following words:

> The History of Japanese-Americans is a story of tragedy and triumph. Few people ever came to American more predisposed and determined to be good Americans. Few met such repeated rebuffs and barriers—including barriers of mass internment camps or more completely triumphed over it all across a broad spectrum of economic, social and political success.[36]

"Triumph and tragedy" are the ingredients of good drama. Both abound in the group career of this remarkable people. The 750,000 Japanese Americans of today are the product of two great nations that entered the Pacific arena of power at approximately the same time and are contemporaneously working through the challenges of their advanced industrial societies. The cataclysmic clash of the two nations in World War II was both preceded and followed by eras of attraction and repulsion and competition as well as cooperation. The ups and downs of international relations have left indelible marks on the Japanese-American people who were caught by events of which they had no control.

The love-hate relationship goes back to 1853 when Commodore Matthew Perry of the United States Navy sailed into Tokyo Harbor and began the process of ending over two hundred years of the self imposed isolation of Japan in its Tokugawa period. It is significant that among the gifts that Perry presented to the Emperor were a toy steam locomotive, machinery, modern guns and one hundred gallons of Kentucky bourbon. For better or for worse, all of these items were prophetic of the commercial and military interactions between these nations in the future. Perry's visit coincided with a time of major governmental changes in Japan. A period of modernization, urbanization, and industrialization had begun which disrupted a feudal society and thereby dislocated substantial numbers of people. Heavy taxation, overpopulation and a growing enthusiasm for all things "Western" provided the incentives for 30,000 Japanese farm workers settling in Hawaii from 1886 to 1894.[37] To the American mainland came 129,000 more in the 1890s. By 1924, when further Japanese emigration to America was stopped, 125,000 more had come.[38]

These large migrations of agricultural laborers were preceded by trickles of Japanese peasants working in the sugar cane and pineapple plantations of Hawaii since 1868. A small number of students also came in the early years. A naive admiration of anything American was characteristic of their mentality. Consider the following statement made by just such a student:

> The desire to see America was burning at my boyish heart. The land of freedom and civilization of which I heard so much from missionaries and the wonderful story of America I heard of those of my race who returned from here. It made my longing ungovernable. Meantime I had been reading a popular novel among the boys, "The Adventurous Life of Tsurukichi Tanaka, Japanese Robinson Crusoe." How he acquired new knowledge from America and how he is honored and favored by the capitalists in Japan. How willingly he has endured the hardships in order to achieve the success. The story made a strong impression on my mind. Finally I made up my mind to come to this country to receive an American education.[39]

Inevitably, Japanese immigration will be compared to that of the Chinese patternmakers of the previous generation. There are similarities as well as some striking differences. At first, the composition of the migration was overwhelmingly male and intended to be a sojourn rather than a permanent relocation. However, as more of the Japanese left for America, a more normal ratio between the sexes was reached. This indicated two things: (1) The Japanese were willing to permanently transplant as evidenced by establishing regular family life. (2) The host society could not make the charges of immorality so often leveled at Chinese men. By 1920, there were approximately two Japanese men for every Japanese woman living in the United States. Another difference was the government sponsored selectivity of immigrants within the old country. The Japanese Government represented a rising but sensitive world power. It wanted to be represented by the best of its subjects from whatever socio-economic class emigration would come. Japanese authorities were well aware of the treatment that the Chinese had received in America. Accordingly, they extended a more protective preoccupation with their subjects abroad. As a case in point, when the San Francisco Public School Board threatened to segregate Japanese students into an all "Oriental" school, the Japanese Government protested vehemently. As a result, President Theodore Roosevelt found it was diplomatically necessary to work out a Gentlemen's Agreement in 1908 whereby the schools would remain integrated; but Japan, on its part, would discourage future immigration except for wives and close relatives of the Japanese community resident in America. The calibre of Japanese migrants was screened by the prefectures (government Districts). Indeed, they selected an interesting sample of Japanese society for emigration to the United States. The cliche "poor but proud" aptly describes the results of such official processing. Neither the affluent wanted or the destitute were able to make the big trip across the Pacific. The "Issei," as this first generation were to be called, were tough, resilient, proud, ambitious, self disciplined, polite and literate. Because of Japan's compulsory education laws, almost all could read and write in their native language. When the U.S. Commissioner of Immigration went to Japan in 1899, he reported, "It is a feature of the law (that) the government has acted upon the theory that the character of the Japanese abroad will be taken as an index of the character of the nation at home. Hence, these regulations provide for the careful inquiry into the character of those going abroad and also required that provision shall be made for the return of the emigrant, in the event that he becomes sick or a public charge in a foreign country, before the passports are granted."[40]

Forty percent of the "Issei" went into agricultural work especially in Hawaii and California. They helped fill the shortage caused by Chinese exclusion. Mining, fishing, lumbering, domestic service and ethnic-business and services account for the rest of their jobs. Only 10% could be considered clerical or professional. Almost from the start, they established a reputation for hard work and reliability. Noteworthy is the fact that though white farm laborers were paid more by the hour for their work, the Japanese made more money when paid by the piece or package in the sweating system. The historian Bradford Smith maintained, "The Issei contribution to America was not in great men but in the anonymous little men who made the desert spaces green with the labor of their hands, who kept the track even so that Americans could ride comfortably across the land, who tended the comfort of the well-to-do and grew vegetables the poor could afford to buy, who sacrificed for the welfare of their children."[41] Some notables in this generation do stand out despite that truism. None more than George Shima who came to be called "the potato king of California." Coming to America in 1890 as a common laborer, he was destined to drain thousands of acres of Sacramento River lands and then made a fortune growing potatoes on them. Horticulture is a related area in which Japanese-Americans made legendary contributions. Kosaku Sawada moved from Osaka to Mobile, Alabama where he became famous over a fifty year career as the pre-eminent grower and hybridizer of camellias. Botanists credit him with developing thousands of new varieties. One of the most interesting of this generation was Kataro Suto who was the landscape engineer and nurseryman who helped create Miami Beach, Florida.

On a less grand scale, but no less significant in the overall picture of the rise of the Japanese Americans, is a general pattern of improvement. Farm laborers contrived every possible way and means to become farm owners in the period of 1900 to 1940. The cycle of their progress usually involved contract farming, sharecropping, leasing and ultimately owning farm land. The laws of California from 1913 on, made it extremely difficult to reach the goal of ownership. However, various subterfuges were used to get around the legal prohibitions. In 1900, there were only 39 Issei owned farms in California totaling 4,700 acres. Twenty years later there were 5,000 Issei farms with more than 460,000 acres under cultivation.[42] As late as 1940, the majority of Japanese-American males were farmers. As a measure of their productivity, in that same year, they were the creators of about one third of the commercial valuation of California truck-farm crops. During this period, the Japanese gardener became one of the stereotypes of Asian-American life. By 1940, 5,000 Japanese had gone into gardening and landscaping.[43] This was the opportunity that many grasped at. Gardening was a small business with little need of capital in order to get started. Skill, trustworthiness and intense labor (often performed by the entire family) was what was needed to serve the homes of middle and upper class America. This the Japanese-Americans had in abundance. For the same reasons, Japanese entered the corner grocery, restaurant and small hotel businesses.

"It's going to be better for my children" is a refrain found throughout the pages of American immigrant history. The Euro-American boast of "My son, the doctor" resonated in Issei hearts. Great sacrifices were made for the second generation—that is, "the Nisei." As one reaches the 1940s, the native-born Japanese-Americans were increasing in numbers. The advantages of being born American (hence citizenship) along with education, facility in English and the hard work foundation of their Issei parents were pushing the second generation into what Harry Kitano called "the middleman minority status." What happened to the Japanese in America bears some remarkable resemblances to what happened to the Jews in Europe. Restrictions in land ownership and discrimination from unions in the skilled work trades forced the Nisei into intensified small business ownership and professionalism.

It is not uncommon for the sons and daughters of immigrant parents to want to be "more American than thou" or to use the contemporary ethnic jargon to "out-Anglo, the Anglo." Peer group pressure and generation gaps were not invented in the 1960s. The values the Nisei learned in public schools and absorbed in popular entertainment were often in conflict with their parents. Most of the Nisei spoke very little Japanese beyond home necessity. Half of their members became Christians. They formed their own separate organizations such as the Japanese American Citizen's League (J.A.C.L.) that rejected close national ties with the mother country. When the general society permitted, they joined any and every service organization from the Cub Scouts to the Kiwanis Clubs. When the general society refused to accept them, they formed parallel organizations. It is this wholehearted acceptance of all things American that makes the 1942-1945 imprisonment of the entire Japanese-American mainland population so bitterly ironic.

Anti-Japanese sentiment certainly did not begin with the attack by Imperial Japan on the American fleet in Hawaii, on December 7, 1941. What American's entry into World War II did was to bring to a head four decades of opposition and discrimination. Dennis Kearney switched his slogan to "The Japs Must Go" in 1892. Exactly fifty years later, the wish was literally fulfilled. There is a line of continuity between the sentiments expressed by Mayor Phelan seeking reelection in 1900 by denouncing Japanese-Americans from the steps of the City Hall to the editorial that appeared in the San Francisco Chronicle in 1942. Consider how war hysteria intensified what was already there in the following incendiary words from two eras:

> The Japanese are starting a tide of immigration which we thought we had checked twenty years ago . . . The Chinese and Japanese are not bona fide citizens. They are not the stuff of which American citizens can be made.[44]
>
> The Japanese should be moved to a point deep in the interior. I don't mean a nice part of the interior, either. Herd 'em in the badlands. Let 'em be pinched, hurt, hungry, and dead up against it. . . . If making one million innocent Japanese uncomfortable would prevent one scheming Japanese from costing the life of one American boy, then let the million innocents suffer . . . let us have no patience with the enemy, or with anyone whose veins carry his blood.[45]

Physical and verbal abuse made life a nightmare for Japanese-Americans in the early weeks of 1942. Fear of a West Coast invasion by Japan plus frustration over American military defeats in the Southern and Western Pacific led many to scapegoating. The sentiment prevailed that all Japanese, whether citizens or not, were threats to national security. The concentration of the Japanese-Americans in relatively few areas made them all the more vulnerable to popular attacks. A second "day of infamy" was not long in coming. On February 19, 1942, President Franklin Roosevelt issued Executive Order 9066 which ordered the relocation of all mainland Japanese Americans. This affected 110,000 people which consisted of 40,000 Issei and 70,000 Nisei. Biological inheritance rather than loyalty, citizenship or even generation was the sole determinant as to who this order was to be applied. Homes, businesses and farms had to be liquidated within a few days. The financial loss of the Japanese-American community has been conservatively put at $400,000,000 (by 1942 values). The entire population was removed to ten concentration camps that resembled minimum security prisons in isolated areas that ranged from Arkansas to California.

Roy Yanno, a young Nisei in those tragic days has left us a vivid account which telescoped the collective misery into his personal experience.

> The government didn't tell us whether we would be able to come back or not. They didn't promise us anything. So I told my wife that perhaps the best thing would be to sell our furniture and buy food and medicines and things like that. Our youngest daughter was only four months old, and we didn't know if there would be doctors or hospitals in the camp. . . . There were a group of vultures who came in knowing that we had to leave. . . . These barracks were built in such a hurry that there was no paved road or anything like that. It was just full of dust. Every time you walked all the powder would fly up and from top to bottom we were covered with white powder. . . . The barracks was built in such a way that there was no ceiling above each room—just one high ceiling. . . . When a person cannot have privacy, that is really bad. For myself, my children were young and it didn't matter too much but I felt sorry for the people with teenage children.[46]

The great tragedy of this wholesale violation of the civil rights of American citizens is compounded by their overwhelming loyalty to the United States. Almost all went to the camps quietly, respectful of authority. There is not known of one case of espionage. In fact, thousands of young Nisei men volunteered to serve in the armed forces. The all Japanese 442nd Regimental Combat Unit was the most decorated in World War II and, indeed, in all of America's history. Nine thousand casualties earned them fifty two Distinguished Service Crosses and A Congressional Medal of Honor. The most curious aspect of this unpleasant episode in America's ethnic history is the fact that in Hawaii, the 150,000 Japanese-Americans (who constituted 20% of the Islands' population) did not have to undergo this incarceration. It would take forty-six years for this all to come to a closure. In 1988, President Reagan signed a bill which provided $20,000 payments to the 60,000 Japanese Americans who were internees of the camps and who were still alive. The law included a "Statement" of the Congress recognizing the grave injustice committed against American citizens and permanent resident aliens of Japanese ancestry and extended an apology on behalf of the nation."[47] The payments began in 1989 and total approximately $1,250,000,000. Those three lost years are a great dividing line in Japanese-American history. Thousands of lives were injured in ways for which no statistician can account. Farms, businesses and homes were lost forever. Someday, someone will write the saga of the Japanese-American Scarlet O'Hara coming back not to a ruined plantation as in the 1860s but to a stolen nursery as in the 1940s.

As is evident from the preceding pages, the wartime internment of the Japanese was not the causal point but the accelerator of the phenomenal progress so characteristic of the postwar years. As a catalyst, the trauma of the incarceration stimulated the Nisei to intensify their already evident drive for education. It should be remembered that as early as 1940, the Japanese-American has surpassed the whites in years of education achieved. How often would a Japanese-American father of the 1950s and 1960s point to his head (when encouraging his offspring to study harder) and say, "What's up here can never by taken away." As with the Chinese, the college degrees were usually in the scientific and applied fields of engineering, architecture, optometry, medicine and business administration. The semanticist S.I. Hayakawa actually credits the internment with stimulating long range mobility. Within the camps, the internees worked a wider range of jobs than they had known in civilian life. Then too, family businesses were usually now no longer there to be taken over. In this sense, there was a freeing from restrictive parental expectations. Wider distribution of occupations resulted. The energy and courage released by having to start all over again seems to have suffused and uplifted the whole community. "As American as John Wayne" can contemporaneously be translated as American as Minoro Yamasaki and Daniel Inouye. Both of these prominent Japanese-Americans exemplify the accomplishments of the post-war generation. Yamasaki, as a world famous architect, has graced America with such buildings as the St. Louis Airport, the Seattle World's Fair and campus structures at Oberlin and Princeton Universities. The struggles in Inouye's life perhaps even better summarize in human terms a half century of Japanese-Americana. His eminently readable autobiography contains passages that trace his reactions to Pearl Harbor Day through his career as a captain of the 442nd Regiment to his election as the first U.S. Senator of Japanese ancestry.

Nothing succeeds like success. A growing sense of toleration in racial and religious matters has diluted much of the initial hostility that Japanese Americans encountered as they returned from the concentration camps. The little Tokyo ghettos were never fully reconstituted. As early as 1946, California voters ended the ban on "alien" (Issei) ownership of land. The 1952 McCarran-Walter Act allowed Issei to become citizens. This same immigration law granted an entrant quota to Japan for the first time since 1924. Approximately 150,000 Japanese have emigrated to the United States by 1990, as a result.[48] With educated middle class status has come residential dispersion and a surprisingly high rate of inter-marriage with whites. In this otherwise positive picture of a minority that has fully arrived, there are some negative trends. The accommodationist, restrained and self-effacing traits so necessary for survival in the past may be holding back Japanese-Americans in the present. However stereotypical these qualities may be, their internalization by Japanese-Americans and their image-externalization by the public at large may be a factor in preventing otherwise qualified people from obtaining high level decision making positions in corporate America. A potentially more ominous development, (considering the past half century) is the currently popular Japan-bashing in the press and in common speech. Undoubtedly, the trade wars and economic competition of the United States with Japan in the 1990s has fueled the phenomenon. Unfortunately, there is still that sector of the American population that did not then and cannot now make the distinction between Japanese and Japanese-American.

THE FILIPINO, KOREAN, AND VIETNAMESE AMERICANS: VARIATIONS ON A THEME

Between 1950 and 1990, Asian Americans came from an increasingly greater spectrum of countries in "the Orient." Filipino, Korean, and Vietnamese are filling out the contemporary definitions of Asian-American. It is not coincidental that each of the just mentioned ethnicities come from countries that have been intimately associated with the United States through the 20th Century. The Philippines existed as a colony of the United States from 1898 to 1946. The Korean War of the late '40s and early '50s and the Vietnam War of the '60s and '70s were the initial and tragic phases of encounter between the Americans and these Eastern peoples. Though there are patterns that can be compared, there are unique characteristics for each of these three distinct peoples.

Filipino emigration has come in two waves. The earliest reached its crest in the 1920s; the latter is in full tide in the 1990s. From a socio-economic point of view, the kind of Filipino coming to America in these two time periods is different. After the Philippine Islands were annexed, there were no restrictions to its people from entry into the United States. Filipinos filled the need for cheap agricultural labor after the passage of the Chinese Exclusion Act and the Gentleman's Agreement with Japan. Hard labor in the plantations of Hawaii and then on the ranches, truck farms and canneries of the Pacific Coast states was the lot of most fleeing the rural poverty of the islands. Like the earlier Chinese, most Filipinos were young males thinking of their work in the United States as temporary. Once here, however, they got caught in a cycle of wages and prices that prevented a return for the majority. Sizable populations of this group developed in Honolulu, Los Angeles, San Francisco and

Seattle. By the 1920s, the Filipino population resident in Hawaii and on the mainland was approximately 26,600. Unfortunately, the legacy of racial discrimination left over from the campaigns against the Chinese and Japanese followed the Filipinos. The stereotypes that developed drew much from those already used "Yellow Peril" images. But the exuberant fun loving Hispanic aspect of Philippine culture added another note that can be perceived in the following slander:

> The Filipino never has a dime . . . His money goes for cards, women, clothes and the like. The Filipino contractor furnishes some of these things. He brings women (white women) into the camp as well as booze and gives each laborer who cares to indulge a ticket. That is he takes it out of wages . . . The Filipinos are . . . a social menace as they will not leave our white girls alone and frequently intermarry . . .[49]

Looking from the inside out, a Filipino-American reminisced about living conditions in those days when the image of his group crystallized in the Americans' eyes

> We lived in the red-light district where pimps and prostitutes were as numerous as the stars in the sky. It was a noisy and tragic street, where suicides and murders were a daily occurrence, but it was the only place in the city were we could find a room. I often wondered if I would be able to survive it, if I could be able to escape from it unscathed.[50]

Though the majority were common laborers, it is interesting to note that the very first Filipino immigrants in 1903 were students and teachers. A small percentage of professionals (and those preparing for that status) accompanied the mainstream. In those days, they came in order to become acquainted with American values and systems. Indeed, they were sent to the homeland of an empire that included their islands. In 1934, the Philippines were upgraded from colony to commonwealth status. As a result, future Filipino immigration was put on a quota basis. By 1946, the Philippines was an independent nation and like other Asian countries was all but barred from sending immigrants until 1952. However, after the end of the quota system in 1965, approximately 20,000 to 25,000 Filipinos enter the United States each year. The professional, well educated middle class person who was once the exception is now the rule of Philippine immigration. Sadly, the "newcomer" must fight not only ignorance about his homeland but the stereotypes passed down concerning the Filipino-American population. Because of an exceptional educational system in the Philippines, the country produces more college graduates and professionals than its economy can employ. The same could be said of Korea and Taiwan. The United States with its advanced post industrial service economy is the natural magnet that will continue to attract this sector of the population from around the world. In recent years, there has been a steady flow of Filipino engineers, architects, dentists, doctors, nurses and teachers to the West Coast cities. Many have found their qualifications not recognized and some have been refused jobs because of being "overqualified." But the long range picture is bright because America needs their skills. Filipinos share in a striking pattern that says something about the importance of human capital. By the beginning of the 1980s, it is recognized and proven that immigrants begin economically below the level of the existing members of their own ethnic group resident in the United States but within a few years surpass them. With the Filipino, the process takes about thirteen years.[51] Along with this economic phenomenon, there is a political motive for immigration from the Philippines. The repressive years of the Marcos dictatorship that extended from the '60s to the late '80s forced many (especially among the professionalized middle class) to seek political as well as economic opportunity in America. The oft and proudly repeated story of this nation's boast that it was peopled by generations of freedom fighters and seekers renews itself with the Filipinos. Also, the stream of 170,000 from Vietnam after the fall of the Saigon government in 1975 has added a large chapter to the saga of the flight to freedom. America's political involvement in Asian wars has brought love as well as hate as the means of cementing East-West relations. Vietnamese and Korean war brides, children and orphans have been the vanguards of immigration from these two countries. But it has not stopped with this personally based exodus. From South Korea as with the Philippines, an American presence in their countries opened the door to the middle and upwardly mobile working classes to seek better opportunities in a "Western" nation with which they now had some contact. The business instinct of the Koreans along with their renowned toughness has found in small businesses in inner city America in the 1990s, a challenge that would have made an "Andy Grant" cringe in the 1890s. The case histories of Vietnamese "Boat People" refugees or Korean immigrants going from menials to owners of a franchise store in a few years will be their turn of the century version of the American success story.

Rather than seeing Asian-Americans as exotic transplants, it might be well to think of them as the regenerators of this nation as it enters the 21st Century. If America was truly built on (1) the Work Ethic and its attendant virtues of frugality and self discipline, (2) strong family life both nuclear and extended, (3) business expertise and skill, (4) a love of education and (5) an enthusiasm and involvement in voluntary self-help organizations . . . then, it may be that the Asians exemplify this heritage more than the biological descendants of the Anglos by the 1990s. Confucius rather than John Calvin may be the inspiration point of many of our people but the results may be similar. Perhaps in some mystical way beyond the ken of this author, America is renewing itself by finding people who can perform the necessary jobs for great nationhood. Our essay has moved from present to past to present again to prove this. Historically, Asian Americans have played important roles in the building of this country. Ethnic studies are helping us to acknowledge this long overlooked contribution from the past. More to the concluding point, this historic past is a fitting prelude to the obvious accomplishments of Asian Americans in the present and future. ✦

NOTES

1. Gardena, California is the largest community of Japanese-Americans in the United States. Though an independent city, it is situated in the greater Los Angeles area.
2. These statistics are based on an analysis compiled by the Population Reference which in turn based its figures and approximations for 2000 A.D. on Bureau of the Census data and material compiled by Leon F. Bouview and Anthony Agresta. Table of estimates are quoted in "Asian Americans," *Editorial Research Reports* (Washington, D.C., 1986), p. 57.
3. "A Capsule View of American Immigration Legislation from Cafferty, Chiswick, Greeley and Sullivan," *The Dilemma of American Immigration* (New Brunswick, 1984), p. 58.
4. The term "Oriental" though not offensive in itself is falling into disuse. As with other racial and ethnic designations from the past, it comes freighted historically with a set of images and associations that are unflattering to the people so designated.
5. "Asian Americans," *Editorial Research Reports,* op. cit., p. 44.
6. "To America With Skills," *Time Magazine,* 8 July 1985, p. 49.
7. "Asian-Americans: Are They Making the Grades?" U.S. *News and World Report,* 2 Apr., 1984, p. 41.
8. Diane Divoky, "The Model Minority Goes to School," *Phi Delta Kappan,* Nov., 1988, p. 222.
9. "Asian-Americans," *Editorial Research Reports,* op. cit., p. 46.
10. Stan Steiner, *Fusang: The Chinese Who Build America* (New York), p. 3.
11. *Ibid.*, p. 3.
12. *Ibid.*, p. 113.

13. *Ibid.*, p. 116.
14. *Ibid.*, p. 121.
15. *Ibid.*, p. 120.
16. *Ibid.*, p. 124.
17. *Ibid.*, p. 132.
18. *Ibid.*, p. 146.
19. *Ibid.*, pp. 144-5.
20. Carey McWilliams, *Southern California: An Island on the Land* (Santa Barbara, 1973), p. 90.
21. *Ibid.*, p. 88.
22. *Ibid.*, p. 87.
23. Victor G. Nee, and D.E. Bary, Brett, "*Longtime Californin'*," (New York, 1974), p. 36.
24. This account is a description from the "San Francisco Bulletin" quoted in McWilliams, op. cit., p. 91.
25. These are the lines of a popular song published in 1877—quoted in full in Linda Perrin, *Coming to America: Immigrants from the Far East* (New York, 1980), pp. 32-33.
26. Newspaper quote is found in Lee, *Chinatown, U.S.A.* (New York, 1965), p. 67.
27. Thomas Sowell, *Ethnic America* (New York, 1981), p. 146.
28. H.H. Bancroft quoted in Steiner, op. cit., pp. 196-197.
29. Sowell, op. cit., p. 139.
30. Steiner, op. cit., p. 198-9.
31. Sowell, op. cit., p. 143.
32. *Ibid.*, p. 144.
33. *Ibid.*, p. 152.
34. David Olson, *The Ethnic Dimension in American History* (New York, 1979), p. 395.
35. *Ibid.*, p. 395.
36. Sowell, op. cit., p. 155.
37. Olson, op. cit., p. 333.
38. *Ibid.*, p. 334.
39. Perrin, op. cit., p. 65.
40. Bill Hosokawa, *Nisei: The First Americans* (New York, 1969), p. 46.
41. Hosokowa, op. cit., p. 133.
42. Olson, op. cit., p. 334.
43. Sowell, op. cit., p. 133.
44. Perrin, op. cit., p. 72.
45. *Ibid.*, p. 86.
46. *Ibid.*, p. 87-91.

47. Text is quoted from the Japanese-American newspaper publication in Los Angeles: "Rafu Shimpo" 10 Aug., 1988, p. 1.

48. Olson, op. cit., p. 398.

49. Perrin, op. cit., p. 119.

50. *Ibid.*, p. 118.

51. Sowell, op. cit., p. 283.

SELECTED BIBLIOGRAPHY

Archdeacon, Thomas. *Becoming American.* New York, 1983.

Barth, Gunther, *Bitter Strength: A History of the Chinese in the United States 1850-1870.* Cambridge, Mass:, 1964.

Corpuz, Onofre. *The Philippines.* Englewood Cliffs, New Jersey, 1965

Daniels, Roger, *Concentration Camps U.S.A.*: Japanese-Americans and World War II. New York, 1971.

____, *The Politics of Prejudice, the Anti -Japanese Movements in California and the Struggle for Japanese Exclusion.* Berkeley, Ca: 1962.

Hata, Donald & Nadine. "Asian and Pacific Americans: Still Strangers in their Own Land," Essay found in *American History and Culture: a Reader*, editor Joseph Collier. Los Alamitos, Ca., 1977.

Hosokawa, Bill. *Nisei: The Quiet Americans.* New York, 1969.

Hoyt, Edwin. *Asians in the West.* Nashville, Tenn., 1974.

Hsu, Francis, L.K. *Americans and Chinese.* New York, 1971.

____. *The Challenge of the American Dream: The Chinese in the United States.* Belmont, Ca., 1971.

Hundley, Norris. *The Asian-Americans: the Historical Experience.* Santa Barbara, Ca., 1976.

Kim, Hyung-Chan. *The Koreans in America.* New York, 1974.

Kitano, Harry. *Japanese-Americans: the Development of the Middle-man Minority.* In *The Asian Americans*, edited by Norris Hundley. Santa Barbara, Ca., 1976.

Kuhn, Delia & Ferdinand. *The Philippines: Yesterday and Today.* New York, 1966.

Li, Dun J. *The Essence of Chinese Civilization.* Princeton, 1967.

Lyman, Stanford. *Chinese-Americans.* New York, 1971.

McWilliams, Carey. *Southern California: an Island on the Land.* Santa Barbara, Ca., 1973.

Munoz, Alfredo. *The Filipinos in America.* Los Angeles, 1971.

Nee, Victor G. & de Bary, Brett. *Longtime California.* New York, 1973.

Olson, David. *The Ethnic Dimension in American History.* New York, 1979.

Petersen, Wm. *Japanese-Americans.* New York, 1971.

Perrin, Linda. *Coming to America: Immigrants from the Far East.* New York, 1980.

Saxton, Alexander. *The Indispensable Enemy: Labor and the Anti-Chinese Movement in California*. Berkeley, Ca., 1973.

Smith, Bradford, *Americans from Japan*. Philadelphia, 1948.

Sowell, Thomas. *Ethnic America*. New York, 1981.

____, *The Economics and Politics of Race*. New York, 1983.

Steiner, Stan. *Fusang: The Chinese who Built America*. New York, 1979.

Sung, Betty Lee. *Mountains of Gold: The Story of the Chinese in America*. New York, 1967.

Tiedemann, Arthur. *An Introduction to Japanese Civilization*. Lexington, Mass., 1974.

PEOPLES OF THE CARIBBEAN: NEW AMERICANS

RAFAEL L. CORTADA

THE ISLANDS

The Caribbean islands reflect cultural and ethnic pluralism more than any region on earth. The original Arawak inhabitants were misnamed "Indians" by Christopher Columbus. A warlike nation called Caribs migrated northward from the South American mainland, and drove the peaceful Arawaks before them. These "Indians" were joined in the Caribbean by Africans, Asians, East Indians, Frenchmen, Englishmen, Danes, Dutchmen, Spaniards, Portuguese, and finally, Americans. Thus the islands have accommodated people of every race and many cultures.

European involvement in the Caribbean began on October 12, 1492, when Christopher Columbus sighted an island in the Bahamas, which he named San Salvador, but which the native Arawak Indians called Guanahani. From there, Columbus went on to touch upon Cuba and Hispaniola. On subsequent visits, he visited most of the Caribbean archipelago and the north coast of South America. Columbus claimed the lands he touched for Spain. The race for empire had begun. From the sixteenth through the eighteenth centuries, England, France, Portugal and Holland competed with Spain for treasure and control.

The Caribbean Islands comprise some 90,000 square miles, a bit over one-third the size of Texas. The Greater Antilles, comprised of Cuba, Jamaica, Puerto Rico and the historic Hispanola are dominant. The Lesser Antilles extend in an arc reaching south from the Virgin Islands, through Anguilla-St. Kitts-Nevis, Antigua, Montserrat, Guadeloupe, Martinique, Dominica, St. Lucia, St. Vincent, Grenada, Trinidad and Tobago, and Bonaire, Aruba and Curaçao. The 166 square miles of

Barbados represent the eastern extremity of the islands. The Bahamas, 760 islands stretched over 700 miles, are the northern tier. Bermuda, 1,000 miles to the north is relatively isolated. "The three Guianas," Cayenne, Surinam and Guyana, are often viewed with the islands due to strong cultural and economic ties. The entire area is tropical, characterized by only wet and dry seasons and fall hurricanes.

THE PEOPLE

There is probably no place on earth that is so intensely diverse. The Spanish explorers quickly eliminated the original Arawak inhabitants by disease and intermarriage. The combative Carib Indians were systematically killed. but the islands were useless without a labor supply. So it was to the Caribbean more than to North America that the African slave trade was aimed. A mulatto population became truly indigenous, joining the African and European and merging their blood, language and cultures. Thus the concept of race in the Caribbean is far more complex than the mere dichotomy of black and white. And all became more complex after the British abolished slavery in 1832, and brought in a steady influx of East Indians and Chinese to do farm work and add new diversity to the already complex human equation.

The Caribbean Islands, then, are populated by a virtual microcosm of all humanity. There are blacks, whites, mulattoes, East Indians, indigenous people called Amerindians, and Chinese in greater or lesser numbers and in every combination on all of the islands. They speak Spanish, French, English, Dutch, Papiamiento, and Patois, and offer, in various settings, every example of the fusion of these cultures. The Spanish culture is dominant in Cuba, the Dominican Republic, and Puerto Rico. French is dominant in Martinique and Guadeloupe, and in Haiti. English is generally spoken in Jamaica, Trinidad, Barbados, the Bahamas, and in the Lesser Antilles. Thus when we speak of the Caribbean, we refer to diversity itself, rather than a dominant culture, race, or language.

THE ECONOMIES

The islands are veritable gardens for tropical agriculture, with sugar, coffee, coconuts, pineapples, citrus, tobacco and bananas as the historic cash crops. In fact, sugar dominated the world economy in the seventeenth and eighteenth centuries as oil and steel did in the twentieth. This gave the islands a value that far exceeded their size.

In modern times, the islands have developed the tourist industry. However, it has become clear that tourism alone cannot carry a modern economy. In diversifying, Cuba, Puerto Rico and the Dominican Republic have industrialized to a significant degree. Haiti has moved toward light, cottage style crafts. The Bahamas have diversified through banking and finance. Trinidad, Jamaica, and Guyana have used minerals, oil in the former case, and bauxite in the latter, to generate jobs. But overpopulation threatens every gain. And industrialization brings urbanization and environmental problems. So immigration will continue to be a vital safety valve for these small nations for the foreseeable future. This makes aid to these nations to develop their economies in the direct interest of the United States. Economic development will require establishment of markets, infrastructure, and facilities to move goods. Development, coupled with regional integration, may ultimately stabilize populations.

POLITICS AND GOVERNMENTS

While there have been exceptions, democratic government is the norm in the Caribbean. Strong British and American influence has achieved this much. The large Anglophobe islands, Jamaica, Barbados, Trinidad, and Tobago, have well established and orderly democratic governments based upon a parliamentary model. Even when Jamaica coped with violence in the electoral process, democracy was never seriously threatened. Puerto Rico and the Virgin Islands, closely allied with the United States, have deep democratic traditions and stable governments.

Haiti and the Dominican Republic have divergent political histories. Both have experienced decades of dictatorship. While the Dominican Republic has moved toward stability and orderly electoral processes since 1965, problems continue to torment Haiti. The brutal dictatorship of François "Papa Doc" Duvalier was followed by that of this son, Jean Claude Duvalier. The latter was unseated and sent into exile by a mass protest of the common people. But military rule has replaced the dictatorship. Haiti suffers from extreme poverty, exhausted and eroded soil, and the absence of a democratic tradition. It seems unlikely that Haiti's development will move toward democratic government in the foreseeable future.

Cuba has a similarly divergent history. The harsh dictatorship of Fulgencia Batista until 1960 has been followed by the "Marxist-Leninist" rule of Fidel Castro. The Cuban middle class was largely uprooted to Miami. The Castro government has improved literacy in Cuba dramatically over the past three decades. But it is impossible to speculate about the nature of the government that would replace Castro's through natural evolution.

Democracy dominates the Lesser Antilles. Martinique and Guadeloupe have been absorbed as provinces of Metropolitan France, and the islands are fully represented in Paris. The smaller English-speaking islands of the Lesser Antilles have strong democratic traditions and orderly electoral processes. Their problems stem from the economic dilemmas facing any mini-state, rather than political instability.

These deep democratic traditions, and the high levels of literacy that prevail in most of the Caribbean, orient the island populations toward Canada, the United States, and Great Britain. This facilitates immigration and the movement toward citizenship in the adopted country, since basic values, language, and political traditions are shared.

U.S. INVOLVEMENT

Cuba's alienation is a deviation from history. The United States has generally been viewed by Caribbean peoples as either the model for progress and opportunity or the "Colossus of the North" at various times. The polarized views of race on the mainland have been seen as convoluted and curious. But these have never provided reasons either for any hostility to Americans in the islands, or barriers to migration to the United States. There were elements in the American South even in the Jeffersonian era, who saw U.S. expansion into the Caribbean as inevitable. The Cuban wars of independence saw Jose Marti use Florida and New York City as staging areas, while Antonio Maceo, a black general, led Cuban guerrilla forces in the field. U.S. intervention in the final years led to the "Spanish American War" in which the United States took Cuba and Puerto Rico from Spain. The Virgin Islands were added in 1917 by purchase from Denmark.

THE PUERTO RICANS

Puerto Rico is undoubtedly the Caribbean Island most deeply entwined with the United States. The Spaniards found this to be a peaceful isle populated by Indians, the Tainos and the Boriquens, who had no weapons and contributed only the hammock to the world's "technology."

Africans were imported. But landholdings remained small, and plantation gang labor never proved feasible. Since 65% of the 100 mile by 32 mile island is mountainous, arable land proved scarce and heavily populated. The lack of violence on the island made it possible for significant numbers of Spanish women to settle. Thus agriculture became based upon family farms cultivated by the patron and one to three slaves. Even slavery deviated from the English model in North America.[1] The slaves had defined legal rights, and there were many avenues to freedom. One could even purchase one's own manumission on credit. Thus the number of free blacks in Puerto Rico generally equaled the number enslaved. By 1873, when Spain abolished slavery, fewer than one-fourth of the Africans in Puerto Rico were in bondage.

The American forces were generally welcomed by Puerto Ricans in 1898. And the United States quickly justified this feeling. Military forces made improvement in health and education their first priorities with the eradication of malaria, and requirements for free compulsory education. Efforts to impose English as the official language, however, were abandoned.

The United States' goals in seizing Puerto Rico were purely military. The island offered a choice naval base commanding approaches to Florida, Panama, and the north coast of South America. The people were a secondary concern, and studies on the feasibility of relocation to such areas as the Amazon Basin were undertaken by the United States government. However, the United States Congress instead deepened ties by unilaterally granting citizenship in 1917 through the Jones Act. By this legislation, all Puerto Ricans became United States citizens with full and open access to "the mainland." They became subject to all federal laws including military conscription. On the continent, Puerto Ricans have the right to vote, and pay federal taxes, rights and obligations not extended to the island. The island was granted a Resident Commissioner with voice but no vote in Congress. Thus insular Puerto Ricans joined residents of the District of Columbia and southern blacks as citizens without full rights. By 1920, there were only 20,000 Puerto Ricans on the mainland, generally in New York City.

Until 1948, the Governor of Puerto Rico was appointed by the President of the United States. Some were political hacks, others were excellent. Rexford Tugwell brought the humanism and momentum of the New Deal to the island. However, the island remained one of the poorest places on earth through the first half of the twentieth century.

The election of Luis Muñoz Marín as Governor of the island in 1948 brought a new era of self-government. He moved immediately to implement Operation Bootstrap, an economic plan to attract industry to the island though a program of tax incentives supported by the stability of the American flag and U.S. citizenship. In 1952, a new constitution was adopted making Puerto Rico a Common-wealth, an autonomous state in voluntary association with the U.S. A middle ground between independence and statehood had been found, for the moment. By 1970 Puerto Rico had blossomed, moving from the low-est to the highest per capita income in Latin America, with a gross national product that surpassed Cuba and the remainder of the Caribbean.

Throughout these years, a steady flow of people moved between the United States and the island. From 1950 until 1975, rural people migrated generally to New York City. Since 1980, the migration has been comprised of a college-educated, bilingual urban middle class. With a population of 4 million, the island is one of the most densely populated spots on earth. There are about 1.5 million Puerto Ricans in the New York metropolitan area, and another million throughout the nation, so migration was a vital safety valve that enabled the island's economy to mature. the contrasts remain, however. Puerto Rico's economy, the richest in Latin America, is still poorer than the poorest of the 50 states. Yet the island provides the third best market on earth for U.S. goods. Modernization has brought other stresses. Illiteracy has been totally eliminated, creating greater demand for middle class employment, and keeping unemployment rates at 20%. Automobiles choke the island's roads, with the 26,847 cars of 1940 growing to 489,576 in 1984. The very closeness to the United States creates a tension in the culture, and an uncertainty as to what will emerge from Commonwealth status.

A second generation of Puerto Ricans has been born, now, on the mainland. Some are bilingual, but most are English dominant. But Puerto Ricans both on the island and the mainland are a youthful people, with 60% younger than 16. They are a strange phenomenon to North Americans, since blacks, whites, and mulattoes share a common culture and at times emanate from the same family. In effect, Puerto Ricans born on the mainland are relative aliens in their own birthplace. On the mainland, they have defied assimilation, "bilingualized" New York, and created a new urban speech pattern drawn from Black English and Spanish. It has been said that some can think in one language, speak in another, and read and write either or both. The first and second generation Puerto Ricans born on the mainland represent a unique cultural synthesis; a blending of North American and Caribbean Hispanic cultures. They survived the crucible of the barrios of New York, and in the process, forged a new urban culture.

The culture that Puerto Ricans bring to the mainland has been highly traditional, conservative, and Hispanic. Their value system is rooted in the five "pillars of *Hispanidad*": traditionalism, familism, paternalism, humanism, and fatalism. Their traditionalism has created a hesitancy to yield inherited values without valid alternatives, and these do not seem to be offered by the "pop culture" of the mainland. The second and succeeding generations may well find themselves alienated from the traditions of the island, without having accepted fully the mores of urban America. It is more likely that they will shape these. The Puerto Rican family remains extended and close, with roles defined by age, sex and kinship. Success is shared, hardships are deflected. The feminine role faces the greatest challenge in America, since it has been deeply rooted in the family. It is unlikely that the paternalistic role of men will change. They see dignity in work and in nurturing and protecting the family. The tradition of *machismo* implies these obligations, as well as the sexual double standard. The humanism of the value system has enabled Puerto Ricans to judge one another according to personal qualities, separate from roles in society. If traditional North American competitiveness imbues succeeding generations, it is likely that a materialistic outlook will prevail. The fatalism that has imbued the Puerto Rican value system is also likely to change.

Latin people have accepted man's subservience to nature and God's will. Hardship was to be accepted, not necessarily overcome. This has affected the Hispanic concept of time, efficiency and achievement. Puerto Ricans, however, have been closest to the North American's confidence that man controls his universe and his fate, and that every barrier is to be overcome. The transformation of the island's economy was proof of what was possible. It is likely that the Puerto Rican world view will be altered. But they will retain unique perspectives, and are not likely to see the world through North American eyes.

Puerto Ricans have had success in government, the arts, athletics, and in public education, with the public often not fully cognizant of their roots. Roberto Clemente, Tony Orlando, Rita Moreno, Jose Ferrer, Herman Badillo, Geraldo Rivera, former Mayor Maurice Ferre of Miami, and Irene Cara, are all island-born or first generation mainland Puerto Ricans. There is now a viable Puerto Rican middle class on the mainland, composed of both island- and mainland-born people. The current migration that reversed the net outflow to the island after 1980 consists primarily of better education, bilingual professionals. There is every indication that the Puerto Rican community in the United States will become economically stable, as the community establishes itself beyond New York City.

THE CUBANS

Cubans had always come to America for political reasons. During the wars of independence, Cuban liberals used Florida and New York City as staging areas. Thus small Cuban communities were already established in the mainland before 1898.

The United States did grant Cuban independence after the 1898 war with Spain. But strict controls remained, that antagonized many Cubans. Cuba relinquished a naval base at Guantanamo for 99 years, and the United States reserved rights of unilateral intervention through the Platt Amendment to Cuba's Constitution. In the 1930s President Franklin D. Roosevelt's Good Neighbor Policy eliminated some of these antagonisms and eased relations. Nevertheless, Cuban politics remained volatile through the dictatorship of Fulgencio Batista.

Until 1950, immigrants from Cuba were counted among those from the West Indies. So it is difficult to tell how many among the 500,000 people who entered the United States from the West Indies between 1820 and 1950, were from Cuba. It is certain, however, that older communities of Cubans developed at Ybor City and Tampa, Florida, and in northern New Jersey. These older communities were never threatened by the "mainstream" culture of the United States. They learned English, became bicultural and economically productive. The immigrants tended to be politically liberal and reformer-oriented, disenchanted with difficulties faced in Cuba in securing a stable democracy. These older communities tended to preserve their Ibero-Cuban heritage and an expression of pride.

Since 1959, 800,000 "new" Cuban immigrants have entered the United States. Immigration surged after the Castro revolution, then it ebbed and flowed responding to U.S. and Cuban policy shifts. The first wave of refugees were a displaced bourgeoisie, well educated professionals, and entrepreneurs and government. They tended to settle in major urban centers and in Puerto Rico, especially New York, San Juan and Miami. Initial fears that public services would be overloaded or that squalid new barrios would develop proved groundless. The Cubans made rapid economic progress. By 1976, their median income was only $2,000 below the national norm, but still surpassing other Hispanic groups and Blacks. This created tensions, above and beyond those already existing between older and newer Cuban communities.

The largest single influx of Cubans came in 1980, when the Mariel boatlift brought 150,000 Cubans into Florida. The Marielitos, however, were different from the first Cuban refugees of two decades earlier. These were poorer, urban working class people. Some were black. And Fidel Castro emptied his prisons and mental hospitals to include several thousand hardened criminals and mentally ill people. The new immigrants brought the Cuban population in the United States to about 950,000, of whom about 85% are first generation Americans. The first refugees of 1960 expected a temporary political exile. Their children and the Marielitos, like the "old Cubans" of Tampa and Ybor City, do not expect ever to return to Cuba.

Cubans at times found themselves disparaged by Anglos who did not differentiate them from other, poorer Hispanics. Thus the Cubans refugees tended to cooperate at times with other Caribbean peoples in America, whom they had viewed with disdain in the past. Although they settled in blighted areas, the Cubans brought new vitality and stability, and they aided restoration. The Cubans converted Miami from a winter resort city to a year-round banking and commercial hub, and a bilingual cultural center. As entrepreneurs, the Cubans brought a brashness, shrewdness and willingness to risk, that aided their success. Unemployment remains a problem mainly among the Marielitos, who brought problems and the burden of color to America.

The Cubans generally share the cultural values of other Latinos. They pursue material wealth as a vehicle for freedom, rather than as an end in itself. A generation has passed since the first refugees fled Castro. The Cubans have become a permanent part of the economic and cultural fabric of this nation.

To some degree, the Cuban immigrants and their children have become a success story. Governor Robert Martinez of Florida and Mayor Zavier Suarez of Miami are both of Cuban origin, and Cuban-Americans have won representation in Congress. But this success has caused tension. Cubans are politically conservative due to both their anti-communist focus and their economic success. The Black population in Miami has expressed frustration and alienation at their lack of economic improvement and political impotence. To a degree, the success of Cuban political leadership will be affected by their ability to respond to concerns of long term resident minority groups, and the alienated Anglo population.

THE DOMINICANS

Immigrants from the Dominican Republic have always come to the United States, through Puerto Rico, where their numbers are significant. However, Dominicans have rarely attracted notice, since they are generally submerged in larger numbers of Puerto Ricans in New York, or Cubans in Miami.

After the Dominican Civil wars of the mid 1960s, immigration to the United States increased. By 1980, perhaps 200,000 Dominicans had entered the United States. Since then, they have generally filled the 20,000 person quota on immigration from a single country.

Many Dominicans are dark skinned. Thus they have had to contend with prejudice, language, lack of skills and unemployment. While Dominicans have tended to settle in urban areas, some have branched out to do agricultural work. The Dominican population faces the classic problems of all immigrants, compounded by color and lack of visibility. It is likely that their situation will improve as other Latino communities cope and progress.

HAITIANS

Haitians fought with Lafayette in the American war for independence. Their bloody struggle against France for freedom[2] made Haiti the second independent nation in the Americans. Their victory left Napoleon in an untenable position in the Caribbean, inspiring him to sell the Louisiana territory to the United States for $12 million. Thus American's history is entwined with Haiti's, generally to American's benefit. But Haiti's history as a nation is a sad one. Haiti is a mountainous country in which the little land that is arable has been exhausted for generations. Poverty is grinding, and has been compounded by the dictatorships of the Duvaliers, *pere et fils*. Illiteracy, hunger and disease have left the population too exhausted even for political turmoil. Immigration to America has been the only hope for many.

By 1980, 60,000 Haitians had entered the United States legally. Perhaps a greater number entered illegally. Public attention was drawn to this quiet stream of migrants in 1980, and 1981, when about 30,000 boat people arrived in Florida, fleeing the Duvalier regime. They were declared ineligible for asylum since the Duvalier government was not officially deemed "oppressive." It was presumed, then, that the boat people were fleeing for economic rather than political reasons. The placing of the black Haitians in seventeen detention camps differentiated them from other immigrants, until a federal court ruled the federal policy illegal. The Coast Guard has since intercepted and turned back Haitians at sea, to prevent further immigration. The 1980 census found 100,000 Haitian-Americans. However, this would not detect illegal immigrants, and those using the guise of other cultures for self identity.

Haitian communities in Dade County, Florida, and in New York city face similar problems. Language is a serious barrier. Thus farm labor and low paying jobs in service industries have been the prime employment outlets. As language skills improve and a second generation takes root, it is likely that the willingness to work that is innate to Haitians, will begin to allow greater mobility and options. There is already a small middle class of professionals who were among the earlier arrivals and the more recent legal immigrants.

Most Haitians are patois- or French-speaking Catholics, with fierce pride in themselves and their heritage. They will resist absorption into the racial structure of Black Americans, since they feel this would lead to worse treatment and reduced opportunity. Haitian-Americans can be expected to be quite slow to make any identify transitions in future generations.

ENGLISH-SPEAKING IMMIGRANTS

Immigrants from the former "British West Indies" (Trinidad, Barbados, Jamaica, the Lesser Antilles and the Bahamas), have always been a sizeable minority in the United States. Common language, access through commonwealth ties in Canada, the ability to move easily through black American communities, and sensitivity to educational and economic opportunity have made residence in the United States a desirable alternative.

Historically, these British colonies were attractive during the sugar era and even more valuable later due to mineral resources. While the islands have always been relatively poor, they generated profits for England, and the people have always been upwardly mobile. The British left a viable middle class, and a well established civil service in the islands. Education is deeply valued, and the traditions of stable parliamentary government have been absorbed. In a sense, the West Indian population has viewed their insular existence as a constraint to their achievement. Thus significant populations of well educated and successful West Indians have always resided in Great Britain and Canada, as well as in the United States.

It became clear after World War II that colonialism would end. In the West Indies, Britain faced particular problems, since many of the islands of the Lesser Antilles were quite small. Thus it was questionable if they would be economically viable as independent mini-states. The first effort to integrate the islands was through the West Indies Federation, which lasted only from 1958 through 1962. The Federation included Trinidad, Barbados, Jamaica, and the islands of the Lesser Antilles, and excluded British Guiana and British Honduras. The Federation faltered almost immediately. There was no common thread to link the interests of the islands. Economic competition and political independence were too strong. By 1966, the three larger islands and Guyana had become independent. Even today, the islands of the Lesser Antilles exercise internal self government, while relying upon Great Britain for defense and foreign affairs. Many, however, still see advantages to integration. But it is clear that this will have to evolve through regional economic ties rather than political mergers.

The people of Trinidad and Tobago have been particularly influenced by American mores since U.S. bases were placed there during World War II. The people are a richly diverse lot, including Blacks, mulattoes, East Indians and Chinese. They are inventive, optimistic about life and filled with initiative. The economy of Trinidad has been accelerated by oil, which the island has produced over the last four decades. At least 200,000 Trinidadians have entered the United States since 1970, but total populations would be difficult to determine. Many entered under British immigration quotas or through Canada, and they have not settled in any one place or in ethnic-cultural communities. Trinidadian immigrants and their children have enjoyed some success in the United States. Mervyn Dymally, the current Congressman and former Lieutenant Governor or California exemplifies these achievements.

Barbados is a lush coral island 21 miles long by 14 miles wide, characterized by pink sandy beaches and friendly, stable people. As an independent nation. Barbados is one of the world's most literate, with literacy rates that rival those of the Japanese. the presence of "Bajans" in the United States is difficult to determine due to relative dispersal on the continent. Shirley Chisholm, the first black woman to serve in the U.S. Congress is of Barbadian ancestry. And it is likely that success and achievement such as hers are not unusual in that population.

Jamaicans have become a significant minority population in the United States. Perhaps 250,000 have entered the country since 1970, settling mostly in eastern urban centers. They come from a pluralistic, tired society comprised of whites, mulattoes, and Indians, that is about 80% black.

Jamaica is unique in the English-speaking Caribbean in that its folk culture, drawing heavily upon African and Caribbean slave cultures, is especially strong. The Maroons, the offspring of slaves who escaped into the mountains of Jamaica, are still an identifiable population in Jamaica's remote "cockpit country." They still exhibit the fierce independence that led the British to grant them manumission and land by treaty. English is the first language of Jamaicans. However, their rapid speech patterns, coupled with a clipped accent, can cause difficulties on first contact.

Economics is the prime stimulant for immigrants. Jamaica's tourism and bauxite economy cannot support the growing population base. While they adapt easily to American society, Jamaicans react with particular bitterness when confronted with American racism and discrimination. Marcus Garvey, a Jamaican-born Black nationalist of the 1920s, exemplifies this. But discrimination has been seen as an even greater stimulus to excel for those Jamaicans who remain. Second generation Jamaicans have tended to merge into the American population as Black Americans. So Jamaican communities have not survived per se beyond the first generation.

GUYANESE

British Guiana became an independent nation in 1966. The 83,000 square mile country is one of the world's last frontiers. It is rich, undeveloped, and populated by only about 900,000 people, mostly along the Atlantic Coast and the Essequibo River. The population is a rich polyglot of "Africans," East Indians, Chinese, Amerindians, mulattoes and whites.

When slavery was abolished, the Africans moved toward Georgetown and became urbanized. To secure farm labor, the British imported Indians who became a rural people, before they too moved toward the city. The independence period has been characterized by some tensions since East Indians have become a strong majority, while Africans hold political power. Guyana has turned to socialism through a "Cooperative Republic," in an effort to address the extreme poverty and the limited tax base that hinders progress. Some have even speculated that the three Guianas (Cayenne, Surinam and Guyana), could well benefit and accelerate their development by encouraging immigration from the over-populated islands, After all, the people do have deep cultural and ethnic ties. but that neat theory overlooks the nationalism that has developed, and the bitter memories of imported slave and indentured labor that are still fresh. Perhaps in time, as economic integration proceeds and politics become regionalized, solutions of this sort can become feasible. In the interim, Guyana struggles to progress, confident that the untapped wealth of their country, coupled with high literacy rates, will work to their benefit.

There are significant numbers of Guyanese in the United States, with the largest concentrations in New York City and Washington, D.C. Some move easily through Black American communities. However, those of Indian and other extractions have no visible counterparts in the U.S. population. Guyanese are deeply sensitive to the benefits of education, and they tend to be highly successful as immigrants. The Guyanese may never be a visible minority in the United States. They have no desire to be. But they are and will continue to be successful, and to move into the professions.

THE BAHAMIANS

When the West Indies Federation broke up in 1962, the small islands were big losers. They had dominated the Federation through the ballot box, and this fact helped to alienate the larger member islands. The failure of the Federation made it necessary for the Bahamians to replan their future.

The British had been involved in the Bahamas since 1629. However, their history was turbulent with Americans capturing the colony in 1776, and the Spaniards in 1782 before the advent of the British. Piracy mars all of the early history of the islands.

The Bahamas have developed strong, stable parliamentary traditions despite their history. For a period of years after the disintegration of the West Indies Federation, the White minority "Bay Street Boys" of Nassau continued to rule through election, despite the black majority of voters. The election of Lynden Pindling ultimately brought a black government to power.

The Bahamas are one of the most successful examples of economic progress in a small country. This has been no small achievement in a scattered island country that is hard to administer, that is closer and more economically dependent upon the United States than Great Britain, and that is vulnerable to hurricanes. All this is complicated by economic and political power split among whites and blacks. Their economy has been fueled by a healthy tourist industry, augmented by high levels of foreign investment and banking. The clever use of exemption from income tax, very favorable estate taxes upon death and tax exemptions for new businesses have created a relatively healthy economy. Overseas banks, trust and insurance companies have been particularly attracted. The islands have maintained relative racial harmony through a thriving economy and high literacy that has moved everyone into or to the threshold of the middle class.

There have always been Bahamians in the United States. Our proximity all but guarantees such easy access. However, there have been no mass migrations, due to the economic vitality of the islands.

OVERVIEW

Caribbean immigrants are helping to change the face of America. They bring distinct values, new perspectives and a drive to excel that will be an asset to the nation over time. But their growing numbers have generated hostility over race and language not unlike that faced by other immigrant groups. While the Hispanic populations have maintained ethnic communities that provide a buffer against hostility, this can delay merger into the competitive economic mainstream. The English-speaking immigrants have "blended" more quickly. but this too can be a "mixed blessing," since the umbrella is offered by a Black American community that is itself disadvantaged, and has been subjected to hostility over centuries.

It is clear that the key to mobility for each of these communities will be education, which can lead to improved job opportunity. This is in the best interests of the United States, since an underclass spanning generations cannot be condoned without undermining fundamental concepts of personal rights, fairness and cultural diversity.

It is vital that the American public comprehends the full magnitude of the diversity coming to our shores. Convenient rubrics such as "Hispanic" or "Caribbean," we must understand, shelter diverse groups with varying histories, cultures, values, languages, diets, music and recreation preferences. Similarly, we must avoid "blaming the victim" for the poverty that haunts the immigrants. They came here, as did others, to escape poverty. Education and fair opportunity will be effective antidotes to poverty for these new groups, as they have been for others.

Education can abide well with distinctive cultural patterns, as long as these are needed for self identity. This diversity will not create an "American Quebec" as many fear. The new immigrants come to share in, not weaken, America. ✦

NOTES

1. Frank Tannenbaum, *Slave and Citizen: The Negro in the Americas* (New York, 1946).
2. C.L.R. James, *The Black Jacobins* (New York, 1963).

SELECTED BIBLIOGRAPHY

Fagg, John E. *Cuba, Haiti & the Dominican Republic*. Englewood Cliffs, NJ, 1965.

Fitzpatrick, Joseph P. *Puerto Rican Americans: The Meaning of Migration to the Mainland*. Englewood Cliffs, NJ; 1971.

Hauberg, Clifford. *Puerto Rico and the Puerto Ricans: A Study of Puerto Rican History and Migration to the United States*. New York, 1974.

Hawkins, Irene. *The Changing Face of the Caribbean*. Bridgetown, 1976.

Horowitz, Michael M. *Peoples and Cultures of the Caribbean*. New York, 1971.

James, C.L.R. *The Black Jacobins: Toussant L'Ouverture and the San Domingo Revolution*. New York, 1963.

Knight, Franklin W. *The Caribbean: The Genesis of a Fragmented Nationalism*. New York, 1978.

Lewis, Gordon K. *The Growth of the Modern West Indies*. New York, 1968.

Lowenthal, David. *West Indian Societies*. New York, 1972.

Millett, Allan Reed. *Politics of Intervention: Military Occupation of Cuba, 1906-1909*. Columbus, Ohio, 1968.

Mitchell, Sir Harold. *Contemporary Economics and Politics of the Caribbean*. Athens, Ohio, 1968.

Parry, J.H. and P.M. Sherlock. *A Short History of the West Indies*. London, 1963.

Price, Richard (Editor). *Maroon Societies: Rebel Slave Communities in the Americas*. New York, 1973.

Sexton, Patricia Cayo. *Spanish Harlem: Anatomy of Poverty*. New York, 1965.

Sherlock, P.M. *West Indies*. New York, 1966.

Tannenbaum, Frank. *Slave and Citizen. The Negro in the Americas*. New York, 1946.

Williams, Eric. *Capitalism and Slavery*. New York, 1966.

Williams, Eric. *From Columbus to Castro: The History of the Caribbean, 1492-1969*. New York, 1970.

Williams, Eric. *The Negro in the Caribbean*. Westport, 1971.

INDEX

A

B

D

E

F

G

H

I

N

T

U

V

W

Y

Z

◆◆◆

ABOUT THE AUTHORS

◆

Maria A. Brown, is a professor of American and African American history and ethnic studies at El Camino College. She received her B.A. in political science and history from the University of California, Santa Barbara and her M.A. from Syracuse University, New York. She has contributed articles to *American History and Culture: A Reader* and *Unity and Diversity: 13 Original Essays on America's Ethnics and Minorities*. Professor Brown is currently at work on a study of women of color and projects on cultural diversity in the curriculum and the use of interactive media in the classroom.

◆

Joseph Collier is a professor emeritus at El Camino College. He holds a Ph.D. in American Studies from the University of Kansas. He has edited and contributed articles to *American History and Culture: A Reader* and *Unity and Diversity: 13 Original Essays on America's Ethnics and Minorities*. Dr. Collier has also edited *This Living America* and *Forces in the Shaping of American Culture*. He taught for many years the College's courses in ethnic literature.

◆

Rafael L. Cortada is currently in educational administration. He was formerly a professor of history at El Camino College. Dr. Cortada has published extensively in the areas of ethnic and minority history. Born in New York City, he received his B.A. and Ph.D. degrees from Fordham University. He earned his M.A. from Columbia University.

◆

Robert D. Cross is a professor emeritus at the University of Virginia whose special interest include immigration history, American Church history and social history (twentieth century). Among his prominent publications are *The Emergence of Liberal Catholicism in America* and (as editor) *The Churches and the City*.

✦

Roger Daniels is a prominent authority on Japanese Americans. Among his many publications are *The Decision to Relocate the Japanese Americans, Asian America: Chinese and Japanese in the United States since 1850*, and *Coming to America — A History of Immigration and Ethnicity in American Life*. He has served as a consultant to the *Commission on Wartime Relocation and internment of Civilians* and has been involved in such television productions as *Nisei Soldier* (1984) and *Unfinished Business* (1985). He is a professor of history at the University of Cincinnati.

✦

Donald J. Haley is a professor of history at El Camino College, where he has taught United States, World, Mexican, and Latin American history for the past nineteen years. He previously taught in high school, and at one time was a social worker for Los Angeles County.

✦

Donald Haydu received his B.A. in history from Loyola-Marymount University of Los Angeles in 1957. After completing an M.A. at UCLA, he joined the Department of History at El Camino College in 1965. For the last twenty-five years Professor Haydu has taught ethnic studies and American intellectual and cultural history at El Camino.

✦

Gloria E. Miranda is a graduate of the University of Southern California where she received her Ph.D. in history. She is currently the Dean of the Division of Behavioral and Social Sciences at El Camino College. Formerly, she chaired the Department of Chicano Studies at Los Angeles Valley College where she taught history and ethnic studies for nineteen years. Dr. Miranda's research interests include Mexican American family life. Her publications include articles on early California marriage and child-rearing patterns and the Mexican immigrant family.

✦

Michael Novak is a resident scholar at the American Enterprise Institute in Washington, D.C. As a social philosopher, he has written extensively on the relationship between the principles of Democratic Capitalism and Judeo-Christian teachings. He is the founding director of *Ethnic Millions Political Action Committee* and entered public service as chief delegate to the 1981 and 1982 sessions of the *United Nations Human Rights Commission* in Geneva Switzerland. He is the grandson of Slovak immigrants.

✦

Richard P. Sherman is a professor emeritus at El Camino College. He holds a Ph.D. from the University of Southern California. He completed his undergraduate degree at The Citadel: The Military College of South Carolina-Charleston, along with an M.A. from UCLA. He is the author of *Robert Johnson: Proprietary and Royal Governor of South Carolina.*

✦

Arthur Verge is an assistant professor of history at El Camino College. He received his Ph.D. under the direction of Franklin D. Mitchell at the University of Southern California. He is presently completing a book on the impact of the Second World War on Los Angeles.

✦

Alfred J. Wrobel is a professor of history at El Camino College. He received his Ph.D. from the University of Southern California where he completed a study on the impact of the American Revolution on the Poland of Stanislaus August Poniatowski. He also holds degrees from Swarthmore College and Columbia University. In addition to teaching at the University of Saskatchewan (Canada) and California State University (Dominquez Hills), Dr. Wrobel has been a recipient of a Fulbright Scholarship to the University of Warsaw (Poland).